teaching MUSIC

in the secondary schools

WADSWORTH MUSIC SERIES

Basic Concepts in Music by Gary M. Martin
Basic Piano for Adults by Helene Robinson
Basic Resources for Learning Music by Alice Snyder Knuth and William E. Knuth
English Folk Song: Some Conclusions, 4th edition, by Cecil J. Sharp (edited by Maud Karpeles)
Exploring Music with Children by Robert E. Nye and Vernice T. Nye
First Experiences in Music by Lyman C. Hurd, III, and Edith J. Savage
Five Centuries of Keyboard Music by John Gillespie
Foundations in Music Theory by Leon Dallin
Harmony and Melody, Volumes I and II, and *A Workbook for Harmony and Melody, Volumes I and II,* by Elie Siegmeister
Help Yourselves to Music by Beatrice P. Krone and Kurt R. Miller
An Introduction to Musical Understanding and Musicianship by Ethel G. Adams
Introduction to Music Reading by William Thomson
Keyboard Skills: Sight Reading, Transposition, Harmonization, Improvisation by Winifred K. Chastek
Music Essentials for Classroom Teachers by Robert Pace
Music Fundamentals by Howard A. Murphy with John F. Park
Music in the Education of Children, 2nd edition, by Bessie R. Swanson
Music Reading through Singing by Charles W. Walton and Harry R. Wilson
Planning Music in the Education of Children: A Personal Handbook by Bessie R. Swanson
Rhythm in Music and Dance for Children by Sally Monsour, Patricia Eckert Lindell, and Marilyn Chambers Cohen
Singing with Children by Robert and Vernice Nye, Neva Aubin, and George Kyme
Talking about Concertos by Antony Hopkins
Talking about Symphonies by Antony Hopkins
Teaching Music in the Secondary Schools by Charles R. Hoffer
Toward World Understanding with Song by Vernice T. Nye, Robert E. Nye, and H. Virginia Nye

teaching MUSIC *in the secondary schools*

CHARLES R. HOFFER

WADSWORTH PUBLISHING COMPANY, INC.
BELMONT, CALIFORNIA

Credits for chapter-opening photographs: Chapters I, III, XIV, XV—Charles R. Hoffer; II, IV, VI, VIII, IX, XVI—Fred S. Heywood, KMOX-TV, CBS outlet, St. Louis, Missouri; V, XII—Frank Siteman, Clayton High School, Clayton, Missouri; VII, XIII—American Music Conference, Chicago, Illinois; X—Collegiate Cap and Gown Company, Champaign, Illinois; XI—Oakland Public Schools, Oakland, California; XVII—Music Educators National Conference, Washington, D.C.

The pictures on pages 231, 232, and 235 are from the Grand Ledge, Michigan, Public Schools and were taken by LeClear of Lansing, Michigan.

Sixth printing: *March 1969*

L.C. Cat. Card No.: 64-14244

Printed in the United States of America

to my mother and father

preface

This book was written primarily for those who plan to teach music or are now teaching in the secondary schools. It seeks to cover in a practical, thorough, and comprehensive way those things that a music teacher needs to know and do in order to be successful. My hope is that this book will help the new teacher to explore and understand the profound and challenging aspects of what sometimes appears, deceptively, to be the simple job of being a school music teacher. In addition, the book may stimulate experienced teachers to compare and test different ways of teaching, and to take a new look at some old problems.

Before writing this book, I made a survey of eighteen teacher-training institutions, asking questions about how music instruction is organized and what a textbook should cover to be of the most value. The replies were influential in the organization and orientation of the manuscript. Also, as a teacher and administrator of music in the secondary schools, supervisor of student teachers, and teacher of music methods courses at the college level, I have had my own experience from which to draw. Throughout the time of writing, and in the more than five years that this work was contemplated, many valuable comments and ideas came from teachers, student teachers, administrators, and from possibly the most important source of all—the secondary school students themselves.

The book is organized around the factors involved with formal education: the subject, the student, the teacher, and the process of getting the subject across to the student. While the ways and means of teaching music occupy the greater share of this book, the other essentials are not overlooked. The actual teaching of music is greatly affected by decisions regarding the nature of music, the reasons for music in the schools, the nature of the group being taught, and the role of the teacher. These matters must be understood before an elaboration of teaching procedures can be undertaken.

The book departs somewhat from the traditional organization of chapters according to the name of the class: band, chorus, small ensembles, etc. Rather it stresses the underlying aesthetic, philosophical, and psychological foundations of all music instruction in the school. It then proceeds to deal with a music teacher's work: rehearsal, selection of music, interpretation, intonation, performance, and the like. Some special areas—the repair of instruments, the design of music rooms, and marching-band techniques, to name three—are not included because excellent publications on these topics are available.

Throughout the book I have attempted to present points in a practical fashion. Because teaching music is a matter of experiencing as well as knowing, I have sought to make the writing alive and vivid, reproducing as fully as possible the "feel" of actual teaching. Also, I have tried diligently not to state the obvious generalization without thoroughly examining the implications of and reasons for the statement. Research findings and other means of substantiation are used when appropriate to give the basis for positions taken.

In the process of teaching, the profound and the practical are interrelated. A simple act on the part of a teacher is usually based on a fundamental philosophical or psychological consideration. And the reverse is true: profound principles, if followed consistently, lead to practical conclusions. Yet a false dichotomy between the two exists in the minds of many people. In this book, I hope the two aspects have been fused in a meaningful way.

This book takes the position that music is music, whether instrumental or vocal, whether performed or studied academically. All music teachers should seek to increase the student's comprehension of melody, musical expression, tone, and other musical concepts as he matures and learns. The means and organization for doing this vary, but the essential task remains the same. True, a choral teacher is not going to teach his students a new bowing and the orchestra director does not work on vocal production, but the similarities far overshadow the differences. In fact, there are basic similarities of teaching procedure in the illustration just cited.

The main objective toward which the book is oriented is the teaching of music, the gaining by teen-age students of more of the warp and woof of music. To the extent that students learn music, the teacher is successful. Music should be taught in the schools for the sake of the students who take music courses, and not for the benefit of the teacher. A band or chorus exists because, all things considered, that is the best way for that particular group of students to learn music. Such an organization does not exist to entertain at athletic events or civic clubs, or to satisfy a hidden psychological craving of the teacher for recognition, or to provide teenagers with a "happy time" for one period each day. No one is against entertainment, recognition for the teacher, or pleasure when they are kept in their proper place. The point is that learning music—the gaining of musical appreciation, knowledge, understandings, attitudes, skills—must be paramount.

I am grateful to the many people who inspired, encouraged, and enlightened me in my efforts to be a teacher and writer. Citing a few names here would not be fair to the greater number who are not mentioned; therefore I can only thank them as a group and hope that the sincerity of my gratefulness is evident. For their specific help on this book I wish to acknowledge Donald K. Anderson for his review of the portions on instrumental music; C. Bud Welch of St. Ann's School Music Service for assisting with the listing of materials; and Washington University for the use of its library.

The author would like to acknowledge those music educators who contributed through questionnaire or interview their views on a textbook in the teaching of secondary school music.

Varner M. Chance	Illinois Wesleyan University
Irving Cheyette	State University of New York at Buffalo
Kenneth L. Dustman	Southwest Missouri State College
Mary E. English	State University College, Potsdam, New York
Neal E. Glenn	State University of Iowa
Roderick Gordon	Southern Illinois University
Lewis Hilton	Washington University
Charles Leonhard	University of Illinois
Newell H. Long	Indiana University
Paul Mathews	University of Missouri
William McBride	Ohio State University
Jack M. Pernecky	Northwestern University
Ralph E. Rush	University of Southern California
William R. Sur	Michigan State University
Robert M. Taylor	Kansas State Teachers College, Emporia
Robert E. Thomas	University of Illinois

Finally, special thanks go to my wife, Marjorie, not only for her valuable suggestions, excellent editorial work, and the typing of the manuscript, but even more for her patient confidence that the efforts on the book would reach fruition.

contents

I

so you are going to teach music

One who chooses to teach music in the schools has selected a profession that is interesting, worthy, and difficult. Certainly few would maintain that the subject of music is lacking in interest or excitement. Nor would anyone say that the modern American adolescent is a dull species of *homo sapiens*. Music, and especially the teaching of music to young people, is to be esteemed. After all, it involves the transmitting of a significant part of Western culture to younger generations. The place of music in contemporary society and the position of music instruction in the schools make music education an area worthy of one's best efforts, and a field requiring the respect of society and education as a whole.

Teaching music in the schools is difficult. The word "difficult" here is not meant to imply that the task is frustrating, onerous, or unsatisfying. Rather it means that teaching music requires a complex of abilities. A successful music teacher needs to have more than innate musicianship, more than "a way with youngsters," and more than good training for the work he will undertake. He needs all three—plus the imagination and intelligence to apply his talents creatively to the teaching situation in which he finds himself. Music teaching is not for the prosaic, the lazy, or the faint of heart.

TEACHING MUSIC

What music shall be taught in the schools? Simple though it may appear, this question has many complex facets. Music has existed in every historical epoch, in almost limitless forms, and for a great variety of reasons. The amount of existing music is so vast that one can encompass only a small portion of it in an entire lifetime. Clearly, the number of hours available for music study in the schools is much more limited. The question then is "*what* music shall be taught?" more than "*shall* music be taught?"

Further, there is some confusion between the study *of* music and the study of information *about* music. The two are by no means identical. The exact date of Brahms' birth, the fact that A above middle C vibrates 440 times each second, or the fact that the violin bow is made of Pernambuco wood constitute information related to music, but they are not the essence of music. Factual material has its place, but it should not be so mingled with the aesthetic aspect of music that the teacher or student loses sight of the distinction between them.

The heart of the matter is this: music is the sounding of a series of related pitches in a space of time. *When one guides the students to comprehend and manipulate related sounds, then he is teaching music.* The music of Brahms comes alive only when pitches are sounded in the time-space framework indicated in the notation of his manuscript. The phenomenon of A440 becomes music only when it is sounded in conjunction with other pitches in a meaningful way, and the Pernambuco bow has significance only as it affects the tone quality of the violin and the finesse of the phrasing. Music, then, does not exist apart from the aural experience of musical tones.

In this respect, the music class should theoretically be wordless. Words can only say something *about* music. The instructor and pupils would be better off to pull up their music-making device (be it an instrument or voice) and "discuss" in the musical medium. Good players of jazz, in their "sessions," carry on musical conversations. They achieve a purely musical experience, even though their "points of discussion" are usually improvised and not of a deliberate, serious nature. The quality of a good melody, in music of any type, is something that can only be perceived aurally, and not described in words or proved in a formula. The same is true when examining the development or variation of a melodic theme, or when judging the effectiveness of a musical line in relation to a text. Musical phenomena must be understood musically, rather than verbally.

From a practical standpoint, a music class cannot operate only musically with time and pitch. As desirable as such a class might be, the need for leading the student from his usual verbal manner of thinking to a more musical and aesthetic type of mental activity demands that words be used, and that methods be utilized which will enable him to think better musically. Granting the claims of practicality, a music teacher should never depart from the ideal any more than necessary, and he should be aware of the reason for the departure.

It is often disturbing how unmusical some music teachers can be in their teaching. Harry R. Wilson reported this experience in his travels around the world.

> Athens offered the opportunity to visit a class of thirty eighth-grade boys during a music lesson. Boys are the same in Greece as in America. The lesson was on sixteenth notes. I listened for forty-five minutes to the singing of the ascending and descending scales using syllables in the key of C major to this rhythm on each note:
>
> 
>
> First the group sang the exercise while beating time with the arm; then different individuals sang the exercise while the remainder of the group continued to beat time. The class became restless, as one can imagine—and I did too.[1]

Dr. Wilson's experience could be approximated in too many classrooms in this country, though possibly not to the degree he relates. Mere blowing into an instrument while fingering the keys does not constitute music, nor does vibrating the vocal cords while singing. The sounds and pitches must have some coherence, some logic, before there is music; and then the students need to be made aware of the musical qualities. One does not learn to understand, appreciate, and manipulate music by working with material that is basically lacking in musical sense, or by working with music without being conscious of the properties in it.

Granted, there are times when the mastery of motor skills does not require much intellectual comprehension. The note

demands a certain fingering; the sustaining of a long tone requires the development of certain muscles. These skills, however, are only necessary steps to be taken so that music can be performed. No singer could hope to attract the attention of an audience by his ability to sustain a tone, and no violinist could go far who only responded in a robot-like manner to one notational symbol after another. Motor skills are means to an end, and not ends in themselves. Necessary though they may be, they should not be permitted to dominate the musical instruction process.

The burden of proof is on the teacher when he departs from the teaching of related pitches in a time framework. He must be confident that the less musical procedure will achieve something that cannot be attained in a more musical way. He must be sure that the drill activity will achieve a result that has a lasting effect. Nor should the teacher mistake the effort

[1] Harry R. Wilson, "Impressions from a Trip Around the World by an American Music Educator," *Music Educators Journal*, XLVI, No. 1 (September–October 1959), 79. Reprinted by permission.

and hard work of drill activity for learning. Great effort and learning are not necessarily related. Rigorous exercise of the leg muscles is of only limited value in playing well the complex game of football. The same is true of the use of bodily muscles in the making of music.

Most important, the teacher himself must be musically sensitive. He must have in some degree the understanding and feeling of a concert artist. He must be more than someone who reacts automatically to the stimuli of musical symbols. He must, for example, have some sense of phrasing; otherwise, how can he teach it? He must know the style of a work in order to convey the mood in which it should be performed. If a teacher is going to instruct beyond the bare rudiments of the musical nomenclature and performance—that is, actually teach music—then he must have proceeded well beyond the rudimentary stage himself.

TEACHING TEEN-AGERS

The music teacher needs to understand his students for several reasons. First of all, if the age group being taught has characteristics that call for the adaptation of method or materials, it would be folly not to have the flexibility necessary to make the teaching effort successful, providing, of course, that the integrity of the subject is retained. Second, since motivation is of such importance in teaching any subject at any level, the teacher must understand some of the factors that motivate students. A horse cannot be motivated with cash awards; a person who wishes to train the animal must realize this and use other means to inspire the beast to learn. Teen-agers as a group have interests and behavior patterns which, while not universal, do predominate and characterize them generally. As much as one might wish they would shed certain of these traits and gain others, a wise teacher does not bemoan the fact that he must teach such young people; nor does he become embittered and cynical. Rather he adjusts his approach to the group he is seeking to teach, at the same time preserving the basic goals of the subject. True, this is not an easy thing to do; it requires skill, effort, and imagination.

A good teacher can put himself in the place of his students, taking into consideration their interests, needs, and backgrounds. He can to some degree see the subject through the eyes of the pupil. This ability is necessary not only to allow for the adaptation of methods and materials; it is important because the teacher-class relationship can affect the students' attitude toward the course. Teen-agers are sometimes slow to distinguish between their feelings toward the teacher and their feelings toward the subject. And in an art such as music, which is so dependent upon sensitivity of feeling and perception, attitude becomes crucial. Once the students realize that a teacher is sensitive to their interests, the relationship between pupils and teacher is greatly improved, with the result that more learning ensues.

At stake are the long-term results of music teaching. What is learned in class today determines how much understanding and skill there will be for the student in the future. Also, the attitude toward music controls the carry-over value of music into other areas of the school and into adult life. A teen-ager who has nurtured a hearty dislike for music is not a likely candidate for joining a church choir, purchasing a good recording, or supporting the fund drive of the local symphony orchestra.

THE TEACHING PROCESS

A music teacher organizes, selects, presents, and involves the students with music so that they gain new insights and skill. This is the great challenge, the unending excitement of being a teacher. An example from the elementary school will illustrate the point. Suppose a teacher wishes to have a second-grade class sing a song with pleasing tone and accurate pitch. Because the song is simple, it presents the teacher with no serious technical challenge. The children themselves are interesting and a pleasure to know, but offer the teacher little challenge in the guidance of the class. The excitement comes in taking the great art of music and so presenting it that it becomes meaningful to the seven-year-old youngsters. How can the good design of the melodic line be impressed on them, on children who scarcely know what the word "design" means? How does one make second-graders conscious of pitch and exact in its rendition? Certainly not by telling them, "Watch your intonation!" Does a gentle sweep of the arm truly aid a child in feeling the shape of the phrase, or doesn't it? Are there other means that would be more effective?

One could go on at length posing such questions about the teaching of a simple song in the elementary school. The problems are no less demanding at the secondary level. A multitude of problems—some involving technique, some interpretation, some style—crop up constantly in music that is studied at this level, and at all times the teacher must remember that he is dealing with that lovable combination of idealism and deviltry, the teen-ager. Teaching does not consist only of knowing something oneself; it is the ability to guide people and organize subject matter so adroitly that learning takes place.

In considering the word "teach," one must guard against thinking of it in superficial terms. A teacher may talk and talk to a class about rhythm, for example, but unless he has in one way or another presented rhythm so that the students leave the class knowing more about it than when they entered, no teaching has occurred. A band director may spend rehearsal after rehearsal playing through happy tunes and cut-and-dried marches; but at the end of the year, if the students know little more music than when they started, it cannot properly be said that much has been taught. Teaching produces changes in the students—it results in new meanings, knowledge, skills, understandings. It is a two-way proposition, as Nathaniel

Cantor's book *The Teaching⟷Learning Process* ably emphasizes—a process of interaction between pupil and teacher.[2] It is not merely the dispensation of facts without regard for the results of the dole. A teacher is not like the milkman who faithfully supplies the contracted amount of milk, and then moves on without knowing or caring if the milk is consumed and by whom. The dispensation of facts is frequently and loosely called "teaching." But only the implanting of new understandings can justify the honored term "teaching," and carry with it the excitement and rewards which mark the profession. This is what the word "teaching" means as it is used throughout this book.

Much has been discovered about how methods and conditions affect learning, and there is much more to be discovered. Educational psychologists and other professionals have developed a body of knowledge, a discipline if you will, about the teaching⟷learning process. For example, it once was believed that reading should be introduced by first teaching the letters of the alphabet, since words are made up of letters. Then when words were learned, they were put into phrases, and finally into sentences. Logically this method, generally called the ABC method, seems reasonable, but psychologically it simply did not work. Today teachers know that words are comprehended as a whole. Without this knowledge, and without training in how to use it, the teacher would waste a great amount of time and introduce habits that would need to be broken later. Fluent reading ability and a gracious way with children are not sufficient qualifications for the teaching of reading. The same is true of teaching music.

Frequently a teacher entering the profession is tempted to teach as he was taught. Sometimes a conscious attempt is made to emulate a former teacher. This approach is found wanting in several respects. First, the situation which the new teacher will encounter and the one in which the model teacher operated are different. Second, as has been pointed out, there has evolved a body of knowledge which is greater and more precise than that available to the earlier teacher. Each generation of music teachers should hope to surpass the level of its predecessors, because it can build upon the work of former generations. Third, some students achieve much *in spite of* the quality of their past instruction. A good student is not necessarily the product of a good teacher. In fact, he might have been better, had he had a better teacher. Training, work, and ability are what the new teacher needs, and not a model to be mimicked.

What is a good music teacher? He is one who feels music fully. He comprehends the place of music in the educational process. He understands the students he is to teach; he finds out what motivates them, and what their hopes and fears are. Then, knowing music and understanding his students, he organizes the music program to reach each student. He selects music

[2] Nathaniel F. Cantor, *The Teaching ⟷ Learning Process* (New York: Dryden Press, 1953).

that provides for maximum learning. He presents the concepts of music—melody, counterpoint, intonation, pitch, rhythm, style—in a manner that will be meaningful to the class. The good teacher is known by what he *does* (he brings students to a greater understanding of music), and not by what he *is* (a musician, administrator, congenial fellow). He needs to "be" certain things in order to "do," but the teacher is primarily concerned with accomplishment—effecting musical growth within his pupils.

II

the need for music in the secondary schools

Sometimes music teachers are reluctant to think through fundamental questions about what they are teaching and why. Can't they just go ahead and do a good job of teaching and leave the discussion of "remote" and "impractical" questions to college professors and their classes? No, the consideration of basic matters cannot successfully be left to someone else. There are at least four reasons which compel every music teacher to think through such matters for himself.

REASONS FOR CONSIDERING BASIC OBJECTIVES

To begin with, a teacher's educational philosophy and objectives are so involved in what he does in teaching that he cannot avoid taking a position on them. True, he does not often state his position verbally, but he does make decisions and take actions that are necessarily based on his beliefs about music education.

> Mr. Atkins thought that the first thing a choir should do at each rehearsal was go through ten minutes of warm-up routine. So, almost without exception, the first ten minutes of every period were spent singing vowels, triads, and other vocalization figures. The interest in the choral music program lagged, and the choir was small. But Mr. Atkins kept up the routines because he felt that this was the way to train singers.

By this action, Mr. Atkins has defined one of his fundamental beliefs. He has clearly said, "Thorough warm-up first, an interested group second." The correctness of Mr. Atkins' decision is not the point at issue here. What is significant is that this practical action tacitly reveals one aspect of his philosophy of music education.

Second, there is still a need to "sell" music in the secondary schools. Many times the problem is not one of coping with obvious and deliberate doubts about the value of music in the curriculum. Rather the director has to do some "convincing" for music so that he can work out schedule conflicts, upgrade the music-course credit, secure an adequate budget, and handle many other problems.

> Miss Green, teacher of general music at South Junior High School, discovered that the contemplated curriculum for the more academically able seventh-grade students contained no music requirement. Furthermore, it allowed for only one elective class, which would meet for only one period every other day, and the elective field included four courses in addition to music.
>
> Miss Green found that she had to convince the school administration of the need for music for all seventh-grade students, including the able, and then establish the fact that music was of sufficient importance to warrant adjustment in the curriculum in order to allow room for it.

The job of promoting music education rests primarily on the music teacher. How can he convince someone else if he is not sure himself! He needs enthusiasm and conviction in what he does and says. He must remember that *he* is music to the students and faculty; he is the leader, the spokesman, the promulgator of music.

Third, for the teacher's own sake he needs to be clear on what he is trying to do.

> Marian Knowles was tired. It had been a hard day; nothing seemed to have gone right. The classes had been talkative, their singing dull and often flat; and as an added disappointment she had just realized that she had used up much of the money available for music, with none of the music for the spring program yet purchased.
>
> As she dropped into a chair in the teachers' lounge after school, a veteran teacher noticed her dejected air and said, "Don't worry so much, Marian. Why work so hard? After all, who wants to be the best teacher in the graveyard?" As Marian heard her words, she wondered, "Just what am I accomplishing here? Is it all worth it?"

A teacher must be able to answer these questions, if for no other reason than to clarify his own perspective and objectives.

This assessment of objectives is necessary if the teacher is to improve upon his own work. An evaluation can be made only in terms of some standard or goal. Therefore, in order to better himself, the teacher must know what his goals are and must re-examine them from time to time with a bit of honest soul-searching. The teacher himself is the only one who can bring about changes in his teaching; no administrator or colleague can do this for him.

In the fourth place, a teacher needs to be clear on his basic objectives in order to be consistent.

> Because it was Neal Groton's first year as band director at St. Mark's High School, he was anxious to have his marching band make as big an impression as possible. Accordingly, he enrolled in band almost anyone interested enough to join, even students with substandard training. By doing this, he was able to field a large but poor-sounding aggregation. Not only did Neal want a big band for marching, he simply had a good feeling about having so many students involved in instrumental music.
>
> At the end of marching season, he realized that he should eliminate about one-half the players if the concert band were to be able to study and play music at the level appropriate for a high school group. Because students were not allowed to be dropped in the middle of the course, Neal made rigorous demands for extra rehearsals and made caustic remarks to less-able players in class, hoping thereby to encourage unwanted students to quit. At semester time a sizeable group of players did drop band, but among them was the first clarinet and second chair trombone. The remaining band members resented the affronts to fellow students and became indifferent to learning.
>
> About March, smitten by his conscience (which was aided by some searching questions from his principal), and struck by the fact that his method of treating the students was not in the interest of education, Neal changed to a more "good-humored" approach, coupled with a greater interest in the welfare of the students. But the time was late. The students did not forget so easily their experience of the past months. His more relaxed handling of the band initially brought forth more talking and "fooling around." After a month the behavior did improve somewhat, and the band did expend some effort to prepare for the spring concert. As the year finishes, Neal wonders what he will do next fall when he again wants a big group to march. He feels torn between a desire to present an outstanding musical group and a desire to help and teach students.

Neal Groton's vacillating sense of direction is not only making him miserable, it is also robbing his students of the best music education he can give them. He needs to realize that the band cannot be and do everything. In short, he must make the best choice of goals he can, and then stick consistently to them. He must do this so that the action he takes in December will not tear down all that he sought to do in November.

For these reasons, then, all music teachers must understand the basic purposes of their job. One: A teacher cannot avoid acting on fundamental propositions, even if he can avoid talking about them. Two: There is much need for convincing others of the place of music in the curriculum. Three: A teacher needs clarity of purpose so that he can do his job and evaluate it accurately. Four: He must know his purposes in order to be consistent.

THE BASIC NEED FOR MUSIC

The "bedrock" foundation upon which the music teacher must act lies in the answer to a simple question: why is music needed in the schools? The answer determines in large measure what the goals of the teacher should be, which in turn determine the practical actions he takes in the classroom and at rehearsal. Every music teacher is involved with aesthetics, and the discussion of aesthetic experience gets right to the heart of the music teacher's work.

The use of the word "need" in conjunction with music in the school may on the surface appear to be an exaggeration, particularly in view of the fact that from time to time music is decried as a "frill" in the curriculum. With each challenge, music educators have clamored to maintain that music has a rightful place in the schools. But to say that music is a necessity is a stronger and more unusual statement. Be it frequently or rarely made, however, the statement is true.

It is true in the sense that some education in music is necessary for a well-educated person. It is untrue in the sense that music is necessary for existence. Music is not necessary in order to build a fire, erect a shelter, or grow a field of wheat. If mankind were interested only in existence, then music would indeed be a "frill," a pleasurable diversion. But the human race since the time of the Cro-Magnon man has been seeking something more than mere existence. Man contemplates and thinks. Furthermore, he places a value on the quality of objects and on his own experiences. This is essentially what makes him different from all other creatures in the animal kingdom.

An outstanding physical scientist, Lecomte du Noüy, in his fascinating and profound book *Human Destiny*, discusses in detail the evolution of man from the standpoint of its ultimate meaning and purpose. Of the Cro-Magnon man and his significance in the history of the human race, du Noüy says:

> . . . the Cro-Magnon was above all a great artist. The paintings which adorn his caverns are often admirable. His sculptures, his engravings on bone and ivory are wonderfully realistic, his tools and his weapons are superbly decorated, his jewels and ornaments are remarkably ingenious and graceful . . . These *useless* manifestations—the word is taken in the sense of "not absolutely necessary to maintain or defend life"—mark the most important date in all the history of mankind. They are the proof of the progress of the human spirit in the direction of evolution, that is, in the direction leading away from the animal. The primitive "useless" gestures of man are in reality the only ones that count.[1]

[1] Lecomte du Noüy, *Human Destiny* (New York: Longmans, Green & Co., Inc., 1947), pp. 125–26. Courtesy of David McKay Company, Inc.

What du Noüy states regarding the importance of artistic, aesthetic activity for the development of the human race could be substantiated by many other scholars. The point is that when man seeks something higher than existence he turns to reflective activity such as the arts represent. Music and other aesthetic experiences are necessary if man is to reach his full stature; he is not fully human without them. Not fully human without the arts and music—a shocking and untenable proposition? Not when it is closely examined. An idea of greatest importance? To the music educator, it is the foundation of his profession.

Education for centuries has sensed this fundamental point. Plato placed music high in the curriculum of the school (although partly for reasons

The Cynic's Corner

"The maddening thing is knowing that even at this very moment, in some lonely garret somewhere, some guy is painting something that'll be remembered long after we've been forgotten."

Interlandi, 1955
The Register and Tribune Syndicate

which are no longer held valid). In the medieval university, music was a part of the quadrivium of studies necessary for a master's degree. Today the curriculum has enlarged and changed, but the attitude still prevails that the well-educated person needs among other things an aesthetic sensitivity.[2]

Since music needs to be in the schools because of its aesthetic qualities, it is essential that the word "aesthetic" be clearly understood. For some people the word connotes something vague and far removed from ordinary life, and something terribly difficult to understand. In the sense of a thorough, intellectual, verbalized probing of beauty and its meaning, this thought is largely true, since aesthetics involves a basic and complex examination of psychological and philosophical factors in human existence. The sensing of aesthetic quality is another matter. A high school student can sense the quality created when a line of music is artistically set contrapuntally against another, even though he cannot launch into a discourse on the aesthetic need for symbolization of the ebb and flow of life's rhythms. Almost all people can to a certain extent sense aesthetic quality; it is not limited to a few artistically elite individuals. Children likewise have this ability to a degree commensurate with their age. What is being discussed here is the need for a sensitivity to aesthetic qualities, and not a journey into the intellectual discipline of aesthetics, even though the latter provides the foundation of the former.

While aesthetic experiences are common, they differ from common experiences. When a man builds a chair, he fashions it primarily to serve a specific practical function. As he works, he experiences the pleasures and discomforts arising out of the making of it. He expects to attain a specific goal—a chair to sit on or to sell. All of this is in the realm of ordinary experience. Aesthetic experience occurs when he contemplates the beauty of the grain of the wood, the shading of the finish, the grace of the design, without any thought as to the practical value of the chair or pride of workmanship. For the chair-maker the aesthetic experience is the act of stepping back and perceiving the beauty and artistic meaning of the piece of furniture.

The chair-maker could, if he had the ability and inclination, put into a work of music or another art form a symbolization of his experiences with the making of the chair, the joy and effort it demanded. Then other people could contemplate this work of art and gain aesthetic impressions from it. This is what composers throughout history have done, except that the experiences and musical thoughts compacted into their music are considerably deeper than those associated with making a chair.

Aesthetic experience does not attempt to solve problems or reach con-

[2] As an example, see: Education Policies Commission, *Policies for Education in American Democracy* (Washington, D.C.: National Education Association, 1946), p. 207.

clusions. It is valued for its own sake. Generally, the working out of a mathematical problem is less important than attaining the proper answer. But in sonata-allegro form the coda is not the "answer" to the movement. What is valued is the experience of hearing the array of sounds as they progress from one to another. The coda has value only as it is related to the rest of the music in the movement.

Aesthetic sensitivity, then, is the ability to gain meaning and pleasure from the experience of contemplating an object or event, and this sensitivity needs to be imparted to students. What does this mean for the music teacher? Many things. For one, it means that he must present music in such a way that its aesthetic properties are grasped. The students should be taught to be sensitive to the qualities of the sounds, the rise and fall of intensity in the harmony and melody, the organizing force of the rhythm, because it is these and similar characteristics that give music its aesthetic qualities. The music itself should be stressed, and matters related only to music minimized.

Second, learnings about music derive their meaning from association with the qualities to be found in music. This applies equally to concepts such as melody, harmony, and rhythm, as well as to facts, such as the pitches to be sounded in the dominant seventh chord in the key of G. The implications of this point for the music teacher will be examined at length in Chapter Seven and elsewhere in the book.

Third, education which makes students alert to aesthetic qualities requires that good music be used. As Chapter Sixteen will disclose, no one can teach such values from compositions that are trite, superficial, or highly temporary.

Fourth, to acquire aesthetic sensitivity, the student should be guided toward musical independence. When there is no teacher present, how much can the student accomplish on his own? If he has gained some understanding of what the art of music is all about, something more than an ability to follow directions in class, then there will be lasting, truly musical results. And no teacher should settle for less.

Fifth, the evaluation of a teacher must be made in terms of his ability to impart musical learnings, which include both an understanding of and a feeling for the music, as well as skill at producing it. It is easy to tell the violin section to play more softly during a certain passage, but it is more important to have the violinists understand *why* they should play more softly at that point. It is relatively easy with a recipe-like procedure to get a student to write the major scales correctly. It is far more difficult, and significant, to guide him so that he understands the transposition of a scale pattern or the tonal relationships in the major scale. The teacher is successful to the extent that his students are brought to a point beyond merely reacting to the printed page. Teaching which seldom touches on the understanding of the qualities to be found in tone and the combination of pitches in a space of time is form without substance. In the deepest sense, it has failed the art of music—and the students.

Finally, making students sensitive to the qualities in music is something that must be done deliberately; the attention of the students must be focused on the qualities. A teacher cannot expect a student to grasp the essence of musical feeling by merely counting and fingering the notes. It is possible for a student to be a member of a music group throughout high school without gaining an awareness of what is really happening musically.

> At a meeting of music educators, one teacher commented that so many high school second trombonists, when they play, ignore the rest of the band and are conscious only of the first and third trombone parts. A college band director answered, "I disagree. They aren't even aware of the first and third trombone parts!"

NONMUSICAL REASONS FOR TEACHING MUSIC

Absent from the discussion so far has been a listing of the reasons usually presented for the inclusion of music in the schools: it encourages teamwork among the students, development of character, emotional release, social or group adjustment, and so on. Such justifications indicate that music classes and organizations are regarded as means to some desirable, but nonmusical, goal. Fine as these reasons are, however, they are secondary, occurring as by-products of good teaching. If, for instance, a student gains self-confidence by appearing before the public in the choir, this will happen in the normal course of affairs. The teacher does not need to de-emphasize music just because he wants to stress the psychological value of musical participation.

Happily, music can contribute to educational goals other than the aesthetic one already cited. This enhances its place in the curriculum, although none of these benefits is by any means exclusively the property of music.

Personal Development of the Student

Music contributes to a student's growth in many ways. Public performance provides an especially important outlet for personal and group development. The value of being able to stand in front of an audience is inestimable, and some persons have done much to promote training that will develop this ability. Dale Carnegie built a tremendously successful speech course on the need of people to face audiences of all types. The Future Farmers of America makes a deliberate effort to encourage as many boys as possible to speak publicly, conduct meetings, and, in many places, to sing. Do the students in music organizations feel the need of being able to perform in front of an audience? They most certainly do!

> Roger was a senior. As a hot-rod enthusiast and a poor academic student, he liked to be considered somewhat of a "tough" guy. He took choir because he needed the credit, and because he had heard that choir could be enjoyable. On a questionnaire he was asked what day he remembered most clearly in his choral experience. His answer ran something like this: "The day I remember best was the day we sang for assembly on Veterans Day. It was the first time I ever did anything in front of the students. I sure was scared. But our first song went real good, and I felt much better after that."

Whether he realized it or not, Roger had succeeded at something besides getting into trouble. Now he had a good feeling about music, which, incidentally, was the key to getting him started in the right direction in other areas. Of course, music cannot be advocated mainly as a "reformatory" for maladjusted students, but it can be a big help toward changing the outlook of many young people.

Personal development also comes from the recognition awarded to members of a successful music organization. The choir gave Roger for the first time in his school life an opportunity to be recognized for his positive rather than his negative accomplishments. As an avenue for gaining recognition, music has an advantage usually enjoyed only by the extracurricular activities that the school offers. Music, especially vocal music, is probably used as a means of achieving recognition more often by girls than by boys, because boys have opportunities for athletic recognition that are not open to girls.

Several studies have shown a positive correlation between participation in music and student leadership and acceptability. In one study, students in the top quarter on a social acceptability scale were compared with students in the lowest quarter on the scale.[3] The students rated themselves in singing ability. The testing procedure involved subjective evaluations and thus reduced the validity of the musical judgments. But it did reveal the correlation between social acceptability and confidence in an area of musical endeavor. The results showed that most students in the lowest quarter did not sing at all, while two-thirds of the boys and seven-eighths of the girls in the top quarter were average or better in singing.

In another study it was found that a high percentage of school leaders were active in music.[4] A survey by the LeBlanc Corporation strongly indicated that students who undertook instrumental music were more likely to be better students in almost all respects.[5]

[3] Raymond G. Kuhlen, *The Psychology of Adolescent Development* (New York: Harper & Brothers, 1952), pp. 340–41.

[4] Clarence E. Garder, "Characteristics of Outstanding High School Musicians," *Journal of Research in Music Education,* III, No. 1 (Spring 1955), 13–20.

[5] Unpublished study, LeBlanc Corporation, Kenosha, Wisc., 1961.

One must be careful to avoid confusing correlation with causation. The fact that two events are related does not necessarily mean that one causes the other. In these studies one cannot be sure whether the good students select music, or music makes good students; but that there is a relationship is clear.

The social aspects of music can be far-reaching. For example, music provides a point of rapport among students from different schools. They can meet at festivals and concerts, under circumstances in which success does not depend upon directly competing with the other fellow. This is an aspect of social interchange that athletic events seldom provide.

Psychological Factors

The problem of mental health is becoming increasingly important in our society and our schools. Authorities on mental health estimate that one child in twelve born today will at some time in his life be confined to a mental institution. Recently an extensive survey in New York City revealed that 81 per cent of the population in Manhattan could be classified as being "emotionally disturbed," 23 per cent severely so.[6] Such facts are shocking, and clearly place the psychological and personal adjustment of the student, as an objective of education, in an important place.

Music can play a significant role in helping students emotionally. Music has value not only because it is an *expresser* of emotion, but also because it is a *releaser* of emotions. In 1951 the *Music Journal* began publishing the results of a survey that covered some 5,000 children across the United States. The children were asked to respond to questions on their likes and dislikes in music, among other points.[7] The results were eye-opening. They indicated that the youngsters liked music not because it was culturally good for them, or because it improved them personally, but rather because it made them "feel good." They wrote comments such as "I can't describe how I feel when I play—it's wonderful, that's all." And, "When I get moody and down, I get away from the family and listen to my record player. . . ."

These remarks are significant because they were made by normal children. The need for emotional catharsis is common to everyone, and this is especially true of young people who are going through so many rapid changes. The problems of the teen-ager may seem simple to an adult, but they often cause more frustrations, fears, and repressed feelings than adult problems cause for a mature person. The secondary school student needs some means other than a racing automobile for emotional release. Admittedly, mere release of personal feelings does not solve a student's

[6] L. Srole, et al., *Mental Health in the Metropolis* (New York: McGraw-Hill Book Co., Inc., 1962), p. 138.

[7] Jack Dolph, "Teen-Agers and Music," *Music Journal* (September 1951), pp. 27 ff.

basic emotional difficulty, but it can help to prevent the intensification of these problems and take much of the "sting" out of them.

Although music does not always have the power to "soothe the savage breast," it can do wonders with many abnormal and exceptional people. The whole professional field of music therapy has grown in the last few decades. Universities have instituted training programs for persons who will use music as a means of curing mental illness. Certainly it is impressive to hear a performance by the Glee Club of the Moore School in Detroit, Michigan. In this school for delinquent boys, the Glee Club has successfully helped many of the boys adjust so that they can "graduate" into the regular public schools.

Avocational Value

A great deal has been said recently about the worthy use of leisure time. William G. Carr, Executive Secretary of the National Education Association, has this comment about the future of education in a world of increasing leisure:

> A fourth aspect of quality in education during the next 20 years will be a great enrichment in art, in music, in literature, in all those occupations of mankind which we broadly call cultural. Since 1900, the average life span has increased by 20 years, while the average work week has decreased by 20 hours. These trends will continue.
>
> Will these added years, these new hours of freedom from toil, be spent to any real advantage? Will they be used to refine life or to cheapen it? In the coming years the schools will respond to these questions by a new emphasis on the pursuit of happiness. And by happiness, I do not mean merely the alternation of benumbed idleness with sensory excitements. I mean that self-realization which comes from a purposeful and abundant life.[8]

Music is one of the most common avocations in modern-day America. The most desirable form of avocational activity from the music educator's point of view is that of active participation—playing in a community orchestra, singing in a church choir, or playing chamber music. Fortunately, the growth of local opera groups, orchestras, and choirs has been gratifying, although there is still much room for further growth.

Far greater than the number of people who take part in musical groups is the number who listen to music. Because of mass communication and recordings, practically the entire population of the nation is involved with music as listeners. Thus, the training of intelligent listeners is one of music education's greatest challenges and opportunities.

An additional point can be made about music's avocational value. In

[8] William G. Carr, "What's Past Is Prologue," *NEA Journal*, XLVI (December 1957), 605.

many communities parents have been "sold" on music for their children with slogans such as, "A boy who blows a horn will never blow a safe." Although the matter of guiding juvenile behavior is far more complex than the statement indicates, it is true that a musical activity gives a youngster a worthwhile way to spend his time and efforts. Teen-agers are going to use their energies in one way or another, and music is one excellent means of occupying them constructively.

Doubtful Claims

Just as there is a need to state those points that recommend a place for music in the curriculum, there is likewise a need to guard against making claims that are not significant. Advocating music for reasons that have no supportable basis only diverts attention from the truly valid reasons for music's place in the curriculum, weakens the justifiable claims, and makes music educators appear to others as careless, wishful thinkers. As an example of this, overzealous promoters of music in the schools have made the claim that music is a health builder. To build a case for school music on such a premise is a mistake. For one thing, there is almost no evidence to support the conclusion that music is particularly beneficial to physical health. In the second place, there are such subjects as physical training and health education in the curriculum. The contributions of these subjects to physical well-being are so much greater than those of music that a comparison between them in this regard becomes almost ludicrous.

The same might be said of music as an agent for developing patriotism or citizenship. Singing patriotic songs may help somewhat in making the student more sensitive to patriotism. But when compared with courses in citizenship, government, social science, and history, can music be considered a significant promoter in this respect? When a school official wants the students to have more work in citizenship, he assigns additional time to courses whose major purpose is instruction in citizenship, and not to music, in which citizenship is only one of several purposes.

Music teachers would do well to question one other claim: music teaches moral and spiritual values. The word "spiritual" may require definition in this case. If spiritual means incorporeal or nonmaterial, then music does have great spiritual value, and offers the students a worthy experience with something nonmaterial. But if the word "spiritual" is used to mean sacred or ecclesiastical, then the claim, along with the claim of moral value, is on shaky ground for three reasons. One: The principle of the separation of church and state prohibits the public school from delving deeply into this area. If a religious number is sung in the public school, it is for the musical value of the song, and not for its religious message. Two: Even though a student may sing songs of patriotic and moral worth, there is no evidence that he thereby becomes a more responsible citizen. Three: Rightly or wrongly, the public has heard much about eccentric and immoral musicians and artists. It would be difficult indeed to convince the layman that music is a builder of morality, rather than a hindrance to moral conduct.

THE TEACHER AND EDUCATIONAL OBJECTIVES

The teacher's role in determining goals in public education is ambiguous, presenting as it does both limitations and opportunities. A teacher in the public schools of the United States is limited in the sense that he has to accept the broad objectives endorsed by the educational system. No teacher can go contrary to these goals without harming in some way the total effectiveness of the educational effort. For instance, no teacher can ignore the many for the benefit of the few, without detracting from the accomplishments of the schools. Such a practice is contrary to the tenets of public education today.

The objectives of education apply to all areas of the school, including music. Sometimes music teachers feel that since music is a specialized activity, there is no need to be concerned with what the rest of the school is trying to do. Music *is* a specialized study, but it operates within the framework of the school. Everyone wants to have student music organizations perform well, but not at the expense of everything the school seeks to accomplish.

The educational mandates that guide the individual teacher are broad and general. This is quite proper because room must be left for individual initiative and operation; this is one of democracy's great strengths. The teacher fills in the details, deciding what shall be taught in a particular school with its unique combination of students, musical backgrounds, and facilities. It is the teacher who gives substance to the general objectives of education. Without this "filling in" process by the teacher, the general goals of education would not be met.

The forces at play in developing a curriculum are diverse, and often conflicting. Many teachers and teachers-to-be must wonder where they fit into the picture. Is the teacher the one to determine what should be taught in music, or is he to teach what he is told? Who finally decides such matters: teachers, administrators, school boards, state offices of education, or the public? Unlike European countries, the United States government has no agency which possesses authority over what the schools shall teach. This matter is left to the states and local school boards. Most of the people holding positions of school governance are elected by the people or appointed by elected officials. Basically, therefore, the curriculum derives its authorization from the public at large.

But the matter does not rest there, because the public in turn looks for guidance from the professional educator. The views of educators nationally are articulated by professional associations such as the National Congress of Parents and Teachers, professional writings in books and journals, and in the local community by the local teachers and administrators. Therefore, the relationship between the public and the teachers is active and dynamic, with each influencing the other. In this relationship the teacher has a definite role to play in providing the public with the benefit of his expertness in matters of education.

In a similar manner, the teacher can influence decisions within the school system. The superintendent of schools is employed by the board of education to administer the total educational effort of the school district according to the policies established by the board. He must consider not only the curricular problems of music, but also the effect of the program on the finances of the school district, the building space available, and the support and interest of the public. Because the superintendent cannot know all and do all, he must delegate much of his responsibility. He must depend upon the music staff for recommendations concerning the music program. In light of the other educational demands on the school system, he will render a judgment as to how completely the suggestions of the music faculty can be followed. Unless he is informed about what the music teacher feels is necessary, he will assume that the present situation is satisfactory.

When a teacher thinks about his role in matters of curriculum, he is likely to ask, "Yes, I understand the need for the aesthetic in the educated human being, but my superintendent has had little training in such things. Building a music program on such a basis is something he doesn't understand. What should I do?" This is a difficult and crucial problem. The superintendent represents much of contemporary American society, which esteems practical accomplishment and the production of goods. Achievement can be recognized and measured rather easily in the fields of science, foreign language, and physical education. When the objectives are less tangible, as in music, the teacher needs to educate not only the students in his class, but likewise the public and often the school administration. To answer the question specifically, the teacher must inform the administrator about what the music program is seeking to do. It is not enough to let him know what is wanted; the *why*, the basis for the teacher's view, must be made clear. The teacher should never abandon what he knows to be good music education, nor embrace what he thinks the administrator wants taught. Rather he needs to educate his supervisor patiently, persistently, and tactfully, as to why music is included in the schools and what is needed to accomplish its goals.

If music is to be regarded as a curricular subject, then it must be considerably more than "show biz." Everyone likes to be entertained, especially when it is free. Service clubs are delighted to have luncheon entertainment provided by the schools, and football fans are happy to be treated to a band show at half-time. Attractive as this prospect may be (it's fun for the students and an ego-builder for the teacher), the public must be educated to the fact that music is first of all a school subject, and in common with other subjects in the school, it seeks to teach the students something.

Many times school music has been "sold" to the public and the school administrator on the basis of its public-relations value. Music, along with physical education, is especially susceptible to this use (or misuse). Too often superintendents are urged to buy a sousaphone because the band needs it to look good on the football field or win a higher rating in the festival, not because the sousaphone is necessary for a better instrumentation by which the students can learn more adequately how the music should sound. The fact that a neighboring school band, orchestra, or chorus might "show us up" has been used more than once to sway the thinking of a superintendent, who because of his position is sensitive to public opinion. The attempt to achieve the right ends by the wrong means has come back to haunt some teachers. When the music program becomes a servant to public relations, its emphasis is changed from education to entertainment. Its tendency is to concentrate on the most talented young persons and to brush over the mass of the students, who some day will become the public which elects school boards who in turn hire superintendents.

Strong, articulate teacher guidance is vital in establishing an effective music curriculum. The music teacher must know why music is needed in the schools and what course content will best fill this need. Then he must educate the school administration and the public on these points.

Questions

1. Is Mr. Atkins' devotion to warm-up routines (page 9) justifiable philosophically? Why, or why not?
2. Suppose that you are Miss Green (page 10). How would you justify the inclusion of music in the curriculum for all the seventh-grade students? Would the reasons differ significantly from those used for inclusion of music in the senior high school?
3. The foregoing chapter stressed that the primary reason for music in the schools is to give the students an understanding of its aesthetic qualities. Is this also the primary function of art? of English literature? of typing and home economics? of mathematics? of extracurricular activities such as scout-

ing and interscholastic athletics? If the reasons are not the same, in what ways are they different?

4. Assume that an instrumental music teacher believes that one of the major purposes of his job is the development of self-confidence and poise in the students. In what way, if any, will his teaching differ from that of the teacher who is primarily interested in the development of a knowledge about and sensitivity to music? What, if anything, does a music teacher do specifically to develop character or provide emotional catharsis for students in his classes?

5. Suppose that you are teaching in a school whose music budget is very inadequate, especially in relation to the support given other areas of the curriculum. The members of the music faculty decide to go to the superintendent to present their case for increased financial support. What points would you make as reasons for the increase? Would comparisons with the amount spent in other schools for the music curriculum be a valid technique? Suppose that the average size of the general music classes is seventy. What points could be made for reducing their size?

6. Assume that you are asked to give a fifteen-minute talk for a local service club on the local school music curriculum. How would you explain in good, practical terms about the goal of aesthetic sensitivity? Or would you just ignore the subject, and talk about the more obvious features of the program?

7. How consistent with the objectives of education in the United States are the following statements by music teachers?
   a. "You can't make a silk purse out of a sow's ear. No use straining yourself over a kid who just doesn't have it."
   b. "I've one of the best positions in the state. Three fine junior highs feeding in well-trained players, and I use the best of these."
   c. "I know that not many youngsters take choral music. But if the few I have get a good music education—not just the milktoast so many teachers hand out today—it will be worth it."
   d. "I don't care how poor they are, or what color their skins happen to be. I'm determined to teach them as much as I can about music and what makes it tick."

Suggested Readings

Leonhard, Charles, and Robert W. House, *Foundations and Principles of Music Education.* New York: McGraw-Hill Book Company, Inc., 1959. Chapters IV and VI.

McMurray, Foster, "Pragmatism in Music Education," *Basic Concepts in Music Education,* 57th Yearbook, Part I. National Society for the Study of Education. Chicago: University of Chicago Press, 1958.

Meyer, Leonard B., *Emotion and Meaning in Music*. Chicago: University of Chicago Press, 1956.

Reimer, Bennett, "Leonard Meyer's Theory of Value and Greatness in Music," *Journal of Research in Music Education*, Fall 1962, p. 87.

————, "What Music Cannot Do," *Music Educators Journal*, September–October 1959, pp. 40–45.

III

teen-agers: their manner and motivation

The promise and problems of the youth of today have not suffered from a lack of attention in television, newspapers, magazines, and professional journals. Despite all of this attention, the path of the adolescent into adulthood has become no easier; indeed, with the rest of the modern world, it has grown more complex. Nor has the abundance of attention greatly helped the teacher, who finds some of the discussion contradictory, inconclusive, or applicable only to specific problems which the teacher seldom encounters.

What, then, must the music teacher know about teen-agers in order to teach them properly? He must be aware of the factors that have the greatest influence in shaping the adolescent. Knowing these, he can develop his procedures toward maximum effectiveness.

EMOTIONS AND ATTITUDES

Between the ages of twelve and eighteen a young person makes a transition from childhood to adulthood that requires much adjustment, even under the best of conditions. He passes from a state of limited responsibilities to adult responsibilities of such magnitude as serving in the armed forces, deciding upon a vocation, and selecting a partner in marriage. The adolescent of today finds the transition difficult, in part because society has poorly defined what an adult is and what he should do. "A woman's place is in the home" was an apt aphorism one hundred years ago. Today it is not. The lack of social definition has been caused by two world wars, tremendous technical advances, a severe depression, a change in the status of women, a seemingly permanent state of international tension, and many other changes—all within a generation or two.

The process of emancipation from adult authority causes the teen-ager much anxiety. Learning to live without adult supervision is a necessary part of life. But what agonies it can cause the teen-ager, the parent, and the teacher! The adolescent wants to be free from adult control, and yet at the same time he wants supervision because he does not know how to get along without it. The question of how much freedom to give the child is of deep concern for conscientious parents and teachers.

Traditionally there has been conflict between youth and the adult community. Older people tend to look upon youth as impractical, brash, and foolhardy; young people sometimes regard their elders as old-fashioned and insensitive to change. Margaret Mead, outstanding American anthropologist, has said that the rapid pace of our changing civilization has made children at the age of five accept as commonplace some ideas to which many adults will never quite become reconciled.[1] This, of course, causes much lack of understanding between students and teacher, and between children and parents.

Another adolescent problem is the growing awareness of sex. In addition to learning an adult role and freeing himself from adult authority, the adolescent has this mysterious and powerful force with which to contend. Society has no well-defined attitude toward sex. The adult world preaches chastity before marriage, and yet a novel with a goodly dose of promiscuity can easily become a best-seller. Little wonder that the adolescent may become confused in understanding this growing force within him.

Finally, the adolescent is forming new concepts of himself and of his capabilities. Kuhlen says of this problem, "The desire to achieve and maintain satisfactory personal status seemed especially important during the teens."[2] Concern over self-capabilities and status makes the teen-ager particularly wary of doing something in which he is not sure of himself. The teacher must be careful in the attitude he takes toward mistakes in learning. These four problem areas—adult expectations, emancipation from adult authority, awareness of sex, and the formation of concepts about self—cause the adolescent to behave in ways that are sometimes disconcerting.

A primary characteristic of the emotional behavior of the teen-ager is intensity.[3] Emotional reactions are often entirely out of proportion to the stimuli that precipitated them. Adolescent emotions are marked by

[1] Margaret Mead, *The School in American Culture* (Cambridge, Mass.: Harvard University Press, 1951), pp. 33–34.

[2] Raymond G. Kuhlen, *The Psychology of Adolescent Development* (New York: Harper & Brothers, 1952), p. 274.

[3] Elizabeth B. Hurlock, *Adolescent Development* (McGraw-Hill Book Co., Inc., 1949), p. 114.

inconsistency and extremes of feeling. Within moments the mood can change from sorrow to joy, from pride to humility. These emotions are easily set off because teen-agers possess what might be called a low emotional "boiling point."

Teen-agers, especially those of junior high school age, lack control in expressing their emotions. Crying, giggling, poking a neighbor, squirming, tugging at clothing, and tapping a pencil all indicate a lack of proper channels of expression. Because music provides an avenue for expression, it can be especially valuable to students of this age.

SOCIAL DEVELOPMENT

The process of maturation also gives rise to social difficulties. Generally, as the child reaches adolescence, the approval of adults is no longer as important as the approval of the peer group. Teen-agers need to feel that they "belong" and are accepted by their fellow students, so they frequently form cliques. A publication of the U.S. Department of Health, Education, and Welfare states the problem in this way:

> Adolescents today are cut off, probably more than ever before, from the adult society. They are still oriented toward fulfilling their parents' desires, but they look very much to their peers for approval. As a consequence, American society now has in its midst a set of small teenage subcultures which focus teenage interests and attitudes on things far removed from adult responsibilities, subcultures which may develop standards that lead away from the goals toward which the schools are intended to lead.[4]

The monograph goes on to point out that for most boys being a good athlete is far more important than being a good student academically, and that for girls pretty clothes and popularity with other teen-agers are the most important.[5] Although it may distress the educator, most teen-age boys worry more about having a car than about earning good grades.

Many times the teen-ager is especially interested in being accepted by members of the opposite sex. Both popular notion and scientific data point to the importance of boy-girl relationships. One study showed that as a topic of conversation among adolescent boys, sports led the list, the subject of girls was a close second, and the third topic, school, ran far behind.[6] Some adolescents go to all sorts of ludicrous extremes to have themselves accepted by the opposite sex. Fads come and go, creating many a strange spectacle—boys and girls with eccentric hair styles and

[4] James S. Coleman, *Social Climates in High Schools,* U.S. Department of Health, Education, and Welfare Cooperative Research Monograph No. 4 (Washington, D.C.: U.S. Government Printing Office, 1961), p. 7.

[5] *Ibid.*, pp. 10–15.

[6] Urban H. Fleege, *Self-Revelation of the Adolescent Boy* (Milwaukee: The Bruce Publishing Co., 1945), p. 234.

unusual manner of dress. Underneath the fads there are strong motivating forces.

The importance of peer acceptance suggests two practical considerations for the music teacher. First, he must be extremely careful about any action which may cause the teen-ager to "lose face" in front of his friends. Adolescents do not want to be isolated. This feeling is so strong that many of them are even sensitive about being singled out for praise. Another practical application of peer approval is seen in the performer-audience relationship when a school music group appears before the student body. The judgment of peers affects the attitude of the members of the organization toward that organization, which in turn affects the kind of musical learning that can take place.

PHYSICAL AND VOCAL DEVELOPMENT

Particularly in the seventh and eighth grades, the girls are often physically and mentally more mature than the boys. This condition exists to some degree throughout high school, although boys tend to catch up. Individual variations are striking, especially in junior high school. Differences in height of a foot or more are not uncommon. Because growth can occur rapidly, especially in boys, there is a tendency toward physical awkwardness, with a limited level of endurance.

Less well-understood are the changes that occur in the voice. When the boy reaches puberty, the voice box enlarges to about twice its former size. Because the vocal cords double in length, the pitch of the voice drops about one octave. More boys experience voice change at thirteen years of age than at any other, with a lesser but equal number changing at age twelve and fourteen, and an even smaller number at eleven or fifteen.[7] In most cases, the voice change occurs simultaneously with other bodily maturation. With the change in the size of the vocal apparatus, the boy experiences difficulty in regaining muscular control over the voice. He is more awkward vocally than he is in other physical movements. In a real sense, he must learn to use his voice all over again. Hence the changing voice is marked by instability and inconsistency; some boys for a period of a month or two can sing either a treble or bass part with equal ease. The teaching of boys whose voices are changing is a complex and important subject which is discussed in some detail in Chapter Twelve.

Girls' voices change also, but because there is no drastic change of pitch, there is no particular vocal problem. Most girls in junior high school have voices which are light and fluty in quality, with a limited volume. Maturation brings about the distinctive tonal characteristics that differentiate between alto and soprano. There is usually a widening of range

[7] Glenn V. Ramsey, "The Sexual Development of Boys," *American Journal of Psychology*, LVI, No. 2 (1943), 217.

also. The voices of both boys and girls deepen and become richer in quality.

TEEN-AGE MUSICAL DEVELOPMENT

It is easy for musicians who have had training at the collegiate level (especially beginning teachers) to overestimate the musical background of most teen-age students. The disparity in background between teacher and pupil becomes more striking when one considers the musical history of a typical school music teacher. He had private instruction in voice or an instrument before entering high school. He continued private study and played or sang in several high school organizations. He was one of the minority of high school seniors who went on to college. At this stage he was already marked as being above average musically. In college, music was his major field of study, and, in addition, he may be working on a graduate degree. One would have to search among hundreds of people from the general population in order to find another with as much background in music.

Little wonder, then, that it is often hard for the music teacher and the student to understand each other. The teen-ager has had vastly fewer experiences of almost all types than the teacher. Granted, some students are exceptional, but the average student is musically so far behind that it is even difficult to communicate with him about music. He is likely to regard Broadway musical comedies as "classical" music, and he may think that Baroque refers to a salad dressing. When a trained musician sees an A sharp appearing on a piece of music in E major, something clicks within him that says this is an altered tone or a modulation. This same A sharp means very little to most adolescents. The teacher has developed a concept of tone quality. But what about the teen-ager? Where has he had the chance to hear a good tone? on the radio or television? from the jukebox? in the movies? How many good concerts does a high school student hear in a year? In the small towns there are almost no performances, save by local amateur organizations. In the cities, concerts are expensive, and frequently the distances to the downtown area are great. Besides, children from the lower economic areas and minority groups feel out of place among the well-adorned patrons of many concert halls, and therefore do not attend such programs. The teacher has had experiences with music that his students have not had. He may have played or sung under a fine director when the music thrilled him "to his toes." Can anyone describe this to a person who has never experienced anything like it?

A teacher has to be careful what he says when he tries to convey his feelings to the students.

> A fine, devoted choral director from a college was leading a massed high school choir at a festival. The music was a beautiful Bach chorale. Throughout the rehearsal the director yelled directions such as,

> "Now you are on your knees pleading before God! Shake your hearts! Shake your hearts!"
>
> When the students returned to their schools the next day, some of them asked their own teachers, "Was that director a little 'off' in the head?"

It is easy for the trained musician to understand what the director meant by his exhortations. The students, however, simply did not have enough experience to understand.

Some music teachers talk about "covered tones" to their vocal students. This is fine *if* the covered tone has been demonstrated to them. Words such as "light," "intense," "intonation," and "sustain" also need careful demonstration, and the difference between tone quality and pitch has to be clarified. The teacher must be constantly aware of the lack of musical background in his students, so that he can present the material in an understanding and patient manner.

MOTIVATION AND INTEREST

There is little agreement among psychologists and educators as to why and how a person is motivated. It is declared that:

1) Students are naturally interested, and the teacher need only open the doors of learning so that interest may be satiated.
2) Students are interested in something when it becomes involved with self.
3) Students are interested in something which has a fascination for them.
4) Interest is intrinsic (coming entirely from within the person) and is based upon the student's prior experiences; therefore the teacher can do little to whet this interest.
5) Interest is a state of tension in the student, which can be relieved by fulfilling some purpose.
6) Interests are the result of basic biological needs that must be satisfied.

There is some truth in all these statements. Since biological motivations are based on physical needs of the human organism, they are easily understood. Other motivations, however, are so complex that one can only theorize about them.

Three points seem significant for the music teacher. One concerns the relationship between the intrinsic and extrinsic theories. It is clear that interest is not entirely extrinsic. If it were, then would not everyone be interested in the same things? On the other hand, interest is not totally intrinsic. It has to come from somewhere; except for biological motivations, people are not born with interests. Clearly, a person's experiences are a prominent factor here. For the music teacher, then, the answer lies in a synthesis of the two positions. Extrinsic motivation, yes; but the teacher cannot expect lasting success merely by concocting a mechanical rabbit which the students by their natures will chase. Intrinsic motivation, yes; but the teacher must not assume the fatalistic attitude that he can do nothing to spark the students' interest.

The second significant fact is that adolescents' interests are not yet fully stabilized. To many adults, teen-agers appear fickle and impulsive, and to an extent this is true. A boy or girl at fifteen has not established permanent beliefs and interests. A student may like music under one set of circumstances, and heartily dislike it under another. There are a few students whose intrinsic interest in music is so great that it can scarcely be daunted no matter what the conditions may be; and by the same token, there are others who can never become interested, regardless of favorable circumstances. But with the majority of students, interests are flexible enough to be influenced by the quality of teaching.

The third point is that people become interested in activities in which they can enhance the status of self. Interest is further stimulated when the self becomes identified with the group. Who has not observed the brother and sister who say nasty things to each other? Yet, when an outsider makes a disparaging remark about either of them, almost miraculously they are united. What has happened is that an attack on one necessarily involved the ego of the other.

MOTIVATION TECHNIQUES IN MUSIC GROUPS

Nearly everything a teacher does in guiding the learning experiences of his students is related to motivation. Motivation cannot be separated from the process of teaching. Motivation influences how much learning takes place, and it is equally true that learning is a motivator. If, for example, the students are helped to understand better what accurate intonation is and are better able to perform in tune, then their success in learning will motivate them toward further study and enjoyment of music. Therefore, a teacher's best motivational technique is his ability to teach.

In discussing motivation in music, some distinction must be made between an organization, such as a band, and a class, such as music theory. The performing group meets as a class in which music learning should take place. But it is more than that. It needs to possess a group spirit of persons united in the achievement of a common end: the presentation of successful musical performances. A student in band can have a sense of belonging that the student in theory cannot have. A theory class does not present its efforts before the public; therefore it is not evaluated as a group. In a class, the students succeed or fail largely on an individual basis, but an orchestra succeeds or fails much more as a group. Both class and organization derive their motivation from the attraction of music, and from the excitement and satisfaction of learning it. The chief difference is that a teacher of a musical organization can make use of several techniques in addition to those normally employed in good music teaching. Each of the following ideas seeks to involve the students more fully in the welfare of the group so that they will gain additional nonmusical motivation.

1) Give awards for service rendered. This recognizes the faithful, and lets the rest of the students know that good service is esteemed. There is divided opinion about the use of awards. Some educators feel that the student should give a course his best efforts not because he will receive an award, but rather because the course seems worthwhile to him. Such motivation is certainly to be desired. Nevertheless, in our society, public recognition is so much a part of life that, practically speaking, the teacher can ill afford to disregard the fact. True, awards are a form of extrinsic motivation. If they are not over-emphasized, they can be regarded not as a mere motivating device but as a means of recognizing those students who under any circumstances would do better-than-average work.

2) Have a group uniform for use in public performances.

3) Let the students invest in the group. This gives them some equity in the success of the organization. One choir had each new member buy a stole with the school letters embroidered on it. The stoles were worn with the robes for all performances, and each year a service bar was added. The stoles gave the choir a better appearance, and hence a morale boost. Members were encouraged to keep their stoles permanently after graduation. In instrumental music most students have purchased an instrument, therefore they already have an investment in music.

4) Have the graduates of the group come back and sit in on rehearsals when they can. One choir has a particular number that it performs at every spring concert. All the choir alumni in the audience are asked to come up to the stage and sing with the group for that number.

5) Make sure that names of all members are printed in the concert programs. Double-check to make certain that they are spelled correctly, and that none have been omitted.

6) Involve as many students as possible in the operation of the organization—set-up committee, uniform committee, library committee, student officers, and so on. What director would object to being relieved of some of the routine duties! Occasionally teachers complain that the students do not do a good enough job, and that a few students do not take any assignment seriously. In the first case, it should be remembered that the students are far younger and less capable than the teacher. They need much guidance and frequent checking to see that they are doing their jobs properly. As for the students who cannot fulfill their obligations, it is wise to talk with them in private about the situation. If they are not interested, let them resign and have the group elect someone else to replace them.

7) Help the students plan a "Parents' Night," when their parents come for an informal orientation to the organization. A potluck supper can be

held, after which the group performs some music. The numbers need not all be learned and ready for performance, because parents frequently enjoy seeing the stages of development through which the music is perfected. The group might even try sightreading a number. Then the students can explain about awards, committees, and other features of the organization.

8) Make use of good group pictures. Besides being used in the school yearbook, they can be placed in the school and town newspapers and on posters advertising the performances.

9) Investigate the possibility of making a recording of the group. Some companies will make recordings from a tape which is supplied them, and from this they make a standard microgroove recording, complete with a printed label.[8] A few of these companies will improve the sound of the finished product by re-recording through an echo chamber, a device used in most commercial recordings to add life to the sound. These records can then be bought by the group members. More important than the keepsake value of the recording is the obvious incentive this gives the students to produce a high-quality performance.

GROUP MORALE

An effective means of increasing interest and ego-involvement on the part of the members is through the development of a group spirit. Persons have made tremendous efforts and sacrifices for a group, team, or nation. Group consciousness is a major reason for the use of uniforms, flags, emblems, and organized cheers—all symbols of solidarity. In musical performance, *esprit de corps* has a decided effect upon the actual musical results that are achieved, and the musical result, in turn, is a strong influence in building group feeling. When a spirit of unity prevails in an organization, a student will *not* reason, "Well, the band was poor, but I did a good job, so I'm satisfied." Rather he will think, "The band was poor, and I'm sorry. After all, I'm a little bit of the band."

Morale, motivation, and group success are necessary in achieving good performing organizations in which a high level of learning takes place. Teen-agers hunger for a favorable response from other young people; few are unmoved by an appeal for group success. The teacher should realize that he is on firm ground psychologically when he says, "Look, no one wants to be a member of a group that is the laugh of the school. The way for you to succeed is to learn the music so that the audience will enjoy hearing it." The teacher should realize, too, that the vast majority of teen-agers do not want the less-motivated students to detract from the

[8] Permission to record copyrighted songs must be obtained from copyright owners through their licensing agencies.

group's efforts. The teacher must protect the interests of the conscientious students.

Since "success" affects greatly the motivation and morale of teen-agers, it is necessary for them to understand what constitutes "success." How they arrive at an evaluation of the group's work is a matter of the first importance.

Three opinions will influence the students' evaluation of their performing ability. The first, though not the most important, is the opinion of the teacher as revealed in his comments and reactions. The students are interested in specific comments; they want to know how well or how badly they did. For instance, "It was quite good (very good, rather good), but we still need to be more careful about our attacks and entrances."

The students would be less than human if they did not rate highly the response of the audience and the remarks of the audience to them after the program. Because of the importance of peer groups, the musicians are particularly sensitive to the response at a school assembly. A wise teacher makes an effort to receive a positive opinion from this diverse group. The topic of presenting performances is covered in detail in Chapter Eleven.

In time, a third evaluation should become more important, and that is the members' own opinion. As the year progresses, the students should be given standards by which to judge their own work. This is an integral part of their education in music. They should learn to be on the alert for poor attacks, faulty intonation, and inappropriate tone quality. The development of critical listening is the key to mature evaluation.

ATTITUDE OF THE TEACHER

A significant factor in personal and group morale is the general spirit established in the classroom by the teacher. Since the subject of music is so closely intertwined with feeling, a music group requires a higher degree of pupil-teacher rapport than almost any other organization. The teacher cannot help being aware of the feelings of his students, and the students, in turn, are quickly conscious of a teacher's attitude and his mood. If he is unenthusiastic, so are they.

Students will not try to improve if they are criticized constantly. Everyone is sensitive about being criticized, music teachers included. Therefore, the teacher should adopt an attitude of "honest optimism." He must honestly evaluate the playing or singing; no good is accomplished if he tells his group their work is fine when really it is not. Optimism is essential, too, because teen-agers need encouragement, and the teacher must constantly be setting goals for the group. There is no need to become overwrought if one section can't master a particular point; almost always they will get it in time. Certainly they should not be punished over the passage: "Listen, we're going over this until you do it right!" It is infinitely better to be good-natured and say something like this, "Go home, get a good night's sleep, and eat a good breakfast. Then, when you come to class tomorrow, it will seem easy!"

It is important to be diplomatic in criticizing student musicians. In fact, it is a good idea to preface a criticism with a compliment: "Trombones, your tone was good right there at letter B, but the intonation was off. Check your pitch on that E natural; you were flat the last time you played it." The teacher should impress upon the students that their music has good points, but it can be still better. He should encourage them to improve and yet not frustrate them with ideals that are beyond their reach.

Much of the classroom atmosphere depends on the attitude of the teacher toward mistakes by the students. Most adolescents are not sure of themselves and are genuinely afraid of making an error. As a result, when they feel inadequate, they will "fake" their way along. The teacher must let them know that mistakes are common to every member of the human race, including the teacher. It is wise to encourage openness about errors. The teacher might say something like this: "Don't be ashamed of making a mistake; we're ashamed only of those we make over and over. If you're going to make a mistake, make it a *good* one; then we can correct it. Don't 'fake' in rehearsal and save your error for the concert. It's too late to do anything about it then." Such a statement is psychologically and educationally sound, because it leads to the correction rather than the suppression of errors.

The effectiveness of the teacher's admonition here depends, of course, on the degree to which the students feel confident in his word. He must, in effect, be able to look at the student who has made an error and say, "That's all right." The natural tendency is to be irritated and impatient. It is easy to forget that the football player who drops the touchdown pass in the end zone feels worse about his fumble than any of the spectators; the same is true in music. On the other hand, there are some instances in which a student makes the same mistake many times. If he is unwilling or unable to rectify his error, he needs private assistance from the director.

Educational psychologists have demonstrated the comparative effectiveness of praise and reproof.[9] In two different experiments, best results were shown by the praised group, next best by the reproved group; the poorest results came from the ignored group. However, only the praised group gained a statistically reliable amount over the ignored group. In another study, an educational psychologist secured subjective reports from graduate students as to practices that had affected their performance in high school. The findings are most revealing:

[9] G. S. Gates and L. Q. Rissland, "The Effect of Encouragement and Discouragement upon Performance," *Journal of Educational Psychology*, XIV (1923), 21–26.

Judgments as to the Effect of
Various Kinds of Incentives, in Per Cent[10]

	Effect on Work		
	Better	Same	Worse
Reprimand before others	40.4	13.3	46.2
Reprimand in private	83.1	9.9	6.9
Sarcasm before others	10.0	12.9	77.1
Sarcasm in private	18.2	16.9	64.9
Ridicule before others	7.2	23.8	69.0
Ridicule in private	21.2	15.2	63.6
Friendly conference	95.6	3.9	.4
Public commendation	90.6	8.3	1.1
Work for teacher best liked	95.1	3.8	1.0
Work for teacher least liked	5.9	26.9	67.2

One can see from these figures the importance to high school students of "saving face" in front of their peers. It also demonstrates the value of praise, the need for honest optimism, and the importance of the feelings of the student toward the teacher.

Good rapport between students and teacher is essential in the music class. It is achieved largely through the attitude of the teacher. In neither of the illustrations that follow does the example represent a single act that won the students over forever; rather the incidents were typical of the teacher's actions throughout the year.

> At the conclusion of a general music class which had been excellent in every regard—learning had been going on, participation had been high, singing enthusiastic and of good quality—Mr. Johnson found that he had just under two minutes left; not enough time to start something new. It was nearly 12:30 and the students would leave directly for the cafeteria.
>
> "Let's read the menu," he suggested. A boy was asked to go to the bulletin board which contained the week's menu, along with other school announcements. "Wait till I set the proper mood, Jeff," and he began to improvise on the piano the most pompous, booming fanfare he could muster. One would have thought the king was coming. Finally, the climactic, final chord. Jeff began to read, "Onion soup," then more thunderous piano music; "Wiener on a bun,"—more music —all to shrieks of glee from the class.

> The class was attempting to play a tune on the melody bells, with eight class members each holding one pitch of the octave. At a point that required one student to play her note twice, Mrs. Worthington said to the player, "Mary, hit the A twice."
>
> "Oh, no," Mary said quietly, "it's the G that should be struck twice."

[10] T. H. Briggs, "Praise and Censure as Incentives," *School and Society*, XXVI (1927), 596–98. The Society for the Advancement of Education. Reprinted by permission.

> Mary was right; Mrs. Worthington had inadvertently given the wrong note. "Oh dear!" she quipped, "First mistake I ever made in my life! Mary's right. Judy, it's your G that's struck twice."

In the first instance the teacher stopped taking himself so seriously, and sent the students from the room with a relaxed, positive feeling. In the second case, instead of becoming tense and overwrought, and engendering negative feelings in the students, the teacher let the error pass for what it was: a simple mistake.

A touch of humor helps immensely to maintain a relaxed feeling in the rehearsal room. Good humor does not consist merely of telling jokes and engaging in humorous antics. It is an attitude of having fun while you work. Start at "letter G as in goulash" or "C as in caramba." Humor can be worked into the directions given to the group. "Sopranos, you should hand the phrase over to the altos on a silver platter. But you know what you did last time? You tossed it to them on a garbage-can lid."

Another factor in teacher attitude which influences rapport involves the cohesiveness between the teacher and students. Never should the teacher allow a "wall" to develop between the students and himself. There should be no teacher vs. students; the teacher should not even think in terms of two separate interests. Rather, there should be a feeling of "we're doing this together." Inclusion, not separation, will achieve the best results and the most pleasure from teaching music. The students must be included, be "in" on plans, hopes, and the operation of the class.

A pleasant, optimistic outlook on the part of the teacher does not negate the need for firmness and consistency in dealing with young people. Consistency in this relationship gives the students a sense of security and confidence. If they never know what the teacher's reaction is going to be, they will never be quite sure how they should act.

> Miss Martin was determined that there be no "horse-play" in chorus rehearsal. On Monday Jim Norton, a weak bass, was caught tossing a bit of paper at another bass. Miss Martin immediately asked him to leave the room. He was given five hours after school, and his grade was lowered.
>
> On Wednesday Peter Ott, the only good tenor, was caught tossing a little piece of dried mud from off his shoe at another chorus member. Miss Martin just glowered at him and said, "Now look! Let's leave the horsing around to horses." Peter was given no penalties.

Kuhlen sets forth this observation on teacher behavior. In a study made of students' likes and dislikes in teachers, the best-liked teachers were characterized as being both friendly and businesslike; the least-liked, the opposite.[11] According to an extensive study by Hart, teacher actions that have the greatest importance in the eyes of pupils are 1) indications of fairness, 2) indications of cheerfulness, 3) indications of sympathetic

[11] Kuhlen, *op. cit.*, p. 482.

understanding, 4) indications of control, 5) indications of ability to get pupil response, and 6) indications of knowledge and skill.[12]

The attitude of the teacher is not the only factor that contributes to a proper atmosphere within the group. There should be a ban on destructive criticism by the students, especially in performing organizations. Some adolescents go through a stage of making smart and cutting remarks, even when they are totally uncalled for. Bad attitudes can easily "snowball" from a few people to many in a short time. Students who persist in talking negatively should be handled as behavior problems. On the other hand, the teacher should not be afraid of constructive suggestions, which often can be handled through a student officer arrangement. The students should be invited to express their thoughts about class activities, as long as their thinking is sincere and responsible. What should be avoided is the pointless, chronic complaining in which a few students like to indulge.

Finally, the teacher can now and then talk about good attitude. This does not mean long lectures or pep talks, but rather some occasional statements as to the meaning of group endeavor. Say to the students, "You should be proud to be a member of the band. You don't have to go around the school beating on your chest and shouting 'I'm in the band!' But you should feel glad that you're in it, and when you know you're doing good work, don't be afraid to say so." It never hurts to tell the performers, "There are sixty-five people in band, right? So when you hear the applause at the end of a number, one-sixty-fifth of that applause is for you. Enjoy it."

SECURING ADEQUATE MEMBERSHIP

A problem that concerns only elective performing organizations is that of recruiting and maintaining adequate membership. It is fine for a textbook to state that a sixty-five-piece band should have twenty B flat clarinets and two bassoons, or that the choir should have a tenor section nearly the size of the soprano section. But this does not mean that the teacher on the first day of school will find the prescribed membership in band or choir. What can he do about incomplete membership?

The music teacher should be clear in his own mind, and make clear to the administration and other teachers, the reason for seeking students for music groups. It is *not* to build a little "empire" for the music teacher. Rather, it is to have a group of sufficient variety and size to provide a better musical experience. An orchestra without violas and string basses is just as incomplete as a football team without a guard and tackle. The presence of a tenor section in a mixed choral group significantly affects the kind of music that is sung and studied. The performing organization and

[12] F. W. Hart, *Teachers and Teaching* (New York: The Macmillan Company, 1934), pp. 131–32, 250–51, 278–79.

the theory class are affected differently by the size of membership in relation to the results achieved.

Recruiting Members

A singing group can be built much more quickly than an instrumental group, which requires a training program encompassing several years. The problems and their solutions, however, are basically the same for both vocal and instrumental organizations.

The most effective way to get new students to join is to have a successful organization. The clothing store that announced, "Our best advertisements are being worn" had the right idea. The activities and attitudes of the present members are by far the best advertisement. A student who contemplates joining a music group is influenced, in most instances, by three things. First, he wants to know how the present membership feels about the group. If he hears grumbling, he will not feel encouraged to join. Second, the student's own impression, gained from hearing the group, helps him determine how well he thinks he would like the activity. If the choir sings only sacred numbers, and the student does not care for that type of music, he probably will not enroll, no matter how enthusiastic the members seem to be. Third, the impression the student gains about the teacher is important. Many high school students do not differentiate between liking music activity *per se* and liking the teacher. They gain their impression of a teacher from what they hear about him, and what they see of him in the halls and in assembly performances. So if the teacher walks around school with a long, glum face, many students will assume that his classes are similarly dreary.

What specifically can be done by a new teacher who starts the first week of school with only a small, incomplete enrollment of students who signed up the preceding spring? Here are some suggestions:

1) Meet with the school principal or head counselor. Try to get his approval for schedule changes for students who might want to enroll in a music course.

2) Obtain schedules of all students and make a list of those who have time for an additional course. As much as the new teacher may wish to succeed, he must not proselyte from the classes of other teachers!

3) Check the records to discover students who were members of music organizations in previous years but who are not now enrolled.

4) See personally those students who are able to enroll. Be enthusiastic, but don't plead. Some students wait until they have a chance to "size up" the new teacher before committing themselves.

5) Ask the present members for leads on likely prospects—students who have shown some inclination toward music.

6) Solicit recruiting ideas from the members and use them on posters such as the one shown here.

7) In vocal music, arrange a short, private audition for every new member. This is not only an opportunity to assess the student's abilities, but it is also a chance to meet him personally.

8) Make the first rehearsal a successful and pleasant experience. Accomplish something the first day, even if it is only the singing or playing of some simple music, in unison if necessary. Save many of the beginning-of-the-year routines for later (assigning music, robes or uniforms, and checking class lists). Be enthusiastic about the music organization—this is a prime requisite for a successful first rehearsal.

9) Keep up the membership drive for no longer than five days. Then start to make the existing group into the best possible organization.

Some of the suggested steps may seem to encourage membership in the organization by any student regardless of his musical ability. Actually, few students who express an interest in joining a music group are innately incapable of profiting from the experience. Most of them need encouragement in undertaking music study because they have doubts as to their ability.

Encouraging the Boys

So often music teachers, especially in vocal music, bemoan the lack of boys. "If I only had more boys," one vocal teacher complained. "Right now I have only four, and one of them has an unchanged voice." In many schools there is a shortage of boys in the ranks of string players, and even in band. Getting boys into music, and keeping them there, is a special challenge. Generally, male teachers have an easier time involving boys in music. Yet there are many women who have successfully recruited whole boys' glee clubs, so the sex of the teacher is not the crux of the problem.

Sometimes boys feel that music is not quite manly. Fortunately, this attitude has decreased considerably in the last twenty or thirty years, but its remnants still exist. Overcoming such an attitude is one important step in recruiting boys. The teacher can point out many important masculine musicians. There are the fine men's choruses; the outstanding bands in the military services which present excellent male vocalists; and the Metropolitan Opera Company which often features husky men as solo basses and tenors.

The idea that music and singing are not for boys is only part of their attitude problem. Many boys sincerely feel that they are unable to sing. This is probably a reaction to the change of voice and the accompanying uncertain and frustrated feelings it causes. So boys must be given encouragement and understanding. Their singing should never be ridiculed, nor should the girls be allowed to laugh at it. Further specific advice on helping boys vocally is included in other chapters of this book.

In some schools boys have been attracted to singing by the appeal of a barbershop quartet. This type of ensemble is especially useful when there are only a few boys, but it is not easily developed. In addition to a proper voice distribution of bass, baritone, and first and second tenor, it is necessary that the boys possess above-average musical talent. There are several books of barbershop quartet music available, but the parts are more difficult to sing than is generally supposed. Traditionally, barbershop singing is done "by ear," without the aid of notes, formal arrangement, or accompaniment; so a good sense of harmony is indispensable. Probably the simplest way to learn this music is to have the quartet sing along with recordings of barbershop singing. Despite the superficial quality of much of the quartet literature, this type of music can create a great deal of interest in singing.

For some reason, a group of boys who sing with a big, strong tone can capture an audience, even though they are singing a simple unison song with not too much polish. The boys may be in a group of their own, or the male section of the chorus may sing alone. In either case, the group should appear before an audience at a reasonably early date, because a long wait before performing allows interest to wane. It is best not to attempt difficult works; rather, fairly simple music in unison or two parts should be sung. Having undergone a successful performance, the group will be convinced that boys can and should sing. The more exacting work in parts should come after morale and interest have been established.

Both vocal and instrumental music teachers usually welcome a member of the school's football or basketball team. The younger boys look up to athletes, whose entrance into the group seems to place the seal of approval on music—an approval that weighs heavily with the rest of the student body. The blessing of athletes in music can be a mixed one, however. These boys are putting their best time and effort into their sports activities, and music is definitely in second place. Then, they are the object of so much attention that they tend to be a bit harder to handle. The teacher is glad when he gets boys from the school teams in music, but his success need not depend on them.

Care must be used in the selection of music. Boys do not take readily to songs they feel are frilly and meaningless. By contrast, the boys in one high school choir became fond of the work "In Solemn Silence" by Ippolitov-Ivanov. It is a slow, chordal piece—a prayer to God that the horrible sufferings of war may pass. Though not the type of work one usually thinks that a high school student would like, it was one they could comprehend, and they sang it with dignity and understanding.

Talk to boys in concrete terms. Inspirational jargon about "falling on your knees" is the type of approach that many high school boys simply cannot understand. Instead of directing them to use "a more intimate style," tell them to sing the passage like one of the well-known crooners of the day. Rather than saying, "Boys, that sounded just lovely!" shout out, "Hey fellas, that's the way to do it—with some polish!" When boys talk at the wrong time in class, or misbehave in any way, there is no subtlety to it. It is right out where everyone can see it. So don't be subtle about reprimanding them. Instead of squeaking out, "Boys, you behave yourselves now," bark out in a firm voice, accompanied by a forcefully pointed finger (and a twinkle in the eye), "John Jones, you cut that out!" The teacher should be honest, unafraid, and make himself understood; and he will get along fine with the boys.

GRADING STUDENTS

Music teachers often consider grading a necessary nuisance, and feel, with much justification, that any grading system inadequately reflects what the student is really accomplishing in music class. Therefore the tendency is to consider grading as a rather insignificant, routine duty. The students look at grades with interest and concern, even though, paradoxically, in the long run grades as such are not a primary motivation for most teen-agers. Because young people are sensitive about grades received, and because learnings in music class are less often subjected to concrete examination in written form, it is important that the manner of grading indicate to the students that the teacher is fair and understanding. If grading is handled brusquely or carelessly, it can become a barrier impeding the establishment of a good relationship between students and teacher.

The purpose of grading, of course, is to provide parents, student, and teacher with the most accurate picture possible of the student's work. The grading process should be an integral part of the instruction. Tests are given because they are a valid means of extending the learning process, not because they provide the teacher with ammunition to use on report cards. Testing procedures, like teaching methods, will vary according to the level of the students and type of class.

Music teachers face two dilemmas in grading: one between pupil growth and a fixed standard, and the other between musical accomplishment and class deportment. Marks can be determined in relation to some standard fixed by the teacher, with an "A" or 100 representing perfection in this system, or they can be decided in relation to the progress and effort that the student has shown. Both methods have validity when applied to the right situations. In college work a grade should represent the fulfilling of some standard. On the other hand, the concept of rigid standards is quite out of place in the elementary and junior high school, and to a lesser degree in the high school. It is somewhat unfair to grade a child with many musical advantages by the same standard as another child with an impoverished musical background. By the time a student reaches high school, however, one cannot ignore the existence of some standard of achievement.

A report on the student's musical achievement and his contribution to the entire group is especially pertinent in performing organizations. A boy may be the best tenor in the choir; but if his behavior impedes the progress of the group, determining his proper grade is difficult, even in a school that has a dual marking system—one for academic achievement and one for citizenship.

These questions must be resolved thoughtfully by the teacher, keeping in mind the age and musical development of the students, and the type of class. In any case, the teacher needs to make a clear-cut set of criteria for grading, one that is consistent with the over-all evaluation procedures of the school. To eliminate later misunderstanding, these standards can be printed and given to each student. The criteria may or may not carry definite point or percentage values. The assignment of so many points for effort, so many for deportment, so many for technique and the like, gives the students a sense of concreteness, but in fact the teacher can and should adjust the evaluation on each factor slightly so that the student gets the grade the teacher feels he deserves.

It should be made clear to the student that practically speaking the factors forming a grade are interrelated; that effort is usually related to accomplishment, for example. Here is a sample set of criteria, which considers both effort and ability:

Grade of A

1) Has shown much improvement.
2) Has shown outstanding willingness to assume responsibility, to cooperate, and to better the organization.
3) Has shown outstanding ability to perform a part with accuracy and a good sense of ensemble.
4) Has shown exceptional ability to perform with a properly produced, pleasant tone quality.
5) Has shown exceptional understanding of the music performed by the organization.
6) Has learned all assigned music.
7) Has shown outstanding initiative by individual practice and study outside of school time, and by participation in community music activities.

For a 'B' grade the words "good" or "above average" can be substituted for "outstanding" and "exceptional." The 'C' grade can use "average" or "some" as modifiers, and the 'D' grade can use "below average" and "little." Attendance has not been cited in the criteria because it is assumed that the school has a policy concerning unexcused absences and make-up work.

The student's attitude toward music talent can have a considerable effect upon what he does in music, and upon his understanding of the grading system. Many persons believe that either you have talent or you haven't. If a person has talent, they feel, then he need hardly lift a finger —music will just pour from him. If a person does not have talent, then no amount of effort will matter. Of course, such a concept is very much in error. It is the job of the teacher to make sure that his students are set straight on this matter. Especially important is the role of effort in musical achievement. Many students do not realize that much plain hard work is required in order to excel in music. It is advisable, also, to stress that "average and normal" people can perform and enjoy music. Music is not only for the gifted; it is for everyone.

The merit of the curve as a basis for establishing music grades is dubious, especially for performing groups. First, one cannot precisely measure amounts and quality of music learning. (The same is true of learnings in almost all other subjects.) It is possible to measure the speed of someone's typewriting, but not his understanding of a musical phrase. Second, grading rigidly on the curve automatically sentences a certain number of students to failure or a low grade, and they see this as a grossly unfair practice. Third, in high school performing groups which have achieved a fairly high level of advancement, students of lower ability have been eliminated, especially in instrumental music, by the normal vicissitudes of study over the years, or they have been placed in groups which are less advanced. If students are learning well, they deserve to earn reasonably high grades, regardless of any overbalance at the upper end of an arbitrary grading scale. Although the curve can be considered in determining marks, it should not be slavishly followed, unless the idea of earning a grade or meeting a standard is to be completely abandoned.

Some music teachers use what is commonly called a "point system." Under this system a student receives a specified number of points for each rehearsal attended, solo appearance, hour of practice, private lesson, and the like. When enough points have been earned, the student receives a specified grade or award. Point systems are solely concerned with quantity of work, and therefore lack validity for purposes of grading, although they are appropriate for determining awards based on service. The number of points earned may be considered as a part of the evidence upon which a grade is determined if the teacher also includes in the computation other evaluations of quality.

Many teachers have students in performing groups audition as a part of classwork and the grading process. These auditions can be held privately, in which case they will have to be scheduled outside of the class period. Some teachers prefer to have the students become accustomed to performing publicly, and so the young people perform by twos or threes, or alone, in front of the others. The teacher can easily distinguish individual performance in small groups and grade accordingly. The student is often stimulated to better efforts by the knowledge that he will have to perform.

A few teachers have made good use of self-evaluation by the students. Young people are surprisingly objective in rating their own efforts, and often are more critical of themselves than the teacher would be. The exact wording of the points on which they are asked to evaluate themselves will vary with the age and development of the group. The students can be asked about the amount of effort they put forth and their achievement in musical areas. Educationally speaking, there is a strong case for self-evaluation: it helps the student acquire some ability to judge the result of his own work. Whether or not self-evaluation should become involved with the grades given by the teacher is another matter. Such involvement might undermine the usefulness of self-evaluation. However, if students and teacher understand and accept this technique as a valid part of the grading process, then it can be helpful. The teacher should remember that the Constitution of the United States protects all citizens from being forced to testify against themselves; self-evaluation likewise should not force students to do this.

Questions

1. Should students who sing in church choirs or play in community orchestras receive consideration for this in their grades? Why, or why not?
2. Since teen-agers are especially concerned with personal status, what might a music teacher do
   a. to prevent a student's embarrassment during an audition for a choral group?
   b. to tell a student his tone is not good without hurting his feelings?
   c. to encourage the student who worries a great deal about making an obvious mistake during a public performance?
3. How does the divergence of interests between adults and youth affect their respective attitudes toward
   a. current popular tunes?
   b. art songs, such as Schubert's "The Trout"?
   c. old-time favorites, such as "O Susanna"?
   d. Gothic and Renaissance love ballads, such as "Robin Loves Me"?
4. Since girls tend to be more mature than boys in junior high school, what does this indicate to the music teacher in terms of what he expects from each? Should boys be given a little additional consideration when grades are handed out? What does this indicate for difficulty of the respective parts in vocal music?
5. What type of definition has society given the adolescent regarding his behavior in school? regarding his musical tastes and interests?
6. What does the importance of peer-group thinking on the part of teen-agers say to the music educator regarding the relative effectiveness of studying music in a performing organization, as contrasted with studying it in a more academic, nonperforming class?
7. If you were the director mentioned on page 31, whose flowery language left the students wondering, what might you have said that would have made the same point without misunderstanding?
8. Is the learning of music in order to fulfill the desire of the students for recognition a legitimate educational practice? Why, or why not? Is it proper to use the desire of the group for success in the eyes of the audience to coerce the wayward students into line?

9. What type of attitude does each of these statements indicate? How would each affect the teen-age student?
   a. "What's the matter, Pete! Is your third finger frozen? Let's play E flat next time!"
   b. "Altos, that was nice, except for one thing; you didn't sing the dotted quarter followed by the eighth correctly."
   c. "Whew! I've heard better tones from a New Year's Eve noisemaker!"
   d. "Sherman, I know it's hard to play low on a brass instrument and play it soft and in rhythm at the same time. But that's what the music calls for. Would you do some careful, thoughtful practice at home on that place?"
   e. "This melody you turned in doesn't seem up to your usual standard, Clarissa. Did you really write this?"
10. Think of instances in which you have observed a music teacher develop a good rapport with the students through something he did or said. What points did these instances have in common?
11. Why shouldn't a teacher plead with students to join a music organization?
12. Teen-agers are sometimes impressed with a group if they feel that it is exclusive or difficult to get into. Should the "snob" appeal be used to build up music organizations in the public school? Why, or why not?
13. Harold is a rather pathetic, quiet little seventh-grader. He has a poor music background and the influence of the home is negative. He scarcely passes his tests, sings weakly, but tries (for him); he even tried to give a class report on some Civil War songs, which he did with some inaccuracies and in a faltering manner. He is learning–slowly. What grade should he receive, and why?
14. Marcia, a junior, is a highly talented flutist. Her band uniform is adorned with many blue ribbons won at music festivals. She studies privately, and always does well on written tests. But she can't keep her mouth closed in class; she is seldom attentive and quiet even when the teacher is talking. What should be her grade, and why?
15. Mr. Carlson gives his high school orchestra the following grades: A–12, B–17, C–12, D–9, F–0. How can such high grades be justified?

IV

the complete music teacher

About three hundred years ago a celebrated Englishman named Isaac Walton compiled a treatise on what was required of a person to be a good fisherman.[1] His work was logically entitled *The Compleat Angler.* If Walton's words about fishing are true, there is more to being a complete angler than throwing an appropriately baited hook into the water. Likewise, there is more to being a good music teacher than merely leading a class through a song or conducting the band in a march. A person who plans to teach needs to become aware of the components that go into the making of a "complete" music teacher.

Research studies have been undertaken to determine the qualities of a good teacher of any subject.[2] Immediately one problem had to be faced by the researchers: who decides which are the good teachers, and on what basis? The most valid basis was generally held to be that the best teacher is the one who has the greatest educational impact on his students; that is, the one who teaches them the most.[3] After this matter was settled to the satisfaction of the investigators, studies were made of the characteristics

[1] The author uses the word "compiled" because recent investigations indicate that Walton plagiarized large portions of the work. See H. J. Oliver, "The Composition and Revisions of 'The Compleat Angler,'" *Modern Language Review,* XLII, No. 3 (July 1947), 295–313.

[2] Harold E. Mitzel, "Teacher Effectiveness," *Encyclopedia of Educational Research,* Chester W. Harris, ed. (New York: The Macmillan Company, 1960), pp. 1481–86.

[3] *Ibid.*, p. 1483.

of persons considered to be "good" teachers. To date, the results have indicated that there is no one "teacher personality," and that good teachers possess a wide range of characteristics.[4]

PERSONAL ASPECTS

Personality

The word "personality" usually comes to mind first when an attempt is made to account for the differing degrees of success among teachers. Many people are inclined to regard it as a God-given intangible, incapable of being changed. Fatalistically they believe that one is either "born" a teacher or he is not, and that's that. Personality *is* important, but to feel that it is all-important is to overrate it. Some persons do seem to be more naturally inclined toward teaching than others, but essentially teachers are made, not born. To develop music learning, much more is necessary than merely exposing the young people to a "personality."

A few points can be stated with some certainty, however, about the personality of a successful music teacher. He should be an adult in the fullest sense of the word. He must be conscious of the needs of others. The "artistic temperament," with its whims and idiosyncrasies, has no place in public education, if indeed it has a place anywhere. Nor has education a place for the teacher who sees students as means by which to build up his ego. If the teacher's attitude is one of boredom, superiority, or self-aggrandizement, this will seep through any exterior mask that he tries to assume. No matter how much ability, training, and charm he may have, without a genuine interest in doing the job at hand there will be little success. Adolescents cannot respect a person who is not wholly sincere and honest with them. Neither can they respect erratic, impetuous leadership. Sincerity, stability, and good sense, then, form the basis for the effective personality so necessary in a good teacher.

It is self-evident that a teacher should be well-groomed. But how he combs his hair is not going to determine his success as a teacher, providing, of course, that he does comb his hair, and assuming that he avoids extremes in hair style. In the area of personal appearance, good judgment is the most reliable guide.

The speaking voice of a teacher should be pleasing, and, more important, it should carry a quality of decisiveness. During student teaching, the complaint is frequently leveled at the young teacher by his supervisors that his voice cannot be heard in the back of the room. Usually this problem disappears as the young teacher gains confidence and experience, and makes efforts to improve in this area.

[4] David G. Ryans, "Prediction of Teacher Effectiveness," *Encyclopedia of Educational Research,* Chester W. Harris, ed. (New York: The Macmillan Company, 1960), p. 1490.

Facial expressiveness can be of more value than good looks. Through his facial expression the teacher can communicate with the musicians, particularly when he is conducting them. Close-up pictures or movies of outstanding conductors show that facial expressions are as expressive as hand and arm movements. Some beginning teachers are so serious, so intent about their work, that they look doleful while directing a group. A smile of encouragement at a good performance of some passage can do much for the morale of the musicians.

> A teacher was serving as guest conductor of a fine church choir. The choir sang the anthem extremely well. After the service one of the singers asked the director, "How did we do?" "Fine!" was the reply. "Oh," she said, "I was a little concerned because you looked so serious all through the number; I thought maybe something had gone wrong."

The Importance of Being Yourself

Many young teachers have studied under a dynamic, extroverted individual, or have observed such a person in full swing at a workshop demonstration or festival. The question immediately comes to mind, "Is it necessary for me to have that kind of extroverted personality in order to be successful?" The young teacher recalls that when he stands before a performing group it is all he can do to give the necessary directions and go through the conventional conducting gestures. Even though he may try with all the power he possesses, he cannot seem to break out of his "shell." Is he, then, a poor teacher? Is he in the wrong line of work?

First, it should be pointed out that extroversion does not in and of itself guarantee the ability to convey ideas to the students and to draw from them their best efforts. A choral director may don a red sweat shirt for rehearsals and conduct his choir in a manner closely resembling that of a cheer leader. Undoubtedly this would be effective for a few rehearsals. But what about the fiftieth or the hundredth rehearsal? What was once inspiring could conceivably become annoying. Besides, the students become accustomed to such vigor from the teacher that there is little else for him to do when he wants still more emphasis.

Many people are not extroverts; they never can be and would only look silly if they tried to be. Fortunately, extroversion is not necessary for success. The many non-extroverts who are excellent teachers are living proof of this. Their example suggests: be yourself.

Extroversion should not be confused with the quality of decisiveness that is so necessary in an effective teacher. A teacher must be able to get his feelings and ideas over to the students. A "mousy" person cannot do this. There must be a quality of conviction, of cogency. How the teacher achieves this quality depends on his unique personality, but *he must achieve it*. Many prospective teachers do not realize that this takes time and effort. It is *developed* in one way or another through experience in their own lives, through a knowledge and love of the subject, and through working with students.

The key to the whole question of personality is the ability of the person to develop himself in his own way so that he can command the respect of his students and bring forth their best efforts. Every teacher has strong and weak points. He needs to make full use of his strong points in order to earn the respect of his students. One band director played the trumpet very well. He used it often to show the group how the music should sound. Soon the students were requesting him to play an entire solo, which he did upon occasion. Another teacher had a most winning personality. Because of their personal fondness for this teacher, the students would let nothing prevent them from fulfilling his requests. A third teacher was a somewhat scholarly sort, with a deep knowledge and love of music. At first, the students could not understand everything that he was trying to do, but as time passed they realized that he had something significant to offer them. Three different people, meeting a common objective in three different ways—each used means that were natural and effective for him, and yet each one reached the students and drew from them their best.

PROFESSIONAL PREPARATION

Schools and states vary in what they feel a school music teacher should study in college. Some stress the musical aspect of training, others the professional courses in education, and still others a general liberal arts training. The Commission on Accreditation and Certification in Music Education, a committee of the Music Educators National Conference (MENC), recommends this allocation of time in the four-year undergraduate program:[5]

General culture (non-music subjects, but includes music literature and history)	33%
Musical performance (vocal and instrumental study, piano, conducting, ensemble experience)	33%
Basic music (ear training, keyboard harmony, etc.)	14%
Professional education (methods courses and student teaching)	20%

An important part of music teacher training is preparation in both vocal and instrumental music. Not only is this a musically and philosophically desirable requirement; it is a practical necessity for many teachers. In 1961 a survey of the membership of the Music Educators National Conference indicated that 26.1 per cent of the teachers who were primarily vocal music teachers, 34 per cent of those who were primarily band directors, and 25.8 per cent of those who were primarily orchestra directors

[5] Hazel Nohavec Morgan, ed., *Music in American Education* (Washington, D.C.: Music Educators National Conference, 1955), pp. 148–50.

also taught some classes in another area, vocal or instrumental.[6] These figures do not include supervisors who are responsible for both vocal and instrumental music. A study made in the state of New York indicated that over half of the teachers in high schools held positions which covered both vocal and instrumental music.[7] Beginning teachers most often have a dual responsibility because they are likely to work in school systems too small to warrant the hiring of specialists within the area of music. The MENC has recognized this fact by recommending that student teaching be undertaken in both vocal and instrumental music.[8]

The Student-Teaching Experience

Almost every teacher-training institution requires for graduation a practical, supervised teaching experience variously called "student," "apprentice," or "cadet" teaching. To get the most from this experience, the student must understand the reason for it and know what is expected of him.

Student teaching has three purposes. First, it should provide the student with the opportunity to observe an established, successful teacher. The basic educational steps taken by the teacher are what should be looked for in the observation. For example, the teacher is introducing a new piece of music in 6/8 time. How does he present the rhythm? How does this teaching relate to what has been previously taught about 6/8 meter? How do the students react? What other methods might the teacher have considered? This is the type of significant pedagogical procedure that should occupy the observer's attention, rather than extraneous and petty matters.

The second purpose of student teaching is to provide guided teaching experience. The student can move step by step in a situation structured by the supervising teacher. The student is not pushed into a job in which he is allowed to sink or swim without help. Student teaching cannot, of course, completely simulate teaching as it will be encountered in regular employment. The pupils taught are not the permanent pupils of the student teacher, and they know it. The amount of teaching is a half day or less, and the entire experience seldom encompasses an entire year. While in many ways limited time hampers the student teacher, it is good that he is not suddenly overwhelmed with the work of a new, full-time assignment.

The third reason for student teaching is to establish the fact that the student teacher can teach. A prospective employer wants to know, "How did this candidate do when he actually stood before a class?" A good

[6] MENC, 1201 16th St. N.W., Washington 6, D.C., 1961.
[7] "Trends in Job Placement for Music Educators," *The School Music News*, XX, No. 9 (May–June 1957), 12–14.
[8] Morgan, *op. cit.*, p. 150.

college record and good character recommendations are fine, but there is no better test of a teacher than teaching. Observation and guidance are helpful, but the student teacher must prove that he can really teach live students.

The attitude of the student teacher largely determines what he will gain from the experience. He must *look for* opportunities to contribute to the supervising teacher's classes, even in such menial chores as handing out music, adjusting window shades, or moving music stands. He should not sit around, waiting to see what will happen. Most supervisors welcome signs of initiative on the part of the student teacher.

Because of the delicate relationship involved, the attitude of the student teacher toward his supervisor is important. In most cases, the supervisor accepts student teachers for reasons of professional interest. There is seldom any monetary benefit, and a student teacher means *more*, not less, work for the supervisor. Therefore, the student teacher should be grateful for the interest and efforts of his supervising teacher. He need not agree with all the procedures of the supervisor, but he should realize that there is much he can learn from a person who does some things differently. Finally, he should accept criticism and suggestions in the spirit in which they are given, and not as personal affronts.

The student teacher should know what is expected of him. If he is going to be absent, whom does he notify? Who is responsible for his grade and for the report of his student teaching experience? When he is teaching, is he in full charge of the class, with responsibility for discipline? Who decides the interpretation of a particular piece of music? If a vacation day occurs at the college but not at the school in which he is student teaching, is he expected to report that day? Much misunderstanding can be avoided if the answers to such questions are clearly understood. If he has a question on any matter, it is his responsibility to ask until he gets an authoritative answer.

For the student teacher who demonstrates initiative, optimism, and willingness to learn, the apprentice experience will be well worth his efforts.

Musical Requisites

Certain musical abilities are necessary for the music teacher. One of these is an ear that hears pitch accurately and, even more important, picks the individual parts out of a maze of sound. When something goes wrong with the performance of a group, the director has to diagnose the trouble immediately. If the basses are flatting a certain interval, thereby losing their pitch, he must be able to hear this and correct the basses. Anyone who cannot do this is doomed to failure as a teacher of school music.

A new teacher is likely to be discouraged by his first experience in this area. When he begins his student teaching and directs a group for the first few times, the newness of the sound and of the situation will so consume his attention that he will probably feel at a loss to pick out the various parts. He should not become alarmed; this is a natural reaction. With each attempt he should notice a gradual improvement in his ability to identify individual parts aurally. If he cannot do this by the end of his supervised teaching experience, then some serious re-evaluation of his choice of teaching area is called for.

In addition to good aural discrimination, he must be able to read music fluently. A person who teaches five (or more!) periods a day is developing a current music repertoire of considerable size. Unless he spends many hours each week reviewing and memorizing the music, it is impossible for him to recall every phrase accurately. Music reading—the use of the printed page to refresh the memory on the sound of the music—is essential.

Another necessity for the music teacher is a genuine knowledge of and feeling for styles of music from the sixteenth-century motet to works in the modern idiom. No teacher can adequately lead teen-age students on a musical journey to places that he, as leader, does not know or appreciate. When he does not understand a sixteenth-century polyphonic work, for example, it is a safe bet that his students will not gain an adequate understanding of that area of music literature.

Musicianship is of great importance to the teacher in such matters as determining tempo, establishing the proper tone color and mood, and handling the phrasing. He has to be sure of himself on these matters before he steps in front of a group. If he does not know how the music should sound, this fact is readily discerned by the students, and they soon lose respect for his musical judgment. The development of musicianship continues throughout the teacher's career.

A functional piano ability is a valuable asset. It is a requisite for accompanying class singing in general music courses, and for playing voice parts or working with soloists and small choral ensembles. The instrumental teacher uses the piano to study scores and to accompany beginning and intermediate level instrumental classes. Furthermore, both students and the public often equate musicianship with the ability to use the piano effectively.

To round out one's professional training, gaps in musical knowledge must be filled in. Sometimes courses in music literature and history will do this. Various styles of music may be mastered through private study or through participation in a performing group. Finally, it is always advisable to study records and scores, especially those that are unfamiliar.

SKILL IN TEACHING TECHNIQUES

The "complete" music teacher must be able to communicate his ideas to the students. For example, he knows that the band should play a passage in a staccato style. How does he get the idea of staccato over to the players, and how can they best execute staccato playing? Without a knowledge of effective teaching methods, he must resort to pleading, "Now play in a short, detached manner." This is all right as a starting place, but an experienced teacher knows that words are insufficient to insure staccato playing, save that which might occur accidentally by trial and error.

He needs to have in mind various examples, analogies, and explanations for use in teaching. He cannot stop the class, run to his desk, and thumb through a book trying to find this technique or that bit of information. The methods of presenting musical experiences to teen-agers must be learned thoroughly. As Chapter Eight points out, when possible the teacher should anticipate the problems that will be encountered in a certain piece. If the work demands staccato playing, then prior to its presentation to the group, he can review his material on the performance of staccato.

The teacher must also be able to express extramusical ideas that extend the students' range of understanding beyond the mere notes of a work. He should know something about the social setting in which the work was written, something about the intent of the composer, something about his personality, and the meaning of the text, if it is a vocal work. For example, Johannes Brahms wrote a work called *Ein Deutches Requiem.* During what historical period was it written? Where was it written? What is a requiem? Why is Brahms' Requiem called "A German Requiem"? What is Brahms saying in the Requiem? What kind of man was Johannes Brahms? The teacher as well as the students can profit by intelligent probing of these and similar questions. Certainly they must be answered in the teacher's own mind before he can adequately present the work to the class.

PERSONAL EFFICIENCY

Proper planning requires a quality of personal efficiency and organization. Unless the teacher has these qualities both he and his students are apt to find themselves in a state of confusion. Music teachers have been known to forget to order chairs or risers for a performance, to lose their own music, to fail to keep track of uniform and instrument numbers, and to wait until the last day to prepare a program for a concert. What excitement these foibles create! But while confusion reigns, the educational results are being cut down. Musicians, along with almost everyone else, dislike what is jokingly called "administrivia," but trivial or not, details must not be neglected.

A free help to the music teacher in the area of efficiency in handling business details is the *Business Handbook of Music Education* published by the Music Industry Council, an auxiliary of the MENC. The booklet is especially useful in ordering music, materials, and equipment, and in understanding other matters dealing with music merchants.

Closely related to personal efficiency is the matter of planning. This important topic is discussed in detail in Chapters Eight and Fourteen.

RELATIONS WITH PROFESSIONAL COLLEAGUES

In some instances, a music program is hampered because of a poor relationship between the music teacher and the people with whom he works. For example, he may be so disagreeable personally that the guidance counselor is not moved to give any particular encouragement to students who ask about enrolling in a music course. Some instrumental music teachers consider themselves in competition with choral music teachers, and vice versa. Not only do the two factions fail to work together, but on occasion the efforts of one group are deprecated in an attempt to build up the other. This friction undermines the total music program of the school. Music teachers sometimes overlook the school clerical and janitorial staff. A successful concert, for example, depends on the assistance of such people, but too often a thoughtless teacher takes this help for granted and fails to acknowledge it in any way.

The music teacher must take an active interest in school affairs. He cannot say on the one hand that music is an integral part of the curriculum, and then shy away from serving on a schoolwide curriculum committee because he feels that music is a "special" area. Nor should he display disinterest in the fate of the football team or of the winter play, especially if he wants the support of the athletic and dramatic departments for music.

THE MUSIC TEACHER AND THE COMMUNITY

A school music program is affected by the other music activities and interests in the community. A community with an active music life helps the school music teacher, and in turn, an effective school music program contributes to the level of culture within the local area. Cities which have lost their professional orchestras, either temporarily or permanently, know what this means to the school music program. Good private teachers leave the city in search of other employment, and professional musicians are not available for other performances, such as chamber music and educational concerts. But worst of all, the music teacher says to the students, "Music is important in the lives of people," while the absence of an active music life tacitly says, "Music is not important here." School music cannot long flourish in a cultural wasteland.

The school music teacher, then, has a stake in the status of the professional performer. He needs to support the local orchestra and other musical groups in the larger metropolitan centers; in the smaller communities he can work toward bringing in good music through live performances or radio and television. The high school assembly can also be used as a means of presenting good music. There are talented artists, mainly young performers gaining experience, who tour smaller communities. Outstanding musicians' groups such as those associated with Young Audiences, Inc.,[9] are also becoming increasingly available.

Not only should the music teacher support good performers and performing groups; he should work with them, when possible. An educational concert should be planned jointly by teacher and performers. The professional musician is becoming aware of the fact that the way to raise the musical level of a community is through education of the young people. He is generally willing to work with the music educator to make the performance as effective as possible. Sometimes music teachers and performing organizations have not shown much interest in each other's educational efforts, to the detriment of both.[10]

Attempts have been made to define those areas in which either professional musicians or school groups should take precedence. In 1947 the MENC, the American Association of School Administrators, and the American Federation of Musicians drew up a comprehensive Code of Ethics. It carefully delineates which activities are properly in the domain of the music educator and which are in the domain of the professional musician.[11] All music teachers should be aware of and follow the provisions of the Code.

The dealings between music teacher and music merchant must also be on an ethical basis. Because he is employed by the public, a teacher should not accept personal favors from merchants. The choice of merchant and subsequent purchases should be made solely on the basis of the quality of goods and service in relation to the cost.[12] In cases of purchases amounting to twenty-five dollars or more, it is wise for the teacher to secure bids, if the school system does not already have a person to handle such matters. Competitive bidding encourages the best price from the merchants and provides tangible proof that business transactions are handled fairly and openly. The Ohio Music Education Association and the Music Merchants Association of Ohio have drawn up a Code of Ethics which can serve as a reasonable and reliable guide for every music educator.[13]

Finally, the school music teacher should work cooperatively with the private music teacher for their mutual benefit. The school music teacher must never deprecate the work of any private instructor, and should, when possible, supply interested parents with the names of more than one com-

[9] Young Audiences, Inc., 645 Madison Ave., New York 22, N.Y. This organization has chapters throughout the United States. Under its auspices professional musicians give performances of chamber music that are oriented to school audiences.

[10] Charles R. Hoffer, "Common Efforts of the Community Orchestra and the School Music Program in Providing Listening Experiences for School Students," *Journal of Research in Music Education*, VI, No. 1 (Spring 1958), 39–40.

[11] Morgan, *op. cit.*, pp. 316–17.

[12] *Business Handbook of Music Education*, 8th edition, Music Industry Council, an auxiliary of MENC, 1959.

[13] Morgan, *op. cit.*, pp. 317–18.

petent teacher. In some communities the level of the music program has been advanced appreciably by the efforts of a few good private music teachers. This is especially important in the case of instrumental students in junior and senior high school who have progressed beyond intermediate levels. Since few instrumental teachers know the advanced techniques on more than one or two instruments, the progress of the band or orchestra depends in part on the availability of good private instruction.

The American Music Conference and the MENC have long urged the formation of community music councils which have as their objective the coordination and promotion of all musical organizations in the community.[14] In some cities an attempt has been made to ally all the arts under one central board which oversees artistic endeavor in the city and undertakes a common fund-raising effort for community activities in the arts. Such projects are well worth the music teacher's attention.

Other community organizations, such as service clubs, should not be ignored either. They sometimes provide scholarship money to enable worthy music students to study at summer camp, and upon occasion they are willing to finance a modest tour for an entire performing group. In addition to the financial benefits that may be derived for the music program, these community organizations provide the music teacher with a means of disseminating information to the public, a task of major importance.

The teacher has another valuable community contact in the parents of his students. Information can be sent to parents at regular intervals. An attractive booklet can be compiled, explaining the music program. The booklet will have special appeal if it includes pictures of students and teachers at work. In some school systems a set of color slides has been prepared to educate the public about the music program. A good color picture of a group of youngsters playing instruments or singing is sure to draw a favorable reaction. Parent organizations such as "Band Boosters" also provide the teacher with a means of contact with the community.

Students and parents look to the music teacher for guidance when a career in music is contemplated by the teen-ager. The school guidance counselor should also be involved in such a case, but usually his knowledge of specific demands in music is not as great as that of the music educator. To assist students who are considering music teaching as a career, the MENC has prepared publications which can be secured for little or no charge.[15]

For many teen-agers the public library is the best and only source of good recordings. Librarians welcome suggestions from music teachers regarding the purchase of books and recordings.

[14] *Manual for Developing a Music Council,* American Music Conference, 332 South Michigan Ave., Chicago 4, Ill.

[15] *A Career in Music Education* (Washington, D.C.: Music Educators National Conference), 1962.

CONTINUED GROWTH AND SELF-EVALUATION

Growth, largely through self-improvement, is necessary in the development of a good teacher. Fine as are some teachers just entering the profession, they lack the precision and skill that only experience can bring. The dedicated, talented, and ambitious new teacher wants very much to be a master teacher—*now*. Such a desire is not to be discouraged, but a teacher should be able to look back upon what he did as a neophyte and say, "I could do that a lot better now." This is what is meant by growth. Successful teachers are not those who upon taking their first job breathe a sigh of relief that their education is over.

The most obvious method of improvement, and one required in most states before permanent certification can be achieved, is some continued study at the college level during the summer or in the evenings.

Another means of growth is membership in professional organizations such as the MENC, the National Education Association, and the many state musical and educational associations. These organizations keep the teacher informed of current happenings in the field through their publications and meetings. Most colleges and universities now have student MENC chapters in which the prospective music teacher can take an active part.

A knowledge of pertinent research in music education is necessary for professional capability. The teacher should be familiar with the results of new attempts to improve music teaching, especially those studies of direct value to his teaching assignment. He should seek to unearth the reasons for various practices in music education, many of which have never been subjected to rigorous intellectual examination.[16] The music teacher must ask not only "Does a certain teaching procedure work?" but "Would another procedure work better?" He must be alert to the results of research and experimentation.

Even after availing himself of every professional resource, the young teacher should realize that, in a very real sense, he must teach himself how to teach. No course, no professor, no book, no college can impart enough information about the particular school, its students and the unique problems to be faced, to fully train him for his job. There comes a point at which he must succeed or fail on his own. He must undergo the sometimes excruciating process of looking at himself and improving on his own teaching.

Sometimes a teacher feels that other music educators are the best judges of his teaching ability. For instance, he may place inordinate value on the comments and ratings received from adjudicators at festivals, regarding the adjudication form as an evaluation of his success in teaching. Some teachers even send favorable rating sheets along with their credentials when applying for a better job. Such reliance upon the evaluations of others is based

[16] Charles R. Hoffer, "Research and the Music Teacher," *Music Educators Journal*, XIL, No. 2 (November–December 1954), 20–22.

on shaky assumptions. Although outside evaluations are usually objective, they are necessarily made with incomplete information. The adjudications made at festivals are formed on the basis of one segment of the entire music program—the performance of one group on one particular day. The adjudicators know nothing of the total situation, and must necessarily ignore all the factors that make schools and groups different. If the evaluation is made in the teaching situation itself, it is often done by a school principal, who is seldom a musician. In most cases the only outside evaluation which carries much validity is that of a music supervisor who is a musician and is informed about the situation and group.

When a teacher makes as his objective the attainment of favorable evaluations by other persons, he is demonstrating his own lack of conviction by following an aimless, pointless pattern in which he is buffeted from place to place by every comment from other people. He will inevitably receive conflicting evaluations, and will be forced either to flounder in a state of hopeless confusion or to begin evaluating for himself the statements of his critics.

Although self-evaluation has the obvious disadvantage of being subjective, it is the only practical means open to the teacher. For one thing, self-evaluation is a continuous process. It is not something that occurs once or twice a year, but rather it can go on in one form or another during every moment of every class. Furthermore, the teacher alone is thoroughly familiar with his teaching situation.

The most practicable and effective type of self-evaluation is the persistent and immediate appraisal of one's teaching. The teacher must constantly ask himself, "Am I getting the point across? How well are the students responding to this material, music, or method? Have I stayed on this point long enough?" By observing the students carefully, he can sense how they are reacting. With experience he can become more proficient in his appraisal. Even a beginning teacher can determine student reaction with some degree of accuracy because of the transparent nature of adolescents' feelings.

Teacher-Rating Forms

In addition to a continuous attitude of self-examination, there are specific techniques that can be helpful. One is the use of a teacher-rating form to be filled out by the students. It is easy to be cynical about such forms. In fact, some teachers prescribe this formula to insure a favorable rating: easy tests + high grades + lots of jokes. However, when a teacher proposes this formula, he is apparently assuming that the ratings will be seen by his superior and used as a basis for critical judgment if they reflect adversely on the teacher. This assumption is contrary to the purpose of the form. The device is an aid to self-evaluation, and is to be used by the teacher alone with only one thought in mind: the improvement of his own teaching.

Although little experimentation has been done on the teacher-rating form in secondary schools, there are some points which will contribute to its validity.

1) Present the form to the students on an "average" day, a day as far removed as possible from trips, tests, report cards, and concerts.

2) Keep the wording of the questions simple so the students can understand clearly what is being asked of them.

3) Vary the responses from one side of the page to the other so that the filling out of the form cannot become mechanical.

4) Eliminate forms which students have filled out in a haphazard manner. Thoughtless answers can be detected by checking items for obvious inconsistencies. For instance, a form may indicate that this year the teacher was too easy in managing the classroom, and yet the next item may state that the teacher should be easier next year. A few such comparable items should be included in the form to check against careless and insincere student efforts in rating.

5) Generally, use the form only with more mature students, those in high school.

Appendix B contains a form which was created by a choral director for use with his high school glee club. By changing a few words, it could be adapted for use with instrumental groups as well.

In considering the results of such a form, several points should be kept in mind. 1) Some items are more significant than others. For instance, the students' attitude toward the teacher's manner of dress is not as important as their ability to understand his conducting. 2) Students with limited musical background cannot accurately judge the musicianship of the teacher. For this reason questions relating only to musicianship are not included in the sample form. 3) When the results are tabulated, it should be remembered that the median evaluation is more valid than the mean evaluation. Sometimes fifty students will rate a teacher rather high on an item, and five dissident students will rate him low on the same item. The five low ratings will pull down the mean to a lower level than is warranted.

Space should be provided on the form so that the students can make any comments that seem relevant to them. Unless some particular point is mentioned a number of times, these remarks should not be taken too seriously. The "open end" type of question demonstrates the sincerity of the teacher in wanting the students to express any significant feelings, and it serves as a guide in formulating items that could go into a new teacher-rating form.

Rehearsal Playback

Another specific means of self-evaluation is the use of the tape recorder. One college band director makes a tape recording of all his rehearsals. Before each group practice, he listens to the entire preceding rehearsal on the tape recorder. He makes the recordings for two purposes: to allow himself a more leisurely and thoughtful study of what the group has done, and to evaluate his own efforts in leading the rehearsal. In studying a tape for self-evaluation purposes, a director should ask himself these questions:

1) Were there unnecessary delays and wasted time?
2) Were the points on which I corrected the group really those points that needed the most attention?
3) Did my suggestions to the group actually result in improvement?
4) Were my statements clear and decisive?
5) Did I repeat certain words and phrases to such an extent that they became annoying?
6) Did I stay long enough or too long on one number or musical passage?
7) Were there relaxing breaks in the rehearsal routine, a little humor, or music performed just for the pleasure of it?
8) Specifically, what was accomplished at the rehearsal?
9) Did I encourage the students to discover and learn for themselves, or was the class teacher-dictated?

SUPPLEMENTARY EMPLOYMENT

Some teachers undermine their effectiveness by assuming a herculean work load in addition to their regular teaching schedule. One study in Michigan indicated that the average work load for music teachers was over fifty hours a week, running as high as seventy-five to eighty hours in some cases.[17] Similar results were encountered in a study in Indiana.[18] Many teachers are hard-pressed financially, and many times outside work such as teaching piano or directing a church choir is almost a necessity.

Teaching is a full-time job, and the beginning teacher will find that the duties connected with it consume all of his time and energy. He must consider the ethical and practical questions of how much outside work he should do. One of the great pioneer leaders in music education used to schedule one night a week which he spent at home reading, practicing, or in some way improving himself professionally. This example could well be emulated. Every teacher needs time not only to rest himself physically, but also to redirect himself so that his goals become better clarified and his efforts more productive.

The "complete" music teacher, then, is a person with many characteristics. He has an effective personality which brings out the best in his students. He is a sensitive musician, because music is the art he seeks to teach. He develops himself as an educator, because his job is guiding

[17] Olaf W. Steg, "The Total Work-Load of High School Music Teachers in Michigan," *Journal of Research in Music Education,* III, No. 2 (Fall 1955), 111.

[18] John K. Colbert, "Teaching Load and Related Activities of Music Teachers in Indiana Public Schools, 1953–54," *Journal of Research in Music Education,* IX, No. 2 (Fall 1961), 125 ff.

students to learn that art. He relates his educational efforts to the efforts of other professionals in music and education, and sees his work as being involved with the entire community, especially the parents of his students. Finally, he looks honestly at himself and his work in order to achieve his fullest potential as a teacher of music.

Questions

1. Think of two good school music teachers you have had, and of two that you felt were not as good. What, in their personality and work, made them successful or unsuccessful in your eyes?

2. Being as objective as you can be, do some self-examination of your personality and how it relates to teaching music. What are your strong points? What needs your special attention so that it can be improved?

3. Think of a community that you know well, and answer these questions. Between the music teachers and the professional musicians, is there a coordinated effort to promote music? What is the relationship between the private music teachers and the school music teachers? between music teachers and music merchants? Are there educational concerts by the local orchestra? How and by whom are these organized?

4. Suppose that you are responsible for planning a set of slides explaining the music program to parent groups. How many pictures would you use? What would they depict? What would you say to accompany the pictures?

5. Suppose that you wish to look up the available research on one phase of music teaching. How would you find pertinent magazine articles? graduate studies? references from books?

6. Examine the festival rating sheets on page 440 in Appendix D. Are these forms set up as teacher evaluation forms? How adequately do they indicate to a teacher how well he is doing at his job?

7. Suppose that the parents of a boy with above-average musical ability and achievement ask for a conference with you to discuss a possible vocation for him in music. What would you ask them about their son's interests and ambitions? What could you tell them about the various vocational possibilities in music?

8. Suppose you begin teaching in a town of 5,000 with a high school that receives some of its students from the rural area around the town. The level of musical interest is not high. What steps could you take over a period of two years to raise the level of the town's musical interests and activities?

9. During your first year in a new job you take your musical instrument to a local music store for repair. As you pick it up, the merchant says, "Forget the bill. It's on the house." Should you accept this favor?

Projects

1. During your student teaching experience, seat yourself where you can hear the group well. With score in hand, attempt to focus your ear on one particular part, and follow it as the number is sung or played.
2. Make a tape recording of yourself teaching a class during your student teaching experience. If this cannot be done now, tape record yourself teaching a lesson to a fellow student on your major instrument or in singing. Evaluate the effectiveness of what you said, the amount of talking you did, the pertinence of your comments about the student's work, and the general pace of your teaching.
3. Compute the allocation of course hours in your collegiate training according to the categories listed on page 54. Compare your training with that recommended. Discuss with other members of your class what phases of your training might have been stressed more, or less.
4. Visit two identical classes (high school bands, seventh-grade general music classes, etc.) in two different schools. Make some evaluation of the comparative musical maturity of the students, their innate ability, equipment available for music, schedule, and other factors. Make a list of points on which the two classes are different.

Suggested Readings

Benn, Oleta A., "A Message for New Teachers," *Basic Concepts in Music Education*, 57th Yearbook, Part I. National Society for the Study of Education. Chicago: University of Chicago Press, 1958, pp. 339–55.

Coutant, Madeleine F., "Public Relations and the School Music Program," *Music Educators Journal*, February–March 1954, pp. 68–70.

Davis, Ennis, *More than a Pitch Pipe*. Evanston, Ill.: Summy-Birchard Publishing Company, 1941.

Ernst, Karl D., "Quality Teaching Is Our Answer," *Music Educators Journal*, April–May 1959, pp. 27–29.

Hoffer, Charles R., "Research and the Music Teacher," *Music Educators Journal*, November–December 1954, pp. 20–22.

"Music Education in a Changing World," Report for the Music in American Life Commission on Music in the Community, Max Kaplan, chairman. Washington, D.C.: Music Educators National Conference, 1958.

V

guiding student behavior

In some ways, a detailed discussion of student behavior focuses too much attention on an area that does not deserve it. However, deserving or not, the subject is very much in the minds of most beginning teachers. Its seriousness is brought out in a study by Lawrence E. Vredevoe. He asked 3,000 prospective teachers, "What gives you the greatest concern or worry as you plan for your first teaching position?" Of these, 2,480 answered, "Discipline."[1]

The problem of discipline needs to be brought out into the open, therefore, and examined. Just as one learns first aid not hoping or expecting to use it, a young teacher should be prepared to deal with students when their actions deviate from the accepted standard. By knowing how to handle such situations, the new teacher is more confident in his teaching and is better able to concentrate on the more important matter of teaching the students some music.

While a teacher should take a positive attitude upon entering the classroom (and just by doing this he can avoid some behavior problems), he must be realistic about the total situation. Music lacks the concreteness of other academic subjects; students are less often told to read a certain chapter or write a term paper. An eighth-grader may be held back in school if he fails English, but not if he fails only music. These facts affect a teen-ager's thinking about how he behaves in music class. Furthermore,

[1] Henry Clay Lindgren, *Educational Psychology in the Classroom,* 2nd ed. (New York: John Wiley & Sons, Inc., 1962), p. 374.

with students adjusting to all the changes that teen-agers have to undergo, and with the schools attempting to educate all the youth of the nation, it would indeed be amazing if student behavior were flawless.

NECESSARY PRECAUTIONS

The prospective teacher must keep in mind four precautions when reading about guiding the behavior of teen-agers in music. First, he must remember that no discussion can cover every situation that might arise. There is an infinite variety of ways in which human beings can act, and a limitless number of circumstances in which each act can occur. John talked in class when he shouldn't have. How much did he talk? What did he say? How did he say it? How much did it disturb the rest of the group? Was this the first or the fiftieth time John had talked in class? When did the talking occur—when the teacher was explaining something? when the group was changing from one activity to another? when a record was being played? What type of home background does John have? Is someone else involved with John in this incident? If so, to what extent? Do other students in the group talk when they shouldn't? What has been done about them?

As if the students do not provide enough variables, the teacher brings his share to the situation. For a minor misbehavior, two teachers might call out "John!" with vastly different effects, depending on the personality and prior actions of each teacher. It is a matter not only of *what* is said and done, but also of *how* it is said and done. Sometimes a student teacher consciously attempts to duplicate the methods of an outstanding teacher whom he has observed. Usually there comes to him the inevitable shock when an action, successful for the model teacher, produces the opposite results when applied by the student teacher (sometimes with the same pupils as before). What happened? The situation is no longer the same. The personality of the teacher is different, and the experience of the students with that teacher is different. The best that any book can offer is to give the reader some insight into the most common problems, their significance, and how they might be handled.

As a second precaution, the teacher must not fall back on books as the one means of dealing with classroom misbehavior, while ignoring the development of good, positive teaching. Good teaching is essential, and no teacher should become so preoccupied with worries and fears about student behavior that he neglects for one moment the positive side of his job. In fact, good teaching is the best way to prevent student misbehavior because it draws the students' attention to the benefits of learning and thus discourages them from engaging in divergent activities.

Third, no recommendations should ever be considered as ironclad rules. The suggestions here are based upon experience in teaching music to teen-agers, but that does not mean that these recommendations should not be altered when circumstances warrant it.

Fourth, the effectiveness of a teacher in his relations with his class will bear directly on his effectiveness in guiding classroom deportment. All that was said in Chapter Three about the development of the proper relationship is pertinent here. The specific suggestions in this chapter are offered in light of the points made in Chapter Three.

Lindgren has this to say about the matter of teacher-student relationship:

> The beginning teacher wants specific suggestions—techniques, if you like—that will enable him to handle such problems. It is difficult for him to grasp the point that discipline is partly a point of view, partly a feeling of self-confidence, partly a kind of relationship between the teacher and his class, but mostly a feeling that the class develops about its own behavior. These are the kinds of concepts that defy verbal description. They are the approaches teachers must learn through actual experience.[2]

The average teen-ager is a lovable, wonderful person, and teen-age groups can be lovable and wonderful, too. However, they may not be a joy to work with until some attention is given to the delicate task of developing a good relationship between students and teacher. The plural form, *students*, is used advisedly here. Teachers have long known what the den mother of a Cub Scout troop found out: "Individually those boys are so nice, but when they're together—! !" Most teachers have little trouble in handling a private lesson or an ensemble class. It is when the numbers become larger that unexpected things sometimes begin to happen.

Finally, although policing is by no means a teacher's most important duty, *a music teacher must be able to guide students.* This is as much a part of his job as is teaching the quality of the melody in a sea chanty. And in truth the better a manager he is, the less he will have to bother about discipline.

TEACHER DISCIPLINE OR STUDENT SELF-DISCIPLINE?

If a class of fifty students felt like it, they could get out of their seats, dash out the door, and run down the hall waving their arms and yelling. No teacher would have sufficient physical strength to stop them. Of course, it doesn't happen. Why? Because the vast majority of the students realize that the action would not be in their best interests. Eventually there would be penalties, true, but more important, the students see the sense of what they are doing in class and the lack of reason for running out of the room screaming. In short, they themselves exercise some self-discipline, the ideal form of classroom control. The objective of the teacher should be to encourage development of that self-discipline. A high degree

[2] *Ibid.*, p. 375. Reprinted by permission.

of it is necessary for learning to take place, since no teacher can control all of the actions of the students.

Self-discipline is encouraged when the students are motivated by the classwork. A student is motivated when the class is meeting some need or interest which he possesses. Thus, discipline is involved with the entire act of teaching and the responsiveness of the students to it.

Keeping in mind the ideal of self-discipline, the teacher faces the hard, practical fact that teacher-imposed rules are needed, too. Even adults, who should be capable of self-discipline, need police to enforce traffic regulations, since mature people driving automobiles do not always exercise self-restraint. No teacher, then, need feel bashful about setting up and enforcing rules with teen-age students, especially considering the realistic conditions cited at the beginning of this chapter. Adolescents want to know what the rules are; they want the security of knowing what they can and cannot do, even though they may still attempt to see if they can get away with doing the forbidden. Lindgren ably states the matter in this way:

> One of the perplexing characteristics of children . . . is their need, on the one hand, to have someone set limits for their behavior and, on the other, to test or challenge the very limits that have been set. We often find ourselves drawn into a kind of trap because of these ambiguous and often contradictory motives. Some adults, when confronted by complaints of children that limitations on their behavior are too severe, react by doing away with all or most limits. Thereupon they are appalled when children respond to greater freedom by actually worsening their behavior and blaming the adult in charge for what has gone wrong. On the other hand, adults who attempt to deal with this ambiguous situation by being severe, restrictive, and punitive cannot understand why children are so apathetic and why the behavior of some children actually becomes worse.
>
> Such experiences show that the behavior of children cannot be handled on an "all-or-none" basis. The effective teacher is one who can allow children freedom to develop naturally and spontaneously, but who can also set limits to their behavior at appropriate times. The better the morale of the group and the better the learning situation, the less need there should be to invoke limits.
>
> The problem of the teacher with respect to discipline may be seen in terms of a problem in leadership, to which some of the findings psychologists have made in this field may be applied. One approach to the study of leadership identifies two dimensions: *initiation of structure* and *consideration*. Leadership activities concerned with the initiation of structure include direction, control, punishing, setting limits, rewarding, manipulating, organizing, scheduling, maintaining standards, and the like. Consideration includes such behavior as extending sympathy and understanding, compromising, helping, inviting and using suggestions of group members, being supportive, and the like.[3]

[3] *Ibid.*, pp. 359–60. Reprinted by permission.

GUIDING THE STUDENTS DEMOCRATICALLY

Unfortunately, the words "democratic" and "autocratic," when used to describe teaching, are prejudged by many people. Not only are the words prejudged, but the attitude toward them is formed out of misconceptions of what the words mean in the schoolroom. Music teachers have inherited the tradition of the professional musician who cannot conceive of directing any organization without full leader control in every situation. Yet, educators constantly remind us of the paramount place of democracy in the classroom. Although the positions are oversimplified here for the sake of brevity, there is a tendency for music teachers to disagree with other educators on this point. Music teachers sometimes maintain that the educators advocate letting music classes become a recreation period, with no concern about musical results. At the same time, educators occasionally regard musicians as petty dictators, whose ideas and practices are outmoded. There is some truth, and some distortion, on each side.

It is a mistake to conclude that autocratic teaching is necessarily bad, or that there is no place for autocratic practices in the classroom. Experimental evidence demonstrates rather conclusively that democratic methods are superior. But in most of these studies the autocratic teachers were inflexible and lacked compassion for the students, while the democratic teachers were flexible and warm—a correlation of method and teacher personality which is not always present.[4] Because music classes often engage in group activity, in which all participants act simultaneously, democratic practices are limited. Group activities require good leadership in order to be successful, and music is such a complex group activity that leadership is not easily or successfully delegated to the students. So with or without democracy in the classroom, the music teacher will still have to be the leader. The performing music organization especially is basically a leader-centered activity, and this cannot be changed, no matter how much one might wish to promote democracy in the school. What might be called "benevolent" autocratic procedures have a necessary place in music teaching. For example, the students cannot stop and decide every time what part of the music should be practiced again. Usually they are not musically competent enough to do this, and such a procedure would consume too great a portion of the class time.

Yet democratic practices should play a significant part in the music class. The over-all objectives of the schools demand no less. Besides, democratic practices can be used to increase the musical benefits to the students and the listeners. Students take more interest in an activity when they have had some hand in the operation of that activity, than they do

[4] Lee J. Cronbach, *Educational Psychology* (New York: Harcourt, Brace & World, Inc., 1954), pp. 451–52.

when they are simply led around, no matter how kindly, like a flock of sheep.

It is necessary, then, to clear away a misconception about democracy and to study ways in which democracy can be applied in the music class. Democratic education should not be considered a political system. Grambs and Iverson state:

> After all, the classroom is not at all the area of politics where citizens of equal voting stature discuss, debate, and then cast a ballot. The teacher has knowledge, the teacher is an adult, the teacher is vested by law with authority, and the teacher is surrounded in part with the aura of the parent. These "authorities" of the teacher, both open and hidden, make an important difference. The students had no say in choosing Mr. Griffin as their teacher. Neither of course did Mr. Griffin choose belligerent Tim Atkins or arrogant Jane Boothe for his class. Reluctant subjects and arbitrary leadership do not, in our usual sense of the word, make for a very democratic situation.[5]

Democratic education, then, is more a social system which is concerned with human relationships, and not just with the act of voting. Good teaching in music depends upon discovering the proper balance of group-centered and leader-centered techniques.

CHARACTERISTICS OF DEMOCRATIC PRACTICES

There are four characteristics of democratic practice applicable to the music class. The first characteristic, and the basis for the other three, is the consideration of *the dignity and worth of the individual.* This tenet of democracy simply indicates for the classroom that the opinions and interests of both students and teacher must be respected. It hardly need be said that the teacher should be sincere in setting up circumstances that give the students a feeling of being important and valued; such situations should not be arranged merely to achieve ends desired by the teacher.

As a part of its interest in individual worth, this nation has protected the right of an individual to worship as he pleases. Because of the sensitive nature of religious freedom, care must be taken in the presentation of vocal music that has a religious text. Certain students object to singing Christmas or Easter music, and others do not want to sing "The Rosary" or "A Mighty Fortress Is Our God." Sincere objections to religious songs should not be treated as evidence of misbehavior. If in a particular school it appears that there might be a religious problem, the teacher should talk with the superintendent or principal to find out what policy exists regarding religious music. If the school has no specific position on it, then the teacher should quietly discuss the matter with the student officers of the group. Generally, the student can simply refrain from singing, and this lack of participation will in no way affect his grade. He should, as in the

[5] Jean D. Grambs and William J. Iverson, *Modern Methods in Secondary Education* (New York: William Sloane Associates, 1952), p. 58. Reprinted by permission.

case of laryngitis, inform the teacher *before* the class starts. Notes from home should not be requested. This demand serves only to spotlight a situation that can inflame emotions. The less religious differences are emphasized, the better it is for everyone.

The teacher should explain that the song is chosen for its musical value, and not for its religious message. The class is not seeking to promote religion, and the singing of a religious song does not mean that the singers are endorsing the theology of the text. The music teacher should not discard a good song because of religious objections by a minority, any more than a school cafeteria should be required to serve *only* a certain food on a certain day because of the religious beliefs of some students. If possible a cafeteria director should offer a choice, but he should not require the majority to eat a certain food because of the demands of the minority. For the sake of religious broadmindedness and good music education, the music teacher should select a variety of good music from differing denominations and faiths.

Freedom within Rules

This is a second democratic condition. Initially, it is the teacher who sets up rules for the class. To have the students enter an organization in which there are no rules and expect them to establish their own rules is an impractical, laissez-faire attitude. It is expecting something of the students which they cannot reasonably produce at their stage of development. Rules are a part of democracy, just as they are part of a game. The students should have freedom to criticize constructively and to change the regulations of the classroom in an orderly manner. In this way there can be freedom within security.

Sometimes teachers are afraid to let students determine their own regulations. But odd things happen when students make their own rules—the young people are usually more strict than the teacher would be! In some high schools the students successfully operate the study halls, with no teacher in the room. They have their own aldermen, rules, and even a court to try offenders. In such an atmosphere, students elected to office take their jobs seriously because they have a real function. Students are quick to sense whether the democracy in a classroom is genuine.

Remembering that he must work within the over-all student behavior policies of the school, the teacher should select the precise points at which rules are required. For instance, the student should raise his hand and be recognized by the teacher *before* speaking. A good rule or a bad one? Why? Especially with students of junior high school age, it is wise to discuss each rule briefly. After the regulations have been reviewed, they can be posted in the room, or a copy may be given to each student. Thus the attention of offenders can be called to the rules they themselves agreed upon.

The degree of student sophistication affects the stress to be laid upon regulations. Younger, intellectually less advanced students need the concrete, formal evidence of rules. However, to an intelligent group of juniors and seniors, such techniques as passing out copies of the rules would appear degrading. The more mature and capable class will exercise greater self-discipline and have less need for specific regulations. The teacher must use discretion in these matters. Rules should never become ends in themselves.

Suggested Points of Regulation

There are areas in which rules have to be made by every music teacher. For the new teacher, it is better to err slightly on the side of having too much formal organization rather than too little. After he is established in a position and feels confident in handling the students, he can begin to consider changes that seem desirable. Here are some suggestions for rules that may serve as an initial guide.

TALKING. It is difficult for anyone to sit for a whole hour without talking to someone. A teacher can check himself on this point sometime when he is a member of a group instead of a leader. So it seems unreasonable to expect absolute silence from teen-agers. They should understand, however, that there is a time for talking and a time for silence. Talking might be permitted for about a minute between changes of music, before class starts, and any time that the teacher is not before the class. *Talking should be prohibited at all other times.* Action is necessary early in the school year before bad habits are established. The two times that will cause the most trouble are when the teacher is working with one section and leaves the others sitting unoccupied, and when he stops the group to make a comment on the music. (See page 82 for specific instructions in this situation.) He should not give directions to the class if some students are talking. The persons who miss the directions will make the same errors again, and the directions will have to be repeated especially for them. If this happens often, the class is on the way toward becoming a boring waste of time. Each student must raise his hand and be recognized by the teacher before he speaks. Unless a group is quite small and composed of the better students in the school, this procedure is necessary for the preservation of order.

Just as there is an obligation on the part of the students not to talk out of turn, the teacher is obligated not to demand group silence so that he can make irrelevant statements. If he has trouble with students talking while he talks, it would be a good idea for him to check on the significance of what he is saying.

INABILITY TO PARTICIPATE. In vocal music classes students are sometimes present but unable to sing because of colds or laryngitis. The instrumental teacher must deal with broken or forgotten instruments, cut lips, and sprained fingers. These situations should be handled in basically the same way. The student should report his affliction to the teacher *before* class begins. Then he should sit in his regular place and follow the class activity, learning as much as possible.

Some students who cannot participate ask permission to do homework during the class. If doing homework under such circumstances is allowed, it is sometimes surprising how many students develop throat troubles or broken instruments on days in which there are important examinations in other school subjects!

ATTENDANCE. Many schools have a detention hall or eighth hour to handle excessive tardinesses and unexcused absences. When a schoolwide set-up exists, there is little that the music teacher need do about this matter. If there is no such program, then the teacher must establish rules with his students concerning attendance. One group established this set of rules and penalties: For one unexcused tardiness, one half hour after school; two tardinesses, two hours; three tardinesses, five hours; more than three, suspension. For one unexcused absence, three hours; for two, suspension. Incidentally, being on time should mean being not only in the room, but also in the right seat!

If the teacher demands that his students be punctual, then he himself must not be lax about starting the class on time. This is necessary not only for the sake of consistency, but also for good teaching. A great amount of time can be wasted in getting classes under way. Observing a teacher who is slow about starting class, students may think that he is not concerned about what happens during the period.

Music teachers, who for the most part have been taught throughout their lives a sense of obligation and responsibility, are sometimes shocked to discover that one or two students have failed to appear at a performance of the organization. This action cannot be tolerated. It mocks the efforts of the rest of the students who did show up; it makes a sham of the granting of credit; it demonstrates a complete lack of regard for the group and what it is trying to do. The group and the teacher should establish serious penalties for this, possibly to the extent of failing the offender for the semester or year. The seriousness of the matter should be emphasized *before* the program, so that errant students will have had adequate warning.

OTHER FACETS OF BEHAVIOR. Gum-chewing and music do not go together; students should be asked to dispose of their gum before the class begins. Until the students take responsibility for doing this themselves, some teachers appoint one student as "chief gum-collector" to pass around the wastebasket.

Members of performing groups must maintain good posture. It increases the students' alertness and learning, and it improves behavior. Sloppy posture usually indicates inattentiveness. A sloucher can be reminded that he is beginning to look like a question mark, or a pretzel. A good-natured remark usually succeeds in bringing about improved posture. In classes other than instrumental, slouching can be corrected temporarily by having the class stand.

The students should put all notebooks and purses on the floor underneath their chairs. This will keep them from fooling around with pencils, mirrors, pictures, and other items.

Minor behavior problems are sometimes encouraged unwittingly by a teacher whose attention is focused primarily upon his music rather than upon the students. If he continually hovers over his music, it is likely that some students will lag in participation—they may even engage in activities quite unrelated to music. If looking at the music is such a temptation, it should be closed.

The teacher has to work with one eye on the music and the other on the students. Not only must he know the subject sufficiently to teach it to someone else, but he must also be able to put this subject matter into second place, and focus his major attention on the student response to what is being taught.

Areas of Choice

A third characteristic of democratic education is the provision for significant areas of choice by the students. There are several ways in which students can be given choices in music classes. Two have already been mentioned: consideration of rules, and handling of routine jobs. A third area for significant choice lies in the selection of music. The students cannot be expected to select the major share of the music they will study. The teacher must choose most of the music, but he can let the students select other numbers that interest them.

A fourth area for choice by the students will be mentioned in some detail later in connection with the staging of music for concerts.

Development of Responsibility

A fourth important outcome of democratic education is the development of responsibility in the students. The educational process must gradually prepare the student to direct himself, and give him practice in doing so. The student must be made aware of his responsibility for his own behavior. Some students have the notion that it is the teacher's job to make them behave. The other aspect of training in self-direction is to give the student responsibility in the successful operation of the group.

In most cases of misbehavior, the student who is guilty knows it. So the problem for him is seldom one of not knowing how to act, but rather one of acting as he knows he should.

> Mr. Johnson found that this reminder was effective with his students: "Look, you're big boys and girls now. You know the rules that we all worked out together for conduct in band. So do what you know

is right. If you act like adults, you'll be treated as adults, and everything will be just fine. When you act like children, everyone, including me, will treat you as children. It's up to you to be an adult. Now let's get to work on this music."

The appeal in the example is essentially a good one because it puts the responsibility on each student. Teen-agers want to be free from adult authority, so they need to be given the chance to take care of themselves.

MANAGING RULE VIOLATORS

Many times future music teachers wonder: "How strictly should I enforce the rules? After all, those students are human beings. How can I find out when to clamp down and when to relax control?"

This question is difficult to answer. Because feeling and attitude affect the learning of music, student reaction cannot be ignored. The teacher can learn to sense when he is approaching that middle between too much and too little control. The midpoint is not something that he finds and then rigidly maintains every day and in every situation; no two situations are quite the same. Fortunately, democratic practices allow for communication between students and teacher.

A practical answer can be found in the amount of attention given to rules and behavior. When the amount of attention given to behavior even approaches that given to the learning of music, then behavior is being overemphasized. The point of education should never become proper classroom manners; these are only means to an end. The results that are obtained in the classroom are most revealing. If there is real accomplishment, real learning, then the proper degree of control has been attained; lack of accomplishment may indicate either excessive strictness or laxity.

Students have an uncanny way of knowing when a teacher is confident in what he is doing, and they are especially discerning when he is hesitant. He must make sure that the rules have been clearly established, that the students understand them, and that students are penalized, or dealt with in some manner, when they violate the rules.

To think in terms of penalty rather than of punishment is psychologically more healthful for both students and teacher. The word "punish" connotes the infliction of pain, whereas "penalty" implies a loss due to nonfulfillment of a stipulation, without the involvement of personal feelings. The case against punishment *per se* is well-established.[6] Although punishment or threat of it may appear to work, in the long run it does not obtain a genuine compliance in the teen-age student.

Many a young teacher is afraid that if he reprimands a student, he will be disliked by members of the class, even though the student concerned

[6] Percival M. Symonds, "Classroom Discipline," *Teachers College Record,* LI (December 1949), 147–58. See also Willard Olson, *Child Development* (Boston: D. C. Heath and Co., 1949), p. 338.

is obviously wrong. This fear is unjustified. If the rules are democratically formed, the action of the group will support the teacher in maintaining order. The majority of the class wants the violators dealt with, because they feel that if they behave themselves, so should everyone else.

Objective Attitude of the Teacher

There are several ways in which a teacher can handle a situation more smoothly and effectively. The first involves his attitude toward dealing with rule violators. No matter how disgusted, disappointed, or exasperated he may become, he must not lose his temper. He should be adult enough to avoid the trap of acting childish. A teacher admits defeat when he allows a student to make him angry. Firm, clear, reasonable, and unemotional directives achieve control without harmful aftereffects for students and teacher.

More important, anger denotes the personal involvement of the teacher. By preventing himself from becoming involved personally and emotionally about student behavior, the teacher will be better able to maintain the proper relationship with the students. Noninvolvement is a cardinal rule in handling student misbehavior.

It is difficult for a new teacher to realize that misbehavior by students is seldom directed at the teacher personally. The students sometimes say, when confronted with their acts, "But we didn't mean anything against you." And what they say is true. Students will vent all types of repressions at school. The "smart" talk by the adolescent boy in school may well be the releasing of resentment against an overly strict home. A student's behavior in class may, in some instances, have little relation to what has happened in that particular class, and this is one reason why even a good teacher must expect some behavior disturbances.

The teacher has to make a distinction between disliking the student personally and disliking the things he does. The student must realize, if at all possible, that the teacher makes this distinction.

> Mr. Baker found it necessary to penalize Bill Watson for persistently talking out of turn in rehearsal. "Look, Bill," Mr. Baker said, "personally I like you. But in orchestra there are rules about talking, and we all agreed on them. You seem to have trouble following them. I don't like this, and neither does the rest of the orchestra. Not only aren't you learning anything, but you're keeping the others from learning. Now, I think you'd better put in an hour after school. There are some bowings which should be marked in the violin parts. Why, I'd have to penalize my own mother if she talked as much as you do."

This reprimand is a good one for several reasons. First, it is direct and easily understood. Second, it separates Bill as a person from his actions; and it is the actions that Mr. Baker wants to change. Third, it tells Bill why his behavior was unacceptable. Fourth, it derives its authority from "we" or "the group," and not from Mr. Baker's personal demands. Fifth, the talk ends on a note of humor, letting the students know that Mr. Baker has not involved himself personally in the matter.

Specific Teacher Actions

There are a few suggestions that may help a music teacher to maintain order. For example, a wise teacher is careful about the seating placement of talkative students. When possible, combinations of good friends should be separated. In mixed choral groups, for goodness sake (literally) have the boys sit in the front rows. It may be musically fine to have the lower part soaring out from the back of the group; but before this can occur, the boys have to sing their part well, and before this is possible, it is necessary for them to have training, which requires that they behave themselves and learn something. In performing groups, the seating should be arranged with aisles between the chairs so that the teacher can walk among the musicians to observe their work more carefully. This discourages small offenses, and provides for better rapport between teacher and students.

In handling behavior, *the teacher should mean what he says and follow it up!* If he cannot or does not intend to follow up what he says, he shouldn't say it. Students are quick, very quick to discover idle threats. They will sometimes "test" a new teacher to see if he really means what he says. This test has to be met, or the teacher is in for a miserable time. He must mean what he says from the beginning of the year on. It is too late to wait until after things have gone badly for several weeks or months.

> The chorus students at Farnsworth High School soon discovered that Miss Painter's threats didn't mean a thing. When they came into class, they stood around the room in small groups, talking and laughing. Some students sat down in the wrong seats. Finally, after shouting and pleading, Miss Painter got the chorus seated. She then started to talk about the day's work.
>
> Some members of the chorus began to converse with one another, and Miss Painter barked out, "If you people don't stop talking, I'm going to have you all back here after school for thirty minutes!" The talking stopped for a few moments, then started again. Miss Painter raised her voice so that she could be heard above the sound of shuffling feet and conversation. Finally, after more admonitions to be quiet, the chorus started singing, almost ten minutes after the hour began.
>
> A few students had not bothered to pick up their folders, and Miss Painter noticed that they were just singing along without music. The song stopped. "Where's your folder?" she asked Joe Hinman. "Guess I left it in my locker," Joe replied lazily. "Listen, you people who forgot your folders," she said, "tomorrow I'm going to check each one personally for his folder. If you don't have a folder, I'm lowering your grade." The students weren't worried. Miss Painter had made the same threat before, but had always forgotten to carry it out.

In handling rule-breakers, it is best to follow the advice from *The Mikado* and have the punishment fit the crime. It is often wisest not to make an issue of a small offense. Everyone makes small infractions of rules on occasion. When a motorist is caught over-parking his time on the meter, he gets a ticket. He is wrong, and he knows it; but he doesn't want to be treated like a criminal. Students feel the same way about their small offenses.

When a student misbehaves, what should a teacher say and do? This depends largely on the seriousness and frequency of the misbehavior. No one can supply ready-made solutions to behavior problems without knowing intimately each individual situation. There are many ways to pass out mild reprimands for rule infractions, however. The following illustrations show how two cases *might* be handled.

> Mr. Horvath was explaining to the band how he wanted the accent to fall in a certain phrase. Jane Munson, usually a cooperative student, began to talk with her neighbor. "Jane," Mr. Horvath said, "I hope you don't eat the same thing for breakfast tomorrow that you ate today, because it certainly has made you talkative." He returned to explaining the accent in the phrase.

> Miss Oliver was telling the Girls' Glee Club about the procedures they would follow at the concert for getting on and off the stage. Judy Britton turned and whispered to her neighbor. Miss Oliver stopped talking for a moment, looked at Judy and said in a firm voice, "Judy." She waited a moment more for her to cease whispering. Judy stopped, and Miss Oliver went back to explaining the stage procedures for the concert.

These examples demonstrate the manner in which most of the lesser violations can be handled. In each case, the teacher did not make an issue over the incident, and the entire matter was handled within the class. With less sensitive students it is necessary to be quite blunt, but with most teen-agers a short reminder is all that is required.

What does a teacher do if a student continues to talk even after a reminder? This probably will not happen, but it can. Here is how it might be handled.

> Mr. Winter was working with the tenor section on a passage. Jack Dugan, a bass, turned around in his seat and started to talk and laugh with one of his friends. Mr. Winter said, "Say, Jack, sometimes I think you should have joined a speaking chorus instead of a singing one."
>
> Before Mr. Winter could finish working with the tenors, Jack resumed his talking and laughing. Mr. Winter then said in a firm voice, "Jack, weren't you just told to stop the chatter? Now do it!" Mr. Winter kept looking at Jack until he was in order.

What would happen if Jack still persisted in violating rules? Mr. Winter would have no choice but to deal with Jack outside the class situation. The methods for doing this will be discussed shortly.

Occasionally a new teacher encounters students who are contrary and stubborn. Reasonable requests for out-of-school meetings and other extra efforts are greeted with groans and muttering. Why? A few students, feeling loyalty to the former teacher, may resent the new teacher. Perhaps they are just being adolescent and trying to show their independence from authority. They may want to draw attention to themselves. Such actions are usually of little consequence, and it is best for the teacher to ignore them. Rather than retorting, "Now listen, you *will* do it!" and putting the students in such a position that they will lose face if they back down, it is wiser to pass over the remark and go on, assuming that the students will follow the request in time. In most cases they will. Of course, if a student actually does not follow the directions, penalties must be imposed.

Another type of situation involves no particular individual but rather a sizable segment of the entire group.

> To Miss Babcock, it seemed as though the whole general music class was talking, and not yet ready to work. She held up her hand and said in a loud voice, "A moment of silence, please." She waited about fifteen or twenty seconds while the group quieted down. After a few seconds of silence she said, "Ah, what a wonderful sound–silence." Then she immediately started to work on the day's activities.

> The members of the Girls' Glee Club were generally talking, giggling, and inattentive. In spite of Mrs. Glover's best efforts to teach them, they became noisier and more restless. There were no particular individuals that she could single out as being the source of trouble, so she said in a calm, firm voice, "Look girls, I don't want to treat you like children, but you give me no choice. Now just sit there and be quiet for a few moments." When a minute or two had passed, she said, "I hope we can have an adult-like class now."

How much better these solutions seem than to stand in front of the group and shout for attention, making everyone tense and irritable. Group action is a strong factor in pulling wayward students into line. In the foregoing examples, the action of the group brought the class to order with a minimum of demands from the teacher. His duty is to keep a cool head, get the attention of the students, and give firm, clear requests. He should have the group get to work as soon as possible, and make his own remarks pertinent to teaching the class.

Handling Persistent Rule-Violators

If there are students who persist in violating rules of conduct in spite of good, positive teaching and the employment of reminders and mild reprimands in the classroom situation, the teacher must deal with the students outside of class. A friendly private conference is, according to educational psychologists, the most effective means of dealing with students (see page 38). It does not bring any additional class attention to the troublemaker, and attention in some form is frequently what he is seeking. Furthermore, it avoids embarrassing him before his peers.

The teacher must remember that students who reach this degree of rule violation are motivated by psychological needs.[7] No longer is the teacher dealing with little surface ripples of the undercurrents of teen-agers growing up. Therefore, the private conference is informational in that the teacher tries to determine the cause for the misbehavior, and correctional in that he can work with the student on a course of action to remedy the class situation. If possible, the teacher should secure information about the student from the guidance personnel of the school before the conference.

As for the conference itself, there are several points to remember when talking with a student under such circumstances:

1) Be friendly, honest, and unhurried. Remember to differentiate between disapproval of the student personally and disapproval of what he does. Sarcasm, ridicule, and anger are as ineffective when used in private as they are in the group situation. Allow enough time for a thorough and easy-going discussion.

2) Approach the student positively. Something like this might be said: "Look, John. You could be a lot of help to the chorus. We need tenors, and especially tenors who can carry their part well. You could be a great big plus sign in chorus, if you wanted to be. Why don't you spend your energy building up the group, rather than tearing it down?" This type of approach is so much better than the negative admonitions, "Don't do this. Don't do that."

3) Give the student a chance to talk. This helps to convince him that he is being treated fairly. Learn more about him. Ask him whether there is anything that can be done to help him behave better in the future. He may ask to change his seat, and this may solve the problem.

Many times a student will attempt to talk his way out of a difficult situation. His statements usually fall back on predictable arguments. Some of these defenses are examined briefly here to see how a teacher might handle them, again remembering that the best reply would necessarily depend upon the total situation.

The first argument is basically, "Why are you picking on me?" Most of the time the student knows he is not being singled out unfairly, but he feels in need of some defense in order to save face.

> Henry MacIntyre's plea was, "Why are you picking on me?" Miss Hartman replied, "Believe me, I'm not picking on you or anyone else. The only reason I single out one individual is because he's doing something he shouldn't; and that's why I'm talking to you."

A slight variation of this student defense reaction is one that goes, "Every time there's trouble in my section, you look at me." This argument

[7] Frederick J. McDonald, *Educational Psychology* (Belmont, Calif.: Wadsworth Publishing Company, Inc., 1959), p. 504.

is, of course, limited to students who have been dealt with on previous occasions.

> Fred Travis tried such a defense with Mr. Collins. Mr. Collins answered, "Well, you've caused a disturbance so often in the past that there is a temptation for me to look first in your direction. But it doesn't matter where I look first; the only people I single out are the ones who are actually causing trouble."

If the student chooses to use one type of defense more than any other, it is probably this: "George was doing it too. I wasn't the only one."

> When Fred Travis used this excuse, Mr. Collins replied, "I'm just like a referee in a game. When I see an infraction of the rules, I blow the whistle and hand out a penalty. I saw you this time, so you're being penalized. If George causes trouble, he'll be penalized too."

The statement of the persistent, petty rule violator goes essentially, "All I did was write a note, and I got in trouble."

> When Susan Howard explained to Miss Arnold, "I just asked Judy a question," Miss Arnold answered, "If you had a question about the music, why didn't you ask me? It's my job to answer questions about the music. If your question was *not* about the music, then you should have waited until after class to ask Judy."
>
> On another occasion, Virginia Barrett explained to Miss Arnold, "All I did was laugh at something Donna said." Miss Arnold answered, "What you haven't thought of are all the many other times you've disturbed the class and prevented the others from learning. Remember there was once a straw that broke the camel's back. Well, this incident today is like a straw. So you're being penalized for many small offenses, including today's."

The teacher must not plead with the student to behave. Pleading makes the position of the teacher seem weak, almost desperate. Besides, seldom does it improve the student's behavior in the future.

Handling Serious Infractions

If private conferences with the student do not work, then definite penalties are necessary. A word of caution is in order here. A teacher may be tempted, at the first sign of trouble, to simply lower the student's grade, or send him to the principal's office or to the study hall. But such actions are for the most part negative. Granted they have to be used in some cases, but they can be justified only after the teacher has taken the time and trouble to work with the student privately. Probably there should be at least one talk with the student before resorting to negative measures.

It is best to work with the principal or head counselor on serious behavior problems. A pupil who is causing the music teacher some headaches is probably also causing trouble for other teachers. The principal wants to know about such a student so that an organized program of correction can be effected. He can study the total situation and make recommendations. He may wish to talk to the parents, or he may have the teachers act together to bring about some changed behavior in the student. Whenever possible, the principal should be informed ahead of time if a teacher suspects that he is going to have a serious problem with a student.

Small behavior problems should not be sent to the principal or head counselor. Principals do not like being thought of as school disciplinarians. They want each teacher to take care of his own problems as much as possible, because they realize that eventually the teacher is the only one who can maintain order in his own room. No one else can do it for him. The school administration, of course, will be glad to help in serious and unusual problems.

Besides working with the school principal, the teacher can try several other courses of action. Precisely what is done depends upon each situation. For instance, keeping a student after school or giving him an assignment to do is usually successful only with less mature students.

1) The student can be assigned time to put in after school. This time should be spent constructively doing such things as sorting music or undertaking special assignments. The use of this type of corrective measure is limited because it is often the teacher, not the student, who is penalized by staying later. If the school operates an after-school detention room, then the teacher is not inconvenienced by requiring a student to stay after hours.

2) The misbehavior of the student can be reflected in the grade he receives. Usually, the persistent violator is not the kind of person who cares much about grades, so this is of limited value.

3) The student may be given an assignment that can be done outside of class without supervision. Examples of this would be such activities as reporting on music books, articles, or concerts.

4) The student can be removed from the group for a period of time, and required to sit in the office or study hall. However, one disadvantage limits the use of this appoach. When a student is absent from class, he is obviously not learning, and the teacher will have to devise a means of helping him to catch up.

Permanent Removal from Class

When should a student be removed permanently from a class because of poor behavior? Briefly stated, he should be removed whenever the positive benefits to the individual are outweighed by his negative influence on the group.[8] Any sincere teacher thinks long and hard before

[8] Lloyd Oakland, "Discipline Is Desirable!" in *Music Education in Action,* Archie N. Jones, ed. (Boston: Allyn and Bacon, Inc., 1960), p. 315.

removing a student. Many times the student who gets into repeated and serious trouble has the most unfortunate of home backgrounds. All teachers feel a special obligation to help this student to overcome some of his environment. A teacher feels sympathetic and will tolerate some misbehavior from the unfortunate child that he probably would not accept from other children. On the other hand, he has a clear obligation to the majority of the class who do conduct themselves properly. He owes them the best music education he can give. So comes the hard decision: the chronic troublemakers cannot be allowed to remain. Removal from the class then is entirely justifiable.

A new teacher will sometimes be given this advice by an experienced colleague, "Kick out several students the first week or so, and you won't have any more trouble." There may be some value to this advice, but like an iceberg, only a portion of the matter is immediately observable. To begin with, the teacher is doing more than removing troublesome students; he is defining his beliefs about the purposes of education. Second, the new teacher must have an understanding with the school administration before such action is undertaken. If classroom behavior was very bad during the previous year, drastic steps may be necessary to get order. But such steps should be taken only with the administration's knowledge and support. Third, a teacher must be able to present good reasons for removing a student, and it is hard to build a good case in only a week, especially when the teacher is new. Fourth, a new teacher is often mistaken about who the real troublemakers are. At the beginning of the year, both teacher and students need time to adjust to the new situation. An overzealous teacher can ruin a music group in the first two weeks by wielding the ax too hastily and indiscriminately.

It is far wiser for the teacher to concentrate on effective teaching. Then if a student gets out of line, the teacher can show firmly but pleasantly that he is concerned for the student's improved behavior, as well as his educational well-being. As the teacher demonstrates consistency and reasonableness in his handling of these problems, the students will gain increasing confidence in his judgment, and the spectre of discipline will gradually disappear.

Questions

1. Is it justifiable to lower a student's grade because of undesirable classroom behavior? Is it a good educational practice? Why, or why not?
2. Why does the matter of classroom management become more important as the size of the class increases? In what way do the techniques for manag-

ing a group of eighty vary from those used in teaching a group of five students?

3. Should a student with an unfortunate home background be expected to adhere to the rules just as much as a student from a good home? Why, or why not? If equal adherence is desirable, how might the music teacher make allowances for such a student, while still retaining the integrity of the class?
4. Suppose that through the proper channel of its student officers the band objects to the rule that there be no talking while one section is being given special attention. What should the teacher do to handle the objection?
5. In providing students with significant choices in music, which of these matters are more properly left to the teacher and which can involve a large amount of student participation?
   a. The selection of one of two serious numbers to be performed at a program.
   b. The decision of whether or not the band needs to rehearse again a certain section of an overture.
   c. The selection of the type of stole that will be bought to go with the choir robes.
   d. The decision of whether or not a piece from the Renaissance period shall be studied in the course.
   e. The determination of the order in which the music will be performed in the spring concert.
6. What should the teacher do to manage each of these incidents?
   a. Bob, a sophomore, is somewhat of a "show-off." A student running errands for the principal's office enters the room with a note for the teacher. Bob says in a loud voice to the girl bringing the note, "Marge! Baby!"
   b. Linda is a quiet freshman in the clarinet section. As the teacher is explaining a point, he notices Linda talking quietly to her neighbor.
   c. Howard has caused trouble in the eighth-grade general music class. Feeling that he is seeking attention, the teacher assigns him a report to make to the class, with the hope that this will provide him with attention and the class with useful information. While giving the report, Howard talks and talks, uses the occasion to be a "clown," and is clearly not interested in giving a useful report.
   d. The seventh-grade general music class is attempting to put an Autoharp accompaniment to a song. Herbie is usually reasonably well-behaved. But as he holds the instrument waiting to play the chords the class decides upon, he cannot resist strumming lightly on it.
   e. The ninth-grade Girls' Glee Club is practicing its music for a performance at the annual Mothers' Tea. As the teacher walks by frivolous, talkative Diane, he notices that she is looking at a movie magazine behind her folder.

f. A nearby store is featuring inexpensive plastic water pistols this week. Nearly every boy entering Mrs. Hixson's seventh-grade general music class has a loaded water pistol in his pocket as he enters the room.

7. Why is a private conference the best way to deal with a student whose behavior has become a problem?

8. Are democratic practices suggested for use in music classes primarily because they contribute to the American democratic political system, or because they are the basis for the operation of American society, or because the students will learn more in the class in which these principles are observed?

Suggested Readings

Dodge, Emelie Ruth, "Classroom Control in the High School," *NEA Journal*, March 1958, pp. 180–81.

Grambs, Jean D., and William J. Iverson, *Modern Methods in Secondary Education.* New York: William Sloane Associates, 1952. Chapter III.

Harrison, Russell M., "Human Relations in Teaching," *Music Educators Journal*, February–March 1962, pp. 122–26.

Larson, Knute G., and Melvin R. Karpas, *Effective Secondary School Discipline.* Englewood Cliffs, N.J.: Prentice-Hall, Inc., 1963. Chapters III, IV, and XI.

Lindgren, Henry Clay, *Educational Psychology in the Classroom.* New York: John Wiley & Sons, Inc., 1962. Chapter XII.

Oakland, Lloyd, "Discipline Is Desirable!" in *Music Education in Action*, Archie N. Jones, ed. Boston: Allyn and Bacon, Inc., 1960, pp. 312–15.

VI

organizing and administering the music curriculum

Every music teacher is to some degree an administrator of the music curriculum. Every music teacher is involved with and affected by the type of course offering, the money available, and the condition of housing and equipment in his teaching situation. In small school systems the music teacher is the administrator for the entire music program because he is the only teacher of the subject. Even in large school systems, teachers exert influence on administrative matters through their membership on district-wide committees and their requests regarding equipment and schedule. And it should be added that the music curriculum demands much management. The amounts of money it consumes are large in comparison with other curricular subjects; its work is displayed publicly more than that of any other area, with the possible exception of physical education; and its course offerings are varied and not as well established by tradition as are those of other areas.

INTERRELATEDNESS OF CURRICULAR OFFERINGS

The first objective of the music curriculum is to teach music. What does this simple statement mean for the type and number of courses offered in the junior and senior high schools? For one thing, it means that there is a unifying focus for all the teaching done in music classes. The high school orchestra may be working on a Corelli concerto grosso; the seventh-grade general music class may be exploring the changing voice and its effect on singing; the junior high school band may be attempting a transcription of the "Largo" from Dvořák's *New World Symphony*. The groups are learning music at different degrees of difficulty and in different ways. But the goal is the same, even though the approaches differ. So any teacher of instrumental (or vocal) music who asks, "Why should I care what goes on in vocal (or instrumental) music?" is revealing his ignorance of the unity of music education, and his lack of awareness that whatever happens in one music class affects all the other music classes. More than one instrumental teacher has wondered why the school and town care little for good music, and has never thought that upgrading the now nearly defunct general music course might make a difference in the reception to the best music his group can perform. In the long-range view, covering five, ten, or more years, the various forms of music education will succeed or fail *together*. It is no more logical to expect vocal or instrumental music to thrive without the other *in the long run* than it is to expect a tree to flourish with branches on one side lush and green while the other side is brown and sickly.

VALIDITY OF CURRICULAR OFFERINGS

Curricular subjects must meet the test of providing organized, valid learning experiences. Because time in the school day is limited, any subject that uses part of that time must do so in an educationally worthwhile way. Curricular offerings in music, therefore, should be those classes that encourage sensitivity to aesthetic qualities and provide greater understanding of and skill in music.

This is not true of extracurricular activities. Extracurricular activities are a valuable part of the total school program, and music teachers should assist in their promotion. Many of the nonmusical values of music education mentioned in Chapter Two are furthered in activities beyond the scope of the formal curriculum. Frequently extracurricular activities are based on student interests and benefits other than the learning of music, as in the case of the variety show, the stage band, and the rendition of the latest popular song. However, some extracurricular activities are logical extensions of curricular offerings, as in the case of the string-quartet club, the madrigal ensemble, and the music-appreciation club. Music teachers especially should be on the alert for opportunities to extend learning in such ways.

Desirable though extracurricular activities may be, the music teacher must recognize their nonmusical aspects and keep them from infringing on curricular offerings. When the training of majorettes, the elaborate band show, the pep band, the extensive operetta or musical become curricular, the teacher rightfully may find that he has difficulty in getting administrative support in matters of academic credit, finances, school time, and enrollment of students. In the long run, the music teacher cannot expect music to be treated as a curricular subject if his classes do not provide valid music instruction. He must not try to substitute the nonmusical values of extracurricular activities for musical values that make necessary music's inclusion in the curriculum.

PERFORMING GROUPS

Unfortunately, music educators have tended to classify music courses as either "performing groups" (bands, orchestras, and choral groups) or "classes" (theory, music appreciation, and general music). The distinction has some justification in that the two types of courses approach music differently, the performing group chiefly by playing or singing music, and the class by means of textbook, test, and discussion. Although both approaches have some validity, unfortunately the two types of courses have seldom made use of the learning of the other, a point which will be further discussed later in this chapter.

Performing groups clearly dominate music education in the high school and, to a degree, in the junior high school. Until recently little question was raised as to their educational value. In the re-examination of all education that has taken place since the beginning of the space age in 1957, some people have looked at performing groups with a hard, cold eye, and asked, "How much music are the students learning in these classes?" An accurate and comprehensive answer has not always been given with assurance. It has even been suggested that performing groups be replaced with a more "academic" type of class.

A performing group has several features that warrant its place in the curriculum. As the pragmatists point out, people learn by doing, by experiencing. A student who goes through the work of learning his part and rehearsing with the group knows the music in a way that someone who only listens can never know it. He has seen the music dissected and put together again; he has heard its thematic material over and over until it is part of him. Many a teen-ager has had an initial dislike for a difficult and profound piece. As the weeks went by he gradually began to comprehend its meaning and beauty. Had it not been for the intensive work required to perform the music, he would have been left with no understanding of it.

A strong case can be built for performing groups on the basis of meeting teen-age needs. The students at this age need the recognition a performing group can provide. They want activity; they want things to happen. The thought of only studying about music is not appealing to most of them. Hence the preparation of music for public performance motivates them very much. Such reasons as these do not negate what was said in Chapter Two about the reasons for music in the curriculum. On the contrary, a performing group can take advantage of adolescent characteristics so that the students learn music more effectively.

A third point in favor of the performing group is the fact that it is now established. This is not a compelling reason, but it must be considered. Teachers have been trained in the instruction of such groups, materials have been prepared, and the place of performing groups in the curriculum is largely secured. Before discarding such assets as these, something must be found to replace them. What is needed is not revolution, but rather evolution toward more musically valid performing groups.

What must a performing group accomplish to merit its place in the curriculum? First, it must do more than present pleasing performances. As a part of learning to perform the music, a member of a band, orchestra, or choral group should gain, commensurate with his musical development and maturity, some understanding of:

1) the total work, not only his own particular part;
2) the musical qualities and elements that go into the interpretation and over-all design of a piece—tone, dynamics, phrasing, rhythm, counterpoint, harmony;
3) the way in which the musical qualities and elements are used in the piece;
4) the historical significance of the work and its relationship to the other fine arts.

In the provocative book *Your School Music Program*, there is a discussion of a hypothetical band director who attempts to give her students an education in more than the playing of the notes.

> Yes, she's limited for rehearsal time, like most of us, but she feels that her responsibility is music education, not simply beating time and calling out an alternate fingering for G-flat.
>
> The same kind of teaching should prevail throughout the music program. Musical skill develops as we relate it to and associate it with the making of music—music made or listened to by any group of children or any individual anywhere.
>
> Each music teacher has literally hundreds of opportunities for doing this every week. No time? Then we say that we have no time to help a child understand music. Too difficult? Then our materials are over the heads of our students. Too much trouble? Then we should be working with musicians who have already mastered their art.[1]

To explain why secondary school music has in many cases become too performance-centered, some historical background may be useful. Although music had been in the American public school for nearly a hundred years, the great leap forward in secondary school music occurred with the expansion of the secondary school itself in the decades from 1910 to 1930, and to some extent to 1940. From 1910 to 1940 the chances of a child's

[1] Frances M. Andrews and Clara E. Cockerille, *Your School Music Program, A Guide to Effective Curriculum Development* (Englewood Cliffs, N.J.: Prentice-Hall, Inc., 1958), p. 115. Reprinted by permission.

attending high school increased from one in ten to three in four.[2] This increase caused curricular changes, because now the schools had to serve many students who were not planning to go to college. In addition, a more enlightened view of what was worth while for teen-agers brought music into the secondary school curriculum with new vigor. Because school music at the secondary level expanded so rapidly, there were few teachers trained for school music instruction. The secondary schools many times turned to professional musicians, a trend that was accelerated with the unemployment caused by the advent of the talking motion picture and the depression of the early 1930's. Because so many former professional musicians were employed to teach music in the schools, their influence on music education was profound. These men, naturally, worked with their groups in much the same manner as the director of a professional organization. The period when the band or choir met was a "rehearsal," and the purpose of the band or choir was to present polished and perfected performances. Any teaching technique that contributed to a top-flight performance was a "good" technique. The teacher was called the "director," a term more familiar to the professional musician.

None of this discussion is intended to discredit the efforts of professional musicians who entered the teaching field. Many of these men made valuable contributions to music education. Even today, the paucity of other professional employment for the musician has turned many performers toward teaching in the schools. Fundamentally, common interests bind the professional musician and the music educator together, and the teaching profession needs capable and sensitive musicians. What must be realized, however, is that whatever is good for a professional organization is not necessarily good for the performing group in the school. Because the two groups exist for very different purposes, they should be approached in different ways.

To contribute to more precise thinking on the subject of school performing organizations, several words should be examined. The words "director" and "rehearsal" are acceptable, of course, but they carry a connotation of the professional performing organization. A rehearsal should be a learning experience for the students; therefore the term "class" seems more appropriate. The usual term for a person who teaches a class is "teacher," not "director."

Making the rehearsal into more of a class is going to take some hard work and careful planning. It is going to require imagination and persistence, perhaps even a little daring. *But there is no more important matter to which music education in the secondary schools can address itself than that of making the time spent in performing groups educationally and musically more worth while.* The thought of working learnings on music

[2] *Status and Trends: Vital Statistics, Education and Public Finance*, Research Report–R 13 (Washington, D.C.: NEA Research Division, 1959), p. 12.

literature and structure into the already crowded orchestra or choir period may sound hopelessly impractical at first glance. And it is impractical, unless some changes are made in the operation of many groups. For example, the number of performances a group presents each year may have to be cut to allow more time for study; the music teacher will have to be as interested in purchasing recordings, books, scores, films, and listening equipment as he has been in getting uniforms and instruments in the past; he will need to select a piece of music because it will provide the students with a particular musical insight, and not because it is sure to please an audience.

On page 415 is a reprint of an article that explains in detail how one teacher, Donald Anderson, attempts to enrich the learning opportunities in his band rehearsals. The article presents in a practical way the kind of learning that should be a part of every group's work.

Not all students can profit equally from music instruction. Students want, and can best use, music that is suited to their ability and interest. When enrollment permits, groups operating at different levels should be offered. There can be a choir for the more interested and talented young persons, and glee clubs for the less gifted. The same arrangement can be set up in instrumental music (although for some reason there are few "second" instrumental music organizations in existence). Such a practice is consistent with the democratic philosophy, which stresses equality of opportunity as one of its tenets. However, the teacher must guard against slighting the less-talented group. The education given students in a glee club is just as important as the education given in a choir; only the level at which the learning takes place is different.

The Need for Orchestras

For a variety of reasons, including the growth of the band and the shortage of teachers during World War II, the number of school orchestras shrank considerably between 1930 and 1950. Since 1950 there has been a slow but steady growth in the number of school orchestras. The dearth of school orchestras is still a serious matter. The main cause for concern is that in instrumental music the orchestral literature is vastly richer than the literature for band. This is a matter which hits right at the heart of what music education seeks to accomplish in the schools. While the band can perform transcriptions of many fine works, the aesthetic qualities of string music frequently do not transfer well to winds. Something is usually lost in a transcription. The band is rapidly acquiring a fine contemporary literature of its own, and possibly in fifty or seventy-five years the problem of literature will no longer be a serious one.

A second reason for concern about the lack of orchestras is the type of experience available to the interested amateur after graduation from high school. The American Music Conference estimates that there are about

1,150 nonprofessional orchestras in the United States as of 1962, and about 300 community bands.[3] The opportunity to continue instrumental music upon completion of school lies largely in orchestras, which use only a limited number of winds and many strings.

When speaking candidly on the matter, many band directors give three reasons for not offering string-instrument instruction. One: students who study strings often represent a loss from the band, and hence a lowering of its quality. Thus the end result is two mediocre groups instead of one good organization. Two: there is no one competent to teach strings—the band director plays a wind instrument. Three: there is no time in the teaching schedule. As for the first objection, in school systems of less than 1,000 enrollment in grades 7 to 12, there is some reason for concern. If the orchestra has only four violins and one cello, it cannot perform much of the good music available to it. However, some smaller school systems have both a creditable band and an orchestra; so it can be done if conditions are right. The plea of incompetency is seldom valid. Most colleges require study on string instruments as a part of the training for an instrumental music teacher, and most instrumental music teachers who majored in a brass instrument, for example, do not avoid teaching woodwinds.

The matter of teacher time and additional expense to the school must be faced. No school can expect to get something for nothing, and if it wants to offer its students the proper curriculum in music, then it must realize that an increase in teacher time will be required. Fortunately, string instruments are no more expensive than band instruments, and their maintenance costs are usually low. The amount of teacher time needed in addition to an already existing wind instrument program amounts to about a third of the existing instrumental teacher load. The time allotted to an instrumental music curriculum that includes strings is roughly one-third each to woodwinds, brasses, and strings, with the percussion worked into either the woodwind or brass classes, depending on which are smaller.

Quality of Performance

A performing group exists to teach students music by playing or singing it. As a part of this assignment, it also presents programs to audiences. These programs must be done in a creditable manner. But what is a "creditable" performance? After all, how good is "good"? Are there "standards"? If there are, how can the person just beginning to teach tell if his performing group is up to standard?

In any art, evaluation is largely subjective; absolute measurements are impossible or meaningless. No one can say that a pianist who plays one hundred notes per second is better than one who plays ninety. It is not the *quantity* of notes, but rather the *quality* of the playing. And judgments

[3] "Report on Amateur Music in the United States—1962," American Music Conference, unpublished study, 1962, p. 9.

about qualities can only be subjective. This does not reduce the validity of a work of art, any more than the validity of love is diminished because it cannot be measured. This fact does, however, rule out any thought of hard and fast standards.

A teacher evaluates his work, even if only for his own development as a teacher, so the most valid and useful way for him to do this must be found. School organizations should not be evaluated in terms of collegiate or professional standards, any more than the school football team is compared with college or professional teams. The basis for evaluation must lie elsewhere. Essentially it lies in the fact that, in order to be considered creditable, a school group should be able to *execute the notes and rhythms of the music with a pleasing tone quality and with the essential musical expression of the piece.* How does this differ from the college or professional standard? Mainly in the music performed and the consistency and reliability of performance. The school music teacher selects music which the students can perform. If the group cannot perform the music at the standard of creditability mentioned, then easier music should be found, or the work should be withheld from public performance. Consistency involves the individual capabilities of the members of the group. A professional orchestra could not tolerate an inexperienced violist; the school orchestra can, if it has other better players, and if the weak player's errors do not conspicuously detract from the group endeavor. Reliability is seen when a top-flight concert artist performs a long concerto seemingly without error; a talented young performer is likely to play the same work with an occasional small mistake.

In the criterion for creditable performance, the words "with essential musical expression" are crucial. Sometimes a group executes the notes of a piece apparently without understanding its musical quality. Debussy, played as if it were a rousing good march, is not Debussy nor is it a march. Debussy should be studied in class and every effort made by the teacher to get across the idea of the music, but if the effort fails, then public performance of it should not be attempted.

A concept of a standard can be gained through participation in the music festivals sponsored by state or county music educators.[4] Festivals do invite comparison because the groups perform one after another, often doing the identical piece of music. The festival can be useful and constructive *if* the proper attitude is taken toward it by teacher and students. The contest, which has largely disappeared from the educational scene, is more often detrimental than helpful. As was indicated on page 63, the

[4] Festivals are of two types. One is noncompetitive, with no ratings given by adjudicators, although comments may be offered. The other type involves ratings by adjudicators according to a hypothetical standard. Thus, any number of groups may be rated in the top classification, as long as they meet the standard. A contest usually means that there can be only one group rated as "best" or "first," one as "second," and so on.

teacher should realize that the evaluation of performance as such is of limited value in evaluating the sum of his work. Several states have ruled that when two or three adjudicators evaluate the same performance, they should discuss their opinions with one another to arrive at a more consistent rating. In cases where discussion between adjudicators is not allowed, there are instances of widely different opinions. This only confuses the teacher whose group is being evaluated and tends to discredit the value of adjudication.

NONPERFORMING CLASSES

The nonperforming class has two advantages over the performing group. One: it can cover certain phases of music in a broader, more comprehensive way. A choir can learn to sing only so much music in a year's time. A class in music literature can cover many more works, but in a less thorough way. Two: the nonperforming class is not tempted to give second place to musical learning because of an impending concert. A teacher would be less than human if he neglected a performance, which the public will observe, in order to stress musical learning that the public will *not* see and hear.

The nonperforming class must not be considered as passive or inactive in its study of music. The theory class, as is suggested in Chapter Fifteen, should have some of its better student compositions performed in a laboratory-seminar situation or before the public. The general music class should certainly engage in music-making, and as Chapter Eleven recommends, on occasion even appear publicly. The music-appreciation course should include the singing and seeing of themes, and should stress the fact that effort and interest are necessary to be a good listener. In short, no music class can afford to be detached and dull. The nonperforming class can increase its effectiveness by making music as well as studying it.

BALANCE WITHIN THE MUSIC CURRICULUM

Nonperforming classes have both suffered and profited from the lack of public attention. Because their work is seldom put on display, the classes enable the student to learn and study what is most worth while, but for the same reason they have been somewhat neglected in music education. Andrews and Cockerille state the situation imaginatively:

> . . . we find a situation such as that in Albert School District, where the marching band dominates the music program—a marching band of seventy members and eighty flag wavers, majorettes, and rifle twirlers. Yes, they look mighty good marching down the field on a bright October afternoon.
>
> Trouble is, while they represent only eight per cent of the school population, they receive approximately fifty per cent of all the money

> that is expended on the school music program. This town doesn't know what the other children are missing. And frankly, there is little appreciative value to be had in listening to this band. It takes so long to teach marching and formations every September that there isn't much time left to spend on the music. The spectators applaud a show, not music. Here is a music director who has given up music education and gone into show business.[5]

The effort in music education should be spread evenly throughout the various levels of the school system, and among the various types of music courses. While balance does include the distribution of money, more important is the teacher's attention and effort. Sometimes the choral director will prepare ever so carefully for the choir period, but just before the general music class starts, he can be seen running into his office to grab at random some records to play for the class that day. Music teachers must ward off the temptation to slight the nonperforming class because no one knows nor seems to care about the quality of teaching for these students.

THE COMPLETE MUSIC CURRICULUM

At this point in the discussion of curricular offerings and balance among them, a summarization is needed of the full music curriculum, both performing and nonperforming. At the junior high school level, grades 7 to 9, the following courses should be available:[6]

1) *General Music.* Required of all students in grade 7, and open to all students in grades 8 and 9 without regard to previous musical experience. A course offering a variety of musical activities, such as playing, singing, listening, reading music, creative activity, etc.
2) *Vocal Music.* Boys' and girls' glee clubs, chorus or choir, small vocal ensembles, assembly singing for all students.
3) *Instrumental Music.* Orchestra, band, small instrumental ensembles, class instrument instruction in winds and strings for beginning and more advanced students; credit for private lessons available in grade 9.

At the senior high school level, grades 10 to 12, the following courses should be available:

1) *Elective Course Offerings.* Music theory, music appreciation or understanding. Some schools offer a broad fine-arts course which includes music, instead of or in addition to music appreciation.
2) *Vocal Music.* Boys' and girls' glee clubs, chorus, choir, small vocal ensembles, voice classes, applied music credit for private lessons.

[5] Andrews and Cockerille, *op. cit.*, p. 103. Reprinted by permission.
[6] This summary has drawn heavily on *Outline of a Program for Music Education* (Washington, D.C.: Music Educators National Conference, 1951).

Some of the large choral groups should be selective and others open for election by any interested student, unless the school is too small for more than one group.

3) *Instrumental Music.* Orchestra, band, small ensembles, dance or stage band. Orchestra and band should be divided into first and second groups if the enrollment warrants such division; applied music credit for private lessons.

COURSE LOAD OF STUDENTS

Sometimes a school's course requirements make it difficult for students, especially those preparing for college, to find time for music. This pressure is reflected in the number of students enrolled in music, and the size of enrollment in turn affects the quality of learning that can be carried on. In most schools the problem is one of degree. It is almost always *possible* for the student to enroll in music, but sometimes he must give up something else of such importance that it is not *reasonable* for him to choose music. For example, the student believes, often wrongly, that by taking music instead of an academic subject, he may be forfeiting his chances for admission to a good college. Choices are a part of life and must be made, but the choices offered students should be reasonable ones, such as between art and music or between practical arts and fine arts for the college-bound student.

Several avenues of action are open to the music teacher. One is to work with the counselor to rearrange a student's program so that he can continue in music. Some courses can be taken a year earlier or a year later. Above all, the music teacher must not assume, unless there is conclusive evidence, that the counselor or principal is "against" music. Seldom is this true, and to think so may lead to an aggravated situation in which the music program is the loser.

Sometimes students give a half-true reason for not continuing in music: "I don't have time." The real reason, which the student is too polite or lacking in courage to give, is a loss of interest in the subject. The teacher needs to be discerning of a student's underlying reasons before he goes to the counselor or principal to try to change a schedule.

Finally, the music teacher can work to install an additional period in the school day. A majority of schools still operate on a six-period day, in which the student is expected to take four subjects required for graduation. A fifth period is for physical education (in many states required by law), and the sixth period is for study hall or an elective such as music. The addition of a seventh period greatly increases the likelihood that the student will be able to take music, and for this reason music teachers should work for an increased number of periods in the school day. In fact, unless another period is added, the increasing requirements in other curricular areas will make it more difficult to keep music in the school day.

COURSE SCHEDULING

The setting up of a schedule for classes within the school day, with the exception of small instrumental or vocal classes which are arranged, is the responsibility of the school principal. When the teacher must work in more than one building, the principal schedules in cooperation with a music supervisor and other principals. The music teacher may indicate preferred periods, but with the many demands for special classes and groupings, making a schedule is a difficult task.

Since most general music classes in the junior high school do not meet daily, the music teacher in conjunction with other teachers in the "special" areas may have some choice in the matter of scheduling. Music classes that meet on alternate days can do so in conjunction with physical education, art, or practical arts. Some schools have blocked out the year so that a class has music daily during a quarter of the year, then art daily for a quarter of a year, and so on.

A rotating schedule, such as the one shown here, can be used throughout the school, but it is most often put into effect by instrumental music teachers who draw students from other classes for lessons or sectional practice. The principle of rotation can be varied and adapted almost without end. For classes that do not meet daily, it may be spread over a five-week period by designating a certain rotated schedule as week one, another as week two, and so on. The main objection to rotation is that the students or classroom teacher may forget the class time because it changes from day to day.

	DAYS OF THE WEEK				
PER.	Monday	Tuesday	Wednesday	Thursday	Friday
1	clarinets	lower brass	percussion	free	saxophones
2	trumpets	clarinets	lower brass	percussion	free
3	saxophones	trumpets	clarinets	lower brass	percussion
4	free	saxophones	trumpets	clarinets	lower brass
5	percussion	free	saxophones	trumpets	clarinets
6	lower brass	percussion	free	saxophones	trumpets

One of the most persistent scheduling problems is the need for having the best winds in both band and orchestra. There are several ways to meet this need. Moving from the least to the most desirable, they are:

1) Have band and orchestra meet on alternate days. In the fall the band can meet three times a week, and in the spring the orchestra can meet three times a week.

2) Schedule one of the orchestra practices each week during out-of-school hours and bring the winds in at that time.

3) If room and teachers are available, have both band and orchestra meet during the same period. The best winds can move twice a week to orchestra, while the remaining winds get more practice on the band music and further ensemble experience.

4) Schedule the best winds into a study hall which meets during orchestra time. Twice a week they can then work with the orchestra.

Small ensembles normally meet during out-of-school hours. However, the teacher should upon occasion be able to allow groups to retire to another room to practice during the regular class period. Some teachers organize ensembles according to study halls. While this does not always mean the better players are together, it does provide ensemble experience which is important for all music students.

The near future may see significant changes in scheduling practices for all secondary school subjects; some of these suggestions are mentioned in Chapter Seventeen. The aim of the new scheduling practices is greater flexibility, which will make possible individual, small group, and large group instruction. It is an area of education that bears close observation by the music teacher.

CREDIT AND GRADUATION REQUIREMENTS

First, if music is to be a curricular course, music classes should meet during the school day. If they are forced to meet outside the regular school hours, then they are not curricular.

In the high school, credit should be offered for music study *on the same basis as all other subjects in the curriculum.* This means one full unit of credit per year for all music courses meeting five days a week and requiring homework, outside obligations, and individual home practice similar to homework. Half credit simply means: music is half as good as other courses; it is only half as valuable to the student. Two excuses are given for allowing only a half credit (or less!) for music. One is that no textbook or homework is involved. The music teacher can answer this argument by pointing out the need for individual practice in performing groups, as well as the homework required in nonperforming classes. If the performing group is made a more educational undertaking, as has been urged, this will better establish the case for equal credit in music.

The other reason given for insufficient credit is this: since students from several grades are included in the same class, and since a student in a performing group takes the same course for several years, no new learning takes place after the first or second year. While this statement indicates an ignorance of how music is learned, on the surface it appears to be a logical conclusion and should be answered thoughtfully. It is obvious that students over the years assume positions of leadership in a group. As a sophomore Joe Green may have played Beethoven's *Egmont Overture* as a hesitant second violinist; in his senior year he is concertmaster and is responsible for leadership of the section and for decisions regarding such musical matters as bowing. Back in his sophomore year Joe got part of the musical idea of the Beethoven work, but as a senior he comprehends more fully the phrasing and the manner in which the thematic elements are put together. As the next chapter will point out, music education is the increasing awareness of musical concepts such as tone and phrase, and concepts are not learned in a year or two.

In most instances, students do not need music credits in order to graduate. Most students now in music would probably have enrolled no matter how little credit was offered. The concern here is for equality and prestige for both student and teacher. It weakens the position of the teacher when he says "Music is important" and the school supports that subject only halfway. And the students, when they study hard and accomplish much in music, rather resent the implication that so little is thought of their effort. If music is taught in the high school, then music, as one of the fine arts which are essential to civilized man, deserves equal treatment in the matter of credit.

Below is a typical listing of requirements for graduation:

4 units in English
2 units in history and social science
2 units in mathematics
1 unit in science
2 units in foreign language
5 units of electives

A minimum of two years of physical education, including the passing of a swimming test

total: 16 units

Eleven of the sixteen requirements are in the traditional academic areas, there is a physical education requirement, and sufficient allowance for electives. What's missing? Any mention of the fine arts. The requirements tacitly say: "The fine arts are not an essential part of a high school graduate's education. We have plenty of requirements in other areas, even to the inclusion of swimming." As in the case of credit, a fine-arts stipulation is not going to affect to any large degree the enrollment in music courses. Most students enroll for one fine-arts course during high school anyway. What the requirement does is to place the fine arts on an equal footing with other studies, and to draw attention to the rightful place of the arts in education.

Credit is a two-sided affair. If the school fulfills its obligation by granting credit to music, then music must fulfill its obligation by providing a course worthy of credit. It was for this reason that the listing of curricular music offerings on page 100 did not include two courses at the senior high school level which have sometimes been advocated: the general music class and beginning instrumental music classes. If a student in high school wishes to increase his musical understanding or gain instrumental experience, and receive legitimate credit for it, he should involve himself in the more intensive study of a music-appreciation course or of private lessons.

CREDIT FOR PRIVATE STUDY

Although the instruction is not handled by members of the faculty, some school systems make arrangements for credit to be given for private study. Again, the credit is seldom needed by the student for graduation, but it does give the study the respect it merits, and places such study on the student's record for all to see, including college admissions officers.

In order to insure its validity, credit earned for private study must be carefully administered as to choice of teacher, enrollment, and method of grading. The private teacher may be approved by the state department of education, the school music teacher, or a local college or university.[7] A panel of two or three uninvolved music teachers can be secured to audition the student for grading at the end of the year. The course of study and standards need to be spelled out before study is begun. This may be done by a group of private teachers for each particular instrument, by the state department of education, or by music education organizations as in the case of *Specimen Examinations for Applied Music at the Secondary School Level.*[8]

THE MARCHING BAND

The marching band has commendable features. It is good public relations for the music department. Many people see the band only at the football game; this is their only contact with the school music program. Students achieve recognition, school spirit is bettered, and good feelings are generated all around as the colorful group parades by. To criticize this is something like criticizing Santa Claus. What could anyone have against something that gives so many people a harmless form of enjoyment and impresses them favorably with the school music program?

The objection is that the marching activity of bands, especially at the half-time of football games, has in some cases dominated the music-education curriculum. Just as Santa Claus may draw people's attention away from the real religious meaning of Christmas, the marching band may

[7] See *Missouri Applied Music Plan,* Missouri State Department of Education, Jefferson City, Mo.

[8] *Bulletin of the National Association of Schools of Music,* No. 20 (January 1945).

divert music teachers, students, and the public from the real purpose of music in the schools. That purpose is to teach music. But consider the music that is played on the football field. When the band makes a formation of a four-leaf clover it plays "I'm Looking Over a Four-Leaf Clover"; Beethoven is not appropriate here. Not only has the marching season robbed the band of time it could have spent working on good music, it has encouraged bad playing, because the heat and cold, dust and dirt, plus trying to play on a bobbing instrument take their toll. How often instrumentalists talk about "getting my lip back in shape" to play well after the marching season is over. The half-time show is fun, but it is largely valueless for the students as far as getting an education in music is concerned.[9] Unless school music is regarded primarily as an activity that gives youngsters a chance to gain recognition and a sense of teamwork, things which scouting and athletics also provide, then marching does not contribute to their musical education.

Now, what should the music educator do about it? To begin with, he can treat the problem honestly. If the appearance of the band at half-time shows is necessary for public relations, then let everyone admit it, rather than try to pretend that the students are gaining a valuable educational experience. In most American communities today the marching of the band at football games is so much a part of life that it is unrealistic to suggest that it be discontinued, and perhaps because of its public relations value this would not be desirable in some communities even if it were possible.

In addition to facing the situation honestly, the instrumental teacher can by himself, or better yet in conjunction with band directors from neighboring schools, reduce the effort expended for the half-time show. One way to do this is to cut down on the number of games at which the band marches. Out-of-town games and the first game in the fall are most easily eliminated. (The band may still play at the games; this is quite a different matter from marching.) The other way to cut down on the time spent in marching is to simplify the band show. With a minimum of strain, a band can form the appropriate school letters in block style and march up and down the field. Considerable effort is required, on the other hand, if the band is to spell out words in script and make automobiles, airplanes, and merry-go-rounds. What makes some of the effort spent on intricate formations rather pathetic is the fact that the low bleachers available at most high school fields prevent most of the onlookers from being able to see what the formation is.

In most schools the band director is also responsible for training the nonmusicians (flag carriers, pom-pom girls, baton twirlers)—students who frequently are not members of the band. Although such participation is

[9] Charles R. Hoffer, "The Marching Band—Why?" *Holton Fanfare* (April 1961), p. 14.

good for the students, because it provides them with recognition and helps develop confidence, their activities are only distantly related to music. If possible, the director should secure the cooperation of the physical education department to assist in the training of these students.

SUMMER MUSIC STUDY

Students are not as busy in the summer, and therefore have more time for music study. Summer study helps to maintain playing skills and interest, which can wane if no music activity takes place for nearly three months. Because of the educational opportunities offered by summer study, music teachers need to become informed about and involved in these programs. Teachers in schools that do not have summer music study should consider the possibilities for promoting it.

Many school systems sponsor summer instruction supported by tax funds. In some cases it is included in the budget of the school board, while in others it is supported by a special tax levy, often as part of a recreation program. Sometimes participants in the programs are asked to pay a small fee. In the great majority of summer programs the emphasis has been entirely on instrumental music, probably as a carry-over from the summer band concerts in the park. There is no logical reason why the program should not include vocal as well as instrumental music. In most summer programs, instruction consists of small classes and ensemble playing, but a large group rehearsal may be held once or twice each week. High school students usually do not participate in large numbers, because many find jobs or attend music camps, and the classes are generally for less advanced players.

A second idea has been successfully tried in a few communities. A tuition-supported summer program in music meets in one school building but enrolls students from many nearby school districts and employs a faculty from several different schools. The advantage of such a program is that the student can study with an instructor who is a specialist in his particular field—woodwind, brass, or string. A second advantage lies in the fact that enough students can be brought together to make a high-caliber performing group and to allow greater variety of instruction, including some theory and literature.

A third type of summer study is that offered at camps and on the campuses of colleges and universities. The school music teacher should encourage worthy students to attend. Many school systems arrange for financial assistance through service clubs or by using the proceeds of concerts. A scholarship gives encouragement and incentive to an adolescent, and serves to stimulate in other students a desire for summer study. Financial assistance should seldom cover the entire cost of a student's summer study, however, because a teen-ager gains more from an undertaking when he has helped to pay for it. The procedure used in selecting recipients of scholarships must be carefully spelled out to parents and students, and a full accounting of the awards should be made with the superintendent of schools.

GUIDANCE OF STUDENTS

Every music teacher in the junior and senior high school is involved in the guidance and placement of students in music. This is a serious responsibility because it concerns the growth and development of human beings; it should therefore be undertaken with care. Guidance in music is, of course, very much enmeshed with the teacher's philosophy of music education. If he is looking only for students who will help build up the choir or orchestra, his guidance efforts will be directed to that end. If instead he is attempting to help each student achieve the most from music study, that is another matter, and a view which calls for another type of guidance.

Placing each student in the course that is best for him does not mean admitting everyone to the orchestra or to the select choir regardless of talent. A student is no more helped by being in a class too advanced for him than he is by being placed in a group too elementary for him. Jim, with his limited musical sensitivity, intelligence, and aural acuity, would be frustrated in a group that sings Renaissance polyphony. If Susie's out-of-tune violin playing significantly damages the efforts of the second violin section, then she should not be allowed to limit what the other students can learn. If she has been given adequate instruction and opportunity, then there comes a time when she must be guided into other school areas that represent a better use of her time. Fortunately, students are usually keen about placing themselves. Susie decides to try an art course; Jim is not interested in the select choir because it doesn't sing music he likes anyway, so he would just as soon stay in glee club.

To insure that a student receives the most he possibly can from the music program of the school, the music faculty must act on the basis of as much information as possible. The music teachers in the seventh grade should fill out a card or sheet (such as the one illustrated here) on each student regarding his musical status. The front side of the sheet is filled in by the student himself—it contains information about his musical background and environment. The other side of the sheet contains space for music grades and at least two comments each year by the teacher. These comments should pertain to the student's growth in music and his level of achievement in the class. The sheet can then be passed along as the student proceeds through school. It would be fine to keep more complete records and gain more information, as Andrews and Leeder suggest,[10]

[10] Frances M. Andrews and Joseph A. Leeder, *Guiding Junior High School Pupils in Music Experiences* (Englewood Cliffs, N.J.: Prentice-Hall, Inc., 1953), p. 45.

PUPIL'S MUSIC RECORD CARD

Name ______________________________ Date __________
Address ______________________________ Phone __________
Have you ever taken private music lessons? If so, what and where? ____
____
What musical instruments are owned by your family? __________
Do other members of your family play musical instruments? ________
Do you have a piano at home? ____________________
Do you have a good record player at home? ______________
How many records does your family own? ______________
Are most of them popular music or serious music? ____________
Have you sung in any glee clubs or choirs after school hours? ________
If so, when and where? ____________________
What is your favorite kind of music, and what is your favorite piece? __
____
Do you listen to music programs on the radio or on television? If so, which ones? ____________________
What do you like best about music classes—listening to records, singing, playing instruments? ____________________
____
____

REPORT OF ELEMENTARY MUSIC TEACHER

____
____
____
____

Musical-aptitude test scores ____________________

but many times the music teacher sees so many different students each week that this is not a practical possibility.

One of the items of information included on the sheet should be the results of a musical-aptitude test. Before using such a test, the teacher should clearly understand its purpose and what it can tell about the student. First, there are some things an aptitude test *cannot* do. One: it cannot infallibly predict success in music. To date, no agreement has been reached among psychologists and musicians as to what music talent is, least of all which test measures it most accurately. Even if there were some acceptable and valid indicator of talent, there are still matters such as intelligence, perseverance, and willingness to work. Two: a test cannot indicate without error that a person lacks talent. Sometimes students are bothered by the strangeness of the test situation, or by a physical condition, such as a cold. At other times they do not adequately understand the directions. On the machine-scored type of test, some students miss a square and proceed to mark the rest of the squares in the line out of proper order, thus making the test results worthless. Musical ability is an elusive thing, and is likely to be misjudged for a number of reasons.

What *can* the aptitude test do? It can, and this makes it worth giving, indicate that a person does have musical aptitude. The laws of chance for all practical purposes exclude the earning of a high score by accident. As long as the results are not accepted as final or infallible, the aptitude tests can provide information which, when combined with other observations about the pupil, permit better guidance. The teacher should use the tests as a doctor utilizes his observations in making a diagnosis. No physician would prescribe treatment solely on the basis of the patient's temperature, although he does want to know it and will consider it in deciding what to do. The aptitude-test scores are especially valuable if the test is given twice in a student's school experience, once in fourth or fifth grade and again in junior high school. Two tests greatly reduce deviations due to chance, and they provide information before instrumental music study is begun.

When the first aptitude test appeared, after World War I, its purpose was to provide an instrument that was to measure native endowments with such validity that the probability of success could be determined prior to music study. It was to serve as a screening device for large numbers of youngsters and to come up with those who possess much natural musical ability. Furthermore, it could prevent the expenditure of limited teacher time and equipment on the unmusical student.[11] In cases in which a school system had very limited resources, the aptitude test was thus used *as an expedient.* Today, music educators know that the aptitude test is a remarkable creation and that it is well worth giving because it provides information that can be gained in no other way. But educators also know that it is far from perfect and is capable of providing only a small portion of an answer to a very big question. The aptitude test is for guidance, not for determining whether or not a student should study music. There is a considerable difference between the two functions.

The pioneer work in musical aptitude testing was done by Carl E. Seashore, whose work is available today as *The Seashore Measures of Musical Talents* (revised edition by Seashore, Don Lewis, and Joseph G. Saetveit).[12] The test consists of six elements—pitch, time, rhythm, timbre, tonal memory, and loudness. It may be administered to students in grades four and up. The student marks an answer sheet as he hears the sounds played on a record. The results of each of the six sections are given in

[11] Peter W. Dykema and Karl W. Gehrkens, *The Teaching and Administration of High School Music* (Evanston, Ill.: Summy-Birchard Publishing Company, 1941), p. 373.

[12] Available from Psychological Corporation, 304 East 45th St., New York 17, N.Y.

terms of percentiles according to the level attained by the student on the test. Seashore himself did not want the scores of the six parts put together to form a composite score, although this is frequently done. The reliability of the various parts is about .75, with the pitch test being .79 to .88.[13] This degree of reliability is quite satisfactory. The validity is well-established in that students with high scores on the *Seashore Measures* are much more likely to succeed in music study. The relationship has been proved in a great number of cases. Its validity has been challenged on the basis that the test is not musical.[14] But the critics have missed the point. Suppose that a test is devised to select safe drivers before they actually climb behind the wheel of a car. The test consists of carrying a glass full of water across the room, with the safe driver spilling almost none of the water and the accident-prone driver spilling much. The fact that carrying water is not like driving a car is irrelevant, as long as the water-carrying test really differentiates between the good and bad drivers. The weakness of the revised edition of the *Seashore Measures* lies in the fact that the number of items in each part has been reduced by one-half. A chance error in the raw score has an inordinate effect on a percentile rank.[15] This can be remedied by giving the pitch test twice, since most teachers consider it to be the most important. The loudness test can be eliminated, and the students then can use the space allotted to the loudness test, following the same pattern as for the pitch test. Of course the scorer must be informed of the change.

Another major attempt in aptitude testing is the *Wing Standardized Test of Musical Intelligence* (revised edition).[16] H. D. Wing was critical of the unmusical, "atomistic" approach of Seashore, and set about to devise a more musical test based on a single or "omnibus" theory that music talent is one talent and not a fragmented thing.[17] Working carefully over a period of years, Wing constructed an aptitude test more musical in nature, and one in which the results are more affected by musical training than Seashore's raw talents. The test, like Seashore's, requires about one hour to administer, but is somewhat more expensive. Its reliability is high at .91, and its validity is based on a large number of cases with the same criterion that Seashore used: the correlation between the test score and success in music.[18] It is interesting to note that although Wing built his test on an entirely different approach from that used by Seashore, the stu-

[13] *The Third Mental Measurements Yearbook,* Oscar Krisen Buros, ed. (New Brunswick, N.J.: Rutgers University Press, 1949), p. 177.

[14] *Ibid.,* p. 178.

[15] *Ibid.,* p. 177.

[16] Available from National Foundation for Educational Research in England and Wales, 79 Wimpole Street, London W.1, England.

[17] *The Fourth Mental Measurements Yearbook,* Oscar Krisen Buros, ed. (Highland Park, N.J.: The Gryphon Press, 1953), p. 230.

[18] *Ibid.*

dents who score high on one also do well on the other.[19] Wing's test may be used for students eight years old and up. Because it was created more than twenty-five years after the first Seashore tests, and almost ten years after the revision of the Seashore tests, the quality of the recording is much better.

The *Test of Musicality, Fourth Edition,* by E. Thayer Gaston is about half the length of the Wing and Seashore.[20] In addition to examples played on a recording, it also asks the student about his musical background. Its reliability is high at .88 to .90, and its validity is good, although it is probably more influenced by musical training than are the Wing and Seashore tests.[21] Another test often used is the *Kwalwasser Music Talent Test* by Jacob Kwalwasser.[22] No figures on reliability or validity are provided with the test, although a reviewer working with about one hundred students got a reliability score of only .48, which is low.[23] The test requires only ten minutes to administer.

Some aptitude tests are intended to be given by the examiner at the piano, but this testing method has two serious drawbacks. First, when the human element figures so prominently in administering the test, the likelihood of error and variation on the part of the examiner eliminates the possibility of comparative norms, and considerably reduces the worth of the results. Second, the piano is inadequate for checking pitch discrimination, since it cannot indicate intervals smaller than a semitone, a pitch difference too wide to be of much value.

Other tests are created and provided by musical-instrument manufacturers. Most of these do not make a valid assessment of ability because they lack sufficient items—sometimes there are only ten for pitch discrimination. On tests provided by instrument makers, a vast majority of the students are evaluated as good prospects for music study.

FINANCING AND BUDGETING

Public school systems are financed from tax monies from local, state, and federal sources, and the detailed budgeting is handled in a great variety of ways. The differences in the minutiae of budgeting are so numerous that it is difficult to discuss the matter in any general way. Besides, the matter of finance and budget eventually rests in the hands of the school administration, and the money spent for music purposes is managed in a manner prescribed by the administration.

[19] *Ibid.*
[20] Available from O'Dell Instrument Service, 925 Massachusetts Ave., Lawrence, Kan.
[21] *The Fifth Mental Measurements Yearbook,* Oscar Krisen Buros, ed. (Highland Park, N.J.: The Gryphon Press, 1959), pp. 252–53.
[22] Available from Mills Music Inc., 1619 Broadway, New York 19, N.Y.
[23] *The Fifth Mental Measurements Yearbook,* pp. 248–49.

If a philosophy of equality among curricular areas is operative, then music should be treated as any other school department—no better, no worse. If possible, the budget should be set up according to the recommendations of the U.S. Department of Health, Education, and Welfare on the basis of function, regardless of which department uses the money.[24] For instance, the repair of equipment should be placed under one heading whether the repair is for typewriters, scientific equipment, or musical instruments. After being so grouped, it can then be further broken down into musical instruments, piano tuning, or typewriters, if this is desired.

Music is a subject area that requires large expenditures for supplies and equipment. If the school has in the past fallen badly behind in its purchasing for music, school finances may not allow for the fulfillment of needs in one or two years. The music teacher should work out in cooperation with the administration and the school board a program of buying that encompasses a number of years, perhaps five. In this way music needs can be met over a period of time without badly disrupting the school financial situation.

The bases for financial requests are the educational needs of the school system. There is no point in comparing one school system's expenditures with another, because one may be well supplied, while the other needs many things. The teacher should work out a list of equipment and supply needs, being careful to avoid equipment of a luxury nature that the educational program can get along without, and attempt in time to secure appropriations to take care of the needs.

Sources for Funds

By training, desire, and employment, music teachers are teachers, not fund raisers. To involve them to any extent in bake sales, tag days, and card parties is a misuse of their time and talents. Besides, fund raising puts the music teacher in the awkward position of apparently raising money to support and enhance his own job.

Yet the financial situation in some schools is very poor. A parents' organization may be one answer. Other sources can provide additional funds. A rental fee may be charged on instruments or a small tuition charged for instrumental lessons. There may be profits from the sale of tickets to public performances or to special concerts by visiting musicians. Advertising space can be sold in the concert program. If a share of the music budget goes for the support of a marching band, it is only fair that a portion of the receipts from the sale of tickets to football games be allocated to the music department. Finally, if the school has a stage band,

[24] *Financial Accounting for Local and State School Systems,* U.S. Department of Health, Education, and Welfare Bulletin No. 4 (Washington, D.C.: U.S. Government Printing Office, 1957).

the income it derives from playing at school dances can be used to help meet music-department needs.

Parents' Organizations

Many school districts have parents' organizations to meet equipment needs that cannot be met by the school budget. The parents' group has much to recommend it. It provides an active core of solid support for the music activity, and in most cases the groups so supported meet their financial goals. Parents can also assist the school in activities such as chaperoning groups on out-of-town trips. This, however, is not the entire picture. In some cases, after the initial equipment goals are met, the parents' organization turns into a pressure group. Besides harassing the superintendent with persistent demands (a procedure that at first glance may appeal to an inexperienced music teacher), the group begins to apply pressure on the teacher for more elaborate concerts, better festival ratings, more community performances. Then he becomes burdened with providing a new and interesting program every month for the group's meeting. Finally, the son or daughter of the president of the group may not receive the opportunity to perform as a soloist—a privilege which the parent thinks is deserved. Such situations can put the teacher in a most uncomfortable position.

Before organizing a parents' group, these suggestions should be considered:

1) Be certain that the organization of the group has the approval of the school administration, and that the administrators understand the purposes of the group. If possible, get the administrative approval in writing.

2) Form a parents' group only if the need cannot be taken care of through the regular school budget. Probably at least two years should elapse before a teacher is satisfied that needs will not be met in the regular manner.

3) If possible, integrate the needs of the choral department and the instrumental music department. It should be Music Boosters, not Band Mothers or Choral Parents' Club. Even inadvertently, music teachers must not appear to pit one type of music against another.

4) Avoid the possibility of a future pressure group by organizing the parents' group on a temporary, one-project basis. When the project is done, the group can disband. In this way, no nonfunctional remains will be around to cause embarrassment or discord.

5) Devise ways of meeting and working with parents other than through a permanent, formal organization. The parents' night suggested on page 34 is an excellent way to establish rapport with the parents of the students.

MANAGING EQUIPMENT

The Music Library

If a library is disorganized or inadequate, the new teacher will have to establish a system for filing the music. Although some variation is possible in the system used, certain basic considerations are important. Music not in use should be housed in cupboards or filing cabinets. All copies of a single work should be placed in manila paper envelopes or folders with index tabs for easy identification. (Several types of inexpensive commercially printed envelopes are available.) Filing in this way is swift and sure, and the music is not exposed to excessive handling.

The system of filing alphabetically by composer is generally not recommended for school choral and instrumental works, because much of the music is derived from folk origins and has been adapted by arrangers whose names are not readily familiar. An alphabetical placement by title is preferable. In order to accommodate music of various sizes—a situation encountered particularly among band publications—the following system allows all music of one size to be stored together for more efficient use of space. Two numbers are put on the file card and on the envelope. The first indicates the drawer and the second the particular piece in that drawer, starting with "1" in the front of the drawer. In this system each file drawer is assigned a number.

Individual 3 × 5 cards should be made up for each selection in the library and placed in alphabetical order in a card filing box for reference. Information on the card should include the following:

Title of composition
Composer or arranger
Instrumentation or voice classification
Number of copies
Publisher
Dates and places of performance

To help the teacher in his planning, duplicate cards of different color can be made up to serve as cross references. In addition to the filing by title, there can be a filing by composer, and a third by the type of music —march, choral, overture, sacred polyphonic, or whatever classification the teacher finds useful.

Once a music library is established, it can normally be maintained by student assistants, with a minimum of supervision from the teacher. Before filing music, the librarians should check the copies for needed repairs. Sheets of music almost always wear out first at the crease between the pages. Torn music can be repaired with commercially made tape.

The inventory of copies and parts available needs to be kept up to date so that the teacher is spared the turmoil of passing out music in class only to discover that the supply is insufficient.

When the music is in use, it should be issued to each student in a music folder of heavy cardboard, with pockets that prevent the music from spilling out when the folder is closed. Inside should be a sign-out card, which the student leaves with the librarian when he takes his music home to practice. The card should include a place for the folder number, date, and student's name. For ease of administration, the student should sign out all or none of his music.

Uniforms and Robes

Uniforms and robes should be kept in a dark, dry closet or room. Light has an adverse affect on some fabrics and the better they are protected from moths, mildew, and dirt, the longer they will last and the better they will look. Unless items of apparel are taken home, they should be checked in and out by a student committee. When students have free run on a rack of clothing, a few of them cannot resist the temptation to take the first robe or belt they come upon.

Lending Equipment

A music department usually loans or rents to students equipment worth a considerable sum of money—uniforms, instruments, music. It is necessary, therefore, that the teacher keep an accurate accounting of all equipment. This inventory may be recorded on sheets of paper, in a book, or on a file card for each item; but it must be kept accurate. For instruments it should include type of instrument, manufacturer, serial number, school number, date of purchase, value, and accessories. For uniforms it should include item, school number, size, date of purchase, and cost. No teacher wants to falsely accuse a student of losing a clarinet, nor does he wish to be responsible for the loss of a pair of band-uniform trousers or a cello

INSTRUMENT LOAN CONTRACT

I, ______________________________, accept full responsibility for loss or damage for ______________, serial number ____________________. I will present it for inspection promptly when called for and return it on or before ____________________. I understand that the approximate value of the instrument at the time loaned is $______________. I agree to keep the instrument in good playing condition and pay for any repairs made necessary by misuse, negligence, or carelessness.

Date: ______________ Student ____________________
Parent ____________________

Date returned: ____________ Teacher ____________________

bow. Every item of significant value that is loaned should be signed for by the parent on a bond, which obligates him in case of loss or damage. If the bond is printed on a 3 × 5 card, it will be more durable and easier to file.

Care of Equipment

Instruments should be cleaned and checked at the end of the school year. If repair is needed, the instrument should be sent out during the summer months so that it will not be out of service when it is most needed. If possible, an instrument repairman should examine each instrument in June, to check on its condition and make needed repairs. Pianos should be tuned at least twice a year. Audio-visual equipment used in music classes should also be checked yearly, although in many schools this servicing will be under the supervision of the school's audio-visual specialist.

Insurance

Depending on the particular policy, the normal fire insurance carried by the school district on its buildings will cover some of the music equipment. For other equipment, usually items such as instruments that are easily moved from the building, coverage is available at low cost. Bids should be called for in order to obtain the lowest price. The policies in most cases cover not only theft and fire, but, of more importance, accidental damage—a far more frequent occurrence. The exclusions of the policies basically are intentional damage and normal wear and tear. The values of coverage are more than financial. The relationship between school and parent is reinforced when a father, whose son has his trumpet stolen on the way home from school, is told that even though there is a bond, in this case insurance will cover the loss.

FUNCTIONAL MUSIC ROOMS

For many years it was somewhat of a tradition that the school music teacher worked in the most proletarian of conditions—in an old coal bin, boiler room, cafeteria, locker room, or at the end of the hall. Recently, however, many beautiful buildings have been constructed to include attractive rooms, well-adapted for music. The rapid increase in the number of students means that many more buildings will have to be built in the years ahead. Because of the great variety in school size, in educational needs, and in construction materials, it is nearly impossible to summarize the information that might be useful in planning for building expansion. The MENC has published a helpful booklet on this subject, *Music Rooms and Equipment*, Publication No. 18, which should be consulted if new facilities are being planned.

New music rooms should take into account the space and equipment requirements of an enriched program. For instance, room-darkening shades will be needed so that the various kinds of projectors can be used. Listening equipment is also needed. Storage space for audio-visual equipment will probably be necessary, as well as electrical outlets properly placed for the use of the equipment.

A good architectural firm should consult with specialists in sound engineering in order to insure adequate soundproofing and acoustical conditions in the rooms. The music teacher should ask specifically about this when a new building is contemplated.

Possibly of greater value than the reading of publications are visits to the music facilities of recently completed schools. The tour should include a visit with the music teachers who are using the new rooms. These people can comment with unparalleled authority on the adequacy of their new quarters.

Many existing rooms are not suitable for good music teaching. A few are too "dead"; that is, they soak up too much sound. Deadness is most often caused by too much acoustical tile and draperies. A room constructed for band rehearsal is usually too dead for choral groups. Such a condition is difficult to correct. The problem can be alleviated somewhat by placing large pieces of hard fiberboard over some of the acoustical tile on the walls, and on the ceiling if necessary. Both instrumental and vocal teachers will have to approve any acoustical changes, of course. Dead classrooms have one important advantage: if the students are to perform in another location, the place of performance will seem "live" in comparison to the regular room, and this can give the performers a psychological lift.

More common than dead rehearsal rooms are those that are too "live." It is easier to correct this condition, which is caused by too much echo. Sound-absorbing materials such as draperies, acoustical tile, or porous insulating board can be placed around the room. Draperies can be made rather cheaply and successfully out of bark cloth. If there is no money available for acoustical tile or draperies, then the ceiling can be made sound-absorbent by the use of heavy paper meat cartons obtained from a grocery store or butcher shop. This type of carton is usually about 9″ × 4½″ × 2½″. These meat trays or cartons can be pasted cup end up against the ceiling, and they do an amazing job of eliminating echo in a room.

The successful teacher is wise in his use of materials—equipment, money, and, most important, the limited time of the students. When matters of finance, curriculum, credit, and equipment are handled efficiently, the learning climate is improved and the teaching of music is more effective.

Questions

1. On page 92 the statement was made that vocal and instrumental music succeed or fail together. How can this statement square with the fact that in some schools a choir or band director has had a top group over a period of years, and yet much of the rest of the music program is weak? Is it possible for a music teacher to succeed personally, and yet have music education fail? Do you agree that the various parts of music education are interrelated? Give reasons for your answers.
2. Suppose that the school in which you are teaching has no orchestra and no strings. You and your colleagues in the music department decide that you will request the school administration to start a string program. What points would you make to present your case to the school administration?
3. Suppose that you are asked to evaluate the balance in the music curriculum of a school system. What information would you need to make an evaluation?
4. Suppose that you are teaching in a school in which your band or choir meets only every other day. You wish to increase to daily class meetings. What points would you make to your principal for the increase in class time?
5. Suppose a principal asks you if you would mind meeting your performing group entirely after regular school hours. What points could you make for performing groups being curricular subjects?
6. Why should aptitude tests and other evaluations *not* be used to select those students who will be allowed to begin instrumental music study?
7. If a performing group is a curricular subject on an equal basis with English or biology, should the music organization have student officers and give service awards for contributions to it? Why, or why not?
8. If the school district is not in a financially fortunate position, should tuition be charged for instrumental music study and a fee charged for the use of school instruments? Why, or why not?

Projects

1. Attend two programs, each by a different secondary school group. Evaluate their performance of each piece of music according to the standard cited on page 98.

2. Find out about the opportunities for summer music study in your state. Compile a list of them, indicating the length of session, age level, expense and scholarship opportunities, and educational activities.
3. Test yourself with two of the musical aptitude tests that are available.
4. Ask members of the class who were members of marching bands in high school or college to describe what effect marching had on their ability to play their instrument, to read music, and to phrase and use dynamics. These students should also comment on the quality of music played for the half-time shows.
5. Interview two high school band directors:
   a. Ask them to describe the values of the marching band as they see them. Determine how the values they state agree with the goal of an education in music.
   b. Inquire whether or not their schools have a parents' organization for the promotion of music. If so, ask their opinion of the idea and their experiences with it.
   c. Find out how budget requests are handled in their schools—when they are submitted and in what form, and who decides on the amount of money to be allotted to the music department.
   d. Request permission to see the music library system that is used, and the instrument and uniform inventory and check-out forms.

Suggested Readings

Andrews, Frances M., and Clara E. Cockerille, *Your School Music Program, A Guide to Effective Curriculum Development.* Englewood Cliffs, N.J.: Prentice-Hall, Inc., 1958.

Andrews, Frances M., and Joseph A. Leeder, *Guiding Junior High School Pupils in Music Experiences.* Englewood Cliffs, N.J.: Prentice-Hall, Inc., 1953. Chapters VII, X.

Graham, Floyd Freeman, *Public Relations in Music Education.* New York: Exposition Press, 1954. Chapter III.

Leonhard, Charles, and Robert W. House, *Foundations and Principles of Music Education.* New York: McGraw-Hill Book Company, Inc., 1959. Chapters III, VII, XI.

"The Music Teacher and Public Relations," prepared for Commission III (Music in General School Administration) by the *Committee on Public Rela-*

tions in Music Education, Edward J. Hermann, chairman, Washington, D.C.: Music Educators National Conference, 1958.

Snyder, Keith D., *School Music Administration and Supervision.* Boston: Allyn and Bacon, Inc., 1959.

Whybrew, William E., *Measurement and Evaluation in Music.* Dubuque, Iowa: William C. Brown Company, 1962. Chapters VIII, X, XI.

VII

principles of learning and effective music teaching

Learning is a many-sided word. It can refer to kinesthetic or muscular-physical skill, as when a violinist learns to shift from first to third position. Learning also refers to memorization of facts; the students may learn that A above middle C vibrates 440 times each second, or that Mozart was a composer of the Classical period. Learning may mean problem-solving. For example, a student may have studied some Impressionistic music and its phrasing. When presented with a Debussy work that is unknown to him, he is able to phrase it properly because he has learned how to perform such music. Finally, a person has learned a piece of music when he can listen to it or play it and understand or convey its aesthetic meaning.

Most learning in music is compound, involving all four uses of the word just mentioned. One phase of learning may be stressed at one time or another, but all are present to some degree, if the learning is to be lasting and significant. When a violinist shifts, he is performing primarily a physical act. But also, he is making use of facts by knowing what shifting is and what notes and positions he is using in the process. He must make a judgment as to when a shift can best be made in the music, and he must determine the proper speed and style of shift. Finally, the violinist uses his understanding of music to achieve an aesthetically satisfying performance.

It is important to keep in mind the compound nature of learning in music, and to be conscious of which, if any, type of learning is being stressed. When reading the results of educational research, the teacher must be clear on how the word "learning" is being used, because the word is by no means treated consistently.

SIGNIFICANCE OF BASIC PRINCIPLES

When buildings were constructed by the laying of one stone upon another, the foundation stones had to be set securely, because if they were unstable all the stones placed above them would likewise be insecure. So it is in teaching music. There are certain basic principles upon which the teacher's work depends. He must understand these "foundation stones" if his efforts are to be effective.

The body of knowledge that comes under the heading of methods can for clearer understanding be divided into two parts. The first is made up of principles basic in almost every music-teaching effort. The second aspect, discussed in succeeding chapters, is composed of the many devices, procedures, or "tricks of the trade" derived from the basic principles.

The nine principles of music teaching, which occupy the attention of this chapter, are derived from musical considerations and from psychological research into the phenomenon of learning. Some of the principles are common to the teaching of any subject; others are applicable only to music. All are fundamental to the teaching of music.

EXPERIENCE WITH MUSIC

The first principle in the teaching of music is that students need to experience the qualities of music. Words are inadequate to express or explain music. As early as the seventeenth century the English essayist John Locke realized that this was true of all learning.

> Let us then suppose the mind to be, as we say, white paper, void of all characters, without any ideas; how comes it to be so furnished? . . . To this I answer, in one word, from experience. . . . I find I am absolutely dependent upon experience for the ideas I can have and the manner in which I can have them.[1]

Because music lies so much beyond the scope of language, Locke's doctrine is especially applicable to the teaching of music. A brilliant moment in a Beethoven symphony may be a musical experience of the highest order, but it is impossible for anyone to relate in words an account that in its impact is even a shadow of the effect of hearing the music itself. The rich sound of a Debussy chord can be appreciated only when it is heard. A music teacher who wishes to have his class perceive such a chord must give up any thought of finding words or devices short of actual hearing to do this.

Making music is the best but not the only way to experience music. Listening with understanding and feeling is also a musical experience.

[1] J. E. Russell, *The Philosophy of Locke,* extracts from *The Essay Concerning Human Understanding* (New York: Holt, Rinehart & Winston, Inc., 1891), p. 35.

In a sense, the term "passive listening" is a misnomer. Listening, if it is more than mere hearing, is an active state, although it involves no overt physical act. The research of Schoen and others into the effect of music on heartbeat and respiration proves this.[2]

A cardinal rule for the music teacher, then, is that *learning in music should be based on structured experiences with music.*

Developing Musical Concepts

One definition of the word "concept" is "a mental image . . . formed by generalization from particulars."[3] In music there are concepts of rhythm, melody, harmony, dissonance, modulation, syncopation, phrase, timbre, and many more. These concepts are very much a part of teaching music because they are the verbal tools for understanding music, for becoming educated in it. They become the means to thinking musically and to being analytical about music. They are necessary if the person is to be more understanding than the old man who, looking at the Grand Canyon, said, "Now ain't that somethin'."

Concepts, unlike facts, cannot be learned once and for all. The definition strongly hints at the method by which concepts are learned. They are learned from many experiences (particulars) which slowly form into an ever-enlarging concept (generalization). Just as John Locke gained his ideas from his experiences, the student gains his concepts of music from structured experiences in music.

The music educator's job is to give the students more and more understanding of melody, for example. Children in elementary school learn what a melody is; they may even use the word properly. In the primary grades their concept is only of simple vocal tunes of limited range. Later they sing melodies of greater range and complexity. This is followed by hearing and studying melodies conceived for instruments, which in turn is followed in later years by melodies for particular instruments–violin, piano, French horn. Hopefully, by about junior high school, the students have experience with a modal melody, melodies using more complex rhythms, and melodies that are through-composed. Later they can study the aria and recitative in a Handel oratorio, a Wagnerian opera, or a contemporary dramatic form.

This abbreviated presentation gives some idea of the great amount of learning that can go into one concept. Music teaching in the schools is a twelve-year project of chipping away on melody, rhythm, dynamics, bit by bit, as a sculptor chisels a block of stone, forming slowly more dis-

[2] Max Schoen, *The Psychology of Music* (New York: Ronald Press Company, 1940), pp. 106–108.

[3] *Webster's New Collegiate Dictionary* (Springfield, Mass.: G. & C. Merriam Co., 1961).

tinct and clearer images. Unlike the sculpturing, the learning is never completely finished. In a real sense students do not "learn" melody, because that implies that a definite conclusion is possible; rather they "are learning" melody and other concepts. When the orchestra director teaches his students about the melody in a certain piece, he is not giving them their first learnings about melody, nor does he expect to complete their understanding of it. Rather, he is broadening and deepening their comprehension of the concept. He does not tell the class, "Today we're going to learn a little bit more about melody." Instead, he prods their thinking by such questions as "What's different about this melody? How would you describe it–smooth, delicate, airy, quiet? How does it compare with the melody we found in the Mozart work we studied last week? Violins, did the man who wrote this melody understand how to bring the best out of the violins, or did he like singers better? Horns, would you call what you're playing at letter E a melody? Why?"

When he does this, he is teaching in just as true a sense as when he presents something totally new. It is for this reason that full credit should be given to Joe Green (page 104), even though he spent three years in the same course called "orchestra."

IMPORTANCE OF AURAL EXPERIENCE

The second principle, one closely related to the first, is that *aural experience is a necessary antecedent to visual experience.* This view, expounded by Pestalozzi in 1801,[4] is pertinent to the matter of music reading. Today music educators express this principle by saying, "Ear it before you eye it." The order is the important thing. Teaching musical comprehension by proceeding from printed symbols to aural experience is successful only to the degree that listening has preceded the reading.

The manner in which a child learns language is very similar to the way he learns, or should learn, music. By the time a child enters first grade, he has an understanding vocabulary of about twenty-four thousand words, and three or four years' practice in speaking the language.[5] It is after all through this experience that he begins to see the printed symbols that represent what he has been saying. These facts about language development, along with research by Penfield,[6] have brought about some new approaches to language instruction in the schools. Today many language specialists introduce foreign languages to elementary school children by

[4] *Grove's Dictionary of Music and Musicians, American Supplement,* rev. ed. (New York: The Macmillan Co., 1947), p. 333.

[5] Ruth G. Strickland, *The Language Arts in the Elementary School,* 2nd ed. (Boston: D. C. Heath and Co., 1957), p. 230.

[6] Wilder Penfield, "A Consideration of the Neuro-Physiological Mechanisms of Speech and Some Educational Consequences," *Bulletin of the American Academy of Arts and Sciences,* Vol. VI.

working mainly on an aural-speech basis, and only after two or more years have passed is the child shown the printed page.

BRINGING OUT MUSICAL QUALITIES

A third principle of music teaching is that *the instructional effort must bring out the aesthetic qualities in music*, which, after all, constitute the main reason for the teaching of music in the schools. The process of studying music should not be so pedantic that it stifles the spirit of a piece, or else a situation exists comparable to the one in the old joke, "The operation was a success, but the patient died."

There are two ways in which the quality of music can be lost. One is by practicing a piece again and again without additional insight. Sometimes teachers have the students go through a number repeatedly, apparently with the hope that through some magical process the music will be learned correctly. The learning that takes place is a random assortment of good and bad. The musicians get into a rut from which they cannot easily emerge. The teacher must remember that teen-agers, because of their limited technical ability, have to rely more on spirit. There is a limit to the feeling that they can give a piece, so this spirit has to be carefully tended.

The other way to stifle aesthetic quality is simply to exclude it from the teaching process. A separation between technique and music can easily occur when the entire attention of the student is devoted to using certain muscles in a certain way when developing an embouchure or proper hand position. Some specific attention to the use of a muscle may be necessary, but it should be put into a musical context as soon as possible.

In teaching fundamentals, the teacher must use a variety of approaches. For example, correct breathing is a complex activity, involving musical concepts and skills and requiring time and persistent effort to learn. The teacher can concentrate first on one aspect of the physical action involved, and later on a different action. The students can first work on a musical passage that especially demands proper breathing; at other times the teacher can stress the need for good tone and show how to achieve it through correct breathing. Such variety prevents boredom for the students and results in better quality.

In order to maintain the quality of freshness in the music being prepared for performance, work on the music must be distributed throughout the weeks prior to the performance. Proper spacing is regulated by the amount of time and the number of classes in which a piece is studied. Ideally, a work of music should be so regulated that it reaches its acme of development at the time of performance. This peak occurs at that point which represents the greatest amount of technical perfection coupled with musical effectiveness. When groups go "dead" in their performance of a program, it is often because they reached their acme of interest too far ahead of the performance.

If a group is performing ten numbers, it is clear that all ten cannot be brought to their height of technical accuracy and freshness simultaneously. What can be done? A piece that is nearly ready for performance weeks ahead of the program will have to be placed in a musical "deep freeze"; it should be withdrawn from regular practice for a few days. Curiously, this "seasoning" often improves the performance of the work. Psychologists refer to this as "reminiscence," and it occurs in a variety of learnings.[7] A few days before the performance, this number can be rehearsed again and given the final polishing touches.

There are instances in which it is necessary to set aside temporarily parts of a piece. Some melodies are easily learned, and it is easy to tire of them. Sometimes in vocal music a peculiar situation develops. The students love to sing certain melodies, and yet the more they sing them, the worse the music sounds! The number of repetitions of these passages has to be carefully rationed. It may be necessary to avoid the easier parts of a work in class, and expend efforts only on the more difficult passages.

To demonstrate how music might be spaced over a period of time, let us assume that a group has eight weeks in which to prepare a program of eight works. In this plan, all the music is assumed to be of equal difficulty, a most unlikely possibility.

First week—Introduce and learn most of pieces 1, 2, and 3.

Second week—Introduce piece 4 and learn most of it. Continue work on pieces 1, 2, and 3.

Third week—Introduce piece 5 and learn most of it. Finish work on pieces 1 and 2, and save them for review.

Fourth week—Introduce piece 6 and learn most of it. Continue work on pieces 4 and 5. Save and only review pieces 1, 2, and 3.

Fifth week—Introduce piece 7 and learn most of it. Continue work on pieces 5 and 6. Save and only review pieces 1, 2, 3, and 4.

Sixth week—Introduce piece 8 and learn most of it. Continue work on pieces 6 and 7. Save and only review pieces 1, 2, 3, 4, and 5.

Seventh week—Continue work on pieces 7 and 8. Begin polishing pieces 1 and 2. Occasional review of pieces 3, 4, 5, and 6.

Eighth week—Polish all eight pieces. Dress rehearsal and performance.

In addition, the teacher should pace the students psychologically to help preserve freshness and interest in the music. No teacher should try to

[7] Arden N. Frandsen, *Educational Psychology* (New York: McGraw-Hill Book Company, Inc., 1961), pp. 370–71.

maintain the same psychological intensity in all practices of a performing group. The students will have a vastly different attitude toward a class early in September than they will have toward the rehearsal the day before the Christmas concert.

WHOLE AND PART LEARNING

The question of whole or part learning represents an area of dispute among educational psychologists. One group, mainly representing the Gestalt school, has maintained that it is only the whole, the total configuration, that has meaning; therefore, a teacher should work to give the student insight into whole sections or ideas. The other group, equally esteemed, has stressed the learning of parts as components of the whole; accordingly the teacher should teach portions of a learning task. There are several reasons for the apparent gulf of difference: too much theory and not enough practical research, lack of comparable situations in demonstrating points, and differences as to what the term "learning" means. As the field of educational psychology matures, the points of difference in this instance and others will be clarified, if not resolved. The division among experts demonstrates the need for discretion and consideration in applying research and theories of learning.[8]

The resolution of the whole-part controversy lies in the type of learning task being given the students. The limited amount of research available in the area of music education indicates that the whole method is superior when the size of the learning project is about thirty-two measures or less.[9] The proponents of whole learning have the weight of aesthetic logic on their side, because one or two notes from a melody have meaning only as members of that melody. A melody with fourteen notes in it is not perceived by the ear as one note plus one more plus one more. The ear (or more properly, the mind) perceives the notes as one complete melody. Aesthetically and musically the students must grasp the whole, be it a phrase, melody, piece, or movement. The whole, however, as research has indicated, is usually too large to be learned in one chunk. It must be broken down. One of the jobs of the music teacher is to dissect music into portions large enough to be comprehended yet small enough to be learned by the students. The music teacher, then, teaches somewhat in the manner of a watch repairman, disassembling so that the smallest part can be studied, and then putting the parts back into a whole. In teaching music, this process goes on continually.

[8] Henry Clay Lindgren, *Educational Psychology in the Classroom*, 2nd ed. (New York: John Wiley & Sons, Inc., 1962), pp. 236–40.

[9] William N. Reeves, "An Exploratory Study of Two Sets of Learning Principles Derived from Learning Theories of Guthrie and Wheeler as They Relate to the Development of Instrumental Musicianship," unpublished doctoral dissertation, University of Southern California, 1954, p. 46.

Pestalozzi maintained that one thing should be taught at a time—rhythm, melody, expression are taught and practiced separately before the child is called to the difficult task of attempting all at once. While this procedure is logical, it does not work out psychologically. Teaching music by the application of one layer of learning upon another, as in the case of the ABC method of reading cited in Chapter One, ignores the fact that people learn music by recognizing configurations (groups or patterns) that have meaning for them. Learning to read rhythms, for instance, without application to music is comparable to learning to play the violin with the bow only. *The music teacher, with skill and imagination, must help the students to see the whole that they are studying, while giving careful attention to the parts.*

SCALE OF REFERENCE

The use of the word "scale" to mean "relative dimensions, without difference in proportion of parts," is not common for a musician, who has had to study musical scales for years. But when used in the term "scale of reference," the word implies a sense of proportion on the part of the music teacher as to the selection of learning tasks appropriate for the age, level of musical development, and innate ability of the students he seeks to teach. Stravinsky's *Rite of Spring* is a monument of modern music, but it is not suitable for a junior high school orchestra. No choral teacher should expect a group of thirteen-year-olds to sound like a group of eighteen-year-olds. Nor should he anticipate that an unselected glee club meeting twice a week will achieve the standard set by a highly select group that practices daily. A sense of proportion is vital to the music teacher. *He must view realistically the variables that affect the level at which a class operates.*

Sometimes the statement is made that all students are pretty much alike everywhere, and so the differences in groups are due to the ability of the teacher; that is, the group is only a reflection of the teacher. Such a sentiment is wanting in logic. Can anyone say that a band from a small school with limited financial resources and frequent changes of teachers reflects poorer teaching than a group from a large school with good resources and a long tradition of instrumental music? The scale of reference must differ for each of these schools, or else real musical advancement in the former school may be equated with failure, and the status quo in the latter school may be maintained without improvement.

Many times young teachers despair because, try as they may, they cannot reach the standards attained in the best schools of the state—schools whose groups are heard at professional meetings and workshops. Prospective teachers should realize that the vast majority of groups across the nation are not highly selected and experienced. One hears about the few high-quality performing groups simply because they are exceptional, not because they are typical.

No teacher should be permanently content with mediocre results, however. There should be a constant effort toward improvement and a desire for the best in performance. A teacher should not be content to let things go along as they are, but neither should he consider himself a failure, an occupational misfit, because his groups are only fair in quality when contrasted with the highest standard of performance.

Briefly, these are the factors that affect the level at which performing and nonperforming music classes operate:

1) The age of the students. This is especially important in vocal music.
2) The degree of selectivity of the members.
3) The amount of class time available.
4) The previous musical experience of the students.

The formula for having one of the best bands or choirs in the state is a simple one: mature students + a high degree of student selection + sufficient time + good previous training + a competent teacher = a top group. With a little thought, one can estimate with surprising accuracy the caliber of school groups without even hearing them. Of course, the notable schools have good teachers, partly because able teachers naturally gravitate toward such teaching situations, and partly because good teaching has made their music program unusually strong.

The teacher must make a realistic appraisal of more than just the level of a performing group. "Scale of reference" applies equally to the type of music studied, the kinds of musical experiences given the students, and the evaluation a teacher puts on his work. For instance, to sing well the "Coronation Scene" from *Boris Godunov* is a reasonable expectation with one choral group, while for another to do the same thing is a teaching accomplishment of the first order. In one case the teacher is doing only "average" work, while in the other, the teacher can be characterized as "outstanding."

DEGREES OF DIFFICULTY

A sixth principle states that *a music teacher needs to evaluate the degrees of difficulty in pieces of music and in the learning tasks presented to students.* No teacher, no matter how experienced and capable, can infallibly predict how difficult a particular piece of music will be for a class, or what places will be the most troublesome. Students do not react with consistency. Even though perfect judgment is impossible, the teacher should gauge difficulty as accurately as he can. He should be aware that one portion of a piece may be more difficult than another. He should also realize that the degree of difficulty will depend on what he seeks to teach with the piece. A work may be technically easy, but musically very difficult. Gregorian chant is an outstanding example of this. If subtle musical understanding is not desired or expected, then chant is not hard;

but if it is to convey its full aesthetic meaning, then it is extremely difficult.

Besides being useful in the selecting of music, an awareness of difficulty is helpful in the act of teaching. In vocal music, as an example, the teacher should keep in mind that each of these group efforts becomes more difficult:

one part with piano doubling
one part with the complete piano accompaniment
one part unaccompanied
(The order of the last two depends on the nature of the accompaniment in the particular piece.)
two parts with piano doubling each
two parts with piano doubling one or the other
two parts with the complete piano accompaniment
(Again the order will depend on the piece.)
two parts unaccompanied
three or more parts in the same order of increasing difficulty

If a vocal teacher finds that the students can easily sing at one level of difficulty, then he might skip over some of the intervening levels. If the group cannot do one step properly, say sing in four parts, then the teacher can "back up" and attempt something easier, such as two or three parts, or the one part that is causing the problem. The same general procedure also applies to teaching instrumental music.

The teacher need not always have a class work at the same level of musical advancement. New learnings require that the student be challenged, and old learnings need to be reinforced by repetition of points already learned. The teacher needs to know when he is challenging and when he is reinforcing.

DISTRIBUTED EFFORT

Educational psychologists have found that *it is far more efficient to learn a skill in numerous short sessions than it is to learn the same thing in a few long sessions.* Some psychologists refer to this as "distributed effort," others as "distributed practice" or "spaced practice." In an experiment by Lyon,[10] the subjects learned stanzas of poetry. When two stanzas were learned in one sitting, it required .38 of a minute per stanza. However, when 100 stanzas were learned in one session, it took 3.85 minutes per stanza, *ten times* as long for each stanza! The significant figure here is the amount of time required *per unit* or *line* being learned. Many other experiments, ranging from juggling to addition, have reached

[10] D. O. Lyon, "The Relation of Length of Material to Time Taken for Learning and the Optimum Distribution of Time," *Journal of Educational Psychology,* V (1914), 85–91.

the same conclusion.[11] Thus it is many times more efficient to practice an instrument for one hour each day of the week than it is to practice seven hours in one day. More learning takes place in the first ten minutes of practice than takes place in the next ten, and with each additional amount of study there is a corresponding reduction in the amount learned. The spacing of short sessions is most useful in situations calling for concrete skill learnings, such as playing the piano or writing minor scales. Class activities that require the integration of many components, such as composing music, are best done in longer periods.[12]

One of the underlying reasons for the principle of distributed effort is the forgetful nature of the human mind. The classic studies in this area were done by Ebbinghaus,[13] and his experiments were later substantiated by Luh.[14]

Two important facts are illustrated by the Ebbinghaus curve. One: a great deal of learned material is forgotten. Two: it is forgotten quickly—

EBBINGHAUS CURVE OF FORGETTING

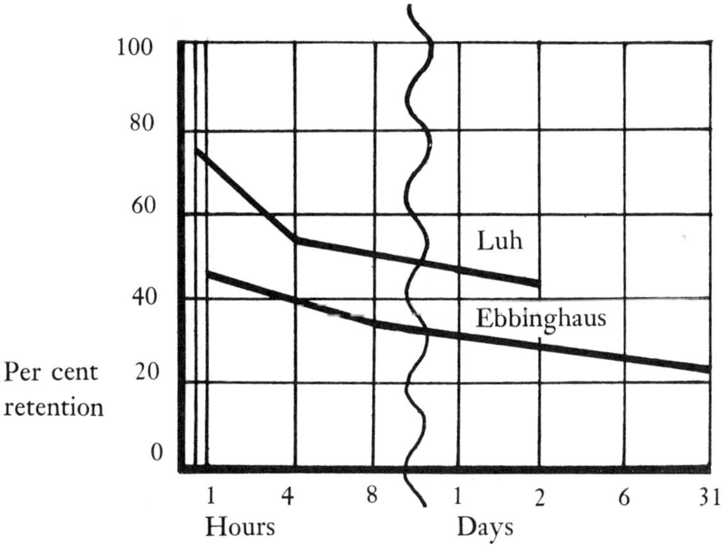

[11] See H. B. Reed, "Distributed Practice in Addition," *Journal of Educational Psychology*, XXVI (1935), 695–700. See also C. G. Knapp and W. R. Dixon, "Learning to Juggle: I. A Study to Determine the Effect of Two Different Distributions of Practice on Learning Efficiency," *Research Quarterly*, XXI (1950), 331–36.

[12] Frandsen, *op. cit.*, p. 300.

[13] H. Ebbinghaus, *Memory*, trans. H. A. Ruger and C. E. Bussenius (New York: Teachers College, Columbia University, 1913), p. 68–75. First published in German in 1885.

[14] C. W. Luh, "The Conditions of Retention," *Psychological Monographs*, XXXIII, Whole No. 142 (1922).

within an hour.[15] To a teacher this means that there must be much relearning and review.

There are additional reasons for distributed effort in teaching. One: fatigue and boredom set in during long practice, and the desire to improve is diminished. Two: mistakes are more likely to be repeated in a long session, thereby becoming fixed in the response pattern. Three: forgetting is a learning experience in that it shows what elements have been inadequately learned. If there are additional practice sessions, these weaknesses can be overcome. Four: a person tends to resist immediate repetition of an act, and this resistance continues as the repetition continues. Five: incorrect acts are forgotten more quickly than correct ones, and spaced practice allows incorrect responses to be dropped.[16]

The music teacher must realize that it is better to leave something unfinished, and come back to it another day, than it is to overwork on it. The principle of many learning periods excludes any thoughts such as "We're going to stay on this until it's right." This attitude brings a negative outlook to the problem at hand. On the other hand, distributed effort should not be a means of escape from hard work. Persistence is still vital to good teaching. But persistence should not be confused with dull repetitiousness.

The maximum amount of time that should be spent on any one activity varies with the amount of concentration required, the age of the students, and their interest in the activity. Students can work for about ten to twenty minutes on a piece of music or on a musical topic in the general music class. In a drill activity, which may require more concentration, the time should be shorter.

A teacher should not overlook the implication that distributed effort has for the spacing of learning sessions within the class. Because much forgetting takes place within minutes after the material is presented, it is profitable to have short learning sessions on the same music two or even three times within the same period. A short review at the end of class is especially valuable. This review can take several forms, such as a quick performance of the music, a resumé by the teacher, a few questions asked of the students, or even a short written quiz.

Distributed effort does necessitate frequent changes from one piece of music to another, or from one activity to another. Far from being a drawback, however, such changes are desirable in the education of the musician. Musicians need to be adaptable, able to adjust from one piece of

[15] The amount of forgetting varies with the type of material being learned. Principles and concepts have the best retention, while material that is meaningless to the students is least retained. See F. P. Frutchey, "Retention in High-School Chemistry," *Journal of Higher Education*, VIII (April 1937), 217–18. Cf. R. W. Tyler, "Permanence of Learning," *Journal of Higher Education*, IV (April 1933), 203–204.

[16] Lee J. Cronbach, *Educational Psychology* (New York: Harcourt, Brace & World, Inc., 1954), p. 368.

music to another. When a group performs, it will have little time to recast its mood for each musical work.

SINGLENESS OF CONCENTRATION

A person can concentrate on only one point at a time. When concentrating, he leaves the remainder of his activities at that moment to fend for themselves as best they can without any conscious aid. The necessity for singleness of attention raises problems for the teacher when he considers all that is involved with the making of music. Tone, words, notes, and style are all present together; and yet an individual can think about only one aspect at a time. The answer lies in emphasizing one phase of the music one time, and another phase the next time.

If a choral group is having trouble with a rhythmic passage, the teacher might focus attention on the problem in this manner.

> The singers first work on chanting the words in rhythm. The concentration here is on the rhythm, and other distractions have been removed. The phrase is then sung, but the singers fail to put in the accent as indicated. They go through the words in rhythm again, and this time speak the unaccented syllables softly. The phrase is again sung with correct rhythm and accent, but with a harsh, nasal tone. The director has the group sing the tonic chord (basses and sopranos on the root, tenors on the fifth, and altos on the third), and hold it while concentrating on voice production and tone. Then the passage is sung again with the correct rhythm, accent, and tone.

Singleness of concentration has significance for the music teacher in determining how rapidly the students can progress. The temptation for the well-trained musician is to cover ground too quickly.

> A supervisor from a large city was discussing the abilities of persons who were teaching voice classes in the various schools. "You know," he said, "year after year the best singers in our all-city recital are from Lincoln High School. And the surprising thing is that George Nelson has a voice like an old crow; he's the worst singer of all the vocal music teachers in the school system. But he sticks to the fundamentals of singing so well that his students get a solid vocal foundation. The teachers who are better singers, it seems, can't resist hurrying on to the 'fine points,' and their students just don't have that wonderful foundation that George's students have."

Probably George Nelson was well aware of the fact that certain things were lacking in the students' singing. He apparently realized, however, that teen-agers cannot jump in a year or two from a state of musical immaturity to a high state of musical development, any more than a boy can grow into manhood in a year or two. He achieved results by concentrating on the most important things first, and leaving the "fine points" until the students were ready for them. He also demonstrated that he knew the primary consideration is whether the students are learning, and not the degree to which they approximate the performance of a professional group.

It is necessary to develop good habits in the making of music. In many respects this is like learning to drive a car. When a person first begins to drive he must consciously think of each step: push the starter button, release the brake, set the transmission, step on the accelerator, turn the steering wheel, and so on. But when he finally does know how to drive, all of these actions are done automatically; he can drive and simultaneously carry on a conversation.

Although the degree is exaggerated for illustration, young violinists are occasionally instructed something like this:

> "Hold the violin under your chin so that it points halfway between straight front and straight to the side. Keep your left elbow well under the violin and your left wrist straight; hold the neck of the instrument between the thumb and the index finger, like this; turn the left hand so that the little finger is nearest you.
>
> "Now, the bow is held in the right hand with the thumb curved a bit so it touches the angle between the stick and the frog; lean your hand inward so the stick crosses under the index finger at the middle joint; the little finger regulates the balance and is curved so only the tip touches the top of the stick. The wrist is flexible but not flabby; the muscles of the bow arm are relaxed, just tense enough to move the bow properly. Now, the bow is drawn at a ninety-degree angle to the strings. Don't let the angle change as you approach the tip. Remember you *draw* the bow gently across the string—don't drag or bounce it."

Then pointing to the music, the teacher says:

> "The note on the second space of the treble staff is A."

If the student hasn't given up by now, the teacher may go on:

> "There are four beats in a measure. You know what beats are, don't you? Each note of this kind, with no stem and not filled in, gets four beats. Now we can figure out all the other note values mathematically."

At least one good thing could be said about this example of teaching, which can only bewilder most students: it is thorough.

MEANINGFUL TEACHING

The final principle for the music teacher is that *whatever is taught must be related to the student in a meaningful way*. A teacher can construct and teach the most masterful and exciting lesson, but if that lesson does not make sense to the student it is valueless. Such a situation is akin to watching a drama in a foreign language, without the aid of translation.

There may be humor, pathos, and philosophical insight in it, but to the viewer it is just a lot of strange words.

How can a music teacher make what he teaches have meaning to the student? First, by relating the learning to what the student now knows. Stroud has this to say on the subject:

> Material is not inherently meaningful; it is endowed with meaning by a reacting individual, and experience or previous reaction is necessary thereto. Similarly, material is not logical apart from someone by whom it is apprehended as logical. To put the matter in another way, meaningful, insightful, and logical materials are partially learned already.[17]

The teacher must determine what the pupil now knows, and start from there, rather than search for pieces of music or techniques which are good for use with any and all senior high school girls' glee clubs, for example.

There are several ways for the teacher to find out what the students know. He has the student information sheet, discussed on page 109. He hears the performance of music in class, and students' comments and questions about the music. After the first few weeks of school, he has the results of tests given to the students. He should have the imaginative ability to put himself in the place of the students so that he can see how the class, subject, and teacher look from their point of view. Hopefully, the years have not dulled the teacher's memory of the year when he was a seventh grader or a sophomore.

There are techniques that help relate the new and unknown to the known. One is to associate the unfamiliar with the familiar in context. Sometimes, for example, a second or harmony part is more easily learned in conjunction with a first part that is familiar.

A second way to make the learning more meaningful is to make it as functional as possible. Isolated drill or facts presented out of context have little meaning. To the inventive teacher, almost every piece suggests points that can be used as teaching tools for work on some aspect of music, a common interval or chord, a certain style of phrasing. The possibilities inherent in a work can also be one of the criteria used by the teacher in selecting music for a particular group.

Another method is to build a learning structure that moves from the simple to the complex. For example, before the class studies an oratorio, they should have a good foundation in how ideas and feelings are expressed in a serious song.

One of the best ways to make an association between the familiar and the unfamiliar is by the use of similes. Since Biblical times people have been teaching and learning from statements such as, "Though I speak

[17] James B. Stroud, *Psychology in Education* (New York: Longmans, Green & Co., Inc., 1946), p. 497. Courtesy of David McKay Company, Inc.

with the tongues of men and angels, and have not charity, I am become as sounding brass, or a tinkling cymbal." Unfamiliar concepts become more meaningful to students when a mental image is suggested: "Ride along with the rhythm, as though you are out in the ocean in a little rowboat, riding up and down with the waves; don't try to plow through them as a large ship would." With a little imagination, a teacher can think of a simile for almost every teaching situation. Tones can be thin and piercing "as a pencil point" or big and easy "as balloons," and the motion of the air coming up through the throat when singing can be compared to heat waves billowing up off the pavement on a hot day. Although the simile should not be overused, it is understandable to the students, and at times adds a note of humor to the class.

The second step to meaningful teaching is that of making the class activity mean something in terms of the class goals. This requires that the teacher make the students aware of the *why* of classwork. Awareness of purpose is especially necessary when teaching something such as breath support in playing a wind instrument or singing. It is fine to say to the students, "This will help your tone and control." (They must understand what is meant by control before the word is used.) But *why* will it help their tone? What do firm abdominal muscles have to do with air passing through the throat? What is different about the air emanating from lungs that are supported as contrasted with lungs that are not supported? Isn't air air? Before much time has passed, each student must become convinced that, indeed, breath support does make for a better tone and more control. He must develop some sense of self-evaluation in order to determine when he does produce a better tone.

The teacher of general music classes faces the same demand. The class has a project of filling twelve water glasses, one for each semitone. The teacher can see the usefulness of this to understanding pitch, tuning, and all that goes with it. But can the students? When the group tries to "tune up" a chord they are singing, the teacher can point out the connection between the activities: "Remember the water glasses we tuned yesterday? What happened when we got to a point where we needed just a little more or less water? We had to listen and work very carefully, didn't we? Try to listen to your singing in the same careful way you did then." The orchestra teacher is in a similar position when he stops the group and says, "Let's go over that again." He had better tell them why. And so had all music teachers.

USING THE PRINCIPLES

A teacher working with a class is not likely to ask himself, "Am I making use of distributed effort? Am I using whole or part learning?" Rather, like gravity, a knowledge of the suggested principles pulls the teacher's actions along certain lines. Subconsciously while teaching, and more consciously while planning, the teacher sees to it, for example, that the students have an adequate aural foundation for what they are asked to read on the page, and that a warm-up exercise makes more sense to them than mere vibration of the vocal cords or of a reed. In planning to teach a song with frequent use of syncopation, he knows that unless the students are musically advanced some means must be devised so that they feel the rhythmic pattern accurately. He knows that telling the students "The quarter note with the accent comes on the last half of the first beat" will probably not bring forth a musically satisfactory rendition of the figure.

The principles are especially valuable to the teacher in determining why the class does not seem to learn a point as it should. When the students do not grasp the lesson being taught, the reaction of the teacher usually is to think that more time should be spent on it. More time may be needed, but sometimes the problem is a basic pedagogical error. Teaching is a bit like playing large chords on the piano; if one of the notes is wrong, the chord usually sounds terrible. By the same token, if one principle of music teaching is missed, the teaching effort will not achieve full success.

The music teacher, then, is faced with a series of searching questions about each teaching action: Do the students really experience the music? Are they developing better concepts of music? Do they have an aural concept of what they see on the page of music? Is the aesthetic quality of the music being brought out? Do the students have some comprehension of the whole piece, and at the same time are its parts being pulled out and studied so that the students can learn them accurately? Is the purpose of the lesson appropriate to their abilities and musical development? Is the work spread out sufficiently to allow for maximum learning? Are they trying to concentrate on too many points at once? Does the learning relate to their past experience in a meaningful way? Finally, do the students see the sense in what they are being asked to do?

Questions

1. The term "scale of reference" was used in the chapter. What are the underlying assumptions made about it when ratings are given at music festivals and contests? Are these assumptions valid in the case of festivals? What changes might be made to better account for variations among schools?
2. What conditions should be fulfilled before warm-up activity can be considered worth while?

3. Which principle of music teaching does each of these examples violate?
   a. The students in Mrs. Schmitt's general music class diligently fill in their workbooks, putting in items such as the number of beats a dotted half note gets in 4/4 meter.
   b. Mr. Garcia rehearses the orchestra for the entire period on the introductory section to Weber's *Oberon Overture*.
   c. Jimmy Johnson has just been told all of this by his clarinet teacher: to watch his embouchure, especially the lower lip; not to lift his fingers so far off the keys; to make sure he taps his foot *evenly;* to play all the first-line E flats with the third finger of the left hand, except where impossible; to be sure to tongue with the tip of the tongue on the tip of the reed.
   d. The band finishes playing a march with a decisive "stinger." "Well," says Mr. Trudeau, "I think we'd better run through it again. We'll have time to do it before the period ends."
   e. Kevin McClean has just taken his first teaching position as band director in Milton. Before leaving for a summer camp job, he orders some music for the band he will meet for the first time in the fall. As he glances through a stack of music, he notices the march "Fairest of the Fair" by Sousa. "Hey," he thinks to himself, "I'll get that. We played it in the band at State U., and I really liked it."
   f. Alice Merkle has her choir work on vowels for five minutes at the beginning of each period. On Monday she works on *ay*, Tuesday *ah*, Wednesday *ee*, Thursday *oh*, and Friday *oo*.
   g. Mr. Newcomb was anxious for the chorus to win a high rating at the festival. He picked the three pieces that the group would sing and worked on them intensively through January and February up to the festival in March. Now, during its performance, the chorus is flatting and lacking vitality in its expression.
   h. In order to improve the sightreading ability of the Girls' Glee Club, Miss Snyder has the girls practice interval-reading. She puts two intervals on the board daily, and then has the girls sing back and forth between the two pitches of each interval.
   i. Mr. Barrow's junior high flutists are encountering difficulty getting into the upper octave when playing B flat, B natural, and C. "Come on! Come on! Try a little harder," he says in a nice tone of voice.
   j. Mrs. Springer has this routine for each new piece her singers attempt. (1) Sing the rhythm of notes on the tonic note until done correctly. (2) Sing through each part until the proper notes are learned. (3) Sing through with the parts together. (4) Put in the expression.
   k. Mr. Albert is a thorough instrumental music teacher. For each important program his band presents, he totals up the number of measures in the works to be played. Then he divides that number by the number of class meetings before the program. Each class session covers the exact number of measures to be learned.
   l. The orchestra is having trouble with a passage in the music. Miss Hedges realizes that the cellos are not getting their part right. However, she

keeps working over the spot with the entire orchestra playing, even though the other parts confuse the cellos.

4. Using the illustration of the violin lesson on page 136, how might the instruction be focused on single points so that the student would not be overwhelmed with so many things to learn?

Projects

1. Think of a simile to use in describing to the students:
   a. how to sing or play in a dry, brittle, staccato style;
   b. how to execute an ascending scale line while making a decrescendo at the same time;
   c. how to produce a tone quality that is dark and round.
2. Assume that you wish to teach proper breath control to your classes. Think of three different ways in which this learning could be presented.
3. Select one work each for band, orchestra, and choir. Study the work, and then decide how you would introduce it to the students so that they could grasp the idea of the whole piece.
4. Observe the same type of class or organization (high school band, junior high girls' glee club) in three different schools. Evaluate each class in terms of (1) age, (2) selectivity of students, (3) time available for instruction, and (4) previous musical experience of students.

Suggested Readings

Basic Concepts in Music Education, 57th Yearbook, Part I, National Society for the Study of Education. Chicago: University of Chicago Press, 1958. Chapters VI, VII.

Frandsen, Arden N., *Educational Psychology*. New York: McGraw-Hill Book Company, Inc., 1961. Chapter VIII.

Leonhard, Charles, and Robert W. House, *Foundations and Principles of Music Education*. New York: McGraw-Hill Book Company, Inc., 1959. Chapters V, VIII.

McDonald, Frederick J., *Educational Psychology*. Belmont, Calif.: Wadsworth Publishing Company, Inc., 1959. Chapters II, IX.

Mursell, James L., *Music Education: Principles and Programs*. Morristown, N.J.: Silver Burdett Company, 1956. Chapter III.

Mursell, James L., and Mabelle Glenn, *The Psychology of School Music Teaching*. Morristown, N.J.: Silver Burdett Company, 1938. Chapters IX, X.

ORCHESTRAL TRANSCRIPTIONS

VIII

teaching music in the performing class

It is a bright, warm day in early September. Joe Fontana, just graduated from college, steps before his band. Before the students is a piece of music, which he promptly undertakes to have them play. Cacophony results! They cannot read through the music as the groups back at college always did. A feeling something on the order of panic springs through his heart. What should he do now? What precisely does he do to begin to teach this, or any other piece of music?

To begin with, there may be a precise answer, but there can be no perfect answer. There are too many variables involved—the musical development of the students, the particular piece of music, the personalities of the teacher and of the group of students. Nevertheless, a precise answer may be helpful for the new teacher, even though that answer will not be the *only* one. It is helpful to see how a problem can be handled under one set of conditions. Possibly then some ideas can be gained as to how it might be managed when circumstances are somewhat different.

PLANNING

As for Joe Fontana's state of panic, it need not have happened; he should have planned for such an eventuality. Planning is a point on which beginning teachers are sometimes confused and have false impressions. In their collegiate musical organizations and in their observation of master teachers, there is seldom any visible evidence of a lesson plan or other preparation efforts. The director to all appearances improvises, using his good musicianship and quick wits. In a few cases, this is true. In most instances, however, a lot of thought and work has gone into the planning of what appears to be made up on the spot, even though much of the preparation does not get written down in the usual sense of a formal lesson plan.

Planning can start only when the teacher decides what he wants to accomplish in his teaching. He should start with a general, long-range idea of what he hopes to accomplish during the year: the music to be played or sung by the group, the programs to be performed, the skills to be developed, and the theoretical and historical knowledge to be integrated into the year's work. Then he is ready to plan what he will do in the particular class period.

The make-up of the individual class will vary to such an extent that no detailed teaching outline is suitable for all meetings of the class. The content will vary according to previous learnings, the closeness of a performance, and the type of music being studied. To begin the period, many teachers use a combination warm-up and technique-developing routine. This portion of the class must be varied from day to day and must be relevant to the other activities in the course. In singing, the attention can be on producing the sound correctly or singing in tune. In instrumental music, playing techniques can be stressed, or a scale or exercise can be played to practice correct fingering or bowing. This type of work should be short, not longer than five or seven minutes. To close a class, the students can review something they do well, or put together in a reasonably satisfactory manner something on which they have been working. The idea is simply not to leave the group hanging in the middle of a specific learning task when the period ends. Between the opening and closing of the class, the group begins study on new music, reviews familiar works, further perfects music it is in the process of studying, and learns facts about theory and literature as these are suggested by work with the music.

To prepare for a particular class, the teacher needs to decide what pieces will be studied, what places in the music should receive special attention, and what learnings are to be incorporated with the music studied. In addition, he needs to study the score and parts to music he does not know well. The teacher's advance study of the music is not undertaken primarily so that he can learn it and decide on the proper interpretation ahead of the students, although this is certainly necessary. Rather, the study should center on anticipating spots that are likely to be difficult for the group. When the students reach a troublesome passage, the teacher must be quick in coming up with the alternate fingering for G on the trumpet, a bowing technique that will help the strings coordinate the bow with the left hand, and a suggestion for getting the woodwinds to play correctly the final eighth note in the 6/8 pattern

No teacher should be caught unprepared on problems in the music; he must have plans for overcoming them.

Need the plans be written down? Should a list of likely problems be drawn up? For the beginning teacher, yes. After a year of experience, his own good judgment can guide him in this. A lesson plan should include a statement of the long-range goals and how the particular classwork fits into those goals. More important, it should include suggestions for warm-up, a listing of the music to be worked on, reminders on the points to be covered in each piece, and an estimate of how much time will be required to accomplish the planned learning. It is wise to write the time not as "5 minutes," but as "10:10 to 10:15." This makes it easier to see whether or not the schedule is being maintained.

Meanwhile, back at the school, Joe Fontana is wondering what to do about his first class. Hopefully, the students' folders contain other pieces of varying difficulty, so the proper step for Joe is to try a simpler number, one so simple that it is certain to be performed with some degree of success. This will salvage some order from a potentially chaotic situation.

But teaching is not merely leading a group through music simple enough to be played almost on sight. So for the next meeting of the class, Joe Fontana must be prepared to teach, in the fullest sense of the word. Let us examine how the process could be undertaken.

THE CONCEPT OF THE WHOLE

As soon as he starts to teach and to perfect a piece of music, the teacher begins the interplay of whole and part learning. The first step in the study of a new work is some activity that will give the students the sense of the whole work.

Several procedures are available for this. The number may be read through at sight, especially if it is quite easy, even though it is a far from perfect rendition. In vocal music, to emphasize the mood the number can be sung the first time on a bright or dark vowel sound, whichever is appropriate. The text of the music may be read aloud in unison with expression, or the accompanist may play the voice parts while the students follow the music. A representative section or phrase of the music can be played or sung to give the students a clear and immediate idea of what the piece is like. If a recording of the work is available, the playing of it is an excellent way to get across the essential feeling of the piece. In contrapuntal music, the teacher can take a thematic phrase and have each part perform it as it comes along. The theme can be learned first, the countermelody second, and the free material left until later. Even when the melody does not appear until a third of the music has passed, as in many popular works, the teacher can start with the melody section for the first reading. If the emphasis is to be rhythmic, the words or rhythms may be chanted or played in unison. In some cases, a technical or rhythmic problem may be studied just prior to learning the new piece, and this can be pointed out to the students. To give them a better idea of the music, they can be told something about the history or the style of the work.

Whatever procedure is used, it should move quickly. The students want to sing or play; they do not want to be told about problems that *might* arise. Sometimes teachers spend as long as twenty minutes preparing to sightread a number, an amount of time that is entirely too long.

INSTRUMENTAL MUSIC TEACHING

Because of the greater number of parts to account for, the teacher of the instrumental class has a problem slightly different from that of the vocal teacher. The logical groupings of instrumental parts vary with each piece of music, and from place to place in the music. For example, the traditional march of the Sousa period often had about six groupings. The excerpt from "Semper Fidelis" shows these groupings in the repeated section: 1) melody—mainly cornets and trumpets, 2) a decorative part in the piccolos and clarinets, 3) a harmony part in the horns, 4) a countermelody in the trombones and baritones, 5) the bass line, and 6) the percussion.

To teach this section of the music, the following steps should be used:

1) Start with the melody, because it carries the main burden of the musical idea. For a reasonably short time, this group of players should be assisted to find the correct notes, rhythms, and expression. Before leaving them to work with another grouping, make sure the essential musical idea has not been lost in working out the technical problems.

2) Turn to the countermelody, which is the next most important part in this music. Assist the players alone for a short time, but as soon as possible have them play with the melody, so that they experience the effect of combining the two lines of music.

3) Assist the bass instruments. In this case, considering the ability of most high school players of the tuba, it may be wise to suggest that they practice the part individually outside of class. Better yet, say "I'll work with you on this again during study hall, or during sectional practice tomorrow." In any event, avoid holding a bass sectional during full band practice. If the basses can play the part reasonably well, combine it at once with the other two parts worked on.

4) Listen to the high woodwind part. Help the players and encourage them to work on their parts outside of class. Again, if they can play the music reasonably well, combine it with the other three parts.

5) Work with the horns. This simple part should require little assistance.

6) Help the percussion as much as necessary, with special emphasis on fitting the part into the entire ensemble.

7) Have the entire band play the section, with special attention to style and balance.

SEMPER FIDELIS

To assist or help means to do whatever is necessary to get the music performed correctly. In the melody parts, it may call for making sure that the students play the line in bugling fashion with the first and third valves for all notes. It may mean achieving rhythmic accuracy by holding the dotted half over into the first eighth of the next measure. It may involve singing to the players the style in which the notes are to be tongued. It may require checking the fingerings of the players on the high woodwind line to see that they use the easiest and best-sounding combination on their particular instrument. And so it goes through each line—counting rhythms, demonstrating style, making sure fingerings are right, adjusting dynamics, bringing out accented notes, pointing out other parts to listen for—until everyone's playing fits into the mosaic of sound that is music.

The teacher must exercise good judgment as to how much attention to devote to the various sections. For example, if a harmony part has many afterbeats, it is fruitless to spend much time on the part alone because it makes sense only in conjunction with the other parts. Discretion is needed in the amount of time given a part and the degree of perfection expected in the first few practices. A teacher might spend fifty minutes in an attempt to achieve a perfect playing of the cornet part, and might even come close to getting the section of the music just right. But what about the rest of the band during this time? Their interest has not been promoted, nor is it likely that their musical insights have been deepened. Besides, if each section receives such attention, the cornets will probably have fallen from perfection when the teacher gets back to them a few days later. The teacher must content himself with cleaning up as many errors as possible in about three or four playings by a section. Further improvement must be left until another day.

VOCAL MUSIC TEACHING

The vocal teacher follows an approach similar to that of the instrumental teacher. After giving the singers a sense of the whole work, the teacher may let them sing the entire number together, if this was not done initially. He must make a judgment at this point, based on how well the students succeed in their attempt at singing the music. It may be that the tenors and basses need only sing their parts again with the accompaniment. Perhaps the altos need to sing their part while the other parts are hummed. More often than not, each part needs some specific help. The procedures suggested here are on the "bedrock" order; that is, they assume that the singers need a maximum amount of assistance. The amount of help called for will vary from one day to the next, from one piece of music to the next, and from one passage to another within the piece.

The usual method for helping singers is the famous and overused step called "pounding parts." The author dislikes the term, but mentions it here because it is in such common usage. "Pounding" implies an activity that is definitely unmusical, and the term indicates a teaching procedure which says that music must be abandoned to learn music, something of a contradiction. Many times the teacher must work out a number section by section, but this can be done with musicianship.

The teacher can do much to retain musical quality by working in musically logical segments, and by pointing out and performing the similar phrases of music as they appear throughout a piece. Students are often surprised and pleased to realize that by learning one phrase they have mastered others that are nearly identical. Above all, interpretation and notes must be learned together. Sometimes inexperienced music teachers think that they will first teach the notes, and then the interpretation. But this idea does not work out in actual practice, nor is it in agreement with the principles of music teaching. After several sessions on a piece with teen-agers, the interpretation has largely "jelled," and changes come only with difficulty after that. Unlike well-trained musicians, adolescents seldom see any difference between learning the notes and learning the style in which the notes should be performed. With teen-agers, first impressions are lasting ones.

When the musical substance of the work has been established, the vocal teacher should follow these steps:

1) Select a phrase of two, four, or possibly eight measures. If the work is SATB, take the bass part and have the accompanist play that line.[1] (A male teacher may want to sing it.) Then have the basses sing their part back in full voice. Have the tenors, altos, and sopranos *softly* sightsing the bass part with the basses. Singing along with other parts strengthens the students' ability to read music in both clefs and contributes immensely to their understanding of the music and its harmony. Naturally the girls will sing the bass parts an octave higher than written. Repeat this unison singing a time or two more if necessary. Then have the section sing the passage alone, unaccompanied by the piano or other singers. Another way to check the section is to select one or two individuals at random to sing the phrase. At this point whatever is not learned adequately will have to be left until the next class.

2) The tenor part should be covered in much the same manner. The girls can sing the tenor part with the tenors. When the tenors have learned their own part, have them sing it again with the bass part, while the accompanist plays the two parts on the piano, and the girls drop out. Depending upon the difficulty of the line, the use of the accompaniment is

[1] A mixed chorus consisting of sopranos, altos, tenors, and basses sings music arranged for SATB, the letters representing an abbreviation of each part. A similar scheme is carried out for girls' glee clubs which sing SA or SSA music, the two S's standing for first and second soprano. The music used with boys' glee clubs is arranged in two parts for tenor and bass (TB); in three parts for tenor, baritone, and bass (TBB); or in four parts for first tenor, second tenor, baritone, and bass (TTBB).

optional. It can be omitted entirely, or the written piano accompaniment can be used, or the accompanist may play all four voice parts.

3) Repeat this procedure for the altos. The sopranos may join in softly on the alto line. The teacher will usually find that the girls are better sightreaders than the boys, and that one singing of the phrase is enough. The altos, tenors, and basses should then combine on their respective parts to sing the phrase.

4) The soprano part is approached last, because it is frequently the simplest and most easily learned. The entire group can then perform the phrase.

Using this procedure, the phrase of music can be built up layer by layer, with everyone singing during most of the process. There are several reasons for rehearsing the bass and tenor parts first in a mixed group. (In teaching glee clubs, the lowest part should also be learned first.) Inexperienced basses and tenors find it tempting to sing the melody an octave lower, rather than to put forth the effort to learn and sing a separate harmony part; this is especially true if the boys know the melody before they learn the bass or tenor. Because the bass part is frequently the most difficult, the boys need the practice of singing in several combinations. Boys are usually less competent musically and vocally than are girls and thus need more attention.

Some teachers prefer to have the other parts not sing while one section is receiving special attention. They object to this method on two grounds. One: a few of the notes are out of range. Two: the singing of four different lines by the sopranos may confuse them. Some of the notes may be out of range for some of the singers, but as a practical matter a few notes in the soprano part are usually out of range for some of the sopranos, and the same is true of every section. As for confusion, it would result if the practice were continued after the initial work on a piece.

The teaching steps are the same whether or not the girls sing with the basses and tenors. Although having the higher parts sing with the lower parts is not essential, it does much to prevent singers from sitting around with nothing to do. Because singers do not have the concrete experience of fingering an instrument, telling them to follow their part silently is not as successful as it is with instrumentalists.

In the early stages of the learning process, humming a part while another section sings is not recommended because it may encourage the learning of wrong notes and careless vocal habits.

KEEPING ALL STUDENTS OCCUPIED WITH LEARNING

Many administrators do not like to see students in music groups sitting and doing nothing while the teacher works with one section. While their concern is due in part to a lack of understanding about how performing groups must be taught, there is enough truth in it to set a music educator to thinking seriously. True, a rehearsal of a professional group is marked by long waits for some players, but in the schools a music class is a learning situation for all students, and the teacher must involve all the students in the classwork as much as possible during the entire time.

The problem can be alleviated by efficient use of teaching techniques. With the instrumental group in the early stages of work on a piece, the students can be told to finger silently through their parts as another section rehearses. (Silent fingering is a good practice pedagogically.) The teacher does not ask students to finger along with another section on a piece that they have been playing for some time. After the fingering activity has outlived its usefulness, the students should be instructed to pay attention to what is going on. By this time, the work with single sections should be largely over.

Many a baritone player is not interested in listening to the clarinet part, even though the second and third clarinets may be playing the same musical line that appears in his part. The same is true of singers in choral groups. What student musicians seldom realize, unless instructed differently, is that there is much that can be learned about music by following what goes on in class, even though it does not directly pertain to their particular part. The teacher should not be hesitant about asking questions of students not immediately occupied. "Altos, at what place are the tenors missing the rhythm?" "Mary, why should the second and third trumpets play the accompaniment figure staccato?" Drawing attention to other sections is especially important in instrumental music because the players see only their own particular part.

WORK OUTSIDE OF CLASS

The steps used in the first teaching of a piece will vary according to the arrangements for additional practice. In one school, the sections of the band have a rotating schedule that allows for a sectional practice weekly outside of the regular period. In another school, the junior high vocal teacher is able to attend two practices of the high school chorus each week. The boys and girls are divided and one group moves to another room so that both can rehearse simultaneously. This arrangement is desirable, if it can be worked out. In another school the teacher has the chorus meet three days of the week together, with one day set aside for work with the boys and one for work with the girls. Some teachers have students practice in a supervised fashion during a study-hall period. The attempt to find a way to work with small portions of an entire group is a matter on which the music teacher will need to advise the administration. It can affect significantly what the teacher is able to accomplish.

The teacher should not overlook the benefits of homework for students in performing classes. Parts can be practiced at home. Singers may also practice correct methods of tone production on their own. A music notebook can be kept, to include information on the music studied, facts about the composer, musical style, technical problems encountered, and other material. On occasion, the students might look up information about the musical work outside of class.

INDIVIDUAL ATTENTION

Since performing groups are usually larger than other classes, there is a tendency for the student to feel unimportant, like a little stick in a large woodpile. The tendency for the teacher is to think only in group terms. When he says, "You did that well," the "you" is usually plural. As a result, the students do not feel sufficiently responsible for their own work. One way in which this can be overcome is through the use of short individual assistance sessions.

> Bill West was an average student and an average clarinet player. Just as the band period ended, Mr. Stafford asked him to remain in his seat a minute. Bill did not feel disturbed, because Mr. Stafford usually had someone stay after class.
>
> "Say, Bill," he said, "let's hear the third clarinet part at letter C in the *Water Music*." Bill played his part in a satisfactory manner.
>
> "That's fine, Bill! You know some of the clarinets were having trouble with that place, and I wanted to make sure that you could play it. You'd better get to your next class now. Keep up the good work."

Such a technique as this is excellent for keeping the students alert, because they realize that anyone can be called upon at any time. In addition, it lets the students know that the teacher is observing their progress and is interested in them.

WORKING OUT TROUBLE SPOTS

One of the keys to more efficient and effective teaching of music is the ability of the teacher to determine the exact point on which the students are having trouble. Many times one note in a phrase is the cause for incorrect performance. It is not necessary, or even wise, to practice again and again all the notes in a phrase just to get a certain note right. For example, the basses in the chorus are learning this phrase from the "Hallelujah Chorus" from *The Messiah* of Handel.

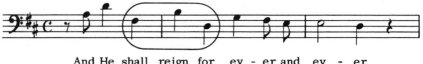

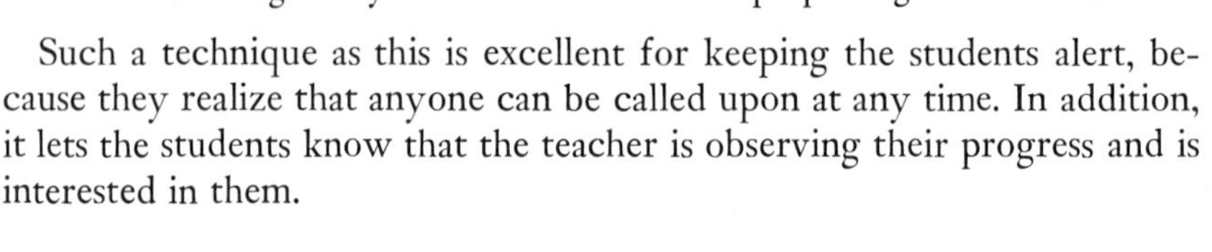
And He shall reign for ev - er and ev - er

The basses may falter on the F sharp, B, and D, missing the B and losing their accuracy. It is useless to sing the entire phrase over and over, mistakes and all. The pianist should play the three tones while the basses sing the pattern. When they do it correctly, they should go over the three notes about three times. Between each repetition the teacher need only say "A-gain" or "Once more" in the tempo of the piece. The whole process would be: SHALL REIGN FOR–once more–SHALL REIGN FOR–sing the whole phrase–AND HE SHALL REIGN FOREVER AND EVER.

Some teachers make a list of several such trouble spots and use them for "spot practice" in the class. This gives the students a quick review on the troublesome passage without the need of performing the entire work. This temporary isolation of the troublesome passages is tremendously valuable in speeding the learning process and in making it more thorough and accurate. Such a technique can be used by the teacher to keep the group alert. An effective way to hold the attention of a class, and to check the learning of a passage, is for the teacher to say suddenly, "We're having trouble with the F sharp, B, and D above the words 'shall reign for.' Perry, let's hear you sing the passage," and have Perry sing it. "Stan, let's hear you sing it," and have Stan sing it.

Prior to working on a trouble spot in the music, the teacher should have worked on the entire phrase or piece so that the students have, as fully as possible, an understanding of its rhythmic, harmonic, and melodic factors –in short, a concept of the whole. Spot practice should never be a series of unrelated little exercises.

Students should be encouraged to inform the teacher of passages that they continue to find difficult to perform correctly. The students themselves know, better than any listener, which passages make them feel inadequate. This technique is more useful in somewhat advanced groups, which do not need to go over music so often in order to learn it and in which the students have a better sense of their capabilities.

INDICATING MUSICAL ENTRANCES

A problem that causes grief among inexperienced teachers is the giving of attacks in the class. Inexperienced musicians are not able to watch the conducting motions and follow their music at the same time. In fact, in some cases the quite inexperienced student can scarcely keep from getting lost when his entire attention is on the music. So in the initial stages of learning a work, some means must be found to supplement the conducting motions. The teacher can mark time by clapping his hands or tapping on some hard surface. At such times, verbal commands may have to be used. After the starting place has been indicated, and in vocal music the opening pitches given either by voice or piano, the teacher says *in the tempo of the music*, "Ready, go," or "Ready, begin." The verbal commands may have to be used the first few times, but then they should be dropped completely so that the students do not become dependent on them.

In vocal music it is sometimes necessary for the teacher to sing with a section the first time or two. It may be especially useful for a man to sing with the boys, because they sometimes lack the confidence and zeal to get started on the right note at the right time. A teacher may occasionally have the unsettling experience of giving a start, and having no one come in. Instead of panicking, he should check to make sure the students understand what he wants, and try again. When students do not come in on an entrance, it is usually due to inattentiveness, lack of understanding, or lack of confidence, rather than to contrariness on their part.

DEVELOPING MUSIC READING

So far little has been said about music reading. In fact, the steps outlined for the vocal music teacher were clearly rote procedures, in which the students heard their part performed and then repeated it. This type of learning is slow, and because it involves small segments of music, it is difficult to keep musical. The teacher must teach the students to comprehend more fully the symbols seen on the page.

Teach music reading? Isn't that the job of the elementary music teacher? Some students can and do sightread well, but most teen-agers *cannot* read correctly at sight the music put before them. There are several causes for this situation, most of which are not relevant to the main purpose of this book. One fact is pertinent, however: many elementary school children are taught to read music—*music of a difficulty appropriate to the elementary school.* Since the music studied in the junior and senior high schools is more advanced, the reading ability of the students will have to be furthered if they are to perform it at sight. One reminder is also pertinent: human beings tend to lose a skill which they do not use with some regularity. No one should be surprised when a student, who has not been in a music class for two or more years, walks into an audition for the glee club and is unable to sightread some simple music put before him. Certainly no music teacher, who can tell the difference when he fails to practice for two or three days, should expect teen-agers with moderate ability and interest to retain for years a complex skill such as music reading.

The ability to read music is a continuum, and not a "can or cannot" proposition. Very few people (even trained music teachers!) can individually and unaided sightread perfectly every piece of music. On the other hand, most persons can ascertain something about the music from looking at it. The elementary schools may be doing their best, but at the secondary level more skill is needed because the group is divided into a greater number of parts, there are changed voices, the works of music are longer, and the technical demands of the music are greater.

Fortunately, the reading ability of a group is always better than the individual abilities of its members. If a performer misses a note, his neighbor can many times supply it. In addition, students are more confident when doing something as a group and have less fear of mistakes.

Although the reading procedures are nearly identical for vocal and instrumental music, a few differences should be mentioned. The main reading problem in vocal music is the maintaining of pitch. Once a singer loses the proper pitch, he must depend upon experience and ability to find it again. Not so with instrumental music. On a clarinet, if a certain arrangement of holes and keys is covered, the player can be sure that he is playing a certain pitch. If a clarinet player misses a note, he usually can find the next one. The singers can be told, "When the notes go up, move the voice up; when they go down, move the voice down; and when they remain the same, do not change." The teacher can then explain that the staff is a graph of musical pitch. Even this simple and limited approach can produce marked improvement in the singers' ability to comprehend the printed page.

Another reading problem in vocal music is the presence of two lines for each part; one of music and one of words. Not only do the eyes of the singer move from left to right; they move up or down to take in the words. To make matters even more difficult, the position of the words below the notes, used throughout elementary school, is now reversed for the boys whenever the tenor and bass parts share a single staff below the body of text. Because of the complex eye movement required, the students should sing most pieces through the first time on a neutral syllable such as "loo" or "lah."

The reading problem in instrumental music arises from the greater number of parts (in some cases there is only one player on a part) and the need for keeping in mind key signature and correct fingerings. The reading ability of the instrumentalist is determined largely by the speed of his reaction to the visual stimuli which the notes represent. A particular F is fingered a certain way, and the wind or brass player reacts to the symbol with a certain combination of fingers and feeling in the lips and mouth.

The way to learn how to read music is to read music. There are no secret systems, tricks, or easy formulas. The teacher may present techniques for better reading, but the only way for the techniques to become effective is for the students to make use of them—often. Notes and rhythmic patterns must be experienced so often that they can be recalled quickly and easily. Reading can hardly be said to exist when a student requires one minute of time to figure out how the rhythmic figure

is executed; he is reading only when he recognizes the pattern and executes it almost instantaneously.

To give students experience in reading, the teacher should have them read a piece of music at a majority of the class meetings. The music should be simpler than the numbers normally performed by the group. When students try to sightread material that is too difficult for them, they tend to become frustrated because they leave the piece without performing it satisfactorily. Some states, such as New York, have music graded by difficulty for use at festivals. If a group is performing music at grade V, then its sightreading training pieces should be at grade III or IV, with an occasional V. As the group progresses, more difficult music can be tried. In every sightreading effort, the group should keep going unless there is a complete collapse. It is hard for a conscientious teacher with sensitive students to keep going when the music doesn't sound good. The temptation is to stop and give some help to make things sound better. The teacher can call out rehearsal or page numbers, letters, or other assistance, but the music must be kept moving if at all possible.

Much of the technique of sightreading can be taught on an informal or functional basis. The teacher should point out various patterns in the music, so that the students can gain a concept of them that is transferable from one piece of music to another. When the problems are derived from the music itself, the training seems logical and necessary to the students. This is certainly preferable to formal schemes which in effect say, "You learn this because you might need it some day."

The informal method will cover almost all the reading problems found in the school music repertoire. The more complex patterns will have to be taught by rote. They are few in number, however, and do not appear to be a serious drawback. Even with a background of training in a formal scheme, in which the student has covered all the possible combinations of notes and rhythms, he almost always seems to have forgotten the exceptional ones when they are finally encountered in the music, and the teacher has to revert to rote methods for a moment.

The functional approach has one other feature to its credit: it allows for retention of the whole-part principle. Essentially, students learn to read rhythm and pitch together, which is the way music is. While teaching the music, the teacher may temporarily isolate a rhythmic problem so that it can be studied. But the occasions during which rhythm and pitch are separated must be short; these elements have to be quickly associated again with the music.

Even the functional, informal approach requires the teaching of such basic music knowledge as common note and rest values, time signatures, accidentals, interpretive signs, and note names. This much knowledge is necessary so that the students will have a basis for their concepts. Although much of this information has been learned in elementary school, review is necessary for maturation at a higher level of musicianship.

As for the teaching of rhythm, it is important to stress the 2:1 ratio, which is the basis of rhythmic notation. The teacher has to remind his students that the rhythmic values of the notes indicate their length as governed by the beat, and that these indicators are so arranged that one is twice or half the duration of the other:

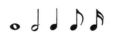

In this way the student is not so disturbed when, after being told that a quarter note equals one beat, he encounters music in 3/2 meter. He can more easily shift from one signature to another. The dotted notes can be explained in terms of an addition to the note. Actually, some students just have to learn that a dotted half note usually receives three beats and a dotted quarter one and a half beats.

To help the students read rhythm, the teacher should have them learn a system for counting it. Several methods of counting are available to the music teacher. The beats are almost universally counted off "one," "two," "three" and so on. Eighth notes in duple time are usually counted by adding "an" or "and." Sixteenth notes are easily counted by "one-ee-an-da," or "one-a-an-da," and triplets by "one-tee-toe," or "trip-o-let." Unless one syllable such as "ta" is used for every note, the counting system should avoid using the same word symbol for different rhythmic figures:

A trained musician can count these patterns correctly, but a student just learning is more confused than helped by them.

Occasionally words can be associated with rhythmic figures, such as

The rhythmic passage

comes up a surprising number of times in music, and it can become known as the "here-comes-the-bride" phrase because of its use in Wagner's well-known "Wedding March" from *Lohengrin.*

It is important in teaching rhythmic understanding to separate the beat from the execution of the rhythmic pattern. Many students are never quite clear on this point. Adolescents are inclined to think that music with a pounding, obvious beat has lots of "rhythm." To keep the distinction as clear as possible, the teacher can have the students tap the beat with one foot and confine the execution of the notes to either the mouth or the hands. Inexperienced students find it difficult to produce even a rudimentary rhythmic pattern while simultaneously maintaining a steady beat.

The process of developing a concept of rhythm can be aided by the limited use of a warm-up routine, which is performed without music. The teacher calls out the type of note just before the beginning of the measure.

Teacher: "Quarters Eighths Quarters Eighths Sixteenths Eighths Halves"
Players: Perform according to teacher's directions, transposing if necessary.
Singers: "1 2 3 4 1&2&3&4&" etc.
"may" etc.
"me" etc.
"mo" etc.

The exercise gives the students effective practice in counting, which is necessary for accurate reading of rhythm. It can be varied by having the pitch move up a semitone on each measure and then return by half steps to the original pitch. Triplets may be added to it later.

The method of presenting 6/8 or compound time has long been debated by music educators. What is sometimes forgotten is that since they first learned "Pop Goes the Weasel," the students have been singing and hearing music in compound meter. So they know about it through experience, even if they do not recognize it in the musical nomenclature. It seems more practical in secondary school music to approach 6/8 by considering it as six beats in a measure, with a strong emphasis on "1" and "4," sometimes stressed by tapping the foot. In this way, the method of counting 6/8 meter remains the same whether a slow or fast tempo is used. The 2:1 ratio is maintained when this is done, e.g.,

and with a little practice the students can as readily read music in 6/8 or 9/8 as they can read in any meter.

Psychologists have discovered that when a person reads, his eyes do not move letter by letter or word by word, but rather by groups of words.[2] The better the reader, the larger are the groups of words he encompasses in a single eye movement. The same principle applies to music reading. The musician learns to react to a note, but in the reading of music he groups notes and performs them by drawing from his previous experience with music. Thus when the flutist sees

he can (or should) grasp the eight notes at once and react with the proper kinesthetic movements in the fingers and embouchure.

The use of patterns of notes is especially valuable to the vocal student, because he does not read by a set reaction of fingers but rather by the relative distance between pitches, which utilizes his mental imagery of the tone and his memory of the physical sensation involved with singing it. Thus, B just above the bass clef feels one way for the male singer and B on the second line feels another. Through experience in the association of notes and their sounds, the singer develops a sense of pattern which helps him in reading. Common intervals and patterns should be pointed out by the teacher as they occur in pieces of music. For instance, when the basses begin to see and hear the similarity between

and

they are learning to read music. The same is true in the reading of rhythmic patterns. The more the students see the dotted pattern

in different settings, the more quickly they can understand and read it.

The vocal teacher can engage in some direct reading practice by use of the chalkboard. He may put a major scale on the board in C, or any key that is comfortable to sing. Under the notes he writes the numbers

[2] William A. Schmidt, *An Experimental Study in the Psychology of Reading* (Chicago: University of Chicago Press, 1917). See also William S. Gray, *The Teaching of Reading and Writing: An International Survey*, Monographs on Fundamental Education, X (UNESCO, 1956), Chapter III.

1 2 3 4 5 6 7 $\bar{1}$ or the solfeggio syllables.[3] Syllables are satisfactory if the students are quite familiar with them; otherwise they should be avoided, as the students feel that they are too mature to spend the time that is required to make the syllables meaningful. The solfeggio syllables are more suitable vocally because they use pure vowels without diphthongs and do not include the problem of the two-syllable word "seven." However, the numbers are in the same language in which the students sing most of their music, so it is clearly suitable. In addition, a number series by its nature implies a relationship between the numbers, and when used to define the distances between scale steps, it clarifies the concept of intervals.

The teacher can start by singing a major scale using the numbers he has written. This establishes the feeling of key center. Once the tonic feeling is established, the students will have some basis for relating the intervals to one another. By pointing to notes on the board, the teacher can direct the class to sing simple three- or four-note groups which begin and end on the tonic–131, 1351, 1231, 123451. Later, longer and more difficult patterns can be sung at sight–1 2 4 5 $\underline{7}$ 1, 1 3 5 6 1, 1 5 1.

After some practice with a scale written on the board, simple tonal patterns in various keys can replace the scale. These patterns should not be haphazard groups of notes, but combinations of three, four, or five notes similar to those found in music the group is singing. When the patterns are sung in unison, the bass clef may be used occasionally in place of the treble clef, because it will do no harm to have the girls become familiar with the bass clef, too.

Because of transposing instruments, the instrumental teacher cannot use the chalkboard for simple reading work. Fortunately, in recent years many supplementary books have been published, especially for band. Some of these stress technique, others rhythm, others style, still others scales and chords, and they have been written at varying levels of difficulty. They are listed in Appendix C.

In any class, sightreading practice should not become segmented from the music used in the class. Exercises in reading are valuable only to the extent that they teach something better than it can be taught through the reading of actual pieces of music. Good sightreading is only a tool, a means to incorporate music into the mind of the person. Reading will help the student reach that goal, but it will not replace it.

REVIEWING LEARNED MUSIC

After the initial work on a piece–after the students have grasped the basic style and are able to execute the correct pitches and rhythms–the teacher must guide them so that they retain what they have learned; he

[3] Scale numbers with a dash above or below the numbers indicate pitches in an upper or lower octave.

must mold the performance of the piece so that they get from it the maximum musical experience.

The amount of forgetting that is characteristic of the mind, as was pointed out on page 133, means that review is certainly going to be a part of every teacher's job. Not only is much of the learned material going to be forgotten by the next time the class meets, but some students may be absent from school and thereby miss the initial presentation entirely. The teacher need not go back to the very first step of learning notes, unless the situation calls for it. Instead, he should have a small group or section perform its part alone. In vocal music, for example, the piano can play the accompaniment with the singers. If the result is satisfactory, then two sections can perform their parts together. The parts can be hummed while the section in need of help sings the words. Essentially, what the vocal or instrumental teacher does is *quickly* move again through a portion of the procedures for teaching the music.

Another helpful device to use in reviewing music is to have a section stand while performing its part (cello excepted). This provides a change of position and allows the group standing to be heard more easily. It also tends to strengthen the confidence and independence of the section and encourages alertness and better posture.

CRITICAL LISTENING BY STUDENTS

To allow for student listening, the teacher can set up "teams" or small groups of students. Each listening group consists of four to eight students, a cross section to avoid, when possible, depleting an entire section, who can be called on quickly to hear the rest of the class perform, or possibly to perform themselves. When given the chance to listen, the group usually stands near the teacher in order to hear better.

After listening to the class perform, the team members can be invited to make comments. Sometimes the listeners will accuse the group of making some error that it did not make, and occasionally the team members will fail to notice some glaring mistake, especially when first given the chance to listen. The teacher should not be discouraged when this happens. As long as the students are learning what to listen for in music, and are improving in sensitivity and in the accuracy of their evaluations, the procedure is achieving its goal. The teacher must guide the students in this evaluative listening process. Here is an example of what might take place after a team has just listened to its own choir.

MISS GORDON: Now, what was the biggest error in the singing?

PETER: The alto part was too weak, I think.

MISS GORDON: Well, that's partly true. But that isn't what I was thinking about.

DIANNE: Well, the tenors let their tone sag as they went for the high note.

MISS GORDON: Yes, a little, but still not what I was thinking of. What was the main fault in the singing?

BILL: They didn't put the "d" on the word "heard."

MISS GORDON: Yes, we're still missing a lot of "d's." But what I heard was the harsh tone quality. It's entirely out of place in this piece. (*To the singers*) Listen, let's sing at letter E exactly as you did it the last time.

Group sings phrase.

MISS GORDON: (*To the singers*) Now let's do the same thing again; only this time, sing it very gently and warmly. Imagine you're saying goodnight to your boyfriend or girl friend.

Group sings phrase.

MISS GORDON: (*To the team listening*) Now, can't you hear the difference? The first time sounded very much like our school fight song, while the second had a tender, serious sound—just what this piece needs.

Admittedly, this process is more time-consuming than having the teacher tell the group what to do. However, the educational values make it well worth while. A student whose opinion is given consideration is less likely to feel lost in the large group, and he will undoubtedly pay more attention to details if he knows he must understand them to form an evaluation. This type of listening activity adds interest and variety to the class. In fact, students are sometimes so eager to listen that the teacher will find it necessary to keep a record of the number of times each team listens.

The greatest benefit of having the students listen in small groups is the clarification it can give the words of the teacher. Such problems as the balance of sections, the precision with which phrases are concluded, the style of an accent, general tone quality, and intonation, become much more understandable to the student after he has heard them in real, live performance. The listening group is one way to give students the aural experience which is a cornerstone to effective music learning.

Since a teen-ager's musical development should include proper listening habits concerned with his own performance of music, he should develop a sense of when he has an important part in the music and when he hasn't. Leopold Stokowski is noted for his insistence that his musicians know this at all times. On a level commensurate with his maturity and musical development, a high school musician should be aware of what is happening in the music from the standpoint of both aesthetic understanding and effective performance. The teacher should stop the group and ask, "Who has the melody here?" "What's happening in the music at this point?"

The students should also develop skill at accompaniment—the performance of subordinate parts within the musical arrangement. Just as it is essential to know what the main ideas of a piece are and who executes them, it is also necessary to allow those ideas to be heard. If a person on a subordinate part cannot hear the melody, it is likely that either he or the other members of his section are too loud. Once the students have learned to execute the accompanying part softly enough, the next step is to vary its dynamics, phrasing, and tone quality to correspond to the melodic line. The students should be taught that in a real sense music is performed "by ear" as well as by sight.

In contrapuntal music the awareness of the main thematic material can be developed within the students by having the subject or main theme performed while the contrasting lines are thought out in silence. In a choral group, subordinate lines can be hummed. Sometimes the seating of the musicians can be arranged according to the order in which the sections perform the thematic material. Or the sections can be turned toward each other in a circular arrangement to enable the performers to hear each other better. When their positions are changed, the teacher should not be surprised if the students have trouble at first; the piece will sound different to them, and they may feel uncertain.

SUGGESTIONS FOR THE TEACHER

Much of the success of teaching music for performance lies in the *way* in which the students are taught. When possible, it is more efficient and effective to communicate with them *while* the music is being performed. The good teacher is the one who foresees a point on which a quick reminder will save a minute of class time. Noticing the pattern

in the trombone part, the instrumental teacher can shout out to the trombones, "Sixth position on F" just before the figure is played. It is not necessary to stop the band and say, "Trombones, in the third measure after letter C, play the F in the alternate sixth position." Not only is time lost stopping the group, giving instructions, and then starting the group again, but the musical flow is impeded. The successful music teacher calls out "Smooth, smooth" at the approach of a legato passage. When the students are slow to cut off a tone before a rest, he snaps out a sharp, distinct, "Off!" just at the beginning of the rest. He may wish to hold his hands still during the rest to indicate the stoppage of sound. The verbal command thus serves the additional purpose of calling attention to his conducting. Commentary from the teacher is a vivid, live way of presenting the live art of music. Its only limitation occurs when the music is too loud for the teacher to be heard. The technique should not replace decisive conducting, nor should it be used right up to the time of performance.

Possibly the following example of how *not* to operate a class will indicate some errors a teacher should try to avoid.

Choir is stopped by Mr. King.

MR. KING: Well . . . (*pause*) . . . Why don't we start at letter A and sing it over again . . . (*pause*) . . . Ah . . . Piano, give us the first chord at letter A.

ACCOMPANIST: Do you want to start with the pickup?

MR. KING: Yes, I guess so . . . (*pause*) . . . Anyway, give us the notes.

Three things wrong here:
1) Director should know what he is going to say before he stops the group; there should be no delay.
2) There should be a reason given for going over the music again.
3) Exact starting place was not made clear.

Notes are played. Choir starts singing, but is soon stopped by Mr. King.

MR. KING: I think you should put a crescendo on the words "o'er all the earth," so that "earth" is louder than the three words preceding it . . . Uh . . . I guess we'll start at letter A again.

Good suggestion.

More delay. The students can't help wondering if the man knows what he wants.

Choir sings phrase exactly as before with no crescendo; sings to end of piece.

MR. KING: (*pause; stands looking down at the music*) . . . That was a pretty good job, I guess . . .

What about the crescendo? He guesses it was good. Doesn't he know? Still is working much too slowly.

Well, let's get out "The Heavens Declare the Glory of God"—the Beethoven.

Good number; the students like it.

You know, I ordered this music from Smith's Music House, and they sent me the music all right, but it was in a book with about ten other pieces. So I sent it back to them and told them about the

Be sure the story will be interesting to the group before you tell it. This one might be—it depends.

mistake they had made in sending me the right music but in the wrong book, you know. Well, you know what they did? They sent me the right music after a couple weeks of delay, but they billed me for the postage *both ways* on the books *they* had sent me by mistake. Was I ever disgusted! So when I sent the money to them for this music, I didn't send the money for postage, and told them why. They sent me a letter apologizing for their error. Guess you have to be firm sometimes.

Just like the time I got a parking ticket because the parking meter was broken. (*Mr. King goes on in detail about how he refused to pay the fine, and was finally vindicated.*)

What, another? When does the group get to sing? What happened to Beethoven?

Oh yes, we were going to sing "The Heavens Declare." (*He smiles at students . . . pause*) . . .

At last!

Oh, oh, another delay. He will be lucky if he doesn't have some behavior problems before the period is over.

Now, at the beginning you should sing with a full, round sound. Basses, do the best you can on that low note. The music is in unison so you shouldn't have any trouble with that part . . . Ah . . . Now along about the middle we have a modulation. Does anyone know what a modulation is? John?

How much of all these comments will the students remember when they sing it through?

A question—good.

JOHN: Yeah, it's when the music goes into a different key.

MR. KING: Right! You'll have a good chance to hear this modulation because the piano plays it for several counts before you come in . . . (*pause*) . . . When you

Delay again.

have the same note repeated, remember to make a crescendo up to the eighth chord. That word "heavens" should go HEA-vens . . . Ah . . . Also you . . . Ah . . . um . . . notice that the first melody comes back here near the end.

Hesitating manner and further delays.

Any questions? . . . (*pause*) . . . Gary?

GARY: Here (*points to the music*) the basses have some little notes written in above the larger notes. What do we do about them?

Good for Gary! Mr. King should have mentioned this.

(*Mr. King walks over and looks at Gary's music.*)

MR. KING: Oh yes! I nearly forgot. Well . . . ah . . . let's just omit them. I think that those notes are there in case you can't get the low ones. You won't have any trouble with those low ones, will you?

He did forget. His lack of preparation on this music is showing. He certainly isn't very convincing, anyway.

Any other questions? . . . (*pause*)

This technique of openly inviting questions is all right once in a while, but it can turn into a great time-waster if used often.

O.K. Let's get going!

Choir begins singing.

Finally! How many minutes have been lost?

This little drama represents only a few minutes out of a single class. Mr. King's slow pace, personal revelations, indefiniteness, and piling up of suggestions could be tolerated for a little while. But just imagine what it would be like to sit through this sort of thing one hour a day, five days a week for an entire semester or year! It would take an extremely patient person, or one who simply hardened himself to be impervious to conditions around him, just to stand it, least of all to be interested and educated by the experience.

Mr. King had no behavior disturbances from the students, even though this type of teaching is an ideal propagator of misbehavior. Neither did he say things that were obviously foolish or contrary to good musicianship. He appears to be a sincere and devoted teacher with a fine musical background. He did, however, make errors in method.

One was his slow pace. To the students, music is only as alive as the teacher makes it. If the learning experience does not move, the students either become mentally numb, or attempt to create excitement. *A quick-moving class is a must.*

Another foible of Mr. King's was his indecisive manner. A lack of self-confidence is shown by tone of voice, lack of eye contact, and general attitude of the individual.

A third error was the fact that Mr. King talked too much. This is not to say that a teacher must never talk about personal matters in front of the group. The students should find out that the director is a human being. However, a beginning teacher should generally avoid this habit until he has had enough experience to be able to sense the type of anecdotes that interest students. Conversational ramblings should be indulged in sparingly, if ever, because they seldom contribute to learning.

There are two ways for a teacher to check himself on overtalkativeness. He can make a tape recording of an entire class period, and then listen to the recording for such faults at a later time. Or he can place a reliable student in the back of the room with paper and pencil, and a watch with a second hand. The student then makes a short note of every activity and the amount of time it consumes. For example, a portion of the sheet might look something like this when it is finished:

	MIN.	SEC.
Band played first phrase		8
Teacher talked		10
Played first phrase		8
Teacher talked		12
Played to end of piece	3	57
Changed to "Noël Français"	1	2
Teacher talked		48

The amount of time spent in the various types of activity can then be totaled. The resulting figures will often be a revelation to a teacher with a penchant for talking.

Closely related to the problem of overtalking is that of making explanations and directions clear. Mr. King had trouble with this. Directions must be complete and exact; if the group starts at a letter where there is a pickup, they must be told whether the pickup is to be included. The instructions should be kept brief, however, in line with the slogan "Don't write; wire."

There was a final point at which Mr. King failed; he ignored the principle of a single point of concentration. The students could not reasonably be expected to assimilate the row of suggestions he pushed at them one after the other.

Time-Savers

Class time in performing organizations can be saved if the teacher will take these easy, practical actions.

1) Write the titles of the music in order on the chalkboard so that the students can locate it in their folders and put it in order before class begins.

2) Have the librarians service the folders by passing out or collecting music during their study hall or after school, rather than during class time.

3) Appoint student assistants to take attendance. One person can be responsible for checking each section in a choral group or large family in instrumental groups. Pupil absences should be indicated on a card for each student or on some kind of class roll, not in the teacher's grade book.

4) Use an electronic tuning device, or provide several tuning bars so that instrumentalists may tune themselves before class.

Objective Listening by the Teacher

Teachers need to provide themselves with opportunities to listen objectively to their own classes. In one large high school the teachers periodically trade groups. While one director rehearses the students, the regular teacher sits in the back of the auditorium and listens much more objectively than is possible when he himself is on the podium. In smaller schools the vocal teacher might exchange classes with the instrumental teacher, or student conductors could be trained. If these procedures are not feasible, the teacher can start the group on a familiar number and walk to the back of the room or auditorium. Holds, rubato passages, and the like can be conducted with oversized motions from the place where he is standing.

The objective quality in listening needs to be emphasized. After the arduous labor required to prepare a performing organization, objectivity will not come easily, but it is necessary in order for the teacher to evaluate his group accurately. He might on occasion imagine that he is an adjudicator at a festival. What criticisms would he make? What suggestions would he offer the teacher of the group?

As an aid to objective listening, good recordings of student organizations are extremely useful, for several reasons. They give everyone a chance to listen. The teacher can take them home and study them, and listen to a passage as often as he cares to. They can be saved as a record of the progress of the group throughout the year, and from year to year. One recording can be compared with another so that the students can be instructed by hearing the results of change in their performance. Furthermore, local radio stations are often interested in airing programs of local interest, if the performances and recordings are of satisfactory quality.

A word of caution: making tape recordings correctly consumes a great deal of time. More than one teacher has suddenly realized on Friday that a whole week has been spent on a few tapes. The first tape will probably require more time than succeeding attempts. Often much time is spent listening to playbacks of the performance, and there seems to be an irrepressible desire on the part of the students to hear everything that has been recorded. To conserve time, one or two of the recorded pieces can be played back in class, and the entire tape can be left until the noon hour or after school. Depending on how they are made and used, tape recordings can be a boon or a bane to the music teacher.

Questions

1. In the early stages of work on a piece, why is it suggested that a particular section be worked over only a limited number of times? What principles of music teaching are pertinent to this practice?
2. How would you explain to a disinterested student why it is important for him to follow what is going on when you work with another section?
3. What principles of music teaching are involved when trouble spots are isolated?
4. When practicing music reading by pointing to a scale on the chalkboard, why is the major scale suggested for the initial work? Shouldn't students learn both major and minor? Is a teaching principle involved here?
5. In teaching parts to an instrumental group it was suggested that the melody be rehearsed first, while with the choral group the recommendation was for the lowest part. What are the differences between vocal and instrumental music that would account for this inconsistency of approach?
6. In concluding work with one section, it was suggested that the part be played or sung with other parts previously learned. Why?
7. In teaching students to play or sing subordinate parts, should these parts be studied by themselves or in conjunction with the melody? Why?

Projects

1. Study the score to a march and a choral number, marking out the melody and other parts as though you were going to teach it for performance. Also mark those spots at which the students may encounter problems of rhythm, pitch, etc.

2. Select three easy numbers (one each for band, orchestra, and chorus), which can be used for a first meeting of the group.
3. Using the same three numbers, decide how you might present the music so that the students gain a concept of the whole piece.
4. Using the scale-interval technique suggested on page 160, direct the class through some simple melodic figures. Use both clefs.
5. Practice starting your college class on a song with verbal commands and without conducting.
6. Select a folk song such as "I'm a Poor Wayfaring Stranger" for the class to sing. As they sing the song under your direction, vary the interpretation by inserting holds, rubato, and so on. Do this through conducting and verbal commands, without stopping the song.
7. Using the same vocal work, mark in those tonal and rhythmic patterns that are common to music in general and/or occur several times in the particular piece, so that they can be pointed out to the students.
8. Observe a teacher rehearsing a school performing group. Note his effective and efficient actions, and those that are not so. Note the amount of time lost between changes of music and in unnecessary talking by the teacher.
9. Visit two secondary school choral teachers and two instrumental teachers. Find out from them
   a. what arrangements are made for sectional rehearsals,
   b. what homework is expected of the class,
   c. what steps they take to enable themselves to hear their own group as objectively as possible.
10. In teaching the parts to a choral group, it was suggested that the lowest be helped first. Examine other collegiate music methods textbooks to see what they recommend, and their reasons for the suggestions they offer.
11. Find out how compound meters are taught to children in the elementary schools. Attempt to determine whether a consistent approach is used, and how much experience pupils have with compound meters. Recall how you were taught to read such meters, and judge the effectiveness of that method.
12. With a college student who has had training in the teaching of language reading, discuss the similarities and differences between reading music and the printed word. Consider such things as eye movement, aural experience, amount of practice, and causes of nonreading.

Suggested Readings

Andrews, Frances M., and Joseph A. Leeder, *Guiding Junior High School Pupils in Music Experiences*. Englewood Cliffs, N.J.: Prentice-Hall, Inc., 1953. Pp. 149–59.

Mursell, James L., *Music Education: Principles and Programs.* Morristown, N.J.: Silver Burdett Company, 1956. Chapters V, VI.

Singleton, Ira C., *Music in Secondary Schools.* Boston: Allyn and Bacon, Inc., 1963. Pp. 236–47, 343–48.

Sur, William R., and Charles F. Schuller, *Music Education for Teen-Agers.* New York: Harper & Brothers, 1958. Chapter XI.

IX

teaching interpretation

An eager young conductor asked a half dozen noted conductors about the interpretation of a piece of music. According to the story, he received seven different answers! Determining an interpretation, no easy job, is a task that every school music teacher faces. It is a crucial one, because only through proper interpretation are the aesthetic qualities of a piece brought to life.

Deciding on the proper interpretation is only a part of the job of the school music teacher. He faces an even greater challenge in getting the teen-age musician to sing or play with the right expression and style. Here the teacher must not only work for the correct rendition of the notes; he must take the students beyond the notation so that the full effect of the music may be realized.

The thought that the music teacher must accept responsibility for teaching students to interpret as well as sing or play music may be surprising to some. The tendency often is to think of interpretation as the duty and concern only of the conductor, and not a realistic goal for school students. Righter speaks to this point as follows:

> Many teachers who admit the possibility of their students' acquiring a high degree of technical skill decline to accept the principle that interpretation can be taught. Possibly one reason for this is that these teachers have devoted so large a proportion of their time to the mastery of playing techniques that they have neglected to study the problems related to the teaching of interpretation. It may even be true that an erroneous conception of teaching *sequence* is the source of the difficulty—the reasoning that physical skills should be taught first, then the interpretation skills. This division of emphasis is fatal to any bal-

> anced progress in music education. All of the essential skills must be taught concurrently in order that one may support the others and give purpose and direction to the entire process.
>
> In searching out the reasons for the failure of so many teachers to teach interpretation one is almost forced to the conclusion that this failure is traceable to the fact that the interpretative values are hidden values, whereas the purely technical problems appear on the surface.[1]

DETERMINING PROPER INTERPRETATION

The interpretation of a musical work is the sum of all the points that affect the sound of the music but are not fully indicated by the printed notation. A discussion of interpretation is necessary because of the inadequacies of the notational system, which does a nearly complete job of specifying pitch and a passingly good job with rhythm. Notation gives a few clues to dynamic level, detachment of notes, and tempo, but that is about all. The interpretation of a work should be the realization of all that the composer intended to convey in that music.

So important is interpretation that the mood and effect of a musical number can be drastically changed by a variation in it. To use an analogy between interpretation in music and interpretation in the spoken word, take the simple question, "Were you there last night?" Notice how the effect of the question can be altered by emphasizing one particular word:

WERE you there last night?
Were YOU there last night?
Were you THERE last night?
Were you there LAST night?
Were you there last NIGHT?

Really five different questions, aren't they? Imagine how many more shadings of meaning are possible if tone of voice, facial expression, tempo, and head movement are taken into consideration.

Traditional Interpretation

A music teacher has several factors to consider in selecting the tempos, tone colors, dynamics, the amount of legato and staccato, and the high points in a particular work. First, he has to know enough music history and literature to be able to match the piece of music with its proper historical style. For example, a Palestrina motet should be sung in a style quite different from that of the Brahms *Liebeslieder Waltzes.* Almost all music that has become a part of the established literature has a basic interpretation that is more or less traditional. This accepted interpretation has grown out of the interpretative trial and error of many music groups in many different places. As a result, this interpretation has a kind of validity about

[1] Charles Boardman Righter, *Success in Teaching School Orchestras and Bands* (Minneapolis: Schmitt, Hall, & McCreary, 1945), pp. 189–90. Reprinted by permission.

it, and it behooves the teacher, especially the novice, to follow in essence the established style of performance.

This is not to say that there is no room left for the teacher's ideas. The historically established interpretation is not so rigid that what is usually taken at a speed of M.M. = 100 cannot be taken at M.M. = 104 or 96. Rather it might be thought of as fencing in an area within which the teacher must work. He can vary slightly the tempo of the chorale "O God, Our Help in Ages Past," but it should not be sung with a rubato tempo and flabby tone; such singing would be a gross musical error. When it is remembered that J. S. Bach wrote most of his cantatas for a small choir of about twenty-eight members, one realizes that bombastic effects are as out of place in his music as a football suit on a basketball floor. There are fine recordings of music from various historical periods, as well as many books with information on interpretation. These can be used as a basis for learning the precedents concerning various styles of music.

Personal Judgment

Although generalizations about vocal teachers and instrumental teachers are fraught with a certain amount of error, choral teachers seem to prefer flexibility of tempo, while instrumental teachers tend to hold to a steady tempo. In the case of vocal music, the tradition of performance of the nineteenth-century art song and operatic music with its artistic freedom probably has been influential. Instrumental teachers have the tradition of the steady beat of the march to account for their tendency toward strict tempos. Generally the teacher should choose the most suitable tempo and stick close to it, since in most works an overuse of rubato distracts from the essential quality of the music. Expression can usually be achieved within the confines of the proper tempo. After various expressive techniques have been tried, the teacher can attempt slight fluctuations of the tempo, if this seems necessary. The order is important here: first the proper tempo, and then slight variations that contribute to the sense of the music.

The teacher has to use his own sense of proportion and good taste. The primary considerations in the interpretation are that it be true to the composer's intent, and that it be sincere. Unfortunately, too many directors interpret with the hope of creating a musical "splash." They interpret to build not the music, but themselves. This, of course, has no place in the school—if indeed anywhere. A lack of musical understanding also accounts for some of the extreme variations of interpretation that are sometimes advocated.

One school of choral directors, for example, has developed a fondness for the *sforzando*, the *fp* < and the exaggerated singing of *m*'s, *n*'s, and *ing*'s (sustaining the sound in a hum). These effects, like bleu cheese or garlic, are fine when used sparingly. The effect is somewhat startling when it is heard for the first time, but with each repetition the ability to arouse interest diminishes until further repetitions are only annoying. In addition, this type of effect tends to detract from the message of the music itself. If a class sings this Negro spiritual,

the effect becomes theatrical rather than religious, and such a turnabout of meaning is hardly in good taste.

Sometimes a director thinks that he needs to alter the interpretation of a piece to make it "interesting." The word "glittering" or "ear-catching" would better describe the effect. Many profound works of music, those of J. S. Bach for example, are not ear-catching or glittering. Good music, like a pretty girl, does not need to be dressed up in a flashy manner in order to be noticed. A teacher who finds himself relying on sensational interpretative effects should check two things: whether he really understands the music his groups are performing, and whether the quality of the music is high enough to warrant its inclusion in the repertoire.

Occasionally one encounters a teacher who has not the slightest desire to overexpress. His conducting beat is of the exact same size and style no matter whether the music should be loud or soft, staccato or legato, fast or slow. His group responds in a similar manner, producing a lifeless, routine performance devoid of feeling. Like the excessive use of interpretative devices, this approach is devastating to real musical qualities.

INTERPRETING WHOLES AND PARTS

Although musical interpretation is a unity of expressive elements, it must be broken down if it is to be taught to teen-agers. The discussion of whole and part learning in Chapter Seven is pertinent to the job of teaching interpretation. Expressive concepts such as rhythm, blend, staccato, legato, balance, and phrasing need to be studied, but in order to be meaningful they must be related at all times to the over-all interpretation.

The student needs a verbal symbol for each concept to aid him in his understanding. For example, Mr. Lawton devises some experiences in which the attention of his girls' glee club is devoted almost entirely to dynamics. The students learn further what the word "dynamics" means in music, they experience the actions necessary to sing softly and loudly, and they become more sensitive and proficient in their response to dynamic markings, crescendos and decrescendos. If Mr. Lawton is to be a successful music teacher, he will relate the study of dynamics to the music the group is singing. In that way the members will better realize how the dynamic contrasts affect the aesthetic qualities of the music.

The adjudication forms created by the National Interscholastic Music Activities Commission (NIMAC) of the MENC, three of which are reproduced in Appendix D, break down the total performance of a group into various elements, so that the adjudicator can discuss them properly. However, at the top of the sheet the adjudicator gives the group one final rating, which represents a summation of all the factors considered. The music teacher must treat the area of interpretation in the same manner by considering the parts that go into it, but then making sure that the whole does become greater than the sum of its parts.

TECHNIQUES OF TEACHING INTERPRETATION

When the teacher has decided upon the proper interpretation of the music, the more difficult task of teaching it to the students begins. Most teachers face several problems at this point. Foremost among these is the fact that many secondary school students seem to be disinterested in subtleties of any type, and their disregard for the subtle makes itself evident in their performance of music. The teacher must remind himself that some students, reared under conditions that are economically or psychologically poor, are forced by their environment to become somewhat insensitive to everything around them, including sound and music. Many students, unless otherwise instructed, will be satisfied to sing or play through a piece of music with little thought as to style or musical meaning. In fact, initially they are scarcely able to differentiate between a performance that contains attention to interpretive detail and one that does not. Until they become aware of the concepts involved in interpretation, they will hardly be able to improve their performance of them.

Sensitivity to concepts involved with interpretation can be fostered in two ways one: by focusing attention on them as the music is being learned, and two: by providing structured experiences that make the students more understanding and aware of all that goes into a piece of music. Both techniques are necessary if successful teaching is to take place. The major effort of this chapter is the presentation of specific, structured experiences for making students more sensitive to music.

Rhythm

Rhythm is essentially an elementary, physical phenomenon, and not an intellectual one. Physical experience must accompany or precede the learning of the symbols that indicate it. Groups that are not musically advanced need many physical experiences related to the rhythm in music—tapping feet, chanting words, counting rhythms. The rhythmic reading methods suggested on page 157 involve this type of response. There is a need to feel the rhythm, and especially the sensation of the beat, which the musician should maintain, inwardly or outwardly, at all times.

When problems are encountered in performing a rhythmic figure, the pattern should be isolated temporarily, and then returned to its proper musical context as soon as possible. Sometimes the students need only to give it concentrated attention and to practice associating the counting syllables with it. Here are two examples of this, the first one from Wagner's *Die Meistersinger von Nürnberg* and the second from "Mary Had a Baby."[2]

Clarinet

Count with syllables, then play:

Then practice with the tie:

Alto

Count with syllables, then sing on "tah":

Specific rhythmic problems can be approached through rote procedures, in which the teacher demonstrates the proper execution of the figure, and the students imitate him. In this way, the students can be given the style and accentuation at the same time. Most of this rhythmic teaching should be done in a "singsong" voice. Suppose that a group of singers is experiencing trouble with the following phrase:

[2] SSA, arr. Theron W. Kirk (Westbury, L.I., New York: Pro Art Publications, Inc., 1959). Used by permission.

The teacher can start by having the singers repeat exactly whatever he says, regardless of rhythm or words. Many times when he works out a rhythmic error he has to break down the wrong pattern before he can establish the correct one. Hence it is best to start with a simple rhythm entirely different from the problem phrase, in order to break away from the incorrect pattern. A quarter note phrase is simple and enables the students to imitate the teacher accurately from the beginning.

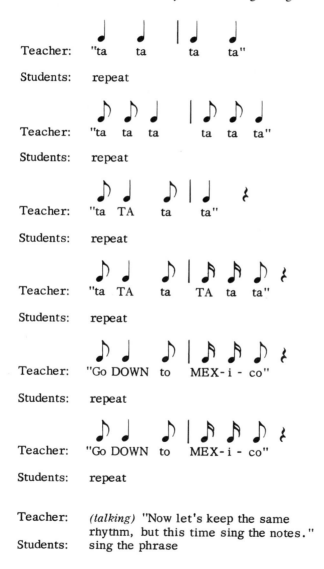

Teacher: "ta ta ta ta"

Students: repeat

Teacher: "ta ta ta ta ta ta"

Students: repeat

Teacher: "ta TA ta ta"

Students: repeat

Teacher: "ta TA ta TA ta ta"

Students: repeat

Teacher: "Go DOWN to MEX- i - co"

Students: repeat

Teacher: "Go DOWN to MEX- i - co"

Students: repeat

Teacher: *(talking)* "Now let's keep the same rhythm, but this time sing the notes."

Students: sing the phrase

The procedure just outlined should be lengthened or shortened according to the needs of the group and the difficulty of the music. The instrumental teacher can use the same technique with the students saying the syllable "ta," then move from that to the playing of a unison tone, and on to the particular phrase in the music.

Some teachers, rather than have the students singsong the words or use a syllable, have them clap out rhythms. This is a good technique, but clapping is not as fast or precise as the articulating action of the tongue.

Once the rhythmic patterns of a piece are conquered, the teacher should make sure that nothing is allowed to impede the surging momentum of the rhythmic flow. A rhythmically dynamic work should occasionally be rehearsed without stops; small errors on such occasions will have to wait for correction until the piece is done. Rhythmic movement is never sterile; it is alive, exciting, and pulsating. A teacher must never lose those qualities by allowing his teaching of rhythm to become academic and banal.

Blend

Although "balance" and "blend" are used interchangeably by some music teachers, the two words do not mean exactly the same thing. Blend refers to the homogeneity of sound, usually within a section, although the term can apply to the uniformity of timbre between sections. Balance refers to the distribution of volume and emphasis among the various sections. Thus, Ronald's voice may not blend (it may be of a different quality) with Allan's, and the cornets may overbalance (be too loud for) the clarinets.

A teacher should not make the mistake of thinking that good blending of tone quality is always desirable or necessary. In choral music some teachers make such a fetish of blend that they drain all the color and character from the voices of the singers. Some instrumental teachers work on blend by striving at all times for a homogeneous tone, even though the instruments are basically different and have highly individualistic tone qualities. This effort may produce an almost perfect blend, but a blend of what? What is left to blend?

The degree of blend to strive for is determined largely by the type of music being performed. A reverent, chordal piece requires far better blending of sound than does an exciting, barbaric selection. In the latter work a teacher should not expect, or even want, a perfect blending. How much more effective it is to let the individual color, emotion, and vitality break through the barrier of blend! Again, good musical judgment must be the guide.

If it is determined that more blend should be achieved, the first step is to make the students conscious of what it is. The teacher has to remind them persistently that it is not necessarily the best musician who performs loudest and has the most "piercing" quality. The comparison with a speaker (the best speaker is not always the one who can talk loudest) can be used to advantage here. The importance of unity must be emphasized again and again. Each section should sound like one performer, and not like fifteen or twenty soloists crowding onto the same part. The idea of each performer trying to fit his sound into the whole group must be carefully nurtured.

In many respects, the secondary school choral teacher does not find the problem of blend as serious as does the collegiate director (or the church choir director!). The lack of mature voices may hinder the school teacher in many respects, but blend is one area in which an immature voice has an advantage. Few teen-age singers have an inordinate amount of vibrato or highly individualistic voices.

Chapter Twelve presents some basic singing techniques for use in choral groups. A good technique encourages uniformity of tone production, and this in turn contributes much to the blending of voices, as does the use of a uniform vowel sound by the singers. With advanced groups the teacher instructs the singers to use a somewhat rounded *oh* position of the lips on vowels such as *ee* and *ih*.

The proper method of tone production improves the blend in instrumental music, too. Unusual embouchures with pinched lips and squeezed tones do not contribute to uniformity. With strings, a good healthy tone and a consistently produced vibrato are required for blend. Instruments and mouthpieces should be as similar as possible. A player with a shallow cup or close lay on his mouthpiece will not normally blend with a player who has a deep cup or open lay on his mouthpiece. Nor will trumpets blend well with cornets, or a wide-bore trombone with a narrow-bore instrument. Stiff-reed players will not blend well with soft-reed players.

Several specific techniques will increase the students' consciousness of blend.

1) Choose two singers with the same range, or two players on the same instrument, who do *not* blend with one another. Have them play or sing a phrase together. Then select another performer who blends well with one of the original two, and have the new duo perform together. In this way, the students can hear blend, or the lack of it, for themselves. One variation of this procedure is for the teacher to sing or play with a student. The teacher can at first use a timbre that does not blend, and then one that does blend with the student.

2) Start with one voice or instrument and then add another. When the two sounds are blending perfectly, add a third, and so on. This technique is generally more successful with college students than with secondary school students, perhaps because it is time-consuming, and to younger musicians it seems rather far removed from the actual performance of music.

3) Make use of student listening groups, as was suggested earlier.

4) Make tape recordings of the rehearsal. When students hear music played back with individual sounds popping out all over, they are im-

pressed. Make sure that the recordings are representative of the sound of the group. It would be unfair to leave a microphone so close to one individual that his sound would stand out unduly on the recording.

5) Work on good unison singing or playing. Outlining triads is excellent for developing accuracy in pitch and blend; singers may use various vowel sounds in so doing. Unison songs are good for choral groups because the same words will be sung by all voices at the same time, and this frequently does not occur when music in parts is used. During unison playing or singing, the students can strive for a more homogeneous tone. In band the cornets can be told to sound more like the French horns, and vice versa; in chorus tenors can work toward a quality that blends better with the basses.

6) Develop the group's ability to play or sing softly.

7) Remind individual students whose tone stands out in a section. If handled with delicacy, students do not mind being asked to hold back, especially if a compliment can be paid them for their above average work.

8) Encourage the more timid students to sing or play more loudly.

9) Work with individual problems in extra, private sessions. In singing, unusual quality can be caused by tension in the throat or overarching of the tongue. An instrumentalist may possess a freak embouchure or an improper sense of tone placement. No amount of classwork on blend is likely to remedy these problems. Individual instruction is the most direct and successful solution.

Finally, many times poor blending is a symptom of more basic problems, such as poor intonation, bad ensemble, or faulty tone production. In such cases, the teacher must work on the cause and not the symptom.

Balance

The school music teacher faces a problem which the professional conductor is spared: unbalanced groups. Except for highly select school groups, the teacher must work out the best balance among the singers or players he has available.

Achieving the correct balance is largely the job of the teacher, since he is the only one who can listen to the entire ensemble, and it is his aesthetic judgment that will determine what the correct balance should be. Good music education, of course, requires that the students learn what balance is, and that they understand why one part should be stressed at a particular moment in a piece of music. However, even though the students understand the music, they cannot tell if what they are emphasizing in their performance is being emphasized in what the listener hears. Only the teacher can determine this.

The director generally controls balance by indicating either verbally or through conducting gestures that one part should be louder and another softer. There are several ways to fortify a part that needs emphasis.

The instrumental teacher may be able to rearrange the parts for one or two instruments, or use two players on solo passages, or have an instrument play a cued-in part. A choral teacher can have a few students that he calls "travelers." These students sit near the boundaries of sections and thus are able to move from tenor to bass, or from a first to a second part. Such changes may have a slight effect on the timbre of the line; this may or may not be acceptable, depending on the particular passage in the music.

Good balance does not necessarily mean equality of parts. In almost all works, there is an interplay between parts as one section is more prominent and then recedes to allow another section to bring out its more important line. This interplay exists even in homophonic music when all parts are marked at the same dynamic level. A particular chord member can be more important, as in the case of a Tierce de Picardie or major third at the conclusion of a work in a minor key.

Balance is often better achieved by bringing the less important lines *down* in volume, rather than by encouraging the performers of the more important line to come out more loudly.

Dynamics

Good control of dynamics depends on two things: a consciousness of dynamics on the part of the students, and facility in making dynamic changes. Building a consciousness of dynamics and attaining skill in their use are, of course, very much intertwined. It may be desirable to offer specific training in performing at six dynamic levels (*pp*, *p*, *mp*, *mf*, *f*, *ff*) and in making crescendos and decrescendos, accents, and *sforzandos*. Many students are hazy about such matters when they first enroll in music. The choral teacher can make up any combination of dynamic markings to serve as exercises, and write them on the board or call them out verbally. An especially good exercise combines arpeggios with crescendos and decrescendos:

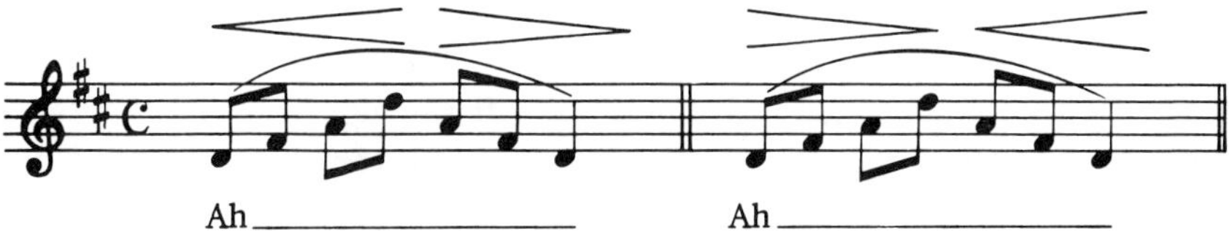

There are several other routines that stress dynamics. One is to hold a long tone or chord for twenty slow counts (see p. 184). The dynamic markings can also be reversed in this exercise. In either case, the exercise is good training in spreading out a crescendo or decrescendo and in sustaining long tones.

Another exercise is to take a technically simple figure and have the students perform it in whatever manner the teacher indicates by his con-

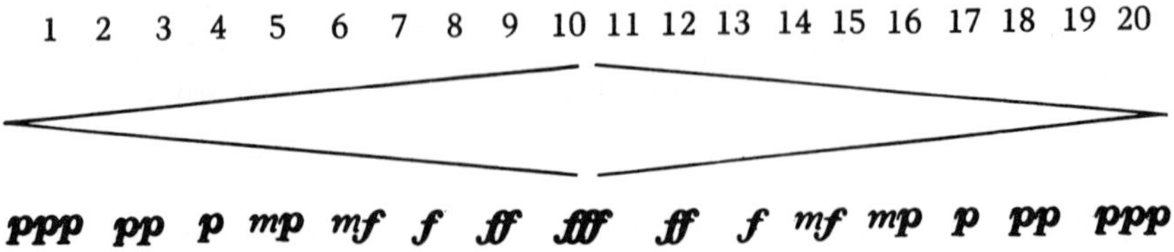

ducting. This makes the students conscious of both the dynamic level and the conducting motions of the teacher.

Fine as such exercises are, it must be remembered that they are not part of a musical context. A group may execute with great accuracy an exercise designed to gain dynamic control, and yet not play or sing expressively when performing a work of music. The principles of meaningful teaching demand that work on various elements of music be functional; whenever possible, such work should be centered in the context of the music being studied.

In the initial stages of learning a number it is usually necessary to exaggerate the dynamic levels. The students need to realize that there is a big "fall-off" between what the performer thinks he is doing and what the listener actually hears. What seems to the performer to be a noticeable crescendo may seem to be almost no crescendo at all to the listener. Therefore the students need to be prodded into exaggerating dynamic levels by such statements as "Make twice as much crescendo as you think you should." A tape recording may be of value here. Tape recorders often do not produce the changes of dynamics that are actually present in the performance. As a result, the dynamics must be exaggerated in order to have any affect on the recording, and an exaggerated performance is good training for the students.

Probably the most important factor in achieving variation in dynamic levels is the use of proper methods of tone production. Although it may seem illogical, a good tone is more easily produced on winds or in singing at *forte* than at *piano*. As described in Chapter Twelve, when singing with a full tone, the chest seems to stay up more easily, the throat is relaxed, and the tone seems to roll out. In soft singing, the chest wants to cave in, the throat muscles become tight and lack responsiveness, and the tone is squeezed out. The result is a flatting of the pitch and tight little tones that can hardly be heard. The singers have to be reminded repeatedly that in singing softly *nothing changes except the amount of air that is used*. The rib cage remains expanded, the lungs are filled with air, and the throat remains at ease. What happens? The muscles of the abdominal wall hold the air back, the mouth is open, and the throat muscles are relaxed. Usually enough breath will escape to support a very soft tone.

It is tiring to maintain the expanded rib cage and the open throat without the aid of a full stream of air flowing by. For this reason, time and conditioning are required for good *pianissimo* singing.

To help the students sing softly and yet maintain intensity in the tone quality (some teachers call this "spinning" the tone), have the group sing a chord or a tone *ff*. Then repeat the chord *pp*, but maintain the identical body feeling, except for the holding back of air, that accompanied the singing of the *ff* chord. Another means of maintaining intensity in singing *pp* is to start by humming the passage. Then sing it, keeping as much of the humming style as possible (somewhat closed mouth, little jaw movement, and a continuous feeling of hum and resonance).

With wind instruments the technique for soft playing is almost identical to that used in soft singing. The correct method of tone production requires adequate breath support and attention to the basic steps outlined in Chapter Thirteen. The throat is not pinched, squeezing the air out and distorting the tone. As in singing, the air is held back by the muscles of the abdomen and the diaphragm. On string instruments there are two variables: the pressure of the bow on the strings, which is controlled by the pressure applied by the forefinger of the right hand, and the extent to which the bow is over the fingerboard. String instruments are designed to produce their biggest tone with the bow drawn quite near the bridge. The farther the bow is from the bridge, the softer the tone becomes.

Unless the adolescent possesses above average voice development and/or tone production technique, his dynamic range is narrow. Junior high school singers especially cannot get volume. There can be only so much *forte*. Any attempt with singers or instrumentalists to go beyond their ability results in a frenzied, distorted tone, which has been aptly compared to "the sound of a piece of canvas ripping." An effective *pianissimo* can be achieved by reducing the number of performers on a part, a technique not unknown in professional music organizations.

It is important to remember that dynamics are relative. Driving one hundred miles per hour may seem fast in an automobile, but for a jet airliner this speed is very slow. Similarly, a *forte* in the music does not mean the same thing to all composers or in all periods. The basic element in dynamics is the principle of contrast. If a performer wants thrilling climaxes in the music, he must save some volume for them. The accented note is a good example of this. If all the notes in this measure are performed *ff*,

it will be impossible to make much of an accent on the notes so indicated. However, if the unaccented notes are executed *piano*, the accented notes will be more prominent. A good way to practice music that contains many accents is to go through it performing only the accented notes. The rest of the notes are heard in the "mind's ear" of the students. Most of the effort should be directed toward keeping the unaccented notes soft, while the accented notes can be allowed to spring out in full volume. Hence the action is as much one of letting the accented notes escape as it is one of "punching" or "kicking" the accented note.

Sustained Tones

At times it is more difficult to interpret long, sustained tones in the melodic line than short ones, perhaps because the greater movement of shorter tones hides a lack of expression by the performer. Sustained tones must somehow convey a feeling of progress. Something must always be happening within a sustained tone, because good music is always evolving.

Two types of sustained tones should be cited here. One is the final chord of a piece, and the other the long tone that leads toward some climactic point. The latter is well illustrated by a vocal work, Handel's "Thanks Be to Thee":

The long A progresses toward the apex of the phrase on the word "be." It is only logical that the tone should increase in volume and intensity as it is held. A feeling of "holding back" at the beginning of such crescendos, and a faster rate of increasing loudness at the end, will make sustained tones more effective.

A final chord can increase or decrease in volume and intensity, depending upon the character of the piece. If the work ends in a triumphant manner, the last tone, if it is long, will probably sound better if the students make a slight crescendo. For some reason, a tone that is held straight at one dynamic level always seems to decrease slightly in volume. Thus the need for the crescendo. On the other hand, if the composition ends in a subdued and pensive vein, the last tone can appropriately diminish in volume. A director can achieve a very dramatic effect by slowly letting the closing tone fade into silence. Even after no more sound is audible, he and the group remain motionless for several seconds. This brief silence allows the effect of the music to become thoroughly absorbed by the listener.

Staccato

One of the most important and difficult elements of interpretation is that of executing separate, detached notes. Staccato style is not as easily perceived by students as legato. The song style, which is basic to music and is the type of music youngsters first learn, is flowing, not abrupt. Staccato is a more advanced and intellectual phenomenon. In addition, it is hard for teen-agers to grasp the idea that there is no one style of detaching notes. The length of note, the separation between notes, and the crispness of the attack vary with each musical work, and often within the piece itself. Composers and arrangers have not always been consistent in their use of staccato markings. Sometimes students are told, "A staccato note means to cut the value of the note in half, so that the latter half of its value is silence." While the statement is true of some phrases, it is not true of others, and it can do harm if it discourages consideration of the musical intent of a particular phrase.

To teach the proper degree and style of detachment teachers must rely largely on demonstration. The proper rendition may be played or sung by the teacher or by an advanced student who has previously been prepared on the passage by the teacher. The teacher may use verbal directions to some extent. But "short" does not mean the same thing to everyone. The phrase "play it shorter than you did last time" is of help, but it still may get across only part of the idea of the style.

On string instruments, short notes are regulated by the style of bowing —staccato, spiccato, ricochet, détaché, martelé. Music teachers who wish to assist their string players with differing styles of bowing should examine one of the books listed in Appendix C.

The achievement of staccato style and properly detached notes on wind instruments, a topic of considerable importance, is discussed in detail in Chapter Thirteen. More than intellectual understanding, wind instrument players need good tonguing, proper breath support, and much practice to develop coordination between breath, tongue, and fingers. With them, the act of tonguing is more than an interpretative device; it is a necessity for good playing.

Staccato singing is difficult, and should not even be attempted until a group has mastered the proper method of tone production. The difficulty seems to arise from the fact that singers want to pronounce the words as slowly as they usually do in legato singing. The vowels must be executed very rapidly in staccato. Some distortion may result when certain vowels and the diphthongs are sung so short, but because of their brief duration this is not serious.

In contrast to wind instrument tonguing, singing requires a short pushing action of the diaphragm in order to produce the abrupt start which is necessary for each staccato note. This diaphragmatic action is similar to that required for the accent and *sforzando*. The latter require a greater push of the diaphragm, and a heavier initial sound.

Tones ending in consonants (except *m*, *n*, and *ng*), are concluded automatically by the formation of the consonant. If the final syllable ends in a vowel, the student is likely to stop the tone by closing the mouth, or by tensing the throat muscles as they clamp down to shut off the flow of air. A more effective way, however, is to keep an open, relaxed throat and to stop the flow of air by a holding-back action of the diaphragm. This latter method is recommended because it retains an open and relaxed throat and thus is more consistent with proper tone production.

When a group sings staccato notes, the teacher must be ever on the alert for sagging pitch. Adolescent singers are prone to go flat on short notes. This can be caused by the practice of "scooping" tones, by failing to make the notes lean toward the logical culmination of the phrase, or by allowing the throat setup to collapse, at least to some degree, when starting and stopping the tones. Another cause for inaccurate pitch in singing short notes is the inability to hear the correct pitch in the "mind's ear." Many young singers find the proper pitch only by "tuning up" the note as they sing it. If the notes are short, there is no time in which to do this, and the result in extreme cases sounds more like talking than like singing. Experience with correct tone-production methods is the best remedy for pitch problems in staccato singing. It is helpful from the standpoint of intonation to sing a staccato passage once in a while in a legato style.

Legato

Music teachers spend a lot of time teaching the *beginnings* of notes. The system of counting beats is very precise as to where a note starts, and students learn to understand and abide by the system. The *ends* of notes are another matter. Many students think that a note which is three counts long stops on the third beat. At best they are hazy on this point. Therefore both vocal and instrumental teachers have to counteract the students' tendency to rob some of the value from the ends of half notes, dotted halves, and notes of longer duration. Gaps caused by incomplete notes, of course, diminish the legato effect. Notes must be held for their full value, and students need to know exactly when a note should end.

Instrumentalists, with the exception of trombonists, do not have any particular difficulty in slurring and thus achieving a good legato. With singers, it is another matter. It is difficult for an inexperienced singer to master a good legato style. Much vocal control is needed to sing with an endless flow of tone which seems to permeate through each word and between words.

The best way to teach legato to the teen-ager is to stress again the idea of continuity of tone. Such expressions as, "Sing through the words," "Keep pulling the tone," and "Don't drop your words" will help establish the concept. The singer can imagine that all the notes are glued together; only at phrase endings should the flow be interrupted slightly. Also, the singer might imagine that in his mouth is a ball of string which is continually being pulled out as he sings. Legato tone is like the string—an endless, constant stream of sound.

The concept of "pulling the tone" can be aided by singing the phrase on a neutral syllable. The point of the exercise is to make the singing with words as nearly as possible like the singing on a single syllable. One other technique may be used. Occasionally during practice the teacher may insert holds at different places in the music, particularly on the last note of the piece. The holds will impress upon the singers the idea of sustained sound.

Phrasing

It is rare indeed to find a phrase of music in which all notes receive exactly the same emphasis. A machine makes identical sounds; human beings seldom do in speaking or in music. Human beings put sounds together into phrases so that they have meaning and logic. Phrasing is primarily the division of music into logical units, and then the rating and relating of the notes within the units as to their importance and purpose. Phrasing in music is not merely a question of where to breathe or when to change bows. Good phrasing is one evidence of genuine musical understanding.

A discussion of phrasing is without limits, because in music there is an infinite variety of phrases, each one requiring a different treatment according to its unique construction. Proper phrasing is dependent upon the musical judgment and sensibility of the music teacher. In teaching correct phrasing to students, the most effective way in the beginning is by rote. Words are inadequate to tell someone how to execute a phrase, to describe exactly how much tenuto to make and how a decrescendo should be integrated into it. As in the teaching of staccato style, the teacher should sing the way the phrase goes. An instrumental teacher may prefer to demonstrate on his horn or clarinet. Initially the student must be told, "This is how it should be done." After a period of years, when he has absorbed a good many phrases, he can begin to figure out phrasing for himself. It is a rare secondary school student who by his own efforts phrases well, especially the more complex music of Debussy, or Bach's unaccompanied sonatas. Some use can be made of the running commentary suggested on page 163. Good musical conducting will also help the students with their phrasing. But the essence of the instruction must be demonstration by the teacher.

This idea can be used to make the students more conscious of phrasing, teach them more about interpretation, and add interest to the class. After the students have some idea of how a phrase should go, they can be asked to sing or play it with the dynamics, note groupings, and style reversed as much as possible. The deliberately wrong rendition draws attention to the interpretation of the passage and adds a little levity to the class. A variation of the procedure is when the teacher offers two or three different ways of interpreting the same phrase. For example, he might put the following on the board

and

and ask the class to perform both. Then he can ask the students which is more suitable in the particular piece of music.

Students should be encouraged to write on their music in pencil. By marking a circle around a phrase unit, they can indicate the notes that are combined into meaningful phrases. For instance, a figure may be written,

but it is musically thought out in this way:

A series of repeated notes can sound monotonous unless handled in a musical manner. The students may circle

to remind themselves about the tendency of the three notes to "lean" or be pulled toward the half. String instrument bowings, which are very much involved with phrasing, should definitely be marked in the music, as should breath marks in wind music.

In melodies containing short note values, the longer notes, *up to one beat in length*, usually receive greater emphasis and volume. For example, in a syncopated figure such as

the eighth notes should usually be thought of as being only half as heavy as the quarter. In most cases a slight separation between the first two notes will improve the musical effect:

Weight value: 1 2 1

The same general idea applies to many other rhythmic figures, such as

and the combinations of

and

in 6/8 meter. To help the students comprehend the idea of volume or weight, when explaining the interpretation of a phrase the teacher might refer to weight values as pounds—one pound for a quarter note, a half pound for an eighth note, or some such allocation. With junior high school students it may be helpful for them to write weight values in pencil on several pieces of music, so that they understand the idea thoroughly.

The beat upon which the note occurs likewise affects the amount of volume it receives. Usually the first beat of a measure receives the most emphasis; the last beat, the least. Emphasis upon other beats will vary according to the time signature.

INTERPRETING VOCAL MUSIC

Unlike instrumentalists, singers pronounce words as they sing and use their voices to create certain musical effects, such as humming. These actions require special consideration.

Phrasing in Relation to Text and Rhythm

There is no fixed relationship between the relative importance of the text as compared to the music. The proper balance can range all the way from Gregorian chant in which the text entirely dominates the melodic line, to a work such as Randall Thompson's "Alleluia" in which the one word "Alleluia" is the text and the music is the essence of the work. The teacher has to make an aesthetic judgment as to the proper relationship between the two when deciding upon the interpretation of a work.

In speaking, certain words are stressed more than others. The same is true of syllables of words. To determine the proper phrasing and interpretation of a particular work, the vocal teacher should read through the text in a careful manner, judging which words are more important, and trying to make himself sensitive to the sounds and colors, the poetry of the words.

Tone Color

Since the tone color or timbre of the human voice shows so readily the feelings of the person, and since a song is the musical setting of specific feelings, the tone quality of a singing group is important in interpretation. Different emotions projected in a song call for different timbres. It comes as a surprise to some students that there is no one, best singing tone.

When a teacher begins to stress to his students that different songs require different tone qualities, it is wise to work on the two poles of tone color: the light and the dark. Choral groups have really accomplished something when they can sing with a light, bright tone when they want to, and a dark, full sound when it is called for. When the tonal extremities are mastered, other types of timbre can be thought of in relation to them.

Change in timbre is brought about partially by specific physical action. The dark tone color is nearer the basic tone quality, which will be described in Chapter Twelve. Adolescents usually find this dark quality more difficult to produce, since their voices tend to be light. The physical setup for the dark tone is a wide-open, relaxed throat, with the tongue relaxed and low. The position of the mouth and lips is similar to the one used for producing the sound *oh*. In fact, the *oh* vowel should be used to practice a dark tone quality.

The light, bright tone quality is produced by raising the jaw slightly from the *oh* position and narrowing the opening of the mouth, as for the vowel *ee*, by bringing the tongue up somewhat. Sometimes the simplest way for the teen-ager to think of the difference between the dark and light timbres is to think of the dark as being vertical and full, and the bright as being horizontal and flat-surfaced. The bright tone should not be squeezed out so that it sounds pinched and strained, however. In such a case the result would not be a bright tone, but merely a poor tone quality.

The other requirement for achieving a change of timbre is for the students to have an understanding of and a feeling for the music. The teacher or a good student may demonstrate the tone wanted, and in effect say to the singers, "This is the tone color we want. Go ahead and get it." This technique resembles an imitative rote procedure, but it encourages the students to base their response on feeling for the music, rather than on conscious physical actions. When a person's voice is filled with anger, grief, or other emotion, he is not aware that he is tightening a certain muscle, closing or opening the back of the throat, tensing or relaxing the tongue. It all happens as the result of a certain feeling. Therefore, the efforts of the teacher to get an understanding of the piece—its text, historical setting, and musical qualities—are helpful in getting the right tone quality. A song with lasting aesthetic qualities should be felt as well as sung, and this feeling will affect the timbre of the voice.

Humming

Many teachers question the usefulness of humming for choral groups. Like several other musical effects that have been mentioned, it should be used sparingly and with discretion.

Students have to be taught how to hum properly. All of them can hum, of course; but often the hum is produced by a squeezing of the throat muscles. The result is a sound that does not project. To produce a resonant hum, students should sing the basic *ah* vowel, and then close their lips. They definitely should not close their teeth! The *ah* vowel can be varied at times with other vowel positions to give the humming tone a slightly different color.

Accurate pitch is hard to achieve when a teen-age group hums. Basically the problem is one of attitude. The singers seem to think that sloppy pitch while humming will not be noticed. In musically less-developed groups it is hard enough to make the singers aware of pitch when they sing, so one can imagine how much harder this task is when they hum.

Runs

Whenever more than one note is sung for a syllable of a word, there exists a situation which encourages sloppiness in singing. One way to achieve accuracy in such passages is to have the singers place a small "bump" or "pulse" at the beginning of each note, much as they were encouraged to do in staccato singing, except in this case to a lesser degree. The phrase

would then be considered as

with the *u* indicating the little diaphragmatic bump at the beginning of each note. Some teachers tell their singers to put a small *h* in front of each note. This technique is fine as long as it is made clear to the singers that they should not stop or break the air stream before each note. The bump or the slight *h* sound will eliminate the siren effect that singers sometimes get on such passages. If this technique is exaggerated, it can ruin the sound when only one person is singing. But when used with moderation by an entire group, it is an inconspicuous aid to clarity. Two more elements are needed to make runs sound clean: accurate pitch and accurate rhythm.

Pronunciation of Foreign Languages

When songs are sung in languages other than English, care should be taken to see that the words are pronounced as nearly correctly as possible. The most authoritative book on the pronunciation of ecclesiastical Latin is *The Correct Pronunciation of Latin According to Roman Usage*.[3] This book is especially useful in giving the correct pronunciation to such often mispronounced words as "excelsis," "coeli," and "nostrae."

For modern languages such as French, Italian, Spanish, and German, several textbooks and dictionaries are available. Many schools own sets of language records or tapes that can be studied. In addition, the language teacher will be glad to assist if he can. If no teacher in the schools is competent in the particular language being sung, the music teacher is advised to look around the community; there may be someone who knows that language well.

MUSICAL FEELING AND TECHNIQUE

In his eagerness for a good performance, the teacher should never become so occupied with the technical phases of the music such as blend, balance, and rhythm that he loses the spirit or the "idea" of the music. Because of the importance of the essential spirit of the music, it is better to let some technical aspect of the music go unperfected than to destroy the heart of the work.

Both technique and musical feeling are necessary, and this fact presents the teacher with a problem to which there is no quick, easy solution. Constant and unhurried effort is required in order to bring each of the two elements into proper perspective. First, the work on various technical phases of music should be integrated as much as possible with the pieces of music currently being studied. Functional learning, not isolated drill, is what is needed.

Second, the teacher should help the students recognize the relationship between technique and musical feeling. A musician has much in common with the actor in this respect. Until the end of the nineteenth century, acting consisted of artificial, pompous, formal motions; techniques were the basis of acting. Constantine Stanislavsky in his books and in the Moscow Art Theatre began a revolution toward a combination of feeling and natural technique. According to Stanislavsky, the actor must project himself as deeply as possible into the character he is to portray, but at the

[3] Published by St. Gregory Guild, 1705 Rittenhouse Square, Philadelphia 3, Pa.

same time he must never lose sight of the fact that he is acting and that a certain amount of objective technique is necessary to project the part successfully.

When a group sings "By the rivers of Babylon, there we sat down, yea, we wept, when we remembered Zion," they must feel the anxiety and privation of the captive Israelites. But more than that they must know the technique required to project the correct feeling through the music to an audience. The students should know in exact, objective terms how to achieve a warm tone or a decrescendo, and at the same time they should understand and feel what it is that the music is trying to convey. When objective technique and subjective feeling are united, a most precious vehicle of artistic expression has been created.

Questions

1. Instead of chanting neutral syllables, is the use of words

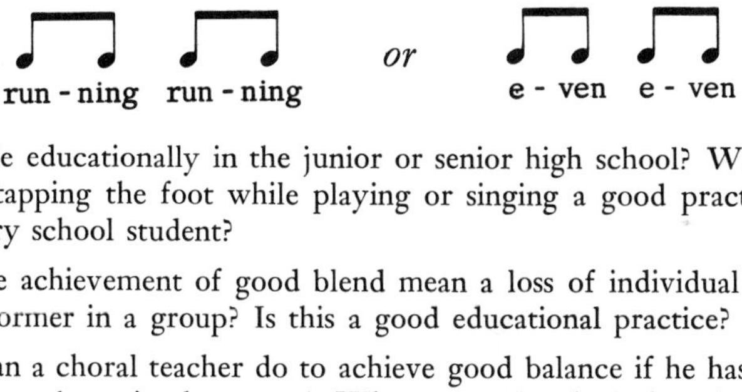

justifiable educationally in the junior or senior high school? Why, or why not? Is tapping the foot while playing or singing a good practice for the secondary school student?

2. Does the achievement of good blend mean a loss of individual quality for the performer in a group? Is this a good educational practice?
3. What can a choral teacher do to achieve good balance if he has forty girls and twenty boys in the group? What can a band teacher do to balance eight clarinets against nine trumpets? What can the orchestra director do to balance a complete wind section with eleven violins, two violas, two cellos, and three string basses?
4. Is it desirable to have each performer learn an exact degree of loudness for each of the six dynamic levels (*pp*, *p*, *mp*, *mf*, *f*, *ff*)?
5. Suppose that the group you are conducting shows no flexibility and does not follow the tempo changes as you conduct them. What teaching device might you use in order to get them to be more responsive to tempo change?
6. Why is it important for students to learn the terms "blend," "phrasing," "tone quality" when they can perform rather well without knowing these words?
7. Examine the adjudication forms in Appendix D. Do these forms give proper emphasis to pertinent musical factors? Are they too much centered on the technical phases of music, and too little concerned with the over-all effect?

Why, or why not? What suggestions, if any, could you make to improve the forms?

8. Page 179 contained the example of a teacher using rote methods to teach his singers the syncopated phrase "Go down to Mexico." Would it have been better to make the students use a system of counting and figure it out for themselves? Which method, rote or reading, is more effective musically in this instance? Which will the students remember longer? Which is more efficient in its use of class time?

Projects

1. There are several recordings available of
   a. "Hallelujah Chorus" from *The Messiah* by G. F. Handel
   b. *1st Rhapsodie Roumaine* by Georges Enesco
   c. *Firebird Suite* by Igor Stravinsky

   Listen to two recordings of each work. Compare and contrast the tempo, dynamic levels, tone color, style or articulation, and other interpretative factors at selected specific places in each work. Decide which is preferable, and be able to state why.
2. Listen again to the opening section of Enesco's *Rhapsodie*, the section that features the clarinet. Decide how you would teach a teen-age clarinetist in your orchestra to play the solos with the necessary musicality and flexibility.
3. Listen again to the middle of the "Hallelujah Chorus." Note the smooth quality of the words "The kingdom of this world," as contrasted with the more martial quality of "and He shall reign forever and ever." Plan how you would work with a teen-age choral group to achieve this difference in the style of singing.
4. Devise some simple unison exercises to be sung or played which will give teen-age students a clearer idea of the exact ending of dotted quarter notes, half notes, dotted half notes, whole notes. Decide upon the verbal explanation that should accompany the presentation of the exercises to the group.
5. Look through copies of choral and instrumental music for works, such as Handel's "Thanks Be to Thee," which are especially suitable for developing an awareness of dynamics and a technique for producing the proper dynamics.
6. Secure two copies of the "Coronation Scene" from *Boris Godunov* by Modeste Mussorgsky, one published by B. F. Wood, and one by E. C. Schirmer. Compare the translated texts in terms of effect on the music, and suitability for performance.
7. Listen to commercial recordings of recognized choral groups singing
   a. a western, cowboy folk song
   b. a chorus from an oratorio

c. an old English folk song
d. Stravinsky's *Symphony of Psalms*
e. Brahms' *Ein Deutches Requiem*

Note the differing choral tone used for each work. Decide how you would work with a high school choral group to achieve the proper timbre for each type of music.

8. Select a phrase of choral music requiring some flexibility and imagination in phrasing. Take it to your class and insist that they phrase it in the way you suggest.

Suggested Reading

Dorian, Frederick, *History of Music in Performance.* New York: W. W. Norton and Co., 1942.

X

achieving correct intonation

"Tune it up, violas," the conductor admonishes a section of his orchestra. A good direction, no doubt about it. A trained musician knows what the conductor means. He responds by careful listening and the slight adjustment of fingers necessary to "tune it up." But what about the thirteen-year-old violist now in his fourth year of study, all of it in group situations? What about the flighty freshman girl in the glee club? To her, "tune it up" may mean to sing in a more lively manner. What about the junior bass who is back in choral music for the first time since seventh grade? For that matter, what about the first baritone horn, a senior with eight years of instrumental music experience? How much does he know about intonation? The school music teacher faces a real challenge. Not only does he encounter all the usual vicissitudes of intonation—acoustical problems of instruments, difficult places in the music, and fluctuations due to heat and cold—he also faces the job of teaching students what it is to be in tune, and what they must do to achieve proper intonation.

Sometimes music teachers, either because they assume that teen-agers cannot perform in tune, or because they do not know how to teach their students to be in tune (or possibly in a few cases because they do not listen carefully themselves) permit their students to have poor intonation. Skill and persistence are required to keep a group in tune, but nevertheless the effort must be made. Although a teacher has not necessarily failed if his group sounds a few notes out of tune, he does bear a large share of the responsibility for achieving good intonation.

The problem for the school music teacher is not primarily one of understanding the physical properties of sound, but of understanding why students may not be in tune, and what can be done to educate them to perform in tune. Of course, many of the causes are interrelated; an instance of poor intonation seldom has only a single cause.

Singing or playing in tune is the assumed, natural condition of music. All the quality recordings which youngsters hear are in tune; music instructors teach with true intonation; keyboard instruments, which so often serve as a standard, are carefully tuned and maintain their pitch for relatively long periods. Why then, after hearing all these models of correct intonation, do teen-age musicians have to be taught to perform with accurate pitch?

There are many reasons, some musical and some physical, for poor intonation; these form the basis of this chapter. In addition, however, there are two factors that give the *illusion* of faulty intonation. One is simply the presence of wrong notes. As an experienced band director once observed, "You know, when everyone is playing the right notes, it's remarkable how much better the intonation is." This observation applies especially to less-advanced instrumental groups.

The second illusion regarding intonation involves the relationship between timbre and pitch. Two tones may be sounding at the same pitch level but seem to be out of tune because of their differing qualities. The amount of brilliance in the timbre has a marked effect on the impression the listener gets about the pitch of the tone. Oddly, a poorer, less distinguished tone quality can more easily conceal its pitch. A fine, alive tone with a solid "center" cannot do this. The phenomenon is best illustrated by a good trombone player. If he blows a firm, well-rounded tone, any movement of the slide is noticeable to the ear. However, let him blow a sickly sound, and he can move the slide an inch or more without seemingly affecting the pitch level. This should not be construed as an argument for poor tone quality, however. It merely means that the teacher must be able to distinguish between pitch and timbre, so that he can trace the problem to its real source.

MUSICAL INEXPERIENCE

The lack of musical experience on the part of many teen-agers, a basic cause of poor intonation, makes itself evident in three ways: poor listening habits, lack of control, and lack of a concept of pitch.

Poor Listening Habits

People are constantly bombarded with sound in supermarkets, restaurants, and stores; their ears are assaulted by sounds ranging from jukeboxes to traffic noise. It is almost impossible to find a refuge from this barrage. Even the silent prayer period in many churches is accompanied by music on the organ. The result is that a person psychologically "tunes out" much of what he hears, and thereby no longer notices the clock ticking, the refrigerator turning on and off, or the noise of cars going by on the street outside. Unfortunately, he develops the habit of "half-listening." Such a habit makes it more difficult to teach students to listen carefully so that they can perform in tune.

As if the habit of half-listening were not enough, many teen-agers for the most part have had little experience in careful listening to parts or themes, or to accuracy of pitch. If the student is merely admonished to "correct the bad intonation," he is placed in an awkward situation. He is like a man who is sent to the scene of a crime to seek clues, but is given absolutely no idea as to the nature of the crime.

Some music teachers think that only a few gifted individuals have the innate ability to discriminate between minute differences in pitch. But Carl Seashore produced evidence to the contrary. His research indicates that the average individual can hear the difference of three double vibrations per second, or about .05 part of a tone at A440.[1] This amount of aural acuity he considers sufficient to make music activity worth while for the student.[2] The student's ability to distinguish fine gradations of pitch may be hidden, but it is seldom lacking. The teacher must find ways to draw out this innate capacity for pitch discernment.

Lack of Control and Coordination

The second manifestation of inexperience is the inability of students to coordinate the directions of the mind and ear with the voice and fingers. This is especially noticeable in boys' singing. Some boys in the first weeks of vocal music will try with all their might to sing a major second, only to sing a fourth, and on the next try a third, and then maybe an out-of-tune second. The adolescent violinist may falter when shifting to a new position, not because he can't hear it and doesn't know better, but because his muscle movement is too inconsistent to enable him to find the same place twice. The teacher must remember that the first efforts in any endeavor are often ineffectual. When a baby is first offered a nice bright object, he moves arms, legs and head furiously in an effort to touch the toy. In time, of course, muscle control will come to him; and likewise control in musical response will come to the teen-ager through practice.

Lack of a Concept of Pitch

The third manifestation of inexperience in music is the lack of a concept of intonation or "in-tuneness." It helps the student little to know that intonation is "the quality of in-tuneness" or that being in tune is "the

[1] Carl E. Seashore, *The Psychology of Musical Talent* (Morristown, N.J.: Silver Burdett Company, 1919), p. 45.

[2] *Ibid.*, pp. 66–67.

accurate reproduction of pitch." These are mere words, and no one can learn about intonation by definitions alone. Words in this case can be used only to help formulate an idea, not to furnish a complete definition.

There are several analogies that can be used to assist in establishing the idea of accurate intonation. One analogy is that of a marksman with his rifle. The marksman aims to hit the center of the target—the bull's-eye. A musician also aims at a target with each note he performs, but the target in this case exists in sound, with the center determined by physical laws of sound. When the student hits the bull's-eye with his tone, his intonation will be good and the sound will have a "trueness" about it. When he starts hitting around the edges of the target, the pitch will be off and the intonation poor. If he just plain misses the target, then he produces a wrong note. In some ways wrong notes are not as hard to correct as faulty intonation, because they are so obviously wrong.

The teacher may also suggest to the students the analogy of tuning in a television set. The selector may be on the right channel, and yet there is a fine-tuning knob to make the picture sharp and clear. Again, achieving good intonation is something like focusing a camera so that the picture is not blurred or fuzzy.

To provide a more concrete experience with pitch, the science teacher might be invited to give the class a short, simple demonstration of the physical properties of sound. Few students fail to be fascinated by a well-planned demonstration of acoustics. It is especially valuable for them to hear the simultaneous sounding of tuning forks that are two or three double vibrations apart. The "beats" created by this phenomenon are a genuine revelation to the students.

POOR METHODS OF TONE PRODUCTION

Poor methods of producing the sound have a pronounced effect on the ability of a group to perform with good pitch. On wind instruments it is more a matter of consistency than it is of the general pitch level, which is regulated by the tuning. There are few things as frustrating for a teacher as the presence of a brass player with a "mobile" embouchure. Each time he plays a tone with a different lip formation he produces a slightly different pitch. It is impossible to tune such a player. Some reed players tend to bite down on the reed when under tension, and a sharpness in pitch is the result. Some brass players when tense press the mouthpiece back hard against the lips, and this causes pinching and sharping, plus other unfortunate complications.

The correction of such problems on winds lies in working not on intonation directly, because in this case it is a symptom, but rather on the fundamentals of playing the instrument. The cure for this type of intonation problem requires attention to points inadequately covered in the early instruction of the pupil.

In singing, pitch is likewise affected when the sounds are strained or inconsistently produced. If no proper singing routine has been established, then the pitch of a tone is subject to every psychological and physiological vagary.

The practice of "scooping" or "shoveling" is harmful to accurate pitch. Although some popular solo singers use the device almost constantly, teenage students need to be told of the damage this can cause in a group. Frequently the cause of scooped first notes is a lack of mental and physical preparation on the part of the singer.

Vowels that are not uniform can be detrimental to intonation. This is primarily due to the different timbres present when the vowels are not produced in a similar manner by all the singers. Uniform vowel production is more easily achieved when the singers retain an open throat position and confine the changes for different sounds to the front of the mouth and lips.

PSYCHOLOGICAL FACTORS

Since music is so involved with emotion and feeling, it is not surprising that pitch is affected by the psychological condition of the students. As has been said, the best corrective for faulty intonation is alertness and understanding on the part of the students. Anything that dulls their acuity will impair intonation. One teacher has been known to spend an entire class period on a single piece of music. Any teacher, vocal or instrumental, who does this should expect the intonation to suffer.

Singing is especially susceptible to the psychological condition of the singers. They can become tired of singing in a particular key. Choral groups do perceive a tonal difference when a piece is transposed a half step up or down. Some songs are rarely sung in tune when performed in the original key. An example of this is the familiar "Silent Night," which can usually be sung with better intonation when transposed up a half step from the original key of C major. Attention should be given to the range when transposing keys. If the top tones become too high, then perhaps transposing down is more practical. However, the basses must not be asked to sing so low that they either rumble or stop singing.

Sometimes students sing the wrong pitch because they are inattentive or indifferent. One individual picks up the pitch from his neighbor, who in turn may be doing the same thing from someone else. If many singers do this, the right pitch can become pretty well lost.

Singers are often affected emotionally and mentally by changes in the dynamic level of the music, and their reactions, in turn, affect the pitch level. This is often found when groups have sung continuously at a *forte* dynamic level. When they attempt to sing a soft section, they will frequently go out of tune; their attention is likely to decrease and a psychological relaxation sets in, resulting in a feeble, unsupported tone, and a subsequent flatting of pitch. The singers should be made aware of these physical tendencies to relax or to overexert themselves as they vary the dynamic level. To overcome such tendencies in his singers, the teacher can provide drills using either simple scales in unison, or four-part chords, with slow changes in dynamics followed by rapid changes of *forte* to *piano* and back to *forte*.

The solution to psychologically caused intonation problems in both vocal and instrumental groups is to re-examine the fundamentals of music teaching discussed in Chapter Seven. Especially significant is the matter of pacing and spacing work on a piece of music, and the principle of distributed effort. Some psychological causes, such as nervousness in public appearances, are overcome only through experience.

Closely related to a person's alertness is his physical condition on a particular day. Colds sometimes affect the ability to hear, and cause general sluggishness. The voice is especially susceptible to the physical condition of the body. Sometimes it is said of a person, "His voice sounds tired," and it is true. When the energies of many students in a group are consumed in an event such as a basketball tournament or a school play, this is apparent in the tired sound and the increased amount of out-of-tuneness.

ENVIRONMENTAL FACTORS

Atmospheric conditions can play havoc with intonation. Not only does hot, humid weather deplete the musicians, causing singers to flat; it affects the quality of tone from reeds. They sound soggy, flat, and listless. Other instruments are affected as well. The tendency for strings is to lower in pitch, and the tendency for brasses and winds is to rise. Probably the most critical problem exists at the outdoor concert on a cool night. The end of the horn nearest the player's mouth is kept warm with breath, while the far end is cool. Each time the player rests for a few moments, the instrument cools and becomes flatter.

Sometimes faulty intonation can be traced to environmental factors in the classroom. Chairs of the wrong type are a hindrance to proper posture. Poor ventilation will affect the physical condition of the students, so one of them can be appointed to be responsible for raising and lowering windows. Overcrowding has an adverse effect on the group. If string players are so confined that they have hardly enough room for a full bow stroke, their physical discomfort will be readily apparent in the sound. Such a situation can only encourage intonation problems.

Acoustical conditions vary from room to room. If the students are accustomed to rehearsing in a "live" room, and are confronted with an auditorium that is acoustically dead, they will tend to overextend in their effort to combat these altered conditions, or they will become frightened and emit only tight little sounds of uncertain pitch.

CHARACTERISTICS OF INSTRUMENTS

The instrumental music teacher has an additional responsibility. He must cope with mechanical frailties and strive to overcome them, and must develop a sense of proper pitch within his students.

Wind Instruments

Errors of pitch are inherent in all wind instruments. The first step is to convince wind-instrument players that they do indeed have to be concerned with intonation. It is obvious to string players and singers that they have to be concerned about pitch, but not so with the student who gets a note by pushing valves or keys. As one student told his teacher, "But I know my clarinet is perfectly in tune. The man at the store who sold it to my dad said so." The techniques suggested on page 208 will help to drive home the need for attention to intonation. The teacher can say, "When you push down the right fingers, you are only in the vicinity of the note, not exactly on it. Getting exactly on pitch is your job."

Next, the student should be taught what tones are chronically out of tune on his instrument. Some of these are predictable, such as the 1-2-3 valve combination on brasses and the throat tone B flat on clarinets, but others depend on the unique qualities of the student's instrument and his manner of playing it. These troublesome pitches become evident through the efforts of the group to achieve good intonation. It is the successful teacher who says to his first flutist, "Barbara, you know that D flat is sharp on your instrument, so humor it down as much as you can."

The teacher's directive to "humor" the pitch down raises the simple question: how? There are both technical and psychological approaches to doing this. Woodwind fingerings can be varied to change the pitch slightly. On the clarinet, covering the holes with the second and third fingers of the left hand when playing throat tone B flat and using the little finger of the right hand on the E flat key on certain high notes are examples of this. Alternative fingerings are available on brasses, especially on the French horn, which can also vary pitch by the degree to which the tone is stopped by the right hand in the bell. Flutes may tip just a bit to alter the angle between the blowhole and the lips, tipping away to sharpen and turning in to flatten. When a flutist does this, he should think of moving his head slightly, and not the flute. The tension or "squeeze" of the lips and jaw on the reed affects the pitch of such instruments. An advanced player can be very precise in his use of this technique, and secondary school players can make use of it, too, provided that they have a fairly well-established embouchure. Brass players also can make slight adjustments by regulating the amount of tension in the lips. The teacher should learn as many special fingerings and techniques as possible, so that he can help his advanced students.

Although it is hard for instrumentalists to realize, just thinking about sounding a pitch sharper or flatter will cause some changes of throat and tongue tension, intensity of the air stream, openness of the throat, and adjustment of embouchure that will effect a pitch change. So when the first flutist Barbara is told to lower her D flat, she is conscious of making certain responses to accomplish this, and she can also "think" of playing the pitch flatter.

Woodwind instruments that have chronic problems can sometimes be improved in the hands of a knowledgeable and skillful repairman. There is hardly a professional orchestra member who has not had some holes made smaller and flatter by filling, pads raised or lowered, or a hole made larger to sharpen it.

Sometimes instruments can be adjusted at points other than the usual tuning place. For example, if a clarinet is sharp on its usual tuning note of C, but in tune on throat tones, it can be "pulled" somewhat at the center joint. On brasses, the entire relationship between fingered notes is altered when the main tuning slide is changed very much. The procedure for getting the individual valve slides in tune is as follows:

1) Play the second open tone (G on trumpet, F on bass clef baritone, etc.).
2) Play the same tone with the first and third valves. Frequently this tone is sharp to the open tone.
3) Pull out the first valve tuning slide slightly and the third valve slide twice as much.
4) Experiment until the pitches of the fingered and open note match exactly.
5) Play one whole step higher (A on trumpet, etc.) with first and second valves.
6) Compare it with same note played with third valve only. If the first and second valve pitch is higher than the third valve pitch, the third valve slide has been pulled too far and the first valve slide has not been pulled far enough.
7) Experiment until the pitch of the two fingerings is exactly the same.
8) Check open tone G against the first and third valve G.
9) If this is not in tune, repeat the procedure until the fullest possible pitch agreement has been attained.

The second valve is so short that it has little effect. It can be checked on the trumpet by comparing B played with the second valve against B played with the first and third valves.

The quality of a student's instrument has much to do with the quality of its intonation. Possibly the most noticeable difference between an economy and a quality instrument is in its tuning properties. The teacher should make every effort to convince parents that a quality instrument, not necessarily a luxury instrument, is well worth the additional cost in terms of the satisfaction the student can get from it, to say nothing of the additional resale value.

A special problem with wind instruments is the influence of the dynamic level upon pitch. Clarinets tend to lower in pitch as they crescendo, while brasses tend to sharpen. This phenomenon causes an interesting but undesirable pitch discrepancy at the extremes of dynamic range. Players must be taught through the use of the techniques cited earlier to compensate for this. It should be added that the stiffer the reed used on reed instruments, the less the pitch is affected by dynamic level.

String Intonation

When instruction is first offered on strings, only students with good sense of pitch should be allowed to start. A string student who cannot hear pitch accurately only frustrates himself and his teacher. For checking pitch sense, the teacher may use the Seashore or Wing tests. Oddly, a lack of ability to sing in tune does not always indicate a poor sense of pitch.

The teacher of strings needs to stress slow and careful work. A primary cause of bad pitch on strings lies in asking the students to play something too difficult for them, something for which they have not yet developed adequate neuro-muscular control. When string players are pushed into higher positions for which they are not ready, the intonation will undoubtedly suffer. Many times intonation is improved when the teacher has the group play the music at half speed. This gives the players additional time to think, move fingers, and listen; and the result is better pitch.

Many times faulty intonation on strings is caused by a poor left hand position. On violin and viola, young players sometimes display three habits that make for a lack of consistency in the placement of the fingers on the strings. One: the player allows his wrist to bend or become unstable. Two: he turns his hand so that he sees the palm rather than the lateral edge. This places his fingers far from the strings and causes him to be less efficient in finding the proper pitch at the proper moment. Three: he allows the neck of the instrument to rest on the joint connecting the index finger and palm. This causes tension and cramping in the hand, and reduces the accuracy and facility of the fingers, particularly on the highest string. This habit can be best observed by viewing the player from his left side.

Inaccurate pitch also results when the string player does not think of the pitch he is trying to get. He must hear the pitch in his mind and associate it with kinesthetic sensing of where the hand and finger should be placed. Slow, careful practice helps to achieve this.

The effect of vibrato on string intonation is a fascinating topic, but it has little practical application for the school music teacher. Vibrato greatly improves the tone of the player, and it may, because of its pitch fluctuations, make the intonation appear to be better, although an argument can be had among string teachers on this point. At least vibrato will not harm pitch if the player is ready for it—that is, if he can place his fingers consistently and unerringly on the proper notes.

Procedures for Instrumental Music Class

1) Teach the students to tune their instruments. As elementary as this step may appear to be, it is surprising and distressing how many teen-age musicians cannot do this properly. Allow sufficient time for the development of such a skill; it cannot be taught in one fifteen-minute lesson. Furthermore, the student himself must be given a chance to judge the tuning. The temptation is to say, "Dave, pull the slide out just a little," without giving Dave the opportunity to find out for himself. In teaching students, their attention needs to be drawn to the "beating" of out-of-tune notes, and the tonal characteristics that identify one tone as being sharper or flatter than another. Strings, of course, must learn to tune fifths. Not only is accurate tuning necessary for good intonation; the process involved gives the students good experience in learning what is meant by being "in tune."

2) Tune wind instruments to pitches other than the usual concert B flat. Because of the construction of many instruments in B flat, this particular pitch may sound good when played on several instruments, while a concert G or F sharp may be quite foul. Tuning on more than one pitch will give a more valid means of setting the over-all pitch of the instrument.

3) Take two identical instruments, perhaps clarinets. Have them tune perfectly on the usual third-space C. As they sound the C in unison and in tune, have one player transfer to the C an octave higher. Nine times out of ten this note is sharp on a clarinet, and the students can hear the "beating" caused by the out-of-tuneness. This technique works to some extent on wind instruments on almost all pitches one octave apart.

4) Instruct two players to take the major third C–E and tune it up to everyone's satisfaction. Then have each player move up a semitone to C sharp–E sharp, or a whole step to D–F sharp. The new third will usually be out of tune and require adjustment. The players can progress to other thirds with similar results.

5) Have the group play Bach chorales, unison scales and arpeggios, and chord studies—slowly and carefully. Tones that are flat or sharp should be corrected on the spot.

6) During practice on the regular repertoire, work out passages in which the intonation is faulty. Learning to play in tune should not be isolated from learning music.

7) Use the tape recorder to analyze intonation.

CHORAL INTONATION

Because of the characteristics of the human voice, and because singers do not have the benefit of the established pitches that instrumentalists enjoy, certain factors of intonation relate largely to choral groups.

Range and Tessitura

The intonation of the human voice is affected by the range of the music and by the tessitura—the average or median pitch of the vocal line, excluding the occasional note at the extreme of the range. Whether strain is caused by attempting to sing a note in an extreme range or by singing too long in an uncomfortable tessitura, the effort breeds out-of-tune singing. When this occurs, it is not so much the fault of the students as it is of the teacher, who selected music too difficult for the voices of his students. Occasionally one or two notes, which might throw an entire phrase off pitch, can be altered or given to another part. For instance, a few tenors might help the basses with some high notes, or a few altos might help the tenors. This gives the line more support and helps retain pitch, while giving the singers more confidence on the difficult passage.

Tempo

A piece of music in a slow tempo is more difficult to sing in tune than one in a rapid tempo. This statement should not be interpreted to mean that if a work such as "Adoramus Te Christe" by Palestrina cannot be sung in tune at a slow tempo, then the tempo should be increased until the piece is in tune. The end—music—should never be sacrificed for the sake of a technical element such as intonation. It may help the singers if they think of a continuous forward motion, or of tonal energy moving ahead; the notes are not static like big stagnant pools.

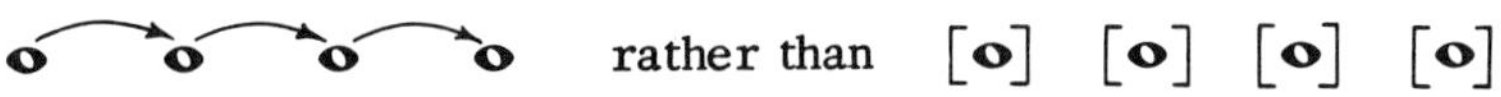

On the first long tones in "Adoramus Te Christe" the singers should mentally lean toward the next syllable of the word. This will help them to sustain their pitch, without destroying the intent of the music.

Modes

Singers, along with string players and trombonists, lack the automatic means which other instruments enjoy of producing a pitch that is at least approximately right. They must hear and produce correctly pitches that are presented in unfamiliar ways. In present-day American culture, the preponderance of music is in the major, or Ionian mode. This cultural conditioning makes intonation difficult in pieces that contain other tonalities.

Before introducing a song in a minor key, the teacher may wish to have his students sing various pentatonic and minor scales, drawing attention to the intervals and how they differ from those in the major scales. In the minor mode, the melodic intervals particularly difficult to keep in tune are the minor third between steps 1 and 3, and the major second between steps 7 and 8 in the unaltered form.

Modulations

While modulation to a closely related key almost never causes a problem, modulations that in one way or another are unusual present difficulties. What the teacher must do is carefully accustom the ears of the students to the musical logic of the harmonies. As the sounds are being made familiar, the teacher may be able to offer tips to the musicians which will help them find the new notes. For example, in the "Coronation Scene" from *Boris Godunov*[3] the solo of Boris ends on a G chord and the chorus, with only the aid of a trilled G, must start singing an E flat chord.

The teaching steps, which probably will have to be repeated on several different days, consist first of hearing the last measure of the solo, then the trill, and then the chorus' chord. Next the teacher can point out that the first sopranos have the same note as the trill, the second sopranos have the root of the chord a major third below, the altos the fifth of the chord, and so on. If the students have had some practice at finding chord members,

[3] Copyright, 1938, by E. C. Schirmer Music Co., Boston, Mass., and used with their permission.

as was suggested earlier, each section may quickly practice finding its note when given the E flat chord, then when given only the trilled note. Finally, the spot can be practiced as written with the piano accompaniment. Similar but less involved procedures can be used with less difficult changes of key, such as the sudden chromatic modulation to a key a semitone higher.

Intervals

When singers and string players perform a series of ascending chromatics, their tendency is to miss just slightly getting all notes up to pitch. With descending chromatic passages, the inclination is to overshoot and end below pitch. There is often a tendency to undershoot all ascending wide intervals. The appearance of the interval—the way it is written enharmonically—also affects the accuracy of its performance. Although the good aural judgment of the students should prevail, with groups that are not particularly experienced it is advisable to say "Lean a bit on the sharp side as you go up for that top note."

The other notes in the chord likewise affect intonation. For example, it is much more difficult to sing an accurate B natural against a C than against a D. One of the most taxing chores for a secondary school teacher is to teach a group to perform a modern work with much dissonance and have the dissonant pitches in tune. What is intended to be a healthy dissonance sometimes becomes discord because of poor intonation. A dissonant work demands slow, careful practice, and much orientation to the new sounds.

Lack of Ensemble

A final reason for intonation problems is what might be termed "lack of ensemble." Sometimes, especially in choral groups, the musician feels much like a man out in the middle of the ocean trying to keep his head above water. The group plays or sings along and the student can scarcely hear himself, least of all hear what the other sections are doing.

There can be many reasons for this inability to hear other parts. The individual, or the people around him, may be too loud; the other sections may be too weak, or located so that they are difficult to hear. It is important, however, that the students develop a mental control of their music-making. Many times the "lost" sensation is prevalent among teenage musicians because they are participating on an instinctive, unthinking level.

In vocal music when a group has been singing in a raucous, out-of-tune manner, a calming effect can be produced by this simple device: have each student place his hand or finger over his ear when singing. This seems to center all his attention on the mental control of his singing, besides permitting him to hear himself. If the student becomes aware of what to listen for in music, of fitting his voice in with the section and the group, and if he is on the alert for sagging pitch and other errors in singing, much of the "lost in the ocean" feeling will disappear.

Another cause of lack of ensemble in vocal music is the inability of the students to hear the piano. If this occurs during public performance, the students are at a distinct disadvantage; the audience is likely to hear both piano and singers and is thereby provided with a constant pitch comparison. This problem can usually be remedied if the position of the piano is changed, or its lid opened. The group can sing more softly and the accompanist can play more loudly. As the group advances, less and less dependence should be placed on the piano. After all, the piano is intended to accompany the singers, not supplant them. When the piano is used to give the pitches of *a cappella* singing, the notes must be struck with sufficient volume to be heard by all the singers. Even if the audience hears these pitches, this is preferable to the hesitant, out-of-tune start that results when singers cannot find their starting notes.

Procedure for Vocal Music Class

Here are some simple procedures that can be used to develop the students' listening powers in vocal music.

1) Play a tone on the piano and ask some individual to match that tone, using a neutral syllable. When he has attempted to sing back the pitch, ask the group or another student if the rendition was flat, sharp, or exactly on pitch.

2) Have the group carefully sing major scales and chords. At first, the students should sing each note simultaneously with the piano or immediately after the piano has sounded the note. When the group can sing accurately in this manner, play the entire chord or scale and have the students repeat it unaccompanied. After several weeks, give the students a pitch and tell them to sing a chord or scale from it. Initially, major scales and chords should be used. If minor chord and scale types are given before the major type is learned thoroughly, the result will be a hybrid of major and minor. Before a group should progress to the outlining of minor triads, it must know and be able to execute major triads very well, which often requires several weeks or months. This does not preclude the singing of songs in minor, however, because if singing in major is accurate, the minor when it appears in a song seems to take care of itself automatically. Accuracy must be emphasized to the students at all times during such exercises. Triads should be sung from the root, third, and fifth. Unless the students are used to the solfeggio syllables, it is best to use numbers or a neutral syllable for the drills on the following page. Do not forget to have a section or an individual sing these alone once in a while.

3) After chords and triads are familiar to the singers, give them a chord and have them trade parts. For example, the first time the basses can take

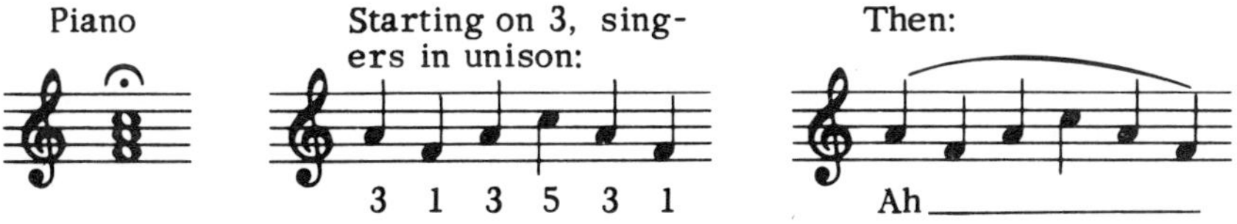

the root or 1, tenors and altos 3, and sopranos 5; the next time the basses take 5, tenors 1, altos 5, and sopranos 3.

4) Play a chord on the piano, call out "one," "three," or "five," and have the entire group or section sing back the proper chord member. This procedure can be made more elaborate by calling out a complete chord with correct doubling, so that there is one chord member for each section. The use of chord imagery not only makes the students more conscious of pitch; it also gives them a technique for finding the correct notes at the beginning of a phrase, a skill that is of the utmost value in choral music.

5) Have the group sing a familiar melody, unaccompanied and on a neutral syllable. Start the singers by using a conductor's beat, and at some given point indicate by a prearranged signal that they are to stop singing aloud. They continue singing silently in their "mind's ear," following the conductor's beat, until they see the signal to resume singing aloud again. This gives them excellent practice in thinking pitches accurately.

6) Encourage the singers to try some harmonizing by ear outside the regular class situation. This makes them conscious of tuning their voices with others. Naturally, harmonizing by ear is not recommended on the regular four-part music, but there are many familiar melodies that are well-adapted to impromptu harmonizing.

7) When the group is singing a work of music, stop on any chord that is being sung out of tune, and rebuild the chord in tune with the help of the piano. It is important not to let the singers become accustomed to poor intonation.

8) Make use of the tape recorder. The students can be more objective about their ability to sing in tune when they hear a recording of their singing.

Questions

1. What reasons might a vocal music teacher give for having a group sing a piece with the piano in order to stay on pitch, rather than sing unaccompanied with poor intonation?

2. Which aspect of unaccompanied singing should the teacher emphasize: staying in tune within the group itself, or being able to finish the song exactly on the properly notated pitch?
3. What is wrong with each of these examples of teaching as it pertains to intonation?
   a. With a pained expression on his face, Mr. Jones complains to his group, "You're out of tune! *Out of tune!* OUT OF TUNE!"
   b. Mrs. Knapp says to her girls' glee club, "Now sopranos, we're going over this piece until you can sing it in tune."
   c. Miss Artz tells her string players, "Just play everything a little higher than you think you should. That will keep us from going flat."
   d. On a warm May afternoon Miss Carson has had her singers sitting for over half an hour. As they finish a song out of tune, she whines, "Now, there you are, flat again!"

Projects

1. Think of two analogies in addition to those mentioned on page 202 which a teacher can use to describe proper intonation.
2. Listen to a trumpet, cornet, French horn, trombone, and tuba each play middle C. Have the players tune to this pitch until the intonation satisfies you. Notice how the timbre of each affects the impression you get of the pitch of the instrument.
3. Talk to a specialist on a wind instrument that is comparatively unfamiliar to you. Ask him which notes on the instrument are most difficult to play in tune, and what he does to compensate for these notes. Ask him how the dynamic level of the music and the weather affect the pitch of the instrument. Request that he play the same pitch several times using a slightly different embouchure each time; as he does this, notice the effect on the pitch.
4. If you are a wind-instrument player, take a trumpet and pull the tuning slide out at least two inches. Then tune the individual valve slides. (If you are not a wind player, observe someone do this.)
5. Have two classmates who play the same wind instrument bring their instruments to class. Listen to them as they tune notes an octave apart. Also listen to them tune major thirds as they raise the pitch level by a semitone.
6. Have the class without accompaniment sing two stanzas of "Silent Night" in C major, carefully checking the pitch with the piano at the end. Then have them sing it in C sharp major, again checking the pitch at the end. Notice which is easier to sing in tune.
7. Have the class sing in tempo a well-known song such as "Dixie," checking the pitch carefully at the end. Then request that they sing through the song

at a much slower tempo, and again check the pitch at the end. Compare the accuracy of pitch of the two singings.

8. In a choral work, find a place that contains a sudden modulation to a foreign key. Plan how you would teach the passage to a school group. Determine what clues the music gives the singers to help them find the new notes.
9. Do some research into the acoustical basis of timbre. Determine why two identical pitches of different tone qualities might give the impression that they are not in tune.

Suggested Readings

Ralph R. Pottle, *Tuning the School Band and Orchestra* (published by the author, Hammond, Louisiana, 1962).

Donald W. Stauffer, *Intonation Deficiencies of Wind Instruments in Ensemble* (Washington, D.C.: The Catholic University of America Press, 1954). Chapters III, VII.

XI

school music performances

Janet Grissom had just started her new job at Westport High School. As she went to check her mailbox in the office, the principal said to her, "Oh, Miss Grissom, better get your concert dates set on the school calendar by a week from Friday, because we want to get the thing mimeographed by then." Janet checked last year's school calendar and set dates for programs at approximately the same time for the coming school year. But as she was making plans for her next day's classes, she wondered, "Just how will the material I'm teaching now be related to the concert I've set in May, or in December, for that matter? I haven't even decided what to do—just set a date for a program." After another moment of thought she pondered, "Really now, why am I having programs in the first place? Why particularly in December and May? Without thinking, I just followed the pattern of the former music teacher. Why should I have these programs? Should I have more? What kind of programs should I present?"

To begin to answer Janet Grissom, one has to go back to the question raised in Chapter Two: why is music included in the curriculum of the school? The goals of music education are crucial for determining why there are performances and what they should be like. Since a performance is so involved with what a music teacher's work is all about, the two should not and cannot be segmented. Performance is a part, not an end, of the educational process in music.

In 1951 the MENC stated that public performances by school musicians should:[1]

[1] *Music in American Education*, Hazel Nohavec Morgan, ed. (Washington, D.C.: Music Educators National Conference, 1955), p. 305.

1) Present a vital goal toward which students may strive.
2) Lead to outstanding programing and achievement.
3) Promote continued interest in and enthusiasm for music in the school and in the community.
4) Bring to parents and others in the community an understanding of the significance of music in education.
5) Improve the standards of musical taste in the school and in the community.
6) Be a means of stimulating creative, artistic, and social growth of pupils.

Generally when a music teacher thinks of the word "performance" he has in mind the formal presentation as done on the concert stage or in the symphony hall. He may even regard a school concert as a diminutive version of a formal professional performance. Yet both logic and the MENC report indicate that the school music teacher needs to think of the word in a somewhat different light. Four of the six points listed, numbers 1, 2, 3, and 6, mention outcomes in terms of education of the participants—points that would not be mentioned in conjunction with a concert by a fine symphony orchestra.

These educational purposes, both for the students and the audience, are the most significant way in which a school performance distinguishes itself. For the students, the program should be an outgrowth of the work carried on normally in class. A good concert will have interest and variety mainly because the class has interest and variety. For the audience, which is usually largely made up of friends and relatives of the participants, the performance should teach something about music and inform them about what the school is teaching in its music courses.

Performances should include all students who study music in performing classes. The temptation, of course, is to concentrate on the most talented students because they present a more favorable picture of what is being done in music. A chorus of seventy-five may present a musical comedy built around two or three principals and five or six minor roles. The other sixty-five students sing a few simple chorus parts, make scenery, assist with make-up, and pull the curtain. The principal performers sometimes get an overinflated view of their abilities and contributions to the good of the group. This is not to say that the talented students should not be given additional opportunities, but they should never be given special attention to the detriment of the others. For example, the teaching of a solo number should take place in private lessons, or before or after school, not during class while the rest of the students sit as onlookers.

Class time is an important consideration in making a performance educationally valid. The unfortunate thing about many operettas and shows is that far more time is required to memorize spoken lines, stage directions, and dance steps than is needed to learn the music. Thus, much time in music class is spent on matters only distantly related to music.

In some cases, however, an operetta or musical is justified by the state of music in the school and community. In one junior high school so little had been done musically that apathy and ignorance marked the reaction of nearly everyone toward the music curriculum. The teacher had the seventh and eighth graders put on a short musical, and although it was, as she freely admitted, definitely of amateur quality, it generated new enthusiasm for the possibilities offered by school music.

A second difference between a school and professional concert is the psychological and social value that should accrue to the participants. This point is mentioned as a part of number 6 in the MENC listing. Since the need for recognition is so great in teen-agers, the necessity for a performance *which the audience regards as successful* is likewise great. A music teacher should not ignore this fact. The listeners should leave the performance with more understanding about music and the school music curriculum, and they must leave with words of praise for the musicians.

How can the teacher help assure a favorable audience reaction and yet maintain good music education? Simply, he must present the music studied in the performing class in a manner that the audience finds interesting and pleasing. In doing this, he should realize that the education of the students and the interest of the audience are not necessarily in opposition to each other. In fact, it is the successful teacher who possesses the ability and imagination to combine the two. It is the less-successful teacher who sees good music education and a high degree of audience enjoyment as irreconcilable, and proceeds either to ignore the listeners or to forget about music education for the sake of audience amusement.

The teacher should realize that success in public performance will in a roundabout way affect the future of his educational efforts in music. Not only will students be motivated to enroll in music courses, which in turn will increase the effectiveness of performing classes, but there will be better support and understanding on the part of the school administration and public. Therefore much of this chapter is devoted to suggestions for making programs pleasing and attractive, while at the same time maintaining their essential purpose in music education.

If performances by school groups are to achieve their goal of being educationally valid and successful in the eyes of the audience, then the teacher needs to keep in mind three additional points. One is the need for informality. Secondary school students are not collegiate or professional musicians, and music teachers should not present concerts that pretend they are. Teen-agers have personality, imagination, and genuine audience appeal, if these attributes are not snuffed out in an oppressive, stiff atmosphere. There is no reason why the teacher cannot offer a few comments about the music during the program; no reason why there cannot be informative notes in the printed program, and no reason why a class activity other than performance cannot be shown to the audience. Music teachers have sometimes overlooked the fact that people may be curious about the simplest things: how a French horn player who has been resting for twelve measures knows when to come in, how the singers know which note of a chord to start on, and what a conductor does to indicate loud and soft.

The second point is the age of the students. Younger students can and should be presented with greater informality. A seventh-grade class can present a program using the water glasses it has tuned in order to study the intervals of the scale and tuning, or it may sing a simple unison folk song with Autoharp accompaniment. A senior high school group, however, should present more polished performances and more sophisticated music, simply because that is the level at which it studies music. The differences between the professional and school concert still exist; there is merely a difference of degree depending on the age of the performers.

The third point concerns the attitude of the teacher toward performance. If a concert is an outgrowth of classwork, then it should be treated as such. Some teachers think that by whipping up effort in the name of the almighty performance, they will achieve the optimum effort from the students. Unfortunately they usually achieve the optimum effort plus tension, fear, and stiffness. Who has not heard groups in which the performers were so afraid of making an error that they just sneaked along through the music? Certainly this is a misuse of performance. A month's work is not ruined because of a missed entrance in a concert; a month's work can only be lost in the classroom. The teacher should not get the cart before the horse here. His primary purpose is the musical education of teen-agers, and not the presentation of flawless performances.

TYPES OF PROGRAMS

All programs by school groups have a common need for the performance of quality music in an informative and interesting manner. However, some of the means used to interest the audience and the general atmosphere of the program will vary according to the age level of the audience.

The School Assembly

Most school groups, with the exception of the marching band, perform almost entirely at school assemblies and public programs at the school in the evening. The two situations, school assemblies and adult programs, are by no means the same. The school assembly involves a highly homogeneous audience, an audience made up of the peers and friends of the performers, and an audience that is volatile and responsive. A stiff, formal assembly will not easily draw a favorable response from the student audience.

The rapport which the teacher sets is crucial to the success of the performance. Basically, he should let the assembled students feel that he understands how they view the program they are about to hear and see. He does this by the manner in which he informs them about various facets of the music and gives them something to listen for in each number. For more serious works, he might give the audience a breakdown of the major themes, with the group serving to demonstrate them. He conveys enthusiasm for the program and respect for the listeners. This rapport is delicate and easily lost. One music teacher during an assembly reprimanded some students in the audience who were inattentive. A few days after the performance, some members of the music group politely suggested that he not do that again. Apparently they realized that his action would only alienate the student body, probably not cure the misbehavior, and would put the performers in the uncomfortable position of having a teacher, representing them, publicly drive a wedge between them and their peers.

For many non-music students, the assembly is their only opportunity to hear and see the music groups. This performance will influence their opinions about music, and may determine whether or not they enroll in a music course. Secondary school groups should also give performances for other schools in the district, especially elementary schools. These are less formal occasions, the purpose of which is to educate the students about music and the school music curriculum.

Whatever the age level of the student listeners, the assembly is important to both the immediate and long-range objectives of the music department. Every effort should be put forth by the teacher to schedule such assemblies and to make certain that they are well received.

Assembly Singing

One type of assembly, mentioned often in writings about music education but not seen often enough in actual practice, is the singing assembly. Dykema and Gehrkens[2] and others early in the 1940's and Sur and Schuller[3] in the late 1950's placed considerable emphasis on this kind of performance. It is difficult to say why the singing assembly is not more prevalent. One conjecture is that the situation reflects the general American tendency to sit and watch someone else play baseball, act in a play, or make music. It may be that as a nation we have forgotten the value of simple pleasures such as singing. In large high schools, it is true, the sheer size of the audience makes the activity unwieldy. Furthermore, high schools often have more assemblies than they can comfortably schedule. These facts, however, do not detract from the basic worth that prominent

[2] Peter W. Dykema and Karl W. Gehrkens, *The Teaching and Administration of High School Music* (Evanston, Ill.: Summy-Birchard Publishing Company, 1941), pp. 41–53.

[3] William R. Sur and Charles F. Schuller, *Music Education for Teen-Agers* (New York: Harper & Brothers, 1958), pp. 176–182.

music educators have attributed to the singing assembly. If music is to reach all students at the high school level, it must be done through assemblies. And if the making of music by people other than trained musicians is to be encouraged, good assembly singing is a significant activity.

How does the music teacher see to it that assembly singing is successful? First, he must make a shrewd assessment of the circumstances in which the assembly will be held: the atmosphere of the auditorium or gymnasium, the availability of a good accompanist, the number of students involved, their experience with such activities and the behavior at assemblies in general, and finally the experience of the teacher in directing community singing. No assembly at all is better than one which is a failure. The teacher must take stock of the situation and correct the weaknesses that can be remedied. If inexperience is the problem, it may be better to start singing in junior high school assemblies, and year by year work them into the senior high school level. The first attempts should not consume an entire period. Possibly during an assembly by a performing group, one number involving the audience could be tried. The teacher can simply turn around and say, "Now, we've sung for you a while; let's try one song together." The student body can sing a well-known tune while the choir sings a descant. This produces a satisfying musical result with a minimum of time and effort.

As part of the preparation, students in choral music classes can learn the songs to be sung. If they are not performing elsewhere in the program, they can be spotted advantageously around the hall in order to take the lead in their immediate area.

Careful attention needs to be given the choice of music for assembly singing. Generally, familiar songs are better choices, as are songs which are "solid," direct, and simple. For example, "Down in the Valley" is better for assembly singing that "Shenandoah," even though the latter is a more aesthetically satisfying piece of music. Some schools may attempt more sophisticated songs and more complex part-singing, but this should come only after other successful singing assemblies on a less pretentious level.

The best way to present words to an unfamiliar song is to project them on a screen. Song sheets or books are all right, but they have to be passed out and collected, and papers are sure to be fumbled by some students. Slides can be made on regular 35mm film by photographing sheets of words, or the material can be printed by hand on sheets of glass 3¼ by 4 inches in size.[4] A motion picture that is easily available demonstrates the necessary techniques for making the slides.[5] The teacher may also want to

[4] Slides of copyrighted words or music may be made only if written permission is secured from the holder of the copyright.

[5] *How To Make Handmade Lantern Slides,* 16mm, sound, color, 20 min. Indiana University.

project still pictures appropriate to the songs. DeBernardis and Ernst report that still pictures hold the attention of the audience to an amazing degree.[6]

A good aggressive accompanist is an absolute necessity for such an assembly. Anyone who has attempted to lead singing with a timid and faltering pianist knows how the entire effort at audience participation can be frustrated, along with the song leader.

Several modern English composers, among them Benjamin Britten and Ralph Vaughan Williams, have written into works of music simple parts for the audience.[7] Before the actual presentation, a few minutes are spent rehearsing the audience on its part.

Informal Programs

So far the discussion of music presentations has centered upon the band, orchestra, or choral organization, each of which is primarily a performance-oriented class. These are not the only groups, however, that appear before the public. General music classes, frequently in combination with other sections of the same course, may perform once or twice a year. In addition, performing organizations make less formal appearances, such as the "Parents' Night" mentioned earlier. On these occasions audience interest should be achieved by showing the learning activities of the class. Students can play portions of recordings they have heard, and offer explanatory comments; they can display the music notebooks they have compiled; they can describe current class projects. The Autoharp can be used to accompany songs, and part-singing can demonstrate the use of changing voices.

With performances of this type, attempts at a formal, professional presentation are out of character. The appeal to the audience lies in the personalities of the students and their own unique response to the music. Instead of entitling a performance "Spring Concert by West Junior High School," it might be called "Music at West" or "Invitation to Music at West Junior High School." People appreciate an unassuming program appropriate to the age and nature of the students.

Programs Outside of School

School groups are often invited to perform for community organizations. It may be necessary for the teacher to apportion carefully the number of such appearances so that the educational purpose of the music group does not suffer. If refusals for performances around the com-

[6] Amos DeBernardis and Karl Ernst, "Pictures and Music," *NEA Journal* (November 1949), p. 616.

[7] *The Little Sweep* and *Noye's Fludde*, by Benjamin Britten, Boosey & Hawkes. *Old Hundredth Psalm Tune*, by Ralph Vaughan Williams, Oxford Music.

munity are necessary, this is usually best handled through a policy statement on out-of-school appearances drawn up by the teacher, student officers, and school administration. In this way the onus does not fall on the teacher individually, and the matter has had the broad consideration of more than one person.

Two special considerations need to be given to performances outside of school. First, they must not infringe upon areas which properly belong to the professional musician. The Code of Ethics, mentioned on page 60, states that school music groups may perform at educational nonprofit, noncommercial functions, as well as at benefit performances for charitable organizations, nonprofit educational broadcasts and telecasts, and civic events that do not usurp the rights and privileges of the local professional musician. Performances by school groups at other civic programs are permissible if they are mutually agreed upon by the school authorities and official representatives of the local musicians' union. Recordings are permitted if they are strictly for education or audition purposes and are not offered for general sale to the public. The professional musician has in his province such events as community concerts and community-centered activities and other nonschool activities, and functions furthering private or public enterprise, partisan or fraternal organizations. The Code says further:

> Statements that funds are not available for the employment of professional musicians, or that if the talents of the amateur musical organizations cannot be had, other musicians cannot or will not be employed, or that the amateur musicians are to play without remuneration of any kind, are all immaterial.[8]

The second consideration is the place of performance. If it is impossible for the group to practice in the new location, the teacher should at least see the surroundings beforehand. Some teachers have had the unfortunate experience of agreeing to sing for the Rotary Club only to find that the Rotary meets in a hotel dining room that is too small to hold both the singers and the Rotarians. If a piano is to be used, the position and quality should be checked.

Television and Radio Performance

Some school groups have the opportunity to be heard and seen on radio and television. The status such an appearance gives a group is great indeed. Because much special preparation is necessary, the teacher should consult the MENC publications on the subject.[9] He should also consult

[8] Code adopted September 22, 1947. Reviewed and reaffirmed in 1948 and again in 1955 by all participating organizations.

[9] Richard Berg, ed., *A Guide to Teaching Music by Television and Radio* (Washington, D.C.: Music Educators National Conference, 1954), and Hazel Nohavec Morgan, ed., *Music in American Education* (Washington, D.C.: Music Educators National Conference, 1955), pp. 220–226.

with the technicians at the local station. Television technicians are generally more concerned with the visual aspects than they are the aural, so the music teacher will need to check carefully to see that the sound is of good quality.

ADJUSTING TO PERFORMANCE CONDITIONS

There are several ways in which a teacher can facilitate the adjustment of the performers to the place of performance and expedite the mechanics of presentation.

If at all possible, the group should practice at least once in the place of performance. The shift from rehearsal room to stage can be difficult for teen-age musicians. The new location sometimes gives the performer an unusual sensation as he plays or sings—sometimes he feels that he is performing alone! The seating or standing arrangement is different, at least to the extent that the distances are altered between musicians and between the conductor and musicians.

During the practice the teacher should check to see whether the students can hear one another, and whether the choral groups can hear the piano. Then he should check the sound from the back of the room. If there are hearing or balance problems, some adjustment of the stage arrangement is called for. Draperies around the back and sides of the stage can be drawn together or apart. The piano can be moved, and its top raised or lowered. In instrumental groups instruments with less volume can be moved forward, and loud instruments can be moved to the back of the stage, where more of the sound is absorbed in the curtains and lost in the gaping ceiling. If seated instrumental risers are available, their use can improve balance and ensemble. The performers should also be forewarned about the effect the audience will have on the acoustics of the room; the sound may be noticeably more "dead."

When a school stage absorbs a great deal of sound, thereby making a group sound weak to the audience, the possibility of a shell should be investigated. Some manufacturing concerns now produce shells that are not only quite adaptable, but even portable. If a commercial shell is too expensive, regular stage flats can be made and painted several times to give them a hard surface. Most important are the overhead panels that keep sound from rising up between the lights and becoming lost. If no other means of support are available, the panels may be suspended.

The choral teacher often finds it feasible to use two arrangements, one for the rehearsal room and one for performance. The rows on the risers may be of a different length from the rows in the rehearsal room. Furthermore, in performance the students are arranged somewhat according to height to prevent unevenness in the appearance of rows, and to prevent tall singers from blocking out the shorter singers standing behind them. When a mixed chorus is arranged by height, the boys, being generally taller than the girls, are often placed in the back and center of the group.

Although a few outstanding collegiate and professional choirs scatter the sections, this technique is too difficult for most school groups. An inexperienced singer needs the confidence and help that are derived from others on his part who are located near him.

The exact arrangement of the vocal or instrumental group is not a vital matter. The traditional seating patterns and placement of sections are based as much on appearance as they are on musical results. Generally the larger and louder instruments are put in the back rows. Considerable experimentation is going on, especially in the case of band,[10] and many unique and valid placement patterns are observed in both choral and instrumental organizations. The teacher should feel free to vary the arrangement according to his personal desires, the size and instrumentation of his group, and the characteristics of the stage, so that the arrangement will produce the optimum in appearance and musical results.

The movements of the groups must be carefully planned. Time and energy can be conserved by having the performers in place when the curtain is opened. Watching one person after another walk onto the stage is not an aesthetically satisfying experience. The girls' heels make a distracting noise, and many of the boys are obviously ill at ease. A row of singers may overshoot its place on the risers and someone from the wings has to signal them all to move back a bit. Why not save valuable class and concert time? Get in place, open the curtain, and start making music.

Upon occasion the group may have to perform where there is no curtain, and the musicians will have to get in place in full view of the audience. With choral groups the simplest way to handle this is to have the front row come out first, then the other rows, starting with the last and working down to the second row. In this way, the first row can somewhat shield the others as they line up. Military marching maneuvers, including the about-face used by some music groups, are out of place. If the students walk in a dignified manner, nothing further is needed to improve their entrance.

If a soloist is to stand in front, provision needs to be made for him. If he is to step forward from his place in the group, a way must be cleared for him, unless he is in the first row. If a music stand is to be moved into position, someone should be assigned this chore. The soloist must know how to acknowledge applause. If he performs from his position in the group, he should be invited to step forward or to stand afterward to receive recognition for his efforts.

The teacher, too, should plan to acknowledge the applause of the audience graciously, with dignity and humility. By stepping to one side

10 Richard Franko Goldman, *The Wind Band: Its Literature and Technique* (Boston: Allyn and Bacon, Inc., 1961), p. 250.

of the stage center and making a modest bow, he subtly acknowledges the fact that the applause is for the students as well as for himself.

Proper deportment before an audience is such an obvious necessity that a teacher may forget to mention it, only to look up at the concert and see a singer chewing gum or a violinist chatting with his desk partner. Each student must be impressed with the fact that his total attention should be on his performance, and that his eyes should be fixed on the director. The students must be strongly admonished about behavior in the event of a mistake. They should not look around, giggle, look startled, or in any other manner show knowledge of an error. They need to be reminded that *someone* in the audience will be looking at each one of them every moment they are on stage.

When students wear robes, uniforms, or similar dress, they should not wear any article of clothing that focuses attention on an individual. Earrings and conspicuous jewelry, hair flowers and ribbons are distracting to the audience and thus are inappropriate, especially for the singing of sacred music.

PLANNING THE PROGRAM

In planning the program, the teacher should keep these points in mind:

1) Select an opening number that will give the students a good start. Choose something that is not very difficult, with a solid beginning and no undue demands for subtleties of intonation or phrasing. The opening number must set a mood of confidence for the performers.

2) Arrange the numbers in meaningful sequence. Some directors make much of putting the heavy, serious numbers at the beginning or end of the concert, the light numbers first or last, and so on. Some go so far as to talk about building up a concert like a crescendo; others mention climaxes. Such considerations seem unrealistic, because what is a high point for one listener may be a low point for another. The only aspect on which there seems to be general agreement is this: works should not be arranged helter-skelter, so that Palestrina winds up next to "De Camptown Races," or Leroy Anderson next to Bach. It is better for the audience and students if the numbers are grouped into logical units such as religious, Baroque, or American music.

3) Check the over-all length of the program. Young teachers in their eagerness sometimes give concerts that are too long. Professional concerts may last for two or more hours, but the patrons of school music programs differ considerably in their musical interests from the patrons of the opera or the symphony. Furthermore, few school groups are of professional calibre. If any misjudgment of time is to be made, err on the side of having the concert too short. It has been said a thousand times: it is better to have the audience leave wishing to hear more, than it is to have them leave glad that their ordeal is over at last. And it is true.

To estimate the length of a program, compute the length of the music, the time for applause between numbers, the time needed to get groups on and off the stage and to move music stands, chairs, and pianos. If an intermission is scheduled, add that time. An intermission is unnecessary when the length of the program is kept within bounds. An hour and fifteen minutes is ample time in which to convince an audience that the music groups are doing fine work. A short concert is easier and more enjoyable for everybody, including the teacher.

4) Plan to keep the program from dragging. Let other teachers or student officers help manage the groups so that when one is through performing, the next is lined up ready to go on stage. Get the performers on and off the stage as quickly as possible. Assign separate rooms to each group so that the students have a place in which to put their coats and cases, do a little warming up, and generally get organized. If the stage has a halfway curtain, small ensembles or soloists can perform from the front half of the stage while another group is quietly getting into place in the back half. If many organizations are participating, it is not necessary to have all groups appear on the stage. A choral group may sing from the balcony of the auditorium, while the band and orchestra remain on stage. In many auditoriums the best place acoustically is immediately in front of the stage in the pit or on the floor. This area can be used just as effectively as the stage area. In any case, plan carefully to keep the program moving.

WAYS TO ENHANCE THE PROGRAM

How is the interest of the audience to be captured by teen-age musicians? What, if anything, is needed beyond the creditable performance of worthwhile music?

One way to add interest is to tie the performance together through the use of a narrator, who may or may not be the teacher. Not only does the narrator integrate the program, he also eliminates "dead spots" between works of music and changes of groups. Another method is to use a variety of groups—ensembles, glee clubs, soloists, stage band, and others. In some cases it is feasible to include groups from both the junior and senior high schools in the performance.

Methods for enhancing the appeal of performances must differ between instrumental and vocal music, for several reasons. The stage setup for a choral performance can be altered rather quickly, since it involves only risers and piano; changes in the instrumental setup require the moving of stands, chairs, podium, music folders, and instruments. Vocal music can, through words, suggest specific actions or props, while even programmatic instrumental music can seldom be treated so exactly. There are differences in length of pieces, with instrumental works usually being longer. Finally, vocal music is generally a more personal, direct experience between performer and listener than is instrumental music.

STAGING VOCAL MUSIC PROGRAMS

The day is passing, if indeed it is not already gone, when a school group can just stand on the risers, sing its program, and thrill the audience. Only groups of exceptional performing ability are able to do this. Motion pictures, television, marching-band shows—all have contributed to the fact that now audiences want programs with some visual as well as aural appeal.

In many communities the concerts have been lifted out of the doldrums by the use of some "staging" of numbers, by no means a new idea in music education.[11] Staging includes many aspects such as props, backdrops, and dress, as well as activities such as dancing and pantomime. For example, in one school a glee club prepared a series of three religious songs. To create the proper atmosphere, the students built a white altar rail to stand in front of the singers, and two artificial stained glass windows. At another concert, the students presented a group of folk songs. This portion of the program was enhanced by having a few students perform an appropriate folk dance to two of the numbers.

Through the use of such techniques, the audience can be educated and interested at the same time. It is easy to forget that many of the listeners cannot fully appreciate what the group is doing. Their attention can be stimulated by a little action or a simple prop. It need not be much, as long as it helps to break what is for them a long spell of watching the students perform from one unvarying position. A program with visual effects permits the performance of the best music under conditions that are far more likely to promote the audience's acceptance of serious music.

Does staging reflect good music education? Yes, if the visual elements are not emphasized to such an extent that they detract from the music. Staging is essentially a means of extending a song from an auditory experience into a visual one as well. The music maintains its proper position as the primary ingredient of the concert.

Staging is good music education because it involves all the students, rather than only the most talented. It presents music in an appealing way without time being spent on spoken lines and complex stage movements. Most important, it allows the teacher to choose the music he wants, rather than accept some second-rate pieces because they are part of a musical play.

The impression should not be given that every number must be staged. Not at all. Probably one out of four is sufficient.

There are many ways in which to develop ideas for visual effects in

[11] George F. Strickling, "Unusual Program Building" MENC Yearbook, XXX (Washington, D.C.: Music Educators National Conference, 1940), 335–39.

choral music. The use of committees has proved to be successful, and, incidentally, it gives the students experience in democratic procedures. Committees of students are formed for each song or group of songs that are to be staged. The categories might include religious music, songs from foreign lands, or excerpts from musical comedies or operettas. The committees meet two or three times during study hall, lunch hour, or before school, to discuss plans. The teacher meets with each committee at least once to exchange ideas with them.

One of the functions of the teacher in these meetings is to point out problems that might arise from some of their ideas. A student may suggest that the group of Negro spirituals be sung in blackface. If the committee goes along with the idea, the teacher will want to point out the amount of effort and time required to put on and remove the make-up, and the fact that it would come off on clothing. It may be advisable to point out the deeper implications of this idea—the social attitudes that are suggested by blackface presentation and the musical inappropriateness of singing serious numbers in a semi-comedy setting.

After each committee, with the teacher's help, comes to an agreement on an idea or two, the thoughts are presented briefly to the whole group, and further refinements are sought. The committees' ideas are usually accepted without change by the entire group.

Next comes implementation of the idea, and another student committee is formed to do this. The membership of these committees is determined by the type of work involved. If a prop is to be built, then boys enrolled in shop courses can do the job. If painting is required, students taking art courses can utilize their talents. Students who have a common study-hall period can work together on a project, and no one will have to be removed from class—always a delicate operation in professional relations. The result is that the greatest share of the planning, purchasing, and actual work is done by the students. Their increased sense of responsibility is a desirable outgrowth of this experience.

Three precautions need to be mentioned. The teacher should never attempt to do extensive staging without the assistance of the students. A little prop may not sound like much work, but when he has to build and paint it himself in addition to his teaching load, that can be too much.

Second, the teacher must *not* assume that he can turn the staging over to the students and go on about his other business. Teen-agers need guidance and assistance—lots of it—in such an undertaking. Many times the teacher will have to tell the students where to go, what to buy, when to work, and how to do the job.

Finally, no group should attempt too many projects, especially the first year. Until the students have had experience in working at such things, they are slow and require much assistance. In addition, the last weeks before a concert are busy enough without the burden of extra projects.

Some props can be used for more than one year, and this makes the second and third year of staged concerts correspondingly easier.

TYPES OF STAGING ACTIVITIES

Here are some staging techniques that students can utilize:

DANCING. Since the whole group cannot sing and dance at the same time, a few individuals are selected to do the dancing. Folk dances, including square dances, are effective, as are tap or soft-shoe dances, if good dancers are available. There are many excellent source books for such dances,[12] and physical education instructors can be most helpful in teaching steps to the students. In selecting a square dance it is wise to choose one in which all the couples are moving most of the time.

A simple idea is to have one or two couples, dressed as they would be for the Junior Prom, perform their own teen-age version of social dancing to one of the better current dance tunes. The routine almost always receives a favorable response from a high school audience.

If at all possible, it is preferable to use dancers who are members of the choral organization. This may create a vacancy in the ranks for some numbers, but the gain in singer morale will make this procedure well worth while. In one school there was a girl who could dance extremely well. She was not in choral music, but came to the teacher to volunteer

[12] Especially good are: Anne Schley Duggan, Jeanette Schlottmann, and Abbie Rutledge, *The Folk Dance Library* (New York: A. S. Barnes and Co., 1948), Edward Durlacher, *Honor Your Partner* (New York: Devin-Adair Co., 1949), and J. Tillman Hall, *Dance!* (Belmont, Calif.: Wadsworth Publishing Co., Inc., 1963).

to dance on a program. When the matter was brought to the students, they flatly turned down the idea of having the nonmember dance with them. They were wise as well as sensitive on this point. Using outside people brings the concomitant problem of when and how to get together for rehearsal.

CHANGE OF DRESS. Variety can be achieved by simple changes of clothing. Since robes hide nearly all clothing worn underneath them, the singers can have one change of dress by merely removing the robe. Many choral teachers feel that it is inappropriate to sing secular and semi-popular songs in robes. Boys in suits and girls in formal gowns are a pleasing sight, and for the singing of less serious numbers, such dress is more appropriate than robes. Cotton skirts and blouses for the girls and bright shirts for the boys give all the change of appearance that is necessary for most folk numbers.

The teacher must allow enough time for a change of dress, designate a place for the change to be made, and provide a room in which to keep the robes or clothing. Boys can usually make such changes faster than girls.

If singers are to wear special clothing in a program, especially suits and formals, they should be given at least two months' notice. Emotional problems can arise in a young person who for reasons of poverty or religious background cannot dress as the other students do.[13] Adequate forewarning cannot solve these problems, but it will give the student more

[13] Frances M. Andrews and Clara E. Cockerille, *Your School Music Program* (Englewood Cliffs, N.J.: Prentice-Hall, Inc., 1958), p. 178.

time to adjust, and allow more time for a solution to be worked out by the school and parents.

LIGHTING. Lights can change the entire atmosphere of a scene. Campfire settings and night scenes with carolers can be suggested with appropriate lights. Many times the mood of the song will suggest some predominant color ("Joshua Fit de Battle of Jericho" might be red); some song titles mention colors. If the stage has a rheostat, infinite variation between dim and bright light is possible. Lighting mixtures should be planned by the teacher with the help of a lighting expert, rather than by a nonmusician. While the lighting should fit the mood of the music, it must never become obtrusive.

PROPS AND SCENERY. The use of props and scenery should be more suggestive than literal. If the action takes place on a Pacific island, then one palm tree is enough to lend atmosphere. If the boys are supposed to be sailors, sailor hats will convey this idea, along with a mop or two for scrubbing the deck, and a few naval flags strung on a rope. To change from one foreign land to another, the flags of the various countries can hang behind the singers, and the spotlight can shift from one flag to another as the occasion requires.

Props and scenery must be kept simple; no waterwheels with real water running over them, please. The school may have pieces of scenery that the dramatics or art teachers have used; these articles may be well-suited to the purposes of the music department. Many stages have a backdrop of a landscape, which is ideal for an outdoor song. The teacher should check with the local fire authorities to be sure that props and scenery do not violate fire regulations.

The music teacher should supervise the building of scenery himself rather than turn it over to the art, shop, or dramatics teachers. It is unfair to burden other teachers with the hard work required by such building projects, when the program is not their responsibility. Also, an embarrassing situation can result if a fellow teacher is not clear on what is wanted. The finished product may not be what the music teacher had in mind. Thus he must either use something he does not like, or break the rules of propriety by not using it at all. There are books available on the building of scenery, but most of them are for complex, literal pieces, unsuited to simple staging requirements. Suggestions for a few basic stage constructions are presented in Appendix E.

ACTION. A few simple pantomime actions can be used to illustrate the words to humorous songs and those with compound repetition, such as "The Twelve Days of Christmas." There is one limitation to this device, however; literal pantomime can make the number look like a kindergarten rendition. For a more mature and effective presentation, attention can be focused on one person who is dressed appropriately and placed toward the front and side of the stage. His actions need not be directly related to the text of the music; in fact, they should be underplayed and completely natural. This technique is well-adapted to songs that are sung *to* or *about* a particular individual. A boy depicting a solitary cowhand can add a lot to the feeling of loneliness inherent in a Western ballad.

A music teacher can become so accustomed to watching the well-coached actions of professional singers that he expects the same enthusiasm and naturalness to be forthcoming from his own students. In one program, three girls were to sing a show tune with certain specific actions suggested by the text. The girls were fine singers, but in the initial stages of preparing the number, they had little idea of what to do while singing. Obviously they could not stand stiff as manikins; that would look ridiculous. First, they were instructed to show the mood of the words by their facial expressions. If they had no other expression in mind, they were to smile. Next they were coached on specific movements of the arms and bodies, but this did not work very well. The actions looked mechanical and the girls had trouble remembering the right action at the right time. Finally, the teacher told them, "Move in any way you like, but just keep moving!" This worked; their actions became natural and pleasing.

In another case, the boys were to sing a humorous song from a current musical. Because it was their first experience with staged numbers, the boys were quite restrained; their motions were extremely inhibited and stiff, even though they were not practicing in the same room with the girls. They were told to exaggerate everything, but this did not help much at the time. Then came a rehearsal-performance for the girls' glee club. A success—the girls loved it! Next came a school assembly, and one could see more inhibitions being thrown aside with each performance. Another success. By the time of the evening program, the problem was no longer how to get the boys to act, but rather how to get them to stop overacting! In any event, they threw themselves into the performance and brought down the house.

LIMITATIONS TO CONSIDER IN STAGING

The type of prop and action is subject to the limitation of the facilities available. These conditions will have to be taken into account:

SIZE OF THE STAGE. The amount of available space should be figured with the curtain closed, since the area in front of a curtain is generally not usable as part of the stage setting. Room must be allowed for the risers and piano. If the singers sit down, as for a campfire scene, more space will be needed. Many times the type of dancing, if any is used, is seriously curtailed by the space available. When action occurs in front of the singers, the teacher must remember that generally the farther back a choral group is placed on the stage, the more its tone will be absorbed by the overhead curtains, and the weaker it will sound to the audience.

SIZE OF THE OFFSTAGE AREA. This consideration determines the ease with which students and props can be moved on and off the stage. A prop that is not in use on the stage has to be kept somewhere, and it must be out of the line of traffic.

AMOUNT AND QUALITY OF STAGE EQUIPMENT. Before planning extensive staging, the teacher should know what stage equipment is available. Is there a halfway curtain? Equipment for raising scenery? Are there rheostats? Colored lights and spotlight? The teacher must also check to see that the equipment is in working order. In some schools the lights and switches are handled carelessly by many students and teachers, and it is difficult to keep stage equipment in repair.

HEIGHT OF PROPS OR SCENERY BEHIND RISERS. It is easy to forget that six-foot boys standing on a two-foot riser are going to block out much of the backdrop. In addition, the audience views the stage at an upward angle, thereby making objects on the stage appear even higher than they are. As a result, the background space available for use is no greater than from five feet above the floor to the bottom of the curtains overhead.

PRACTICE FACILITIES. The amount and type of staging that can be undertaken is influenced to some extent by how much practice the group can have on the stage. If the stage is in the gymnasium, other classes may hamper practice. If the classroom is large enough, it is wise to chalk or paint on the classroom floor the exact area of the stage so that the students can become accustomed to working in the available space.

STAGING INSTRUMENTAL MUSIC

Although bands and orchestras cannot as easily add visual interest to their programs as can vocal groups, there are some steps which can be taken to increase the appeal of an instrumental concert. A few of these suggestions are similar to those outlined for vocal groups.

DANCING. Instrumentalists need not descend into the pit in order to play a number that utilizes dancing. They can leave enough room at the front of the stage for the dancers, or, if the stage is too shallow, a few of the players can move to one side to give the dancers more usable space and hence more freedom.

SCENERY AND STAGE SETTING. Instrumental groups can make use of a backdrop as well as many of the props and flags mentioned for choral groups. Although instrumental music does not have a text to provide specific meanings, there are many descriptive works that suggest visual treatment. In the field of geography alone, the possibilities range from "The Great Gate of Kiev" to the many national anthems and folk tunes from around the world.

The instrumentalists need not always sit in the same arrangement. The use of seated instrumental risers enables all players to be seen more easily by the audience; thus sections can be rearranged and emphasized somewhat according to the needs of a particular work of music.

Neither is it necessary for the players to wear the same uniform or dress on all occasions. On a hot day the band may remove its uniform coats and play in short-sleeved white shirts. Comfort need not be sacrificed for appearance.

FEATURING SECTIONS. Professional dance bands feature groups and soloists as a matter of course. This technique adds interest to the program and permits individuals to be commended on their own merits. The featured section should be placed in a prominent spot. This is especially desirable for antiphonal music. While the following device has been encountered almost too frequently, it is a definite crowd pleaser: the piccolos stand, then all the brasses stand during the trio of "Stars and Stripes Forever." The same type of thing can be done occasionally with other music. In one school system the flutists from every school learned a lovely folk melody, then joined together to perform it with band accompaniment.

In addition to the small ensembles which should be a part of the instrumental music curriculum, the teacher may form a stage band, which is discussed in Chapter Thirteen, or a novel group such as a German band or a "Jug and Bottle" band. One or two numbers that are frankly presented just for fun, and that have not demanded a large amount of rehearsal time, may be worth including in the concert. As a part of the group's performance, the players may adorn themselves with appropriate hats, and in this way add a little more flavor to the musical rendition without a complete change of costume.

MUSICAL VARIETY. Because much prosaic and even crass music is available under the heading "novelty," it is with trepidation that the author even mentions the use of pieces that are not profound. What the instrumental teacher should seek are a few pieces that are skillfully written and musically interesting, but at the same time are not of a serious, complex nature. Such pieces are hard to find. The "Toy" Symphony of Haydn, "Peter and the Wolf" by Prokofiev, and "The Typewriter" by Leroy Anderson are examples. Some of these works are of much educational value because they demonstrate the qualities of instruments so well. Other pieces contain unusual actions, as in Haydn's "Farewell" Symphony, or Johann Strauss' "Clear Track Polka" in which the conductor can add extemporaneous holds and rubato.

VOCAL SOLOISTS AND GROUPS. Not only does a vocal soloist provide variety at an instrumental concert; the combination of voice and instruments can be a musical experience of the highest order. Also effective are some finale numbers that use a large choral group. As a further bonus, this type of presentation brings the vocal and instrumental departments together.

BUSINESS ASPECTS

Sometimes musicians do not want to involve themselves in publicity, printed programs, and the sale of tickets; but these matters need to be handled properly, or unnecessary complications will result.

A practice that has been successful in a few schools is the appointment by the principal of another teacher to manage the business details for the music department. If this can be done, the music teacher can devote his attention to teaching. Even if a formal arrangement is not made, the music teacher may ask for assistance from other teachers when he feels their special training could be used.

Printed Programs

The printed program is a vital part of the concert because it is so closely examined by the public. The audience, before hearing the students, looks at the program and gains an impression of their work. Other music teachers will see the program, even though they do not hear the concert. Programs are mailed to relatives of the students, pasted in scrapbooks, hung on bedroom walls, looked at months and years after the actual performance.

Because the printed program is a permanent item, and because it has a way of getting around, it must include the names of all the students who participate in the concert. If the students are listed by the part they sing or the instrument they play, the lists appear shorter, and each individual seems more important. Above all, the teacher must *make certain that no name has been left out, and that all names have been spelled correctly.*

Everyone who has assisted the music teacher in some way should be acknowledged on the printed program. This includes stores from which props have been borrowed, teachers and departments who have given assistance, administrators who have helped in scheduling, and the school custodians. Such acknowledgments go a long way toward maintaining good relations in the school. Soloists, accompanists, student officers, and members of student committees deserve special mention. This will make the program considerably more valuable for many students, and if they have made extra contributions, they should be recognized.

The printed program can help educate the audience. Although it is easy for the teacher to list only the name of the work and its composer or arranger, a mere list of names does little to enlighten the audience. They wonder, "Which Strauss–Richard, Johann I or II, Oscar? Who is Schutz? Here's a Serbian folk song. Where is Serbia? Must be a typographical error. Do they mean Syria or Siberia?" An audience will derive more learning and enjoyment from a performance in which the music has been explained somewhat.

So it is good use of the music teacher's time, limited as it is, to write brief but informative notes about each piece. Here are some samples:

Soon Ah Will Be Done arr. William Dawson

The early American Negro took refuge in Christianity, finding peace and sometimes exuberant joy. One of the most dramatic of all spirituals is this one in which the slave looks forward to leaving the grief of this world and anticipates the joy of heaven.

First Movement, Symphony in B minor, the "Unfinished" Franz Schubert

This composition is called "Unfinished" because it contains two movements instead of the usual four. Schubert is best known for his ability to write beautiful songs and melodies. He was also one of the first Romantic composers, one who permitted his personal, subjective feelings to be revealed in the music. The movement does, however, follow the Classical sonata-allegro form with its exposition, development, and recapitulation. One of its most melodic themes is beautifully suited for the cellos.

O Domine Jesu Christe Palestrina
(O Lord Jesus Christ)

The outstanding composer of music for the service of the Roman Catholic Church was Giovanni Pierluigi da Palestrina, who lived in sixteenth-century Italy. One of his best-known compositions is the motet *O Domine Jesu Christe.* The text is a prayer to Jesus, with special recognition of his suffering on the cross. It concludes, "I pray that through your wounds my soul may be redeemed." The music is polyphonic, which means that all four parts are equal in melodic importance. The music is restrained and intellectual in character, as contrasted with music that is emotional and sensual.

What is it that these program notes have emphasized? In each case it is the essential quality or message of the music—the Romanticism of Schubert, the humble, pleading quality of Palestrina's motet, and the ecstatic character of the spiritual. This is what the listener must know and understand. Other information about the music or composer is mentioned only as it might contribute to this understanding. The fact that Palestrina composed for the Vatican and lived in the sixteenth century is significant in appreciating his music. Similarly, an explanation of polyphony is helpful to the listener who is oriented to the homophonic music of our era.

Touches of humor may occasionally be injected into the program notes, although a little of this goes a long way. Sometimes the audience would appreciate being forewarned if something unusual occurs in the song. Regardless of what else is included, the essential quality of the work should be stressed in the program note.

Since an understanding of the music is a prerequisite to writing succinct and helpful program notes, a few exceptionally able students might be given an opportunity to prepare the written material. The purpose of this effort is not primarily to lighten the teacher's work load, but to help the students better comprehend the music they are performing.

A program printed commercially looks best, but it is usually expensive. Before placing an order, it is wise to distribute copies of the material to different printers and have them submit written bids for the job. This should be done before any printing is started, because much of the expense occurs at the first step, which is the setting up of a galley proof. If commercial printing is too expensive, the typing teacher can have his classes make up a mimeographed or multilithed program. About 750 to 1000 copies can be made from one set of mimeograph stencils and the results are usually good. Some large schools have print shops that can print programs inexpensively.

Outside pages or covers for programs are available from various firms. There are color pictures from which to choose, and the rest of the folder is blank to accommodate the printing. Original designs by skilled art students also make attractive programs.

The teacher should start working on the program a month before the concert. It will take a week to get bids back, two weeks for printing or mimeographing; and it is desirable to have the programs five days before the concert so that copies can be sent out.

Tickets

Tickets are not required when admission is free. They can still be made, however, and given out for publicity. Making tickets is simple and relatively inexpensive. If there are to be different price levels, each should be represented by a different colored paper. The ticket should state the following information: name of event, presented by whom, where, on what date, at what time, and the price of the ticket. It is wise to print many more tickets than the number likely to be sold.

The policy of reserving seats has good and bad points. It has advantages for the reserved-seat holders (they do not have to arrive early in order to have good seats) and advantages for the organization (a little more can be charged for the ticket). The disadvantages can be considerable. Each ticket must have two parts, one to be taken at the door and another to be kept by the holder as a receipt. The stub and the seat will have to be numbered. The problem arises when the concert is given in a gymnasium and temporary chairs are used. Also, if there should be a mix-up on reserved seats (and this can happen with student ushers), some people will take the incident rather testily.

Tickets to school programs are best sold by the students themselves. People will turn down an adult much more easily than they will a youngster. Giving the students tickets to sell is also one of the best methods of publicizing the event. As an incentive measure, some teachers offer prizes to the top two or three students who sell the most tickets. This is not always effective, because about the second day of the ticket sales someone, perhaps a boy with a newspaper route, will walk into class and say, "Well, I've already sold forty tickets, and I've got promises for twelve more." At that moment everyone else gives up. What seems better from the standpoint of motivating the students, and from the standpoint of filling the auditorium, is to offer the student one free ticket for every five that he sells. He can do whatever he wants with the ticket: give it away or sell it and keep the money. This method makes a small reward accessible to all. Tickets should always be available at the door on the night of the performance.

The bookkeeping of ticket sales is no small item. The easiest method is to give each student a fixed number of tickets, possibly three adult and two student tickets. The dispensing of extra tickets can be recorded. Students should be told to account for all tickets given to them, and they must understand that they will have to pay for tickets that are not returned. When students are told this, they seldom lose any tickets. All ticket collections should be suspended during class periods the final week before the concert. Financial activities can consume valuable time, and most of these business matters can be handled outside of class.

Publicity

The best publicity for a concert is the inclusion in the program of as many students as possible. When a son or daughter comes home from school and announces, "We're having our concert in two weeks—can you come?" the parents are as motivated as they are ever going to be. It is a mistake for a school music teacher to set great store in formal publicity efforts. For the sake of experiment, a teacher with a well-established reputation for good programs decided not to have a single poster or sign made up to advertise the concert. He simply had the event announced in the town and school newspapers. When the night of the performance came, he had another packed house.

If posters are to be made, it is best to assign this project to students who are taking art classes. The public has grown so accustomed to the printed signs stuck in store windows that another sign is seldom noticed. The creations of the students are more eye-catching than commercially printed signs. Besides, the signs made by the students usually cost only the price of the material used.

In many communities, radio stations as a public service will broadcast announcements of school events such as music programs.

Local newspapers should be provided with notices of the event. The willingness of newspapers to publish material about school concerts varies. Many small-town papers are hungry for news and will publish anything given them, including pictures. Larger papers are less likely to print complete write-ups. However, many metropolitan newspapers publish area editions, which contain news of interest to only one area of their circulation. School programs can go into the area section.

All copy prepared for a newspaper should be double spaced. Below is a sample story written in newspaper style:

> The first concert of the season will be presented by the Centertown High School Orchestra at 8:15 P.M. Friday, October 28, in the school auditorium, 1201 Center Avenue. The concert is free to the public.
>
> The sixty-piece orchestra will be conducted by James G. Smith, supervisor of instrumental music in the Centertown schools for twenty years. Featured soloist will be senior Dina Eidelstein, concertmistress, who will be heard in the first movement of the Mendelssohn Violin Concerto.
>
> Also on the program will be the first movement of Symphony No. 2 ("Romantic") by Howard Hanson, American composer and long-time director of the Eastman School of Music. The work is being played in honor of the composer's birthday.
>
> Completing the program will be Schubert's "Rosamunde" Overture, and the Prelude, Chorale and Fugue by Bach-Abert.

The story should contain any items of interest about the concert, director, or soloists, and should be given to the newspaper several days before publication is desired. It should be written in some detail, even though space limitations may require cutting by the editor.

The school newspaper is an important vehicle for publicity. Although it contains little that the students do not already know, it is significant because of the need of teen-agers to be recognized.

One of the most effective means of publicizing the program to the student body is to present a preview assembly from ten to thirty minutes in length. The idea is to show the students the best of the coming program in order to have them attend the actual performance, and, more important, to have them talk favorably about the music group. The parts of the regular program with the greatest student appeal should be used. If the students like what they see and hear, they will attend the complete concert. There need be no fear that a good preview assembly will lose audience for the main performance. Of course, if the preview assembly is *not* good, the results will be worse than nothing. In many respects the success or failure of the preview assembly for the school is more crucial than an evening performance for a largely adult audience. Adolescent listeners never hide their feelings, and their responsiveness to a good program motivates the teen-age performer.

TRIPS AND TOURS

The value of trips and tours for performing groups is a somewhat controversial subject among educators. Much of the controversy has arisen because of the misuse of trips by some directors. Many school administrators' feelings can best be summarized in this fashion: "Trips are fine, *if* they are educational."[14]

What are the characteristics of a properly handled trip by a school organization?

The trip must be an educational venture for the students. Performance should be only one aspect of the undertaking. The students may listen to other music groups, see an operetta or a documentary film, or visit a television station.

The students should be impressed with the fact that the trip is an educational event, and not merely a vacation from school. Naturally students cannot avoid some conversation with their classmates about "getting out of school," but the amount of such talk should be limited. The students should be told that the more "vacation" talk there is, the harder it will be for them to get permission for future trips. The word "tour" may be used even though the students are to be gone only one night. This term sounds more impressive to teen-age students, and seems to have a more businesslike connotation.

The performances should largely be for school assemblies, and, in keeping with the Code of Ethics, no admission can be charged for any performance while on tour. Some schools present "goodwill" concerts in the evenings in churches or school auditoriums, and then take a collection. The results generally are not satisfying. Many goodwill concerts are poorly

[14] For an example of this sentiment see: Harry E. Martin, "For the Good of the Order," *Music Educators Journal*, XLIV, No. 5 (April–May 1958), pp. 30, 32.

attended, and the collection may not cover the small cost of publicity and other items. In such cases, the evening would be better spent by having the students hear or see something related to music. A school assembly, on the other hand, presents a guarantee of a full house and the probability of an interested audience.

The teacher should plan to have his group perform for schools of about the same size as his own school. If an average chorus from a high school of 300 students sang before a student body of 2500, with an average chorus for its size, the small school chorus would be hard pressed to do as well as the home school chorus. It would be difficult for the smaller group to get a good response from the audience.

The trip must be well planned and managed. Arrangements must be made for every meal, every overnight stop. One teacher carefully planned each phase of the journey, but forgot to arrange for a place for the bus drivers to stay overnight!

Of more importance than meals and lodging is the preparation of the students for the trip. The vast majority of students behave splendidly, but there are a few who look upon trips as a chance to get into mischief. Nothing can ruin a trip and eliminate the possibility of future trips faster than misbehavior. Many teachers and schools have found themselves in trouble because students on trips got lost from the group, committed petty shoplifting, damaged property, or threw objects out of bus windows.

What can be done to insure proper deportment? First, the students should be informed that the trip is a privilege—it is up to them to prove they deserve the privilege and can make use of it. Then, with the school administration and student officers, the teacher must establish policies regarding behavior and penalties for misbehavior. These areas should be covered: staying with the group, smoking, hours for going to bed, behavior on the buses, and behavior in public places. Students should know that if they misbehave the penalties will be stiff, including failure in music and suspension from school.

A sufficient number of parents and teachers should accompany the group as chaperones.

The roll should be called or checked by monitors each time before the buses move on.

Limits should be put on the amount of baggage that each student may take.

The financing of the trip must be kept to a minimum and handled in a sensible manner. First of all, the trip should not require an agonizing financial effort. There should be no need for a year of activities such as tag days, collections, dances, sales of baked goods, candy, records, and so on. A trip that requires so much of this sort of thing is out of place in the public schools. A modest money-raising effort should be sufficient to cover all expenses.

Money-raising projects must be considered carefully. Often they require arduous work, and after all the expenses have been paid, there is not much profit. It is true that magazines, candy, and greeting cards are items that do not require the effort of making; but the customer invariably pays a lot for what he gets. If other school groups likewise sell goods to the community, the field can get crowded.

Caution should be used in any money-raising project. After all, the classroom, equipment, and teachers' salaries are already being paid for by the public through taxation. Therefore, school organizations must not be too bold in seeking money.[15] The use of discretion will help maintain the good will of the community, and will serve to impose reasonable limits on the financial aspirations of the group.

One successful method of financing is outright solicitation. Surprisingly, many people prefer this to buying candy or magazines they do not want. In one school there was no charge for concerts. During the intermission of one program a collection was taken for the express purpose of financing a trip. Over half the necessary funds were collected at that one time. In this case, the audience was composed of persons who clearly were interested in the musical organization, and the collection was made at a time when they were receiving something from the music program. Service clubs can be solicited for funds for worthwhile causes.

Funds can also be derived from the sale of tickets to music concerts. Except in the case of an operetta or a musical play requiring expensive costumes, scenery, and royalties, the outlay for a program seldom exceeds the income from tickets. This money can be applied to the cost of the trip, or at least held in reserve in case the actual expenses run over the estimate.

In order to keep expenses down while en route, it is best to eat in school cafeterias and in churches whenever possible. Commercial restaurants frequently cut corners in feeding large groups, and seldom can young people get as much food for their money as they can in schools or churches. For overnight trips, it is desirable to have the students stay in the homes of members of musical organizations from the school that is being visited. A small payment of two or three dollars can be made for each student who is lodged for the night and given breakfast. This practice has several fine features. It gives the students a valuable social experience, and is far less expensive than staying in a hotel. When the group is divided by going to different homes, there can be little running around on fire escapes and general carousing, and therefore little chaperoning is needed.

School buses are less expensive than chartered commercial vehicles. If school buses are not available, the teacher should inquire about regular

[15] Andrews and Cockerille, *op. cit.*, pp. 171–72.

runs of public transportation. Because the cost of chartering a bus is based on miles plus driver time, buying individual tickets on public transportation may prove to be less expensive.

The schedule of the trip should disrupt the normal school routine as little as possible. The trip should not be so long and strenuous that the students come back exhausted. A trip of two days and one night is long enough. The number of performances should be limited to not more than three in any day—one in the morning, one in the afternoon, and one at night. Professional groups almost never perform more than one or two programs in a single day. Scheduling more than three performances involves the risk of falling behind schedule, with its hurried meals and general tension.

When possible, trips should take place during a school vacation time, if the schools to be visited are not likewise on vacation. When students are removed from classes for trips, a sensitive situation is created. The other teachers are naturally a bit envious of the music teacher. He receives frequent public recognition for his work and here he is taking time for a trip. In addition, they are inconvenienced by having students miss their classes.[16] This is another reason why trips should not cover more than two days. The best way for the teacher to approach the situation is to explain carefully in faculty meeting the purpose of the trip and the manner in which absences from class will be handled. The most successful procedure is to have the students get a signed statement from each teacher to the effect that their classwork is of at least "C" quality and that all possible work has been completed in advance. Students who cannot meet these requirements in their classes should not be permitted to go on the trip.

If these conditions are met, a trip can be a wonderful experience for the students. Never do they have such a singleness of purpose, put so much into their performance, as on trips. The students feel as they never have before: "We're really doing things in music!" The social contact, the experience in planning, the musical events heard and seen, all of these make a tour the high point of the year.

There is only one disadvantage to a tour: the students will want one every year!

CHECKLIST FOR PROGRAM PLANNING

The following time schedule is helpful in planning a major performance. Items concerning costumes and scenery can be ignored for the less extensive concert. What is important is that there be systematic and thorough planning.

[16] Andrews and Cockerille, *op. cit.*, pp. 147–50.

September

1) Select and enter dates on master calendar of school activities. If school does not have a central calendar, clear dates with athletic and drama departments and with school administration.

Three to six months before performance

1) Select music.
2) Establish a budget for performance–music, costume rentals, programs, etc. Have approved by administration, if necessary.
3) Secure performance rights on music. Procure music.
4) Make arrangements for costumes.
5) Try out soloists or leads.

Two to three months before performance

1) Establish rehearsal schedule containing approximate dates for learning specific portions of the music.
2) Begin study of the music.
3) Schedule the learning of spoken lines by leads and understudies.
4) Make decisions regarding scenery and props.

One to two months before performance

1) Construct scenery and props.
2) Prepare publicity and program materials.
3) Arrange for tickets and ticket sales. Order tickets.

Two to four weeks before performance

1) Have program printed or reproduced.
2) Arrange for ushers, stage crew, and after-performance cleanup.
3) Put scenery in place and rehearse with it.
4) Arrange for warm-up and dressing rooms.
5) Arrange for piano to be tuned on day of performance, if possible.

One week before performance

1) Mail out complimentary programs and tickets.
2) Have rehearsals consist of complete "run throughs."
3) Set aside one rehearsal for looking over different music; let the students relax and rest.
4) Check stage equipment and public-address system.
5) Check to see that all small props have been secured.
6) Arrange for curtain calls and/or acknowledgment of applause.

Performance

1) Hold a brief warm-up session in which the students perform the first few measures of each number in a thoughtful and careful manner. Check the tuning of instruments.

2) Make sure everyone is in place and equipment is functioning before starting.
3) Start on time.
4) Relax and enjoy the program (as much as possible).

After the performance

1) Return all rented or borrowed music, equipment, costumes.
2) Thank custodians, secretaries, teachers, administrators, and merchants who contributed to the program.
3) Finish collection of money from ticket sales.
4) Initiate procedures with proper school personnel for payment of bills.
5) Deposit with proper accounting the income from ticket sales.

Questions

1. What do these incidents, concerned with performances, reveal about the teacher's understanding of music education?
   a. Mrs. Farnham has five sections of eighth-grade general music. For a PTA program on music, she chooses the best twenty-five girls from the five classes to sing. "After all," she says, "there are a lot of kids in those classes who have precious little ability."
   b. Mr. Pearlman is rehearsing his high school band. The first horn bobbles a note. "If you do that in the concert," Mr. Pearlman says sternly, "I'll clobber your grade, so help me. The audience cannot excuse mistakes."
   c. Miss Hardesty wants the performance of the latest Broadway musical to be as nearly professional as possible. As a result, her singers rehearse only that music for three months in preparation for the performance.
2. Suppose you are asked to have your students provide fifteen minutes of after-dinner music at a service-club luncheon. The performance is strictly for entertainment. Should you or should you not accept the engagement? Why, or why not?
3. Which performances are acceptable under the Code of Ethics with the American Federation of Musicians?
   a. An appearance by the band at a Memorial Day observance.
   b. A performance in connection with the opening of a new shopping center.
   c. A performance at the swearing-in ceremony of county officials.
   d. A train-side appearance by the band when the national vice-presidential candidate comes through town.
   e. A performance by the school stage band at the Senior Prom.

f. A performance by the school stage band at a dance held in a private club paid for by a group of families.

g. A performance by the choir at a hospital benefit dinner.

4. Should the group learn different music for a school assembly, an evening concert, and a performance at noon for a service club? Why, or why not?

Projects

1. Plan a thirty-minute performance demonstrating the various activities of a junior high school general music class. Balance the amounts of time allotted to each portion, and mention points you want the audience to learn from the presentation.
2. Plan a program using two choral groups, one instrumental group, one small vocal ensemble, and one small instrumental ensemble to go on one stage with no halfway curtain but with a good orchestra pit. Arrange the appearances of the groups so that maximum efficiency can be achieved, and state how many numbers each will perform.
3. Think of a simple staging idea for each of the following:
   a. a group of songs from Latin America
   b. "Black Is the Color of My True Love's Hair"
   c. "Johnny Schmoker"
   d. "This Is My Country"
4. Write program notes for the following works:
   a. "How Lovely Are the Messengers" from *St. Paul*–Mendelssohn
   b. *Water Music Suite*–Handel
   c. "Simple Gifts"–arr. Copland
   d. "El Capitan" March–Sousa
5. Select three band numbers, one that features the clarinets, another that features the trombones, and another that features the percussion.
6. Using the criteria mentioned on page 222, select ten songs that are especially suitable for assembly singing.
7. Practice making a bow and acknowledging applause in front of your college class. Offer suggestions to one another to improve this action.
8. Plan a choral or instrumental concert and write up a four-paragraph publicity story about it which could be given to a newspaper.
9. Write a script for the narrator of a program that includes a series of six Christmas numbers. Write a similar script for a program consisting of six works based on American folk music.

10. Set up a sample budget for the presentation of a musical comedy. Include royalties; rental of orchestra parts, costumes, and scenery; and the cost of programs and tickets. Then, assuming a seating capacity of 500 in the audience, compute the minimum ticket cost for one performance, and then two performances.

Suggested Reading

Floyd Freeman Graham, *Public Relations in Music Education.* New York: Exposition Press, 1954. Chapters VII, V.

XII

singing and teen-age voices

Most teen-agers have only a vague notion of the correct methods of singing. In fact, many are not aware that there are correct methods, or that they make any difference in the musical results obtained. These students think that a singer just opens his mouth and whatever sound comes out is all right. This lack of understanding makes more difficult the task of the teacher who wants his students to sing well.

The choral music teacher faces conditions that differ from those of the instrumental teacher. Students in vocal classes are sometimes of a less select quality than are instrumentalists, who usually have survived the normal attrition of several years of study. Some students enter vocal classes after having had no contact with them for a year or two, whereas this almost never happens in instrumental music. Students know that techniques are required to play an instrument; but singing, which has been spontaneous since childhood, does not appear to demand a learned technique. Some popular vocalists, admired by the students, are untrained, and their "singing" earns them a sizeable income.

A well-produced tone may not be required for the singer of folksongs or the recording star whose singing is manufactured by electronic amplification, the echo chamber, and the spliced tape. But at the secondary school level, singing technique must be taught if students are to sing properly music worthy of their efforts. In more sophisticated, serious music the singer needs a supply of air over and above normal needs, and a firm control of the expiration of breath. He cannot sustain tones and phrases, reach high pitches, or attain good tone quality without instruction in how to sing.

Since singing methods in a choral music class must be taught in a group situation, with a variety of student abilities and interests, and with a definite limitation on the time available, the teacher must use a technique that meets the following criteria:

1) It must be usable in a group situation. There is little time for individual instruction, and few students have the time, money, opportunity, or inclination for private voice lessons outside of school hours.

2) It must be simple, direct, and as natural as possible. Few teen-age singing groups could learn much from a singing lesson as it is generally taught in the private studio. Private instruction is often too advanced for them, and it requires for its success much personalized attention by the teacher. Besides, techniques which call for the students to sound like Santa Claus with a series of ho-ho-ho's or to dangle their arms loosely while bending the head and making noises like a propeller-driven airplane are not suitable for a group of sixty-five down-to-earth adolescents. A singing method for secondary school students must be stripped of all but basic learnings.

3) It must be applicable to the music the group is singing. The students need to see improvement in their singing of the repertoire, more than in their performance of isolated and sometimes unmusical drills.

4) It must present the fundamentals of proper singing. Good music education demands a firm foundation for singing, one that will stand throughout all of the individual's experiences in vocal music.

WHAT IS CORRECT SINGING?

It is difficult to get musicians to agree on the right way to do almost anything, but in the case of methods for correct singing, consensus seems impossible. Singing teachers differ on matters of tone, diction, boy's voice change, and range; they further disagree on whether or not the sinus cavities help resonate the tone, whether air is released or "blown out" while singing, what muscles should be used to produce the proper tone quality, and whether or not physical actions should be taught.[1] The differences of opinion cause confusion for the school music teacher who conscientiously wishes to teach his students something about singing.

Many of the differences are due to semantics and a sense of personal allegiance to one view or another. Some causes for the controversies, however, are pertinent for the music teacher. One problem is the differing views on what artistic singing should do. Some singers strive for brilliance and power in singing, others for expressiveness, and others for a contrived

[1] For two writers who are diametrically opposed on this point, see:
Pro: Kenneth N. Westerman, *Emergent Voice*, 2nd ed. (Ann Arbor: Carol F. Westerman, 1955), p. 17.
Con: Sergius Kagen, *On Studying Singing* (New York: Holt, Rinehart & Winston, Inc., 1950), p. 59.

kind of prettiness. The position a singer takes on this matter naturally affects his tone, volume, and diction, which in turn determine to some extent the methods he uses for singing. What is a "big tone" to one singer is "yelling" to another, and what is proper breath support to one voice teacher is muscular tension to another. A further reason for disagreement is the highly individualistic nature of singing. Two excellent singers may have been taught to sing in ways that are in opposition to each other; or the converse may be true: two singers of apparently equal interest and ability are taught by the same teacher, with one turning out to be an excellent singer and the other mediocre.

Although the differences of opinion leave the school music teacher in an uncomfortable position, because almost anything he tells his students could be disputed by some specialist, he cannot stand helplessly by while his students flounder through the music. He must act. Therefore, this chapter will present suggestions for giving teen-age singers a proper vocal foundation. The suggestions are a synthesis of the different views on singing techniques which have proved to be workable and practical in secondary school choral classes. It is *one* method for helping teen-agers to sing; it is not the *only* method. It represents one attempt to meet the criteria listed for a singing method.

The teaching of proper singing should divide itself into two approaches that are used simultaneously. One is the development of physical actions that result in proper singing. The other approach is that of "mind over matter"—the use of aural concepts and psychological attitudes to obtain good singing. Again, it should be emphasized that both approaches are essential and should be used together.

PHYSICAL ACTIONS FOR CORRECT SINGING

The drawings (p. 254) show the position of the lungs, diaphragm, and abdominal wall in a state of inspiration and expiration, the bodily conditions that mark the two extremes of breathing.[2] Below the lungs is the muscular floor called the diaphragm, which is lowered when taking a breath, allowing air to enter and fill the lungs. The abdominal wall moves out somewhat to make room for this action. Then, as the breath is released, the diaphragm moves up and the abdominal wall moves in. The chest and shoulders do *not* move. Although some room for breath can be made by sharply expanding the rib cage (thorax) with each inhalation, it is difficult to control this breath and not as much air can be inhaled as when deeper breathing is employed. Therefore the deep, abdominal breathing is necessary—one point at least on which singing teachers agree.

Since the vocal cords remain silent until activated by breath, the control of the breath becomes all-important. The diaphragm is responsible for this,

[2] Westerman, *op. cit.*, p. 14. Reprinted by permission.

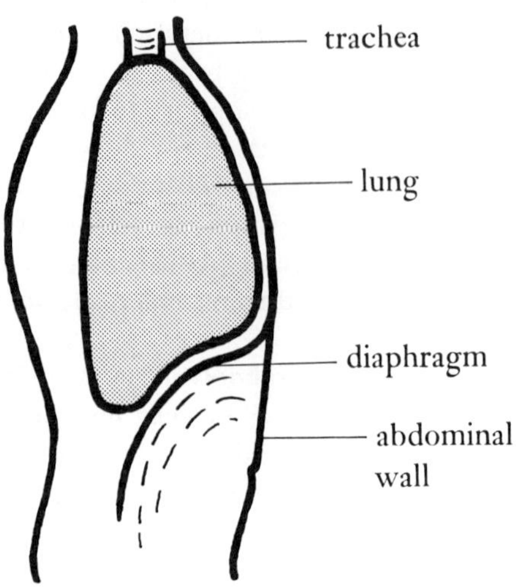

INSPIRATION

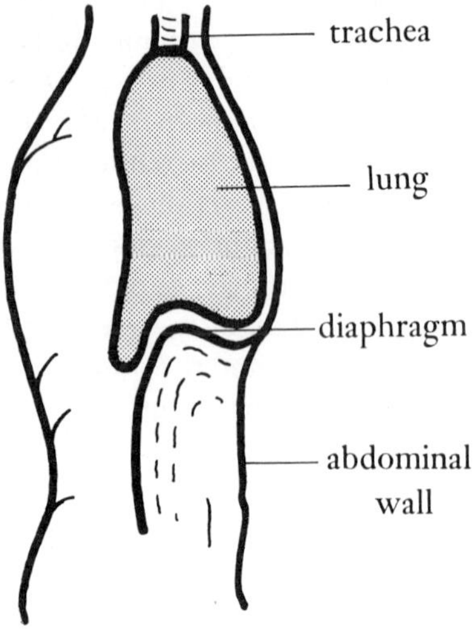

EXPIRATION

and fortunately it can, when trained, do the job beautifully. The vocal cords, upon which inexperienced singers are so prone to center their attention, are merely a passage through which air moves. By slight and almost effortless adjustment, the vocal cords regulate pitch. Since they sound best when vibrating freely, any tension in the throat area is detrimental to both intonation and tone quality. The only place where muscular tension can be permitted is in the large muscles associated with the diaphragm and abdominal area. The cavities of the sinuses, nose, and eyes serve as resonators for the singer.

This brief description of the functions involved in singing covers the essential points, and the points on which there is substantial agreement among voice specialists. An attempt to go into more detail leads directly into areas of disagreement, but fortunately greater detail is not necessary for the vocal music teacher in the schools. If he can get his students to master the fundamental concepts and actions, they will have sufficient technique to sing worthwhile literature.

Now, how can these basic physical actions in singing be organized so that students in a class situation can be taught to do them? Basically, by formulating a simple routine of the physical actions which, if followed religiously, will give the correct bodily movements for singing. The following four-step routine that has proved successful with teen-age singing groups:

1) Without taking a breath, straighten the spine, relax the shoulders, and hold the chest comfortably high.
2) Inhale a full breath, as if the air is going directly into the abdomen.

3) Keep an open and relaxed throat.
4) Sing a full sound that "floats" out.

Correct Position

When being introduced to the first step, the students must realize that to make room for the needed air, the bottom of the lungs and the diaphragm cannot be squeezed or cramped in any way. This is why they are instructed not to take a breath for the first step. Room should be made for the breath, rather than the breath having to make space for itself. The students also need to know that lifting the shoulders is just that—lifting the shoulders, and it has little to do with expansion of the lungs. To help keep the chest up, the students can think of the top of the rib cage as the top of a barrel, the lid of which is extremely light and is trying to float away. Some teachers achieve this in other ways and by the use of other analogies, but the principle is the same.

It is advisable for the students to stand when working on correct singing. The position should not be one of a soldier standing at attention, stiff as a ramrod. Rather, it is a natural but alert bodily attitude. Many voice teachers suggest leaning slightly forward so that the weight of the body is on the balls of the feet. If the students are sitting, they can be instructed to sit straight with their backs two inches away from the back of the chair. The teacher should walk among the students from time to time to correct individuals who are not assuming good posture. Later, when pages of music are held, the students can pretend that they are holding a large beachball between the insides of their arms and the chest as they hold the music.

When the correct position of the body has been achieved, the teacher must stress the maintaining of this position at all times when singing. This is crucial, because once the setup for singing collapses, so does the tone quality. The maintenance of proper singing posture has another function: it gives the student something positive on which to concentrate while singing. If he focuses his attention on the wrong muscles or on his own feelings of inadequacy, tension will result, and tension is the enemy of good singing. The more carefully he concentrates on establishing the proper position, the more he transfers his attention from places that could cause tension to an area that can absorb concentration and improve singing at the same time.

Deep Breath

For the second step, that of the deep breath, the student can place one hand lightly against the abdominal wall. Later, he can place both hands, thumbs forward and fingers to the back, on each side of the waistline, and feel expansion under the hands at those points, too. If he takes a deep breath properly, the wall will expand somewhat around the beltline. The lungs are larger at the bottom than at the top, and so most of the expansion and control comes from the work of muscles in and around the abdominal wall. The expansion should occur not only in front, but also at the sides. The students need to know that during inhalation the abdominal wall moves *out*, and during singing and expending air the wall moves *in*. To get the feel of this action, they can be directed to try this simple experiment at home: lie on the back with arms relaxed at the sides. Keeping the chest motionless, take a deep breath and notice the expansion of the abdomen. Release the breath slowly and there will be a gradual contraction. If one hand is rested lightly on the abdomen, the up-and-down (or out-and-in) motion will be more apparent. The exercise is recommended because in a supine position the deep breathing necessary for singing is natural and practically unavoidable. It then becomes relatively simple to duplicate the action while standing.

The diaphragm itself has almost no muscle feeling, although the results of its action can be felt,[3] particularly when clearing one's throat. Its correct action in singing depends on the correct use of muscles around the abdomen.

To get the correct muscular tension in the abdominal muscles during singing, the teacher can tell his group: "Take in a full breath and hold it, using the *abdominal muscles only*. They should be just tense enough to hold back the breath. The sensation should be one of firm but flexible muscles, something like a light steel spring being gently pulled . . . Exhale.

"Now this time when we repeat the deep breath, make sure there's no tension anywhere else—don't squeeze the throat shut or get a constricted feeling in the chest. Just let the abdominal muscles do the work of holding back the air. Everything else is relaxed. Try it . . . Exhale.

"Now let's see what happens when you sing and use up air. As the abdominal wall moves in, you'll feel an increasing amount of muscle tension there. If you sing to the point where you have no breath left, the muscles begin to feel as though they're in a knot." The students can experience this by singing a long tone to the point of silence and noting how they feel when nearly out of air.

The words of the teacher should suggest a balance between effortlessness, which is impossible to achieve, and tremendous tension, which inhibits action and may cause tension at other places, such as the throat and neck. The teacher can say, "Look, when you walk, your leg muscles can't be completely relaxed because you would just drop to the floor. They can't be too tense, either, because then you would look like a stiff-legged clown. The same is true in singing—some tension is needed but not too much." To give the students another analogy as to the right amount of muscle tension, the teacher might say, "Pretend that you're

[3] *Ibid.*, p. 18.

going to blow the seeds off a dandelion, but stop just before blowing out any air. The amount of tension in your abdominal wall is the amount you should have when you sing."

Relaxed Throat

The third step, attainment of an open throat, is necessary for a full, pleasant, and freely produced tone. The correct throat position is similar to a yawn. In fact, some teachers refer to the tone produced as "yawny." The tongue is low and relaxed; the back of the mouth where one swallows is open and round. It may be helpful to vocalize on the sound "awe," which requires openness in the back of the throat in order to be produced. This sensation should be maintained even when the lips are closed.

The students should be told that the throat is a passageway, and once it is set up, it should not be disturbed. The throat, in singing, is the sphere of calm through which the tone must be allowed to flow freely. The singer must sing *through* the throat and not *with* it. It should not produce the sensation of shifting, even for very high or very low notes. If the position of the throat changes, the swallowing muscles take over and upset the structure, which should remain stationary. Evidence of muscular interference is not hard to find. A high larynx is one symptom of tension, as are raised eyebrows and sluggish articulation. The most common indication, especially among boys, is the protruding, raised jaw, accompanied by a straining of the muscles under the chin. For some reason, boys will try sticking out their chins to sing what are for them high pitches. It never helps, but they keep on trying anyway. The jaw should be relaxed and loose, as if it were suspended by rubber bands.

Action of Breath in Singing

The fourth step emphasizes the term "float" in connection with tone production to indicate that the air is not rammed through the vocal cords; rather it rises slowly through the throat. The teacher can say, "The breath coming out as you sing should move as slowly as if you were warming your hands with it." The singer, to be efficient, must achieve the maximum amount of vocal-cord vibration with the minimum amount of air. This is similar to achieving the most miles per gallon from gasoline in an automobile.

When singers push the tone or expel air carelessly, they achieve a forced, fuzzy quality that lacks resonance, intensity, and solidity. The tone has no center. One way to achieve intensity is to imagine that the air is "spiraling" or "spinning" as it comes from the back of the throat and moves out of the mouth. Boys are familiar with the fact that a football must be spiraled in order to achieve a good pass. This analogy is often helpful in improving the intensity of their singing tone.

If the students are mature and progressing well in their comprehension of the steps for correct tone production, the teacher should seek to develop the resonance in the voices. Although advanced work is best undertaken in private lessons, the teacher can begin the initial steps. First, the students should be told what resonance is. One device that encourages resonance is to have the singers feel vibration in the head. They can place the fingers of one hand lightly on the nose and sing "ping." After experimenting to discover the tone placement that encourages the greatest vibration and resonance, the singers can work to achieve the same vibrant sensation on sounds other than "ng." The object is to encourage resonation by sending the tone through the head and face.

Teaching Suggestions

The principles of music teaching, presented in Chapter Seven, are especially applicable to the teaching of correct singing routine. Whether the four steps should be taught together or independently is a matter of whole-part learning. One step makes sense only as it is related to the others, and yet some attention needs to be given each step by itself, so a process of alternation between synthesis and analysis is called for. The level of development of the group needs to be assessed by the teacher. A musically immature group may not be ready to tackle these techniques for some time. Interest and motivation also need to be present to some degree before the steps will bring forth positive musical results. By way of further preparation, the students should have memorized some songs that can be used in learning the routine. When singing from memory the students can devote their attention to the newly presented steps. In order to be meaningful to the singers, the routine for correct singing should always be presented in association with actual music. As soon as possible, the steps should be applied, even though imperfectly, to the current repertoire.

There is no better instance of the need for persistence on the part of the teacher than the teaching of these singing steps. They involve a complex of skills and understandings, and these cannot be mastered in a period or two. They need to be worked on day after day in a variety of ways, through imaginative use of warm-up and attention to the music. The singer should see the necessity for building good habits, habits which need to become so ingrained that they will not fail the singer even in the face of the distractions caused by singing before an audience on crowded, hot risers.

AURAL-PSYCHOLOGICAL APPROACH

Since the advent of the phonograph, there have been several cases of young singers who without any private instruction have demonstrated rare ability, to the astonishment of auditioning committees from conservatories and opera companies. How was it possible for a totally untrained person to sing beautifully a difficult Verdi or Puccini aria? Simple—the young singers learned the piece by listening to a recording of a renowned artist. Impossible? It has happened, several times.[4] These cases illustrate again the shaping power of a singer's tonal concept. It is no accident that Italian operatic tenors have a similar sound, and Irish tenors, to say nothing of Wagnerian sopranos and French *chanteuses*. They sound alike because they have similar concepts of tone and singing.

Because singing involves so many muscles and bodily parts, and because it is impossible for any teacher to adequately describe all the muscular sensations, no physical routine in itself is sufficient to teach correct singing. Physical steps are needed to get the student started in the right direction and to avoid the development of habits that hinder singing. But complementary to that effort, the teacher needs to convey an aural concept of singing, and then have the students strive for that vocal quality. The human voice is so involved with feeling and thought that what the singer thinks is certain to affect how he sounds. In a very real sense it is the ear (or more accurately, the mind) that controls the throat position, the action of the diaphragm, and the position of the tongue. At times the vocal teacher feels as much like a psychologist as he does a music teacher, and perhaps this is as it should be.

Style and Tone

As a first step toward developing a concept of good singing, the teacher must disabuse the students of the notion that the style used by popular singers represents the acme of vocal performance. The popular song style is fine for the popular song, but for serious music it is badly out of place. Once the students realize that there are distinct styles of singing, they begin to develop a concept of a legitimate, serious style. Basically, they learn good singing by hearing it, be it from other students, recordings, or the teacher.

Students learn more from one another than a teacher likes to admit. One good bass or alto can without realizing it do much to teach the other students in the section. If the members of a section, say the tenors, get the idea that a certain tenor is a good singer, they will imitate him.

When using recordings as models of tone, the teacher must be particular about the choice of singer. A mature performer may have a highly developed tone which no teen-ager can or should emulate. Many times recordings of good collegiate singers are most suitable. The recordings

[4] In fairness it should be pointed out that no doubt some very promising young tenors have ruined their voices trying without proper singing technique to imitate recordings of Caruso or Jan Peerce. These young singers, of course, are never heard from again.

that are made for use with the elementary basal music book series are splendid. They are made by the best professional companies using fine arrangements and singers, and are a pleasure to hear.

A vocal music teacher who is himself a good singer has a distinct advantage. But pianists and other instrumental majors should note that the word "singer" is used and not "soloist." A well-trained voice is usable and fine, but it is not a necessity. What is needed is a voice with a pleasing quality and sufficient flexibility to illustrate different aspects of phrasing, style, and tone. To make their illustrations as effective as possible, some teachers practice singing with a breathy tone, pointed chin, constricted throat, or other handicap. Then they can say to the class, "Look, here's what you're doing—notice what it does to the tone. Now I'll do it right . . . see what a difference it makes?" This helps the student to hear himself as others hear him.

The teacher can strengthen the concept of proper singing by word as well as example. "Hey, that's too rough and blatant. Smooth it up. Be gentler." Or "Guys, that sounds sick. Come on, let's hear some muscle in your tone." He can also use a section as an example. "Now, I want the rest of you girls to listen to the altos at letter G. This, girls, is what I mean by a beautiful tone. Notice that it's warm and flowing, with body to it."

One style, encountered most often among boys, especially in junior high school, is what might be called "piano-like" singing. The boys do not sing through their tones, and the result is a combination of speaking and singing. Each note is a short spurt of sound, usually with a pushed tone of debatable pitch, followed by a rest. Probably this is caused by a lack of self-confidence in singing. The cure may involve singing the songs on a neutral syllable, allowing breaks in sound only at breathing points. Other suggestions for legato singing are mentioned on page 188.

Range

The ease with which a singer adapts to range is affected by his mental outlook. For instance, if a person is asked to walk along a line on the floor, he has no trouble doing so. But if that line were along the roof-edge of a ten-story building, he would find this feat nearly impossible. The way in which a singer thinks about a tone, especially a pitch at the top of the range, will determine in most cases whether or not he can sing it. Some teachers with the best of intentions talk this way: "Now, I know that high A is a difficult note to reach. Why, even professional singers have trouble with it! I hope you can get it, or else we'll have to move it down an octave." The result is, of course, that the students are talked out of singing the note. The teacher should say, "Space suits on, gang. Let's get that A, with a good tone. Sing the line using the technique we worked on—deep breath, open throat." In a relaxed way the students should be encouraged to try. Clearly, they should not be "whipped" into further effort: "Listen, we're going to get that A or else!"

Girls will gain more freedom in the top part of their range by vocalizing on patterns such as these:

With each singing, the pitch should be raised a half step. Altos may sing, as long as they are able, in unison with the sopranos. Perhaps the girls can be held on the high pitch, then cut off and told, "You know, that note is a whole step higher than the highest note in the 'Hallelujah Chorus,' which we're singing." In this way the exercises are made functional. The vocalization should be continued on a somewhat regular basis until the "high-note phobia" has passed.

DICTION

Singing has been defined as sustained speech. Making the words intelligible is one part of the singer's responsibility. Unless the words are understood by the listener, he is receiving only half of what the composer intended. The other part is to sing the words understandably without allowing the act of singing them to detract from the tone quality and musical effect. Many times a singer can vocalize beautifully, but when he begins to put words to his singing he loses his good quality. The words interfere with the singing.

Making words understandable is in some respects the simpler job. First the singers should be made conscious of the need to pronounce words clearly as they sing. In speaking, sloppy pronunciation is more easily covered up because the sounds are relatively short; in the sustained tones

[5] Harry R. Wilson, *Artistic Choral Singing* (New York: G. Schirmer, Inc., 1959), p. 204.

[6] Lisa Roma, *The Science and Art of Singing* (New York: G. Schirmer, Inc., 1956), p. 73.

of singing, such concealment is hardly possible. To some degree pronunciation can even be exaggerated during singing. One simple device that helps here is to whisper the words, since whispering requires extreme clarity in order to be intelligible. A common fault in singing is negligence regarding final consonants, especially *d* and *t* before a rest or breath. The students may be careless, or they may be uncertain as to when the tone should end. If this is the case, the teacher when conducting can close the thumb and second finger of the right hand precisely at the end of a word, and this will help the singers to execute the final consonant together.

The second problem, that of keeping the proper throat and mouth position while forming words, is not so easily solved. The solution requires freedom from tension in the jaw, tongue, and lips, and consistent use of good methods of singing. Both conditions are helped by a minimum amount of jaw movement. As Ehret states, "In *legato* singing, particular attention must be paid to the jaw, which should move very *little* if a legato flow is to be preserved. Actually the jaw has to move only for six letters (B, F, M, P, V, and W), and even in these instances the motions are small."[7] Excessive jaw movement creates tension and often leads to less accurate pronunciation. To correct this, the students can practice singing while touching their fingers lightly on their chins. They will be surprised to discover that they can sing and enunciate just as clearly with more economy of movement.

Some teachers and singers want the different vowels to be sung with almost no change of mouth and throat, but others along with Wilson[8] feel that such rigidity makes the singing lack color and variety. This matter depends on the musical judgment of each teacher. What is important is that the students put first things first. Never should they allow their setup for singing to collapse because they wish to sing a certain sound. They should concentrate on the proper method of tone production and especially on the open throat, so that changes from one vowel sound to another will cause as little disruption as possible.

Since vowels are the vehicles for sustained tone, which is the essence of singing, they are deserving of attention. When singers sing the same vowel but do not all sing it alike, they create an illusion of faulty intonation and they blur the words. Teen-agers, who speak the same language in generally the same way, may not be consistent when singing it. Some students speak a word one way and sing it another. Thus the terms "cleaning up vowels" or "working on vowels" are frequently heard in connection with choral music.

In some cases, good intentions have led teachers into long and complex discussions of palate position, nasalization, and diacritical marks, accompanied by tedious sessions on how to sing the thirty-plus vowel sounds of

[7] Walter Ehret, *The Choral Conductor's Handbook* (New York: Edward B. Marks Music Corporation, 1959), p. 36.
[8] Wilson, *op. cit.*, p. 179.

the English language in conjunction with a labial, aspirate, or lingua-palatal consonant. This approach bewilders the students because for years they have been saying words without being conscious of shaping the palate or moving the uvula. Also, such manipulative efforts sidetrack their attention into areas that are somewhat removed from the qualities of the music itself.

The remedy for the varied phonation of a vowel among singers is to practice singing it uniformly from a model sound in a familiar word. Traditionally, voice teachers have confined their efforts to the five Italian vowels *i, e, a, o, u* (*ē, ā, ä, ō, o͞o*). English is not Italian, however, and these vowels account for only 12 per cent of the sounds on the written page of English.[9] Just the English short *ĭ* as in *sit* accounts for over 12 per cent. Westerman in his book *Emergent Voice* lists fifteen vowel sounds which he says represent more than 90 per cent of the sounds and 95 per cent of the muscular movements involved in singing English.[10]

vē	as in *veal*
si	as in *sit*
tā	as in *take*
thĕ	as in *them*
shă	as in *shall*
lä	as in *large*
gô	as in *gone*
dŭ	as in *dust*
nō	as in *note*
pû	as in *push*
ro͞o	as in *room*
mī	as in *might*
bou	as in *bounce*
few	as in *few*
coi	as in *coin*

A chart of vowel sounds can be made and placed on the wall of the classroom. If a word in a song is not being sung consistently, the teacher can point out the sound for the students to practice.

Some vowel sounds are diphthongs—vowels which are compound when sounded. Perhaps the most common is the pronoun "I." When singers "chew" its execution as

Ah - a - ay - ee,

the effect produced is unpleasant and unclear. For a more satisfying result, the singers should hold the initial vowel sound and then at the last moment move to the second or "vanish" sound. Thus "I" is sung:

[9] Westerman, *op. cit.,* p. 61.
[10] *Ibid.,* p. 63. Reprinted by permission.

Some choral directors feel it is their "deeyooty" to teach a special version of the English language for singing—a version which is aesthetically superior to spoken English. The value of such a project is questionable. There is so much to be taught that represents a more profitable use of time.

Because singing exaggerates the unpleasant as well as pleasant sounds of the language, the music teacher might spend a few moments, but no more, to make the undesirable sounds less conspicuous. One is the sibilant *s*, which if sustained produces a hissing effect. The singers should execute it together and should never prolong it. The conductor can help in some cases by closing his fingers to indicate the end of the sound. Another troublesome consonant is the *r*. Sometimes the word "father" is sung *fahtherrrr*. Instead, the singers should sustain *uh* and add the *r* at the very end: *fah-thuh-r*. Upon occasion, depending on its place in the musical phrase, a vowel may be softened so that it will not be harsh. In most cases this is best accomplished by instructing the singers to open the back of the throat and round the lips slightly.

Whether or not the last consonant of one word should be attached to the first of the next word in legato singing depends on the word and on the musical phrase. For example, the words "lost in the night" can be sung "law-sti-nthuh nah-it." In this case, clarity is improved. However, Mendelssohn's lovely "He Watching Over Israel" becomes comic if this technique is stressed for the words "slumbers not."

GIRLS' VOICES

The voice quality most often encountered among teen-age girls, especially in junior high school, is breathy, thin, or fluty. This is a phase through which many young girls pass in the process of physical and vocal growth. To an extent, the teacher has to live with the problem. It is a result of many factors—muscular immaturity, lack of control and coordination of the breathing muscles, and voice development. Precise and concentrated effort applied to the steps involved in proper singing will help to improve this condition.

In the high school there are few true altos with a rich quality in the low range around A and G below middle C; there are almost none in junior high school. Most teen-age altos sound like second sopranos singing low. A word of warning is appropriate here for those teachers who use some altos as tenors in a mixed four-part chorus. If this practice is followed extensively for any one alto, it will tend to strengthen and overuse the tones in her middle and lower range. In addition, she may develop a fear of singing high. Therefore, regular use of altos on tenor parts should be avoided.

High school sopranos should not sing much higher than G, perhaps an A occasionally. Junior high sopranos should stay about one step lower. The range will depend upon the experience of the singers.

BOYS' VOICES

Boys' voices are usually less breathy than girls'. In the untrained high school boy singer there is often a decided difference between the quality of the low range and that of the upper tones. As long as the bass voice does not develop signs of a raucous, hard tone quality, the teacher can be assured that there will be no strain if the basses are encouraged to sing out in the low part of their range. In baritones and tenors the quality will be especially light and almost colorless in the upper range.

One cannot arbitrarily set up a neat chart of voice ranges, though many authorities attempt to do so. The top note of the average high school tenor may be either F or F sharp, and of a baritone either D or E flat. The top note is that note which is fairly comfortable and which occurs occasionally in an octavo selection suitable for high school choruses.

High Notes for Boys

The topic of an extended high range for boys leads into a matter about which there is some confusion: the falsetto voice, variously referred to as the head voice or half-voice. Music teachers have never been quite sure whether or not the falsetto voice is desirable or usable, and there is even some difference of opinion on what action of the vocal cords causes this sound. There is no doubt that boys can extend their singing range tremendously by the use of falsetto. True, the tone lacks power and healthy masculine sound, and for that reason boys are not eager to use it. However, as Wilson points out, "it is the normal production for changed male voices to use on high tones. It is both easy and natural."[11]

Falsetto is more than a gimmick used to attain a few high notes. Frederick Swanson makes this observation:

> There is another facet about the development of these young tenors that is unique—a facet rarely mentioned in the literature. I refer to the ease with which these boys shift into the falsetto, the mildness of the "break" as compared to the definite "shatter" quite common to their bass class mates. There seems to be a close integration or intermeshing of the full and the falsetto tones, whereas some of the deeper voices develop areas between falsetto and full voice where no sounds can be produced at all.

[11] Wilson, *op. cit.*, p. 206.

> This pattern was first noticed by the writer as he worked with a group of eighth-grade boys in a laboratory situation. The "basses" had been segregated from the "tenors" in a group of nearly 100. Some of the "tenors" were actually less mature boys whose voices had not entered the stage of rapid change. During the school year, the latter dropped quickly into the bass-baritone range so they had to be shifted to the other group. But there was one segment of the class that maintained its tenor range throughout the season, and never developed any tones of "body" below a D.
>
> In this special group, as we experimented with the head-tone and the technique of carrying it down across the break, there emerged for a time a tone quality of a most unusual quality and color. A picturesque writer might use the word "haunting." This writer remembers especially the high a-flat in the spiritual "Were You There," sung with a clear, resonant, entirely unforced tone. Subsequently, in working with other groups, this tone quality has been achieved several times . . .[12]

For years fine professional tenors have been mixing falsetto with the full voice without anyone's being quite sure which voice is being used. The most striking point, which Swanson mentions and trained solo tenors have demonstrated, is the closeness of the voices. With adolescent boys the teacher can say, "Use the falsetto to reach tones you can't get with your regular voice." But he should add, and this is most important, "After you've learned the part, try to sing those tones as much as you can with your regular voice. Approach the high tones easily and freely, almost as you do to sing them falsetto, and in time you can sing them with regular voice." In most cases, in a few weeks the boys can sing the high pitches in regular voice, because their apprehensions over high tones have been eliminated. The boys know that they can sing the note one way or another, so doubt is removed. Falsetto is a good model for singing because it is unstrained and free, thereby encouraging good quality.

Special attention to development of the falsetto will facilitate its use. The object is to effect a smooth transition from one muscle to another. The first step is for the boy to find his falsetto voice. Generally it is easiest to sing the falsetto with an *oo* sound on D, E flat, or E above middle C. After the voice has been found, slur the tone down an octave. Both Wilson[13] and Swanson suggest moving from the light quality *down* into the regular voice. The students should not be taken beyond this point for a few days, although the slur can be slowed down with practice. The next step is to sing a descending scale. At this stage the boys should attempt to make the transfer from falsetto to regular voice as smooth and inconspicuous as possible. Finally, after some experience with the scale on the *oo*

[12] Frederick Swanson, "The Proper Care and Feeding of Changing Voices," *Music Educators Journal*, XLVIII, No. 2 (November–December 1961), 64, 66. Reprinted by permission.

[13] Wilson, *op. cit.*, p. 207.

sound, other vowel sounds may be used. Until the singers are proficient in the use of falsetto, they should start the tone on an *oo* sound and then change to the desired vowel. Gradually the starting note of this pattern should move chromatically from D above middle C up to A. Basses should be included with the tenors in this work, because they also have problems with high pitches.

Procedures for achieving falsetto must be used with caution. The teacher cannot walk into class the first day and ask a healthy teen-age boy who is proud of his new-found manhood to sing a tone that sounds like an owl hooting. The teacher must bide his time until the boys encounter difficulty with a particular note. Then he can say, "I know a way for you to get that note." Another condition must be met: the boys need to have confidence in the teacher. They need to feel that his directions can be trusted to help them sing better. Finally, the beginning work on falsetto should not be done in the presence of girls. The boys will be sensitive at best, so even if it means putting the girls in another room for study hall, it is advisable to separate the two groups. Let the girls hear the results of the work as the music is sung; they need not observe the process.

Voice Change

Miss Miller, vocal music teacher at Thornton Junior High School, looked dejected as she met the instrumental teacher in the hall. "I'm losing my wonderful boy soprano, Tom Jenkins," she said. "His voice is starting to change. Too bad." Too bad? All Tom Jenkins is doing is growing up. What's so bad about that? Besides, what happens now? Does he go into musical oblivion, as so many other boys do when their voices change? Is there something for Miss Miller to do besides shake her head and say, "Too bad"?

For the sake of music education there had better be something more. Tom Jenkins represents every normal boy who goes through school. Most boys at some time or another during the period of voice change are involved in music, often in compulsory classes. What happens to Tom and his male peers during the voice change not only shapes their present attitude toward music, but also influences what they will do with singing during the rest of their lives. For these reasons, the topic of the changing voice cannot be treated as a passing curiosity. It is of first-rate importance, and deserves serious study and thought.

There is almost no subject in the field of music education that is more fascinating, frustrating, and fraught with differences of opinion than that concerning what happens to a boy's voice at puberty and what should be done about it. To begin with, there is the question of whether or not the boy should sing during the period of change. The first published work on the topic appeared in England in 1885 under the intriguing title, *The*

Child's Voice: Its Treatment with Regards to After-Development.[14] It concluded that singing during voice change was injurious and ruinous. This theory in America found little acceptance, nor is it held in present-day England.[15]

The big question to be faced is the matter of what pitches and parts the boys should sing. Competent music educators have reported interesting findings as a result of their work with countless numbers of boys. The writings of three authorities in the field will be quoted liberally here. For the sake of accuracy and clarity, each will be presented as an entity in itself, without being related to the others. There can be no fixed standard to use in determining what is meant by "singing tone," "body in the tone," "straining the voice," or "voice change." Consequently, much of the difference of opinion to be cited here may be due to the writers' definition of words.

Essentially Swanson advocates keeping the boys singing in a range that is easy for them, even if it means some rearranging of the parts. About the bass range, he states:[16]

> Basses who can sing to a low G′ (first line of the bass clef) are quite common in the junior high school. These very "new" basses frequently find middle-c or even B and A quite uncomfortable and must strain to produce these tones. Their "bread and butter" notes are from A′ to G. Boys who can produce an audible low E′ without strain are not at all rare.
>
> These observations are based on actual case studies. They are not drawn from textbooks or stated after theorizing about what *should* logically exist. We have found 12-year-old boys who sing in the lowest reaches of the bass clef easily and happily. In the 13–14-year-old brackets we have found from 30 to 40 of these low basses out of every 100 enrolled in general music classes.

Regarding tenors, Swanson says:

> Yes, there are tenors in grades eight and nine. There are boys who have matured physically rather early who find the range D to e quite comfortable for singing. These boys display the typical "break" at about f, and the lowest notes, D and E, tend to thin out and lose resonance. These boys maintain this singing range, adding only a few tones during several school years, indicating that this is not a transition period but a final "settling" of the voice into its approximate adult range.[17]

14 Emil Behnke and Lennox Browne (London: Sampson Low, 1885).

15 Duncan McKenzie, *Training the Boy's Changing Voice* (New Brunswick, N.J.: Rutgers University Press, 1956), pp. 11, 14.

16 Swanson, *op. cit.*, p. 63. Reprinted by permission.

Swanson's footnote explains: "Pitches in the bass clef are indicated by capital letters, in treble clef by small letters. Capitals followed by the prime (′) are in the second octave *below* middle-c, while the single capital letter indicates a pitch in the octave immediately below middle-c. The prime after a small letter indicates the second octave *above* middle-c."

17 *Ibid.*, p. 64. Reprinted by permission.

Since the handling of boys with tenor range is so crucial, Swanson devotes some space to it.

> One method of accommodating these embryo tenors is so widespread and has been used for so long that it has added several tradewords to the vocal music language. The term "alto-tenor" or "boy-tenor" goes back at least to the early part of the century. . . . The term "cambiata" is a relatively recent arrival in the junior high school music trade vocabulary. At first glance, cambiata and alto-tenor appear to describe the same technique for handling the young adolescent tenor voice. . . . A further inspection reveals that the cambiata parts often extend higher than do the usual alto-tenor parts. Perhaps herein lies the difference. The cambiata is really a low alto part, and is not appropriate for the true tenors we are concerned with here, unless these tenors are trained to sing falsetto. The cambiata parts seem to be based on the assumption (not at all borne out by evidence) that the voice change is a gradual process and that it is advisable to anticipate the emergence of the adult tenor or bass voice by "moving the voice down" to its lowest possible treble register. The alto-tenor technique in contrast seems to make a compromise between the tones available to a true adult tenor and those possible for a boy-alto to sing without forcing.[18]

He urges homogeneous classes for boys, and further segregation into basses and tenors for a year if possible.[19] The music sung should be extremely simple at first.

The most complete writing currently available on the changing voice is Duncan McKenzie's *Training the Boy's Changing Voice*. McKenzie speaks of a "settling" process which other authorities either have not found or have not mentioned.

> Up to a certain stage, the lowering voice is still the boy voice, an unchanged but changing one. It lowers through the second soprano to the alto stage. As the voice continues to lower, it develops to the "youth" stage: the voice sounds neither like a boy's nor like a man's, but has a quality peculiar to this stage. . . . As the changed voice develops and new notes emerge in the lower range, the boy voice gradually disappears until little of it remains. The voice is now at the stage when it can be classified as tenor or bass. The change will occur more rapidly if the voice is destined to be bass than if it is to be tenor.
>
> When the lowering reaches its limits, the lowering process becomes, as it were, a moving-up one; the boy loses some of the lowest notes he has been able to sing. The disappearance of the lowest notes is compensated by an extension of the upper range of the changed voice. Once the moving-up process stops, the voice is said to have "settled"; that is, the range becomes stationary. Not until the voice has settled should a boy's classification be considered his final one, the one he will have as an adult.

18 *Ibid.*, p. 66. Reprinted by permission.

19 Frederick Swanson, "When Voices Change," *Music Educators Journal*, XLVI, No. 4 (February 1960), 50.

> Because of the moving-up of the range, some boys first classified as Bass II have to be reclassified as Bass I, and others first classified as Bass I have to be reclassified as Tenor II.[20]

As for bass range, he writes:

> Considerable differences are found in the comfortable ranges of boy basses during the junior high school period, but by the time the boy gets to high school the voice is nearing the settled stage. This is likely to occur in the eleventh or twelfth year of school.[21]

He then lists bass range as:

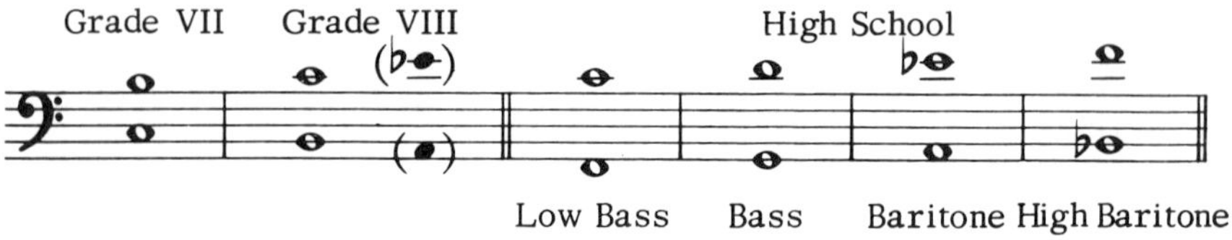

The alto-tenor range he considers to be from G below middle C to G above. The change from alto-tenor to tenor is an almost imperceptible change of quality and an extension of the lower part of the range to C below middle C.

On the assignment to a singing part during the change, McKenzie advocates a "comfortable range":

> The foundation of any successful plan to preserve the boy's singing voice during adolescence is the "comfortable range" policy. As the alto-tenor plan, for example, is carried out in the junior high school, a boy is transferred to the next lower classification as soon as he begins to have difficulty with the highest notes of the one he is in. Thus the lowest notes have an opportunity to develop, while the highest notes, being unused, gradually disappear. Success with the alto-tenor plan lies in encouraging the voice to lower, for that is what nature intends it to do. Accordingly when there is any doubt about the classification of a voice during the adolescent period, it is best to put the boy in the lower one with the proviso that he must never force the lowest notes.[22]

A third view of the changing voice is presented by Irvin Cooper, who has successfully demonstrated his theories at many meetings of music educators. Concerning range, Cooper says:[23]

> Many vocal teachers in Junior High have been misled concerning the vocal ranges of boys and girls in their classes. I will give you a table of ranges below. These ranges are not merely a theoretical dream. They have been proved in hundreds of widely separated

[20] McKenzie, *op. cit.*, p. 28. Reprinted by permission.
[21] *Ibid.*, p. 32. Reprinted by permission.
[22] *Ibid.*, p. 34. Reprinted by permission.
[23] Irvin Cooper, *Letters to Pat Concerning Junior High School Vocal Problems* (New York: Carl Fischer, Inc., 1953), p. 11. Reprinted by permission.

geographic areas, in groups varying in size from a small class of twenty-four to massed choruses of four thousand. Every new clinic corroborates these ranges. Here they are:

Girls | Boys changing (Cambiate) | Boys changed (Baritones)

(small notes indicate general tessitura of each voice)

To indicate a departure from the traditional alto-tenor, Cooper uses the term "cambiata," from the Italian for "changing." Since the definition of this voice part is crucial to his theories, and since it is not yet well understood in the profession, he will be quoted at some length.

> Herein lies the problem: the incidence of the changing voice presents an aural illusion. The illusion is caused by confusing timbre with pitch. In its first major change, the voice of the adolescent boy moves down an interval of a fourth from its preadolescent soprano range. The greatest change though, is in timbre, as the voice thickens considerably and presents a temporary illusion to the listener of sounding an octave lower than it actually sings. Your little fellows who, according to your classification sing very low, strangely enough are one octave exactly below the cambiata range. Could it be that they are in reality cambiate and your ear accepted them as "thin" basses? I am absolutely certain you will find this to be so.[24]
>
> Another point: the cambiata does not achieve its fullest characteristic richness until it has been used a little while within its full new range. Further, if this voice is kept within its natural range it will not break.
>
> Do not attempt classification individually. If you do, the cambiata will escape you again; it is only in comparison with other voices that the cambiata is recognized initially.
>
> Do not try to find cambiate. Find other voices with whose tone quality you are thoroughly familiar, thus:
>
> 1) Segregate boys from girls, . . .
> 2) Confide in the boys what you are going to do, . . .
> 3) Require all boys to sing "The Old Folks at Home," giving the key of B flat major. It must be B flat major. Let us see how this works out for ranges. Baritones will sing in this range,

[24] Very little acoustical research is available on the phenomenon of the boy's changing voice. To date, Cooper has not produced evidence from a clinically controlled experiment. One experiment using the Stroboconn did *not* support Cooper's view regarding an aural illusion, although it did find that adolescent basses had noticeably

while any others will sing thus,

Move around the boys rapidly and tap the obvious baritones on the shoulder with the instruction, "Stop singing." If in doubt about any voice, leave it; it will show up later. Don't spend time trying to decide at the moment. Speed is essential if you want to keep the boys interested in what you are doing. Very shortly you will find that the baritones are all silenced.

4) Ask the baritones to remain silent and let the remainder of the boys sing the song again in the most comfortable voice they can, using the key of G flat major. Boys who still retain their soprano voices will sing thus:

the remainder will sing thus:

Once again move around the singers and tap the shoulder of any boy who is very obviously soprano, with the instruction, "Stop singing." Very soon the soprano voices will be silent, and the remainder are cambiate. You have not even tried to find them, but there they are.

As quickly as possible segregate them into two groups thus:

Baritones	Cambiate	Boy Sopranos	Girls

Piano

To keep things moving, and to give an added stimulus as well as provide a final check, give the key of C major, let baritones sing "Row, Row Your Boat"; cambiate will sing "Are You Sleeping Brother John," while soprano girls and boys sing "Three Blind Mice." It will appear as though a miracle had been performed, not only to you, but also to the youngsters.[25]

The differences among the writers are evident regarding the range of voices and what parts the boys should sing. McKenzie favors the alto-tenor plan of accommodating and anticipating a gradual dropping of the

stronger overtones than collegiate basses. The first octave and especially the fifth above that pitch and the seventh were stronger. See: Patricia Watson, "The Adolescent Boy's Voice," *The Oklahoma School Music News,* XIV, No. 1 (October 1963), 8.

[25] Cooper, *op. cit.*, pp. 18–21. Reprinted by permission.

voice. In a critique of the cambiata plan, he raises questions about how the transition of range should be handled.[26] Swanson appears to be more concerned with helping the boys as soon as they have a significant change of voice, a drop into tenor at least.

In view of the differences of opinion about what should be done with the changing voice, what should Miss Miller and other junior high school vocal music teachers do about it? What should be Tom Jenkins' fate in music? Here are some specific suggestions for Tom's teacher.

1) Take a positive approach to boys with changing voices. Help them understand what is happening to their voices. More important, let them know that this change can add new tones and color to the music sung. Talk in terms of progress. "Doug, let's see, according to my records you could sing from C up to G two weeks ago. Today you got up to A, and with good quality, too, so you're improving. Keep it up."

2) *Never* allow a class to ridicule or laugh at the singing efforts of a boy in the throes of change. Although they may pretend to be unconcerned, boys at this age are extremely sensitive about their new-found masculinity, and one bad experience can cause a permanent withdrawal from further efforts at singing. In addition to ordering the class never to make fun of anyone's singing, an effort must be made to build a feeling of mutual assistance, of understanding, of encouragement in the class. This point is directly related to the first, since to some extent the students pick up the attitude displayed by the teacher.

3) Try the assignment of parts in performing groups according to each of the different views presented in this chapter. It is not necessary now to make a hard and fast decision as to which method is best. Teachers for whom this problem is especially pertinent will have over a period of a year or two more than one group containing changing voices. Try for the cambiata in one class, for alto-tenor in another. Only experience can tell what will work in a particular school situation. It may turn out, and this seems quite likely, that one approach works better with ninth-grade boys than with seventh-graders. The boys' previous musical training, amount of time for class meetings, whether or not the students are selected—all of these considerations affect what the boys can and should sing. Try segregating boys from girls for a semester or a year, if the school schedule will allow for it.

4) Check the range and quality of the boys' voices at least three or four times each year during the period of change. Encourage each boy to ask for an immediate voice check when he feels his range has changed to the point that he is having trouble reaching the notes of his part. The rate and extent of change are highly individual matters, and there is as much variation in voice development as there is in other physical development. Nor is change consistent within the individual. Often there are plateaus, sudden changes, and sometimes inexplicable regressions.

[26] McKenzie, *op. cit.*, p. 83.

By checking and observing the development of each boy's voice, a young teacher can learn firsthand what voice change sounds like and how it progresses. With experience it is possible to judge range by the boy's speaking voice and physical appearance. A short conversation with a boy can in most cases give an accurate impression of the general pitch level of his voice. Heavier facial features, stature, and enlarged larynx usually indicate a maturing voice.

5) Attempt to meet boys' vocal needs in general music classes. Too often teachers in a general music class of thirty teach as if the three boys with changing voices weren't there. Begin by seating them together, in the front row near the piano. Add to the section as other boys join in the change. Then on easy unison songs help the changing voices sing an octave lower by playing their notes on the piano, especially the starting pitch. If the teacher is a man, he should by all means sing some of the time with these boys. Select songs with parts for the changing voices, especially parts that are *easy*. When none is included with a song, try writing a simple part. The part can and often should be as simple as the roots of the chords to a song such as "Down in the Valley," or a short ostinato figure. True, it is hard to do much for the first boy whose voice changes, unless he is a highly capable musician who can sing a part on his own. But what happens to a boy's voice during the change is so important that every effort should be made to help and encourage his singing.

6) Be especially careful in selection of music. Vocal numbers should not consistently violate the tonal limits revealed through checking of the boys' voices. Control of the voice is difficult during the voice change. Choose simple music, especially when most of the boys are changing quite a bit. If a number does not fully fit the needs of the group, do not use it.

7) Stress correct singing, with proper breathing and freedom from tension. The voice is never helped by forcing or straining to reach certain tones, or by singing with a blatant quality in an attempt to sound like a male ten years older. Upon occasion, a boy may be asked not to sing certain notes, although as a regular practice this kills interest and should be avoided.

CLASSIFYING VOICES IN HIGH SCHOOL

The testing of voices has two purposes: to serve as a means of selecting singers, and to get the singer placed in the right part. Initially the teacher should screen the would-be members of performing groups to see that they possess the minimum requirements to profit from choral experience. After hearing the voice and reviewing the information presented on the student information sheet (suggested on page 109), he must make a judgment as to whether or not the rewards of study *for the student* justify the student's expenditure of time and interest.

The best time for auditions is in the spring, so that the class can start right to work in the fall, without delays to wait for the testing of voices.

Voices are generally grouped according to two criteria—range and quality. In high school the most frequently used ranges for the various classifications are:

Soprano Alto Tenor Bass

Many students cannot sing all the notes in any one classification. Such singers are put in the sections that most nearly represent their ranges.

One can become familiar with the tone quality of the various classifications only by hearing them, not by reading about them. There are many fine recordings of bass, alto, tenor, and soprano soloists, and a concept of quality can be deepened by listening to them. Recordings of choral music, especially Baroque works, bring out the characteristic qualities of the various sections. Of course, it should be kept in mind that the recordings are made by adult voices and not by untrained adolescent singers.

For several reasons it is almost impossible to classify adolescent voices with certainty.

1) Adolescent voices, especially the voices of boys, are not stable.

2) The psychological factor enters into the student's performance. Under one set of conditions he may capably sing passages that under other circumstances he could not even approximate. Usually the conditions in an audition are about as unfavorable for the adolescent as they can be.

3) Many students who are auditioned at the beginning of the year do not know how to sing correctly. The development of correct singing habits will make a noticeable difference in a student's range and tone quality.

4) The voices of teen-agers, especially girls in early adolescence, are, like their actions, remarkably homogeneous. What is frequently encountered is an SATB chorus largely composed of second sopranos and baritones with a limited range.

5) The needs of the group have to be considered in classifying the voices, especially in the case of girls. If a girls' glee club consists of one hundred voices, clearly there cannot be fifty second sopranos and only fifteen altos. Some adjustments have to be made. This does not mean that a teacher can or should get an additional alto merely by moving a soprano into the alto section. But whenever possible, the classifications within the group should be considered, in order to maintain a reasonable balance of parts. If good balance is not possible, the teacher will have to do the best he can with the apportionment of voices.

For these reasons, extensive discussion of the "break," color in the voices, and specific tonal patterns to use in classifying does not seem warranted for the school vocal teacher. Some singing teachers even decry the idea of registers in the voice, because they feel the voice is derived from one pair of vocal cords and should have a continuous compass.[27]

Since some classification is necessary for part singing, however, the teacher must make judgments on range and quality, imperfect as these judgments may be. If possible, students should be heard privately.

Place the singer where he cannot see the keyboard, because some students with musical training have preconceived ideas about the notes they can sing. Then have him sing a five-note ascending and descending scale pattern:

Begin girls on middle C and boys an octave lower, and move up stepwise until the top notes of the pattern show strain. Then shift to this pattern, starting at what appears to be the student's middle range and moving down:

Next have each student sing a familiar song such as "America." Transpose the song into three different keys about a fourth apart, possibly into C for a low range, F for a middle range, and A or B flat for a high range. Listen for intonation as well as for range and quality. Other simple testing procedures may be used if time permits. The range, general tone quality, and other pertinent facts about each voice should be written down, dated, and filed for future reference.

Upon occasion, a teacher selects the better students for a select choir or ensemble. In such a case the procedures can be expanded in the following manner.

1) Check the student's ability to match pitch quickly and accurately; play a series of three or four pitches in the singer's range on the piano, and see how rapidly and exactly they are sung back.

2) Listen for a highly individualistic tone quality which may not blend well with other voices.

3) Present the singer with a line of music to sing at sight.

If individual auditions are not possible, group methods will have to suffice, such as those recommended by Cooper for finding cambiate. The patterns recommended for individual testing can also be used for group testing in which changing voices are not involved. Work the boys up to D above middle C. Then arbitrarily place in the tenor section all boys who

[27] Roma, *op. cit.*, p. 36.

can sing the D comfortably; the remainder of the boys will make up the bass section. The same technique can be followed with the girls—all who can sing F on the top line comfortably are placed in the soprano section. An individual audition should follow later in the semester.

"Now remember, girls, we're all sopranos! They get to sit next to the tenors!"

Copyright 1958 by United Feature Syndicate, Inc.

WHAT'S IN A NAME?

Students at the junior high school level sometimes attach much importance to the name of the part they sing. Boys are sensitive about being called "soprano" or "alto"—names associated with girls. To eliminate any problem here, some teachers call boy sopranos "first tenors." Cooper has proposed the term "cambiata" partly because he feels it makes for greater pride among the boys.

Caution must be exercised in the use of the words "first" and "second." No one wants to be second in anything in modern-day America, so the term "high" can be used with the girls' or treble part, and "low" with the boys' or bass-clef part. Because girls' voices are so much alike in early adolescence, some teachers regularly have girls trade parts, one section learning the high part for one song and the low part for another.

To the teacher, who will work on teaching proper singing and musical sensitivity regardless of the size of the group, whether the organization is called choir, chorus, glee club, troubadors, sextet, or ensemble is not a serious matter. As long as the terms are used conventionally—a sextet contains six singers and glee clubs are either boys or girls—almost any name is acceptable. However, sometimes students, especially in junior high school, place much importance on what a group is called. In some schools the "choir"' is for the talented and the "glee club" is for anyone else. Therefore, the teacher may discuss with the group the possibility of another name. In some schools it has been the making of a new attitude in the group, and it is a matter on which the teacher can allow the students freedom of choice.

GROUP SIZE AND SEATING

Generally, the larger a student group, the better it will sound. Teenagers whose voices are not yet fully developed need the support of a number of singers on their part. This gives them confidence and makes their efforts more satisfying. Happily, a group of average voices can, when put together properly, sound very beautiful. The individual voice timbres apparently combine to make a rich tone, and minor pitch deviations are no longer noticeable. If two performers are five vibrations apart, the "beats" are easily heard. But when other voices are added, some of them being one, two, or three vibrations different, the "beats" are no longer distinguishable. A tone with such pitch variation is lacking in brilliance and clarity, but it can still be pleasing.

Group size is relative to the ability and age of the singers, the demands of the music, and the acoustics of the place of performance, so no ideal size can be recommended. Probably student choral groups sound best with forty-five to ninety voices; beyond this point the size becomes unwieldy for the teacher to handle in the regular manner. Nor can the distribution of singers on each part be given with much certainty. Since the lower pitches of a singer's vocal range do not have the "carrying power" of high pitches, and since the lower parts in a choral group are more easily overbalanced, the low voice parts generally need more singers.

In assigning seats in a section, two strong singers should be placed side by side, so that they can support each other. Then less mature singers can be placed on either side of the more able students. In this way, the weaker singers can learn from the better ones. The seating should be changed from time to time so that the singers learn to sing with different persons and have the chance to hear the group from other locations.

SELECTING AN ACCOMPANIST

A poor accompanist can virtually break a choral group by slowing the class pace and confusing the singers by playing the music incorrectly. Therefore, the teacher must select and train the accompanist with utmost care.

If possible, several accompanists should be selected for the organization. One can substitute for another, and an entire rehearsal will not be disrupted because an accompanist is absent. Most teachers must choose their accompanists from within the choral group. In such situations, the use of several accompanists gives more students the experience of accompanying, and also gives them an opportunity to sing.

Unfortunately, a distinction often has to be made between accompanists and pianists. Because of the pedagogical practices of many piano teachers, it is possible for a player to perform a few concertos and etudes extremely well, and still not be able to read the simplest of music. These "rote-type" performers usually make poor accompanists because they have to commit to memory almost every piece they play, and on certain occasions there is not time to memorize the accompaniment. This type of pianist also tends to be inflexible in following a conductor.

In selecting accompanists, three simple tests can be given.

1) Have the applicants sightread the accompaniment to a piece of octavo music, preferably one that is not too difficult. Rate them on their ability to keep going without stopping, and of course on their general accuracy in playing the music.

2) Have the applicants sightread only the voice parts of a choral number. Do not select a work of a contrapuntal nature for this purpose, since music of this type is too difficult for most high school students to sightread. Many times the applicants have trouble reading the voice parts in SATB music.

3) Choose a simple octavo selection and have the applicants learn the accompaniment before the audition. At the try-out, have each pianist play the piece while you conduct. In order to see how well he can follow, go through the piece and alter the tempo several times. Then ask him to play a certain passage—for example, the tenor part on page four, second score, fourth bar. This will soon reveal his alertness in following verbal directions. If the accompanist can transpose and modulate, this is an added boon to the teacher and the class.

Few teachers are fortunate enough to have accompanists who can play fluently through the three tests just mentioned, so some training is in order. Learning to play the notes on the page and to read the voice parts is simply a matter of individual practice. If the accompanist studies privately, his teacher is usually more than willing to give him special assistance. At the beginning of the year, it is wise to hear the accompanists play their music privately *before* the piece is practiced with the singers. The most common cause of trouble for inexperienced accompanists is the clef sign used for the tenor part. It is usually necessary to explain this phenomenon to the pianist. When seen on a tenor line, any of the first four clefs (see below) indicate that the notes do not sound as written, but rather one octave lower. The fifth sign is the tenor clef, on which the pitches sound as written, with middle C on the fourth line.

The main task in training an accompanist is to teach him to anticipate tempos and verbal instructions. The development of this ability will be hastened if the teacher is consistent in his approach to the music. The accompanist should also learn to think of a piece of music by phrases and sections rather than note by note. This helps him to envisage possible starting and stopping places.

USE OF THE PIANO

The use of the piano in teaching vocal music is rather limited. Aside from the initial playing of parts in the rote learning process, the piano should be avoided for demonstration purposes because its tone is so unlike the tone of the voice. Once a tone is struck on the piano, it immediately begins to fade away. In vocal music the objective is a continuous, full sound.

A beginning choral teacher who was not a voice major in college may be self-conscious about singing in front of a large group of students, and consequently he turns to the piano for all demonstrations. To correct this habit, he can at first sing short and easy passages for the group in order to gain confidence in his ability to demonstrate musical ideas.

The question of how much accompaniment should be used depends upon the ability of the singers. Musically advanced groups can and should sing frequently without the piano, even on works that will be accompanied in performance. Inexperienced musicians, too, should do some singing without the piano in almost every class meeting. Care must be taken so that the piano does not cover up faults in the singing. Also, the singers must develop a degree of independence from the piano, because in the unfamiliar circumstances of a performance they may find it more difficult to hear the accompaniment.

MEMORIZING MUSIC

Choral groups almost always memorize the music which they perform before an audience, while instrumental groups never do, except for one or two standard numbers used on the marching field. There are good reasons for memorizing by choral groups:

1) There are no distractions caused by holding music or turning pages. All the singers' attention can be centered on singing the music and watching the director.
2) The appearance of the group is improved; there is no chance for a singer to bury his head in the music.
3) Many annoyances are eliminated—loose pages fluttering to the floor, and music brushing the back of a singer's neck.
4) Memorized pieces are usually thoroughly learned pieces.

It is possible to facilitate the process of memorization by using some of the psychological principles described in Chapter Seven. The principle of distributed effort applies to memorization, which is most easily and thoroughly accomplished in many short periods, rather than in one or two long ones. The recognition of patterns and relationships in music is also directly applicable to memorization, since most works of music have an over-all pattern or form. To illustrate the presence of form in music, the teacher can demonstrate the standard form for popular songs: introduction, eight measures, repeat eight measures, bridge, repeat eight measures again. When singers can recognize an over-all pattern, the learning of music is simplified. The music can be scanned for accents, holds, solos, ritards. Many times these features show a pattern in themselves.

The students should be aware of the fact that the words frequently are poems, and have phrase endings that rhyme. Often the music follows the pattern of the words in such cases. An English setting of J. S. Bach's *Wachet auf, ruft uns die Stimme* will serve as an example.

> Now let every tongue adore Thee,
> Let men with angels sing before Thee.
> Let harps and cymbals now unite!
>
> All Thy gates with pearl are glorious,
> Where we partake through faith victorious,
> With angels round Thy throne of light.[28]

There are several teaching devices to assist the students in memorizing. They can be asked to write the words to the songs, as a test that will influence their grades. A group memorization technique can be operated in this manner: Select a logical section of from two to four lines, and let each student study it by himself for about twenty to thirty seconds. Then have the entire group recite the words together without their music. If

[28] Copyright 1946 by E. C. Schirmer Music Co. Reprinted by permission.

this goes well, call upon two or three individuals to recite the sections. Move on to another portion of the text, and after it has been memorized, have the group recite both the first and second sections. Move the process along as quickly as possible, and do not keep it up too long at one time.

To vary the procedure just described, the words can be passed back and forth between teacher and singers. For example, Now let EVERY TONGUE ADORE THEE; or, now LET every TONGUE adore THEE. Another variation is to recite a line and ask for the first word of the next line. Chorus: NOW LET EVERY TONGUE ADORE THEE. Teacher: "George?" George: "Let." Chorus: LET MEN WITH, etc.

The teacher can facilitate memorization by having the students sing the piece from memory at an early stage of preparation. Singers can become so accustomed to the "crutch" of looking at music that it is difficult for them to break away from it. This should not be urged too soon, however, since it may encourage faking.

The teacher should impress upon the singers the necessity of thinking ahead when singing. Foresight is necessary to prevent such serious mishaps as singing through a break, or starting out on the wrong section of the music. Lines are less likely to be forgotten when the singers think ahead.

Calamity can also be averted by good spot practice. In a piece of music there are frequently a few crucial places at which the music is most likely to break down—changes of section, change of key, and so on. The singers should be made to feel especially confident at these points.

Some teachers in an effort to build the confidence of their singers, unconsciously develop habits which increase the students' dependence. One of these is the habit of singing along with the group. Generally this practice should be used only to help a part that is weak, or to encourage the singers in a strategic place such as the beginning of a new section. The danger is that the singers begin to rely on the teacher's help. Since he cannot sing along in a concert, the students should learn to do well without his support. Another disadvantage is that the teacher's singing tends to make the music sound better to him than it actually is. He should be listening carefully to the group, not to his own voice—even though the latter may sound better.

The teacher should also avoid "mouthing" the words. This technique can be of only limited help to the singers. If all the parts do not have the same words at the same time, the help is negligible; and even if the words are synchronized, it is doubtful how much the singers are able to benefit from lipreading. They should have the words learned well enough to get along without this assistance.

Needless to say, all numbers that are to be performed in public should be memorized by the teacher. He makes a poor impression when he conducts from the printed page while his singers perform from memory. The teacher should maintain eye contact with the singers at all times during performance, and this precludes looking at a copy of the music.

Questions

1. How would you explain to a choral class of high school freshmen and sophomores why it is important for them to learn how to sing correctly?
2. How would you explain to a ninth-grader that the style of singing used by the latest teen-age idol is not usable or appropriate with music of artistic quality?
3. Should a choral teacher attempt to develop an adult-like singing tone in a high school choir? in a junior high school choir? Why, or why not?
4. What analogies can be used to give the students the idea of the open throat?
5. Ronald Clark can sing from C below middle C up to D above middle C. According to Swanson which part should he sing? According to McKenzie? According to Cooper?
6. Suppose that several boys in chorus show a marked tendency to force tones, producing a strained, unpleasant quality. What can be done to reduce this problem? Which step in the singing routine should be emphasized?

Projects

1. Find three choral pieces that contain long tones suitable for work on proper breathing. They should be simple, yet musically worthy of study. Handel's "Thanks Be to Thee" is an example.
2. Review three collections of part songs for boys' changing voices. Note the range and tessitura of the parts in each of the three books.
3. Listen to recordings of solos by sopranos, altos, tenors, and basses. Select one of each voice type that is suitable as a model for teen-age singers to emulate.
4. With your college music methods class, work out a consistent vowel pronunciation on the following phrases: "I'm going away," "Still are your thoughts." Then practice singing these words together:

5. Using members of your methods class, give several an audition for a choral music group. Classify their voices and assign them to an appropriate part.

XIII

teaching instrumental music

Instrumental music teachers tend to think of themselves as a breed apart from other teachers of music. While this is largely not true, the instrumental teacher does face some conditions that differ from those encountered by the vocal music teacher.

The most significant difference is the degree of specialization. Instrumental music involves a conglomeration of fingerings, embouchures, bowings, and other specialized techniques and knowledge. Scraping a bassoon reed, stopping notes on the French horn, spiccato bowing on the violin, the several fingerings for high G on the clarinet—these are all highly technical bits of skill and learning.[1] The teacher of singing faces many challenges, but at least there is only one species of the human voice.

BEGINNING INSTRUMENT INSTRUCTION

In most school systems the custom is to begin instrumental music in the fourth or fifth grade. However, in some districts instruments are first offered in junior or even senior high school. Even in systems that begin instruction in the elementary grades, beginning classes should be offered in junior high school for students who are new in the district or who are just now becoming interested in music study. Therefore, some beginning instrument teaching is a distinct possibility for the instrumental music teacher in the secondary school.

[1] An aid to the teacher in recalling all instrumental fingerings, trills, rolls, positions, and transpositions is *Fingering Charts for Instrumentalists* by Clarence V. Hendrickson (New York: Carl Fischer, Inc., 1957). The book is a handy pocket size.

Pre-Band Instruments?

In some instrumental music programs much value is placed on pre-band instrument classes. These inexpensive and easy-to-play instruments are on the order of modern-day recorders, although they lack the range and gentle tone of the recorder. They are included in the instrumental program in order to weed out the less talented and less interested students, and to provide some training in the reading of notation.

The involvement of the instrumental teacher with special classes of pre-band instruments is questionable on several counts. One: it is a pre-*band* program. What is being done to encourage and train string players during this "band" experience? Two: these simple instruments have little carry-over to real band instruments. There is no transfer of embouchure and very little of fingering. Three: the validity of pre-band instruments as prognosticators of success in instrumental music has not been established. Four: if the training in music reading is valuable, it should be carried on as a part of the regular elementary basic music program, the benefits of which will accrue to all students.

In the elementary music program, the work with keyboard and recorders, or an exploratory program including strings, appears to be more valid from the standpoint of music education. The instrumental teacher can use the time saved from the pre-band class to do a better job of teaching the legitimate instruments, which is after all the surest way to have a successful instrumental music program.

Pupil Guidance

If the instrumental program is to be a part of the music curriculum, then its goals and practices must be consistent with those of music education in general. One point at which instrumental music sometimes deviates from its proper educational function has been in the selection of students to play instruments. The problem has been twofold, in that it involves both belief and validity. Since the music program exists in the schools to educate all students in music as fully as their interest and ability allow, the idea of in some way selecting only those students who are most likely to succeed is objectionable. Unless high school instrumental music is regarded as being akin to the football team in that it must produce a winner, then all except the clearly incapable should be allowed a fair trial. If after a year Donald decides playing the trumpet is not for him, at least he has had that educational experience and hopefully has learned from it what he could. It would have been fine if he had had the interest and ability to continue the trumpet or attempt another instrument, but the music curriculum has not suffered because he was offered the experience.

The other aspect of the problem is that no one could really have determined whether or not Donald would be a success in instrumental music.

Sometimes a student who shows little promise or motivation turns out a few years later to be a fine instrumentalist.

In the 1920's the school board in one city informed a local musician that they would be glad to start a band in the schools *if* he could present a "playing band" in three months. With such a deadline, he gave all interested students a hastily created test before they were allowed to become members of the demonstration band. The students were asked to march around the school gymnasium to the beat of a drum. All those who got out of step were eliminated. The director freely admitted years later, "I don't suppose that test was worth a thing. But I had to do something to cut the numbers down to where I had instruments for them." Such a procedure was understandable in those years and under those conditions.

But now instrumental music has been well-established in the schools for about four decades; expedient actions should have been retired. Today decisions affecting the lives of youngsters should be made with the utmost care and knowledge, and not on the basis of homemade tests by the teacher. The topic of talent testing was discussed in Chapter Six, and the limitations of these carefully constructed, highly scientific efforts were pointed out at that time. How much less valid, then, must be the test that a teacher concocts for his own use?

Furthermore, through rental instrument plans with music merchants, the rental of school-owned instruments, and the cooperation of an informed board of education, all but the most financially depressed districts can now make it possible for sincerely interested students to try instrumental music. It is the teacher's obligation to keep the school administration informed about the needs of the instrumental department, both as to teaching staff and instruments.

Only general guides can be offered with confidence regarding what instruments should be assigned to individual students. If a youngster faces a lengthy session with braces on his teeth, or if he has an underbite (lower teeth in front of upper) or crooked teeth, he should be guided away from brasses. Generally, small students should not try large instruments. Boys who have thick fingers should be encouraged to try instruments other than violin; notes in the higher positions are too close together to allow for thick fingers without some kind of compensatory movement, which is difficult. Students whose pitch sense is below average should especially avoid strings, French horn, and trombone.

The most important point to consider in assigning an instrument is the desire of the student. A teen-ager can accomplish wonders—when he wants to. He can become proficient on an instrument while appearing to defy all the physical qualifications. The teacher should guide students in instrument selection, but he should not require that they take a particular instrument or none at all. The incidence of drop-out among students who begin on an instrument other than their first choice is higher than normal.

Although instrumental music is offered for the values that accrue to the students who take it, the teacher should attempt to maintain some balance in instrumentation, both for playing music in the near future and in high school. To achieve this balance, the teacher will have to rely on his good judgment in guiding students in their selection of instruments, and even then he has no assurance that five years hence he will not have a half-dozen drummers and no baritones. The number of students encouraged to begin on each instrument should be in proportion to instrumentation needs listed on pages 306 and 307, with consideration given the fact that a few clarinet players, for instance, will transfer to oboe and bassoon. It is helpful if the school owns the instruments, so that the inventory available to beginners can be balanced.

Many schools own instruments that are rented to beginning students for a nominal charge. If the school system does not provide instruments, or if its supply cannot meet the demand, students may rent from local merchants. Some school systems closely integrate their activities with a certain merchant, in which case ethics must be closely observed as to bids and equal opportunity for all merchants. If at all possible, the student should not be required to purchase an instrument before study is undertaken, because this entails a financial risk for the parent. Instruments that are relatively expensive, uncommon, or difficult to play (oboe, viola, tuba, bass clarinet) should not be offered beginners, if for no other reason than to cut down on the variety of instruments in the class. Generally beginning instruction is offered on the following instruments: flute, clarinet, trumpet, horn, trombone, baritone, percussion, violin, and cello.

Organizing the Beginning Class

The relationship between instrumental classes in school and private instruction outside of school is not clear at times to parents and school administrators. Private instruction is preferable and should be encouraged because it affords the obvious advantage of individual attention. Class lessons are necessary in school, however, because few schools can support the prohibitively high cost of individual instruction. Besides, in many communities competent private teachers are not available on all orchestral instruments. In a sense, class lessons are an expedient, but they are a good expedient in several ways. There is a unity in what is taught and in the rate of progress, so that within a year or two the students can be put together to form a band or orchestra. Then, there is a certain amount of motivation when students work together and learn that other students have difficulty in playing their instruments, too. Finally, as the teacher becomes experienced in teaching classes, he finds that by the use of good pedagogical techniques he can accomplish during the first year or two of the students' study almost as much as he could in private lessons. Naturally, as students advance and playing problems become more individualized, class sessions rapidly lose their value.

Beginning classes should meet a minimum of two times a week for thirty to forty-five minutes, and each group should not exceed twelve members unless larger numbers cannot be avoided. If this number is consistently exceeded, the teacher should work to secure additional teaching help. With strings, for instance, it takes some time just to tune twelve instruments, and the larger the number, the less time there is in which to teach and give attention to each student.

The class should be as homogeneous as possible, although this will depend primarily on the schedule of the school and teacher. A mixing of strings and winds should be avoided at all cost. Sharp keys are better for strings and flat keys for winds, and the two do not mix well until the intermediate level. Even families of instruments in the same class present problems to the teacher. Just as he gets ready to call out a note to the clarinets he remembers that the note will be different for the flute; when he mentions one fingering to the violins he must be ready to suggest another to the cellos.

Homogeneous classes do have one disadvantage: they can create a problem for the classroom teacher, who may find that he has a few pupils absent during a sizable portion of the day, a situation that can work quite a hardship on him. If the school has two or more instrumental teachers, one can take brasses, another woodwinds, and hopefully a third strings. This removes many students from the class at once, reducing interruptions for the classroom teacher to two each week, and requiring the students to miss only a minimum of regular classwork.

Beginning Instruction Books

Many publishing companies offer inexpensive instruction books for beginning instrumentalists. The books contain simple works that can be played by a complete ensemble at a remarkably early stage. Though generally well-written, many of them reveal distressing similarities. There seems to be an attempt in thirty-two pages to give the player all the signs and notes that might conceivably appear on the printed page, even symbols that are seldom encountered in the beginning literature. Kuhn has observed, ". . . in most instruction books the introduction of technical problems is dry and unimaginative on the one hand and, on the other, does not present enough material to master the problems."[2] He suggests the following criteria for selecting a methods book:

1) Are there general instructions on the care and use of the instrument?
2) Are there correct illustrations of fundamental posture, positions, embouchure?
3) Is there a complete fingering chart?

[2] Wolfgang E. Kuhn, *Instrumental Music: Principles and Methods of Instruction* (Boston: Allyn and Bacon, Inc., 1962), p. 112.

4) What is the value of the musical content?
5) Are technical problems introduced logically and functionally?
6) Are directions given simply and clearly?
7) Is the music edited well?
8) Is ensemble music included?
9) Is there a list of musical terms?
10) Is the physical make-up and appearance of the book appropriate?[3]

Because so many instruction books contain limited material, supplementary music of a simple nature will be needed, especially if within the year the beginners attempt to play for an audience, which it is desirable to have them do. The instrumental teacher can use for this purpose simple, solid arrangements of folk songs and well-known melodies.

Teaching the Beginning Class

The principles of music teaching presented in Chapter Seven have much application to the teaching of beginning instrumental music. The most challenging problem for the teacher is to clarify the complex nature of playing an instrument, as was illustrated on page 136 in the multiplicity of instructions given the young violinist. The beginner cannot do everything at once. Therefore the teacher must settle for concentration on one thing at a time, and by alternation between wholes and parts slowly build the complex action involved in playing an instrument.

Because much kinesthetic learning is involved in instrumental playing, the teacher's efforts should be also directed toward the building of good habit patterns. For instance, the development of an embouchure is largely a matter of muscle movement and strength. A teacher cannot hope to have students play with the proper embouchure if he presents it once, and then proceeds to other things. Embouchure must be taught over a long period of time, using a variety of approaches, sprinkled liberally with short reminders.

Mastery of an instrument, then, requires both complex learning and habit development; the teacher must carefully combine different phases of the learning activity. For instance, the clarinet players may play long tones on open G, checking with their left hand to see that they are "keeping their chins down" as they play. When they are successful at this, the teacher may point to a line of music that has been studied previously, and say, "Now that you have the position of your lower lip and chin right, let's see if you can play this line *while at the same time* keeping your good lip and chin position." If the students have worked enough on their em-

[3] *Ibid.*, pp. 30–34. Reprinted by permission.

bouchures and notes and rhythms, they will be able to put together the two aspects of good playing. If they fail, they should again concentrate on one thing.

Two practical procedures can be helpful in teaching the beginning class. One is having the students sing the line of music *in rhythm* at proper concert pitch, using the note names while fingering the notes on their instruments. Sharps, flats, and naturals can also be sung, using only the note names while the students think and finger the accidentals. The attention of the students should be drawn to the key signature and accidentals before going through the line. A variation is to have the students say "tah" or "lah" for each note. Singing while fingering is especially helpful in the first semester of study. Another practical step is silent fingering, which is useful to students at any level. There is no need to have students sitting idly by in an instrumental music class. While one section is playing, the others can be fingering a new line, or one on which they need practice.

Rote Procedures

Rote teaching is useful in the early stages of study. One of the most confusing things for the students is to put together the mechanics of instrument playing with the reading of the notes. Rote procedures allow the proper mechanical habits of playing to be assimilated without distraction. In addition, when music stands are not needed, the teacher can move about freely to give help with fingering or playing positions. There is no need for him to remain in front of the group, because there is almost no need for formal conducting—it is not meaningful to students at this stage. The class is started by verbal cues instead of hand motions. Usually the teacher should count out a complete measure, inserting "ready, begin" or "ready, play" in tempo on the final two counts.

Sometimes difficult problems, such as crossing the break between registers on the clarinet, are best introduced by rote. A portion of "Three Blind Mice" (B-A-G, B-A-G) can help the player to get across more easily, and also make the relationship between the two registers more clear to him. "Three Blind Mice" is a remarkably useful piece. It can be used to help trumpeters who cannot get low C easily (E-D-C, E-D-C). It also can help trombonists practice slide positions (D-C-B flat, D-C-B flat) or (A-G-F, A-G-F). On violin it can provide practice crossing strings (B-A-G, B-A-G).

Rote procedures are especially valuable on strings because all string instruments are in concert pitch, all use bows, and they have most of their open strings in common. An example from the string class is the pizzicato playing of simple patterns. The teacher can say, "Pluck the notes D and E—open D then first finger. Let's play it this fast (*said in tempo using quarter notes*): D-E-D-E-rest rest, D-E-D-E-rest rest. Instruments in position. . . . (*in tempo*) Ready, play." The class plays the pitches and says the notes and rests aloud. Many variations are possible to enliven the class. For one, the teacher may turn his back to the students, pick up his violin and play a simple pattern (D-E-F sharp-E-D) and ask the students, "I started on D. What other notes did I play?" If the students are quick to tell the proper note names, he can try this step: "I started on D. Don't tell me what I played. Just play it back to me. . . . (*in tempo*) Ready, begin."

Later the teacher may start showing the students the notation for the patterns presented in the rote experience. Three approaches can be used. For the five-note pattern D-E-F sharp-E-D, the teacher can write the notes on the board and say, "Here's a picture of the notes we played. This is what they look like when they're written down." Another approach is for him to write the pattern on the board before the rote instruction, and have the students read it, which is of course the normal reading process. A variation of this is for the teacher to say, "Follow the notes on the board. I may or may not play what's there. Check me and see if I do." The third approach, and in some ways the most educational, is to ask a student to think up a five-note pattern and sing it to the class, being sure to get an accurate starting pitch. Then he can play it on his instrument, and write it on the board. The singing is more likely to be an accurate representation of the pattern he thought up, so it serves as a check on the accuracy of his writing and playing.

Rhythm and bowing on string instruments are closely integrated. Rote work is excellent for getting the bow arm to move properly in rhythm. The teacher can start this early in the study of the instrument. "Now we've played on the four open strings G, D, A, and E. Let's play one note down bow and one up bow, rest two counts, then go to the next string. Do G first, then D, A, and E. After that, we'll come back down E, A, D, and G." The students then do the pattern

Other patterns can be approached in the same manner so that the players will simultaneously gain freedom of bow movement and comprehension of rhythm.

Because time is at a premium in every beginning class, instruction should be as efficient as possible. One way to hear individual students quickly and still keep everyone learning is for the class to play a line together. Then, in rhythm, the teacher can call out, "Ralph, play," and Ralph plays the line alone, as the rest of the students finger along. Then the teacher can call for the entire group again or for another student. Thus there is no break in the music until the teacher calls for it. Another way to be efficient in the use of class time is to hear individual students play their assigned lesson on an informal rotation basis. Only two or three students selected at random need play a line of music alone. In this way, all students prepare because they may be called on.

Stress the Musical Qualities

The teacher of the beginning instrumental class needs to make a special effort to keep the activities musical. As was pointed out, many methods books tend to be unimaginative and dull, with a strongly mechanistic approach to music. Because so much attention needs to be placed on moving a finger and counting a note, musical expression seems to get lost. Finally, when a student knows only three or four notes, and whole notes at that, it is difficult to perform more than a few pieces. A certain amount of technical facility must precede the making of music on an instrument. But the teacher should not give up teaching music. Again, rote and memorization are a real help here. Because of the effort required to learn a piece from the written page, many of the students will have nearly memorized the piece anyway, so not much additional effort is required to have the class play from memory. The distractions of reading the music are thus reduced to a minimum.

When the students learn their first little melody, be it "Lightly Row" or "Twinkle, Twinkle, Little Star," the teacher should work further on the number to bring out its musical qualities. What is the high point of the melody? What are the groups of notes that belong together? Should the piece be smooth or choppy? Books of simply-arranged solos, such as the *Breeze Easy Recital Pieces* by John Kinyon,[4] are available and can be used to supplement the method book. Whatever the material used, instrumental classes should above all make music.

Rhythm

An instrumentalist who gets lost and cannot perform the notes with the rest of the group is learning nothing and hindering his classmates. Therefore, one of the requirements of music instruction is that it give the students training in the execution of rhythm. As a first step, the students can be told to tap the foot lightly on each beat. Unless they have considerable previous musical experience, the students during the first year may continue to maintain the beat with the foot.

If the class has trouble doing a rhythm correctly, they can lay their instruments on their laps and clap out the pattern. If they have trouble with the steady rhythmic feel of a piece, they should practice standing

[4] New York: Music Publishers Holding Corporation, 1958.

up, marking time, and playing the music as they march in place. The most frequent problem among young students is the separation of the beat which they tap and the rhythmic figure which they play. Many times they will do this:

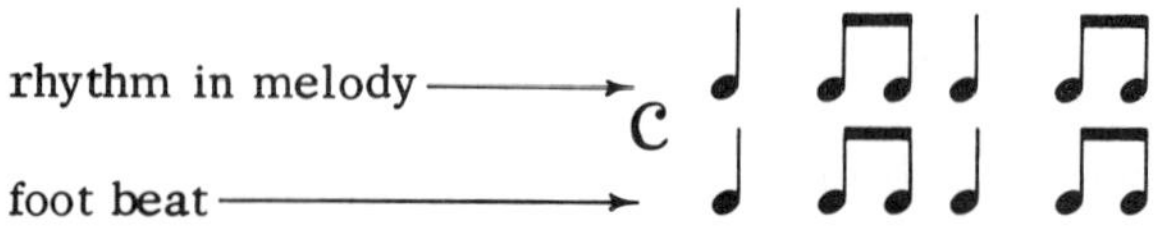

Marching helps to cure this tendency.

In addition to the steady foot beat, a system of counting must be taught. Suggestions for syllables to be used in counting are given on page 157. The students should count out lines of music in singsong fashion before playing them. Singsong counting has real purpose: it accentuates the rhythmic swing or pulse. Never should the beats be recited mechanically; rhythm is not like that.

Practicing

Strange as it may seem, the teacher must teach the instrumentalist how to practice. Telling the young student, "Practice each day for thirty minutes" is comparable to the physical education instructor saying, "Spend thirty minutes a day building up your muscles." How? Doing what? A portion of each class must be devoted to giving specific directions on what is to be done outside of class. The beginning student needs to know how fast the line of music is to be played, and he must know how to make sure he is using the right embouchure or position. Above all, he needs to realize that practicing is not a process of "putting in time." The emphasis should be placed on practicing *correctly*. Shorter practice periods with a high level of concentration are what the beginning instrumentalist needs.

If possible, the student should establish a daily practice time which is respected by his family and friends. Some teachers make a point of having students fill in a card that parents initial indicating the amount of time spent practicing. Such efforts are fine, as long as they do not place too much attention on time rather than results. There is so much to learn about the playing of a new instrument that the student's attention might better be focused on remembering the musical, rather than the clerical, aspects of his instruction.

NEED FOR TEACHING FUNDAMENTAL SKILLS

There is a continuing need for teaching instrumental music skills in a group situation beyond the beginning levels. Most school instrumentalists after a year or two in class lessons move into a band or orchestra. At this point it is unlikely that they have mastered as fully as they should the production of a fine mature tone, the many varied types of articulation and bowings, or the best embouchure or playing position. Clearly, private instruction at this stage is most desirable, but many players lack money or interest, and often there is no competent teacher available. So the instrumental teacher has to do what he can to develop in his players the skills that make for adequate performance of the music they study. He cannot assume that a fundamental like breath support has been learned after it has been taught once. If only it were that easy! Fundamentals must be worked on bit by bit in beginning classes and in the bands and orchestras of the junior and senior high school.

Fortunately, as in the case of singing, if students grasp the fundamentals of producing the sound properly, they have come a long, long way in their study of music.

Instrumental methods classes at the collegiate level normally cover much specialized information necessary for the instrumental teacher: the assembly of the instrument, common fingerings, proper position for playing. These courses tend to emphasize the techniques for teaching the first lesson; they are oriented toward the instruction of beginners. This chapter, therefore, will stress the teaching of certain basic points that need to be taught in some degree to all secondary school students regardless of their level.

The preceding chapter devoted considerable attention to the topic of a correct method of singing. The concern was, as it is in this chapter, for those techniques that can be taught with some success in a group situation. This book does not cover all the worthwhile points that a singer or instrumentalist could learn. Indeed, entire books have been written on just the techniques of playing the clarinet or violin. So the information here should be considered as merely introductory.

Through reading and conversation, the instrumental teacher should gain as much specialized information as he can about instruments other than his own; it will all be useful in his work.

FUNDAMENTALS OF WIND-INSTRUMENT PERFORMANCE

With winds there are three fundamentals that can profitably be worked on in a group situation: breath support, basic embouchure, and basic tongue action.

Breath Support

Rafael Mendez considers breath support alone to be 40 per cent of playing a brass instrument,[5] and wind players are nearly unanimous in agree-

[5] Rafael Mendez, *Prelude to Brass Playing* (New York: Carl Fischer, Inc., 1961), p. 10.

ment with his sentiment, if not with his precise percentage. In most respects instrumental breath support is similar to the breath support used in singing. The same organs and muscles are used and their function is the same. The differences are in the degree of abdominal muscle action demanded, and in the natural resistance offered the air stream by reeds and brass mouthpieces (flutes excepted).

The player should first place his free hand lightly on his abdominal wall to see that the wall moves out as he inhales, and moves slowly and steadily in as the tone is played. In instrumental playing the *depth* of breath should be emphasized. Mendez says to the student, "Think DOWN . . . DOWN . . . DOWN . . . against the belt. Now fill the middle part of the lungs. Think . . . OUT . . . side-to-side . . . front-to-back."[6] Stein tells his students to imagine, if they can, filling only the top half of a pitcher, the point being that the deep part of the lungs must fill first.[7] This exercise can be done by the students in class:

> Stand. Place hand against abdominal wall. Inhale, filling the lungs *deeply*. Then, with the teacher and/or students timing the action, blow out the smallest possible stream of air between the lips, and note the slow inward movement of the abdominal wall. If ten seconds is achieved, do the exercise again, increasing the time to fifteen seconds, then again to twenty, and so on over a period of days until at least sixty or even ninety seconds is reached.

For strengthening muscles for breath support, both Stein and Mendez suggest this simple exercise which can be done at home:[8]

> Lying on the back, feet together, toes pointed away from the body, SLOWLY raise stiffened legs to a ninety-degree angle with body, then SLOWLY lower again.

Other home exercises are:[9]

1) Inhale a deep breath, hold it *with throat open*, and place a mirror close to open mouth. Mirror will get cloudy if breath escapes.
2) Inhale, counting to four, then exhale while slowly counting to eight, again keeping throat open.

The playing of a tone requires the relaxed and open throat, and the slow, billowy air stream that are needed for correct singing. Tension should be maintained in the abdominal muscles as the sound is produced. An advanced player may not require a great amount of abdominal muscle tension, because he knows precisely which muscles to use and how much to use them. But for almost all wind players in secondary school, the

[6] *Ibid.*, p. 12. Reprinted by permission.
[7] Keith Stein, *The Art of Clarinet Playing* (Evanston, Ill.: Summy-Birchard Publishing Company, 1958), p. 18.
[8] *Ibid.*, p. 20; and Mendez, *op. cit.*, p. 15.
[9] Stein, *op. cit.*, p. 20.

abdominal wall should be kept as firm as possible at all times when playing.

It is more difficult to maintain breath support when the player's attention is diverted to fingerings or rhythmic figures. Breath support, therefore, must become a habit. When the students forget about breath support because their attention is on notes, the teacher can refer to the passage and say, "Now, the last time at letter L you got the right notes, but I know you can get a better tone than you did. Do it again, but this time *at all costs* I want you to keep up your support, even if it means a wrong note." Strangely, instead of bringing forth many wrong notes, such a direction usually leads to a better playing from the standpoint of both tone and technique.

Part of the teacher's job in getting students to support tones is to convince them of the need for it. The teacher can demonstrate, if he is a brass or woodwind player. He can play an unsupported, and then a supported tone, so that the students can hear the difference. He can demonstrate the effect of proper control when playing at the extremes of the range of dynamics. The upper range on brasses demands much support, unless these notes are obtained by pinched lips which produce crude sounds or by "squealer" mouthpieces with shallow cups and narrow bores.

Basic Embouchure

The subtleties of embouchure can hardly be taught in a group situation, but by close observation and reminders, the teacher can prevent many grievous embouchures from developing.

SINGLE-REED INSTRUMENTS. The clarinet requires a more carefully developed embouchure than does the saxophone, although proper lip formation is necessary on saxophone. Briefly, the embouchure for both is set in this way: Without pulling the corners of the mouth back, tighten the muscles in the corners of the mouth. Then, with the lips just barely touching, try vigorously to pull them apart in an up-down separation. This will stretch out or thin out the muscleless areas around the mouth, especially just below the center of the lower lip. The result should be a pointed or "Dick Tracy" chin. The reason for the pointed chin may be explained to the students in this manner: "Your car can't go far on a flat tire; the wheel on the road needs to be firm. The lower lip needs to be firm, too, so that the reed can vibrate without being soaked up in a flabby lip." The lower lip in single-reed playing should be the consistency of a pencil eraser. The correct embouchure is needed at all times, but particularly on high notes. The teacher should be on the lookout for lower lips incorrectly "rolled up" underneath reeds. (Note picture of the boy playing the clarinet at the beginning of this chapter.) When playing correctly, most students will show muscle action along a line running two inches down from each corner of the mouth.

The clarinet should be held so that it forms a forty-five degree angle with the chin and teeth. Some students hold it straight out like a cigar, and then try to achieve the proper appearance by tipping the head down until the chin is almost to the collarbone. A forty-five degree angle means that the upper teeth touch the mouthpiece at a point about one-eighth of an inch from the tip of the mouthpiece, while the lower lip touches the reed halfway up the vamp or cut of the reed. The lower lip should rest on top of the lower teeth, with half of it going over the teeth, but half remaining in front. Unless a student has thin lips, some of the lower lip should show when he plays. One suggestion that usually helps all phases of single-reed embouchure is for the player to stick his chin out a little bit, just enough so that the teeth would meet were the mouth to be closed.

The embouchure for clarinet is:

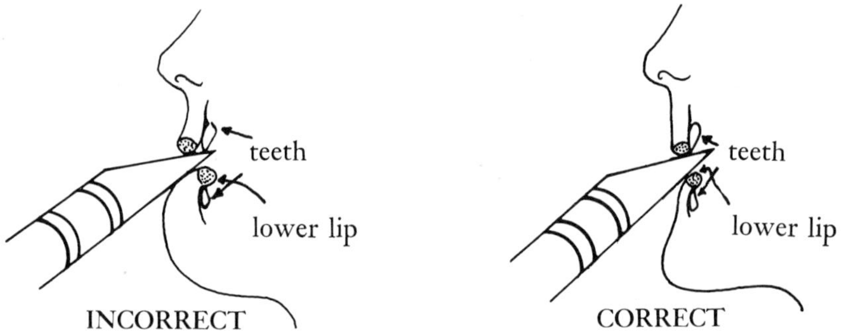

DOUBLE-REED INSTRUMENTS. The embouchure for oboe and bassoon is similar to that used for clarinet. The upper lip is brought more into play because like the lower lip it goes between the reed and the teeth. A little more side-to-side stretch between the corners of the mouth may be required, so that there is a pulling away of the broad outer circle of muscles below the eyes, in the cheeks, and on the chin, and a squeezing in of the inner circle of muscles around the lips.

Much of a player's success on a double-reed instrument lies in the quality of his reed. Commercial reeds are made to one major specification: they must produce a tone fairly easily, even for the immature player. As a result, they are usually too soft, with the raspy sound characteristic of a soft reed. For the good player, the only answer is to make his own reeds. It is an unusual secondary school student who learns to do this, however. What is most often feasible is for the teacher to make arrangements with a professional double-reed player, who can then make suitable reeds for the students. By the way, when a willing professional is found, he had better be treated with deference. It takes time to make reeds, and seldom is it financially worth while for the maker.

FLUTE. The point to watch on flutists is the angle between flute and lips and the degree of tilt at the blowhole. The flute should be held parallel with the lip line, with the edge of the blowhole at the lower edge of the lower lip, and should not tip to the high or low side on the right side of the mouth.

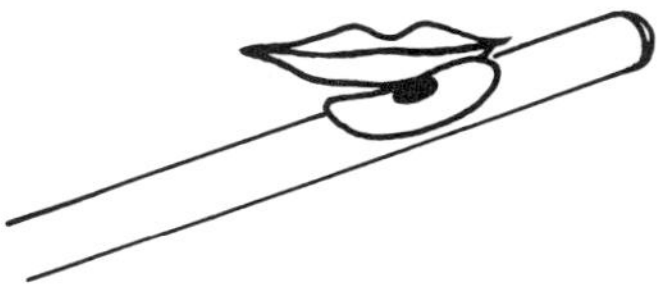

INCORRECT

CORRECT

The blowhole should tilt just slightly toward the player's lips. The precise angle can be determined by the player only after carefully listening to the tone quality.

The flute achieves its change of register by the speed and angle of air going into the blowhole. Many students attempt to play high notes not by making the opening in their lips smaller and by pushing the chin slightly forward, but by blasting out more air. The result is a breathy tone and frequent inability to reach high tones, to say nothing of the unnecessary effort expended by the player. For high notes, the opening of the lips should be made "as small as the eye of a needle." This results in a smaller but faster air stream.

BRASS INSTRUMENTS. The basic formation for the vibration or "buzzing" of the lips on the mouthpiece is the same for all brass instruments. The corners of the mouth should be tightened, and the center of the lips slightly puckered, somewhat similar to the position for a kiss. The mouthpiece is set lightly, *not pressed*, on the lips, in the center of the mouth, with an equal portion of the mouthpiece on each lip (French horn excepted). Slight variations or off-center positions caused by individual differences in facial and dental structure are of no concern as long as the tone is free and clear. French horn players should be taught to rest the rim of the mouthpiece on the rim of the lower lip, thus placing one-third of the mouthpiece over the lower lip and two-thirds over the upper.[10] The adaptation of the embouchure required for trombone, baritone, and bass depends mainly on lip tension and the degree to which the lips are pursed out.

Pressing the mouthpiece against the lips is a poor technique that is too often used as an emergency measure. Pushing the mouthpiece into the lips achieves temporary improvement, especially in reaching high notes. But what sacrifices are involved when pressure is used: feeling is lost in the lips, notes crack or fail to speak, the low register is weak, intonation suffers, slurring is uneven, and permanent damage can be done to the

[10] Phillip Farkas, *The Art of French Horn Playing* (Evanston, Ill.: Summy-Birchard Publishing Company, 1956), pp. 21–25.

lips.[11] This quick solution is to be avoided at all costs. The player should pretend that the instrument is suspended from the ceiling on strings, and that without touching it with his hands he can move up to it, place his mouth on the mouthpiece and play it. Some teachers actually hold the instrument lightly for the student so that he can experience the sensation of playing without pressure. The muscles in the corners of the mouth, plus the support from the diaphragm and the abdomen, should do the work in reaching correct pitches. For this reason, when selecting music the teacher needs to avoid brass parts that move brass players into high notes before sufficient facial muscle or what is loosely called "lip" has had time to develop. One practical remedy to too much pressure on the lip on trumpet or cornet is to encourage the player to try a hand vibrato in private practice. In order to achieve this, he must withdraw pressure, and this can be a beginning to the process of weaning away from pressure.[12]

Brass players should not be seduced into quick and easy playing of high notes by the use of extreme mouthpieces. For whatever is gained in one phase of playing, something is lost in another. Mouthpieces with medium cups, rims, and bores should be used.

Tonguing

The third fundamental of wind-instrument playing which can be advanced in the group rehearsal is correct tongue action. This is more than a mere technique for executing staccato runs in eighths and sixteenths. It is a fundamental action necessary to articulate any note regardless of speed or rhythmic pattern. The playing of "America" requires tonguing involving the same basic action as a difficult solo.

In a way, "tonguing" is the wrong word to use, because the making of a tone depends on air and a vibrating mechanism. So the first requirement for proper articulation on wind instruments is proper breath support. Many times a student complains that he cannot get his tongue to work properly, when the real problem lies in a lack of breath support. Breath support must precede effective tonguing.

Training in tonguing should start as soon as students can support their tone. In some respects, it would be good if they could wait a year, but this is not a realistic expectation. The students see music that calls for tonguing, and even slurred phrases need to have the initial note articulated. Besides, students will experiment with tonguing whether the teacher likes it or not, although they may not do it in his presence.

The tonguing operation is based on the *release* of air, not the *pushing*

[11] Mendez, *op. cit.*, pp. 22–24.

[12] Robert D. Weast, *Brass Performance* (New York: McGinnis & Marx, Publishers, 1961), p. 34.

out of air, as the uninitiated student may think. First, the tongue acts as a dam to hold back the air. Air pressure resulting from continuing breath support builds up behind it. Then the tongue is quickly pulled away from the reed or teeth. At that exact moment the sound starts distinctly. This is referred to as the attack (in many ways a misleading word for the tongue-breath action it describes). The action involved is like turning on a garden hose at low pressure and attempting to hold back the water with the thumb. When the thumb is removed from the opening, the initial forceful squirt is comparable to the "spring" or "kick" of a good attack on a wind instrument. With the hose, it does no good to turn the water on harder, because the initial spurt is unaffected by later increases in pressure. The same is true of the tongued attack. Once the air has started, additional air will merely give a pushing effect that is musically undesirable. Because of this, the attention in tonguing is on the *beginning* of the note. In fact, in rapid tonguing the player can think only about the start of each tone.

Unnecessary movement only complicates the tonguing process. Too often students move the jaw, lips, and throat in an attempt to improve on an action that should involve only continued breath and coordination of the tongue. Since it is difficult for the player to work at just holding still, he can be directed to concentrate his attention on breath support and the quick action of the tongue in pulling away to start the tone. The students should work harder on active breath support when no sound is heard than when it is, illogical as it may seem. To emphasize the build-up of pressure before the note is sounded, the students can be told to feel a "ping-pong ball" of air pressure between the tongue and the roof of the mouth just before the tone starts.

As Chapter Nine pointed out in discussing interpretation, the degree of attack desired differs with the demands of the music. The difference in attack is determined by the amount of air pressure built up (with greater pressure bringing a harder attack) and by the speed with which the tongue is pulled away (the faster movement making for a more distinct start).

On brasses and flute the tip of the tongue is placed behind the upper teeth at or near the point where the gum meets the teeth. On lower brasses some fine players tongue at the edge of the teeth with no audible difference in the quality of tonguing. On reeds the tip of the tongue is placed lightly, not pressed, against the tip of the reed, on the lower reed on the oboe and bassoon. Clarity is improved if the tip of the tongue is made firm and pointed. On all winds, the movement of the tongue to start the tone is largely down, not backwards, and only the tip of the tongue moves. The tongue is large, and if all of it moves, speed and clarity are impossible.

Students who have trouble feeling the tongue movement might try this:

rough the tip of the tongue on the edge of the upper teeth by rubbing it back and forth; then practice flicking the tip against the edge of the teeth.

On brasses the syllable used for tonguing is determined by the pitch level of the note. "Tah" is used for the middle range, "toh" for low notes, and "tee" for high notes. "Tah" is used on woodwinds.

The closing off of a staccato tone is too often hindered by unnecessary effort. On a reed instrument it is not easily noticeable if the tone is stopped with the tongue, but on a brass instrument this action causes a crass and annoying "ut" sound at the end of the tone. The player needs to focus his attention on the start of tones of moderate or long duration, and avoid the use of the tongue to end them. The closing operation will then be taken over by a holding-back action of the abdominal muscles.

FUNDAMENTALS OF STRING-INSTRUMENT PERFORMANCE

After a year or two of class lessons, string players, like their wind-playing counterparts, move into a performing organization, but with a difference. In a majority of schools the strings work by themselves several times a week, while the winds are brought in for only one or two periods to form a complete orchestra. Since string instruments are difficult to play well, and since string parts are often more demanding than wind parts, the extra time is needed to learn the music. Furthermore, the string players, especially in junior high, benefit from the additional work on basic skills.

Bowing

Young string players tend to place their entire attention on the left hand when playing; advanced players at the collegiate level or beyond know that the skill of the bow arm is at least as important as the dexterity of the left hand. Because the right arm is generally neglected, some work on it is well worth the time and effort.

The students should understand the factors that affect bowing: pressure on the bow, length of bow stroke, and speed of bow stroke. Each one affects the quality and volume of the sound produced. A slow bow with much pressure gives one timbre, while a fast bow with light pressure gives another. Several books on bowing are available for school groups (see Appendix C), or if the teacher prefers, he may create his own bowing routines.

Common bow patterns should be learned so well that they become second nature. The first patterns should be very simple so that the players' attention can be centered on drawing the bow properly, and they should be patterns that are common in the repertoire of the group, such as the following:

(WB indicates whole bow, UH upper half, and LH lower half)

Slurred notes of equal value should receive nearly equal portions of the bow so that none of the tones sound cramped or squeezed:

Dotted figures in one bow are more difficult, especially if a change of bow occurs immediately after a short detached note; beginners are likely to become confused over bow direction. Slow and rhythmic practice will establish the feel of the proper bow motion.

Many styles of bowing are best taught in the private lesson, but even in a group situation the students can work on two of the most common styles. *Legato* bowing requires smooth change of bow direction and a rather consistent speed of bow movement. Beginning students should strive first of all to develop a fine legato style, like the singing tone of the human voice. This style is the essence of string performance. A second style of string playing often encountered in orchestral literature is the *détaché*, or full, detached stroke. The secret of détaché is the "catch" at the start of the tone, indicating an abrupt, precise beginning. A slight bit of extra weight on the bow plus a sudden and fast initial movement will produce this effect. It is imperative that the student be able to draw a straight bow, that is, one that is parallel to the bridge. Any lack of bow control will surely show up when détaché is attempted; the bow will either skid out of control or move at an alarmingly crooked angle.

No orchestral string part contains complete bow markings, so the students have a fine opportunity to figure out bowings in an actual work of music. The teacher can give the players an unmarked page of mimeographed music and request that they mark in bowings as homework. These can then be examined in class, compared, and discussed. The string players should be asked questions such as, "Why did you start with another down bow? What is the musical effect of this bowing? What does the music call for here? Could it be bowed another way? Would it be simpler?" The effort is to get the players to understand the mechanical and musical factors involved in bowing a string part.

Left Hand

Intermediate string methods move the left hand into higher positions, and this entails work on shifting. For a few moments the attention of the players should be concentrated on the two pitches involved in the shift. At first, the players can practice the shift silently, using a light pizzicato occasionally to check the accuracy of pitch. The quickness and precision of the left hand should be emphasized. Then the two notes involved in the shift can be played, followed by a playing of the entire phrase.

The real beauty of string tone is brought to life with vibrato. Without it, the quality is sentenced to remain thin and colorless, especially when the players are performing on instruments which are far from the best. Some successful string teachers begin vibrato in the second year of study; others prefer to wait a little longer. In any event, it is started when the teacher feels that the basic playing fundamentals are well established.

A practical method is suggested by Righter:

> The following steps may be helpful, either in first learning to execute the vibrato or in correcting faulty habits: (a) start with the second finger on the second or third string (C sharp or F sharp on violin–F sharp or B on viola); (b) lift all other fingers from the string, but hold them near their normal playing positions; (c) draw the thumb slightly more UNDER the neck of the instrument than would be normal, to provide better support; (d) withdraw the base joint of the first finger from direct contact with the neck of the instrument (these steps will reduce the contact points from three or more to only two–the second finger and the thumb); (e) ROLL the second finger alternately as far forward and as far backward as possible, utilizing the flexibility of the wrist and of all the finger joints; (f) do this very slowly and very evenly at first, gradually introducing rhythmic groupings (twos, threes, fours, sixes) and increasing the speed of the roll slightly; (g) repeat the entire process using the third finger, and eventually the fourth and the first fingers, and also practice the exercise on the first and the fourth strings. These basic exercises will seem cumbersome and difficult at first and they may appear to have little relation to the production of a free and natural-sounding vibrato. Gradually, however, the skill will establish itself and, when this occurs, the rhythmic treatment can be abandoned except as a corrective device. The amplitude of the roll will diminish and its

> speed will increase with practice. The same general approach will apply to the cello and the string bass, on both of which instruments the hand is in a better natural position to start the rolling process.[13]

The teacher may also wish to examine the approach of Waller, which is more specific and detailed.[14] Some teachers feel that it is best not to become too technical with the students, preferring the original advice of Monteverdi to "shake" the hand. Too much technical talk, they feel, may inhibit the proper muscle action. At any rate, teaching vibrato requires much persistence, because the process may take up to two years with some pupils. The goal should be to increase the speed and narrow the amplitude of the vibrato to the extent that the change of pitch is not perceived as such by the ear. Of course it is essential that the students have a chance to see and hear good vibrato, either from the teacher or from an advanced student.

PERCUSSION

Percussion playing requires a variety of techniques, most of which are not as complex as those involved in playing winds or strings. The problem is not usually one of technique but rather of musicianship. Many teen-age drummers do well on the stroke-bounce technique for the roll; the trouble is they cannot put it in the right place in the music. There are occasions—in dance bands and marching bands—when drummers have little need for reading music. Apparently the habit of nonreading carries over to concert playing, with unfortunate results. The students have trouble producing the correct rendition of the printed music and fitting the percussion part into the ensemble. It is hard for percussionists to think of the part they play as being integrated with the group as to phrasing, dynamics, and style. By asking the right question at the right time, the teacher can encourage percussionists to think more musically. "Which snare should you use at letter A, the five-inch or the six-and-a-half-inch? Why? Which stick are you going to use on the tympani at letter G? How important to the music is the roll at the repeat of the melody?"

INSTRUMENTATION

Any suggestions for instrumentation must be considered in light of the quality of players available. One tenor saxophone is sufficient for a band of fifty players, if he is a creditable performer. If he is weak, an additional tenor saxophone is needed. Directors have differing tastes, some wanting more mellowness, others more bass sound, and others more brilliance, all of which will lead to somewhat different instrumentations. Although

[13] Charles B. Righter, *Teaching Instrumental Music* (New York: Carl Fischer, Inc., 1959), pp. 45–46. Reprinted by permission.

[14] Gilbert R. Waller, *Waller Vibrato Method* (Chicago: Neil A. Kjos Music Co., 1951).

orchestral instrumentation has been fairly well standardized over the past 150 years, band instrumentation has changed frequently and is still in the process of being modified, often upon the specifications of the composer or arranger.

In an orchestra, the difference between a large or small group is largely accounted for in the strings, because in the winds only one player is normally used on a part. Therefore the teacher of a small orchestra finds it more difficult to achieve proper balance. Table I gives suggested numbers of players for three sizes of orchestra.

TABLE I

Instrument	*Small*	*Full*	*Complete Symphonic*
Flute and piccolo	2	2	3
Oboe and English horn	1	2	3
Clarinet	2	3	3
Bassoon	1	2	3
French horn	2	4	6
Trumpet	3	3	3
Trombone	3	3	3
Tuba	1	1	1
Percussion and piano	2	3	4
Harp	0	0	1
Violin	12	24	30
Viola	4	7	10
Violoncello	4	7	10
String bass	3	4	6
	40	65	86

Table II represents one concept of balanced band instrumentation. Unless players of unusual ability are available, instruments such as bass saxophone and E flat soprano clarinet should be avoided, because they can easily do more harm than good. If these instruments are vital to a particular piece, it is wisest to have a very good clarinetist double on the E flat clarinet for that number. The division of first, second, and third parts in the clarinets and trumpets and/or cornets can be determined only by the sound of the particular group. Because low notes apparently do not "carry" as well as higher pitches, and because less advanced students often play the lower parts, these parts may require a greater number of players for a balanced sound. The use of trumpets or cornets is a matter of taste for each band director. Traditionally two cornets were recommended for one trumpet, but in smaller groups trumpets are more effective. Double B flat upright tubas are suggested in a ratio of three to one over E flat tubas (if the latter are used at all), because of their bigger tone quality, stronger low notes, and better intonation. A recent report by a committee of the

College Band Directors National Association recommends only BB flat tubas.[15] Generally the E flat tuba has been used to double the BB flat tuba one octave higher, but since these notes are well within the range of trombones and baritones, this function of the E flat tuba is of limited value.

TABLE II

Instrument	*Small*	*Average*	*Large*
Flute and piccolo	2	5	7
Oboe	1	2	3
B flat clarinet	12	20	25
Alto clarinet	1	2	4
Bass clarinet	1	2	4
Bassoon	1	2	4
Alto saxophone	1	2	2
Tenor saxophone	1	1	2
Baritone saxophone	0	1	1
Cornet and trumpet	6	9	12
French horn	3	4	8
Baritone	2	3	4
Trombone	3	4	6
Tuba	2	3	6
String bass	1	1	2
Percussion	3	4	5
	40	65	95

Seating

Traditionally players in a section have been seated in order of ability. If all the players are highly competent, as in a professional symphony orchestra, then this system works well. In a school group where the level of capability may vary greatly from first to last in a section, it is better to assign places by putting the best player in first chair, but then putting the next best in the next chair behind the first (second desk in the violin section or first stand in the second clarinets), the next best on the third stand, and so on to the end of the section. The advantage of the idea is that it puts stronger players on all parts and stands other than the first. In the violin sections, it puts the better player on the outside, where he is most easily heard, and where he can keep playing when a page of music is turned. A minor variation of this plan is to place the best three or four players in the first chairs, and then place players according to ability, moving back a stand or part with each one. These seating systems help to remove the stigma of playing a part other than the first.

In instrumental music, especially band, some teachers have laid great stress on competition for the best chairs. While this motivates some stu-

[15] Richard Franko Goldman, *The Wind Band: Its Literature and Technique* (Boston: Allyn and Bacon, Inc., 1961), p. 167, 169.

dents, it is hoped that the students find the work in band and orchestra of sufficient interest and pleasure to be motivated without the teacher's hanging the carrot of a better chair in front of them. Students can study and learn no matter what chair they are sitting in, and a sour note detracts from the group's performance regardless of its source in the section, so the chair in which a student sits is not the most important matter.

The most educationally valid method of seating is for the teacher to rotate either students or music so that all members of a section get to play first, second, or third parts. Rotation gives the students a greater knowledge of all the parts and more experience in reading music, besides diminishing the emphasis upon sitting in a certain chair. For performance seating, the teacher without much ado should seat players according to ability and seniority. When and if chair try-outs are held, the teacher might have another music teacher in the system also hear them, so that he cannot be later accused of personal bias. To avoid confusing musical ability with personal popularity, students should not be involved in evaluating other students.

Transferring Students to Other Instruments

Students in elementary school are seldom started on several of the instruments listed in the instrumentation tables for band and orchestra. Either the instruments are too large, too delicate, or too difficult for beginners. For this reason, the junior high school teacher must be prepared to transfer some youngsters from one instrument to another. Transfers should be planned well ahead of the time they are made, and they must take into full consideration the student's desires, parents' desires, and the student's musical potential. Frequently a student will begin clarinet fully planning to switch to oboe after a year or two of study. The clarinet training has given him a good musical foundation, and will contribute to his success as an oboist, whereas starting on oboe probably would have ended in failure. Some changes are made to benefit the student, as in the case of a trumpeter who lacks sufficient lip strength and is therefore transferred to tuba. The following list suggests the most logical transfers:

B flat clarinet to any saxophone
: Upper octave of clarinet is almost identical with saxophone; player must learn to relax embouchure for low notes.

B flat clarinet to oboe
: Upper octave of clarinet is similar to oboe; player will require a little time to get used to smaller reed and use of both lips in playing.

B flat clarinet to bassoon
: Fingering of open holes is similar but keys are different; reed change is not quite as difficult as with oboe; player must learn bass clef.

B flat clarinet to alto or bass clarinet
: Fingerings are identical; player needs only a short time to become accustomed to larger reed, mouthpiece, and instrument.

Flute to saxophone
: Fingerings are similar; embouchure on saxophone is not too demanding.

Saxophone to all other saxophones
: Fingerings and notes are identical; very short time is needed to get used to new size of reed, mouthpiece, and instrument.

Trumpet to low brasses
: Basic fingerings are identical; time is needed to learn bass clef and become accustomed to large instrument; change to trombone is more difficult, although slide positions are related to valve combinations.

Trumpet to French horn
: Fingerings present only a minor problem; main difference is in concept of tone; some change of embouchure is necessary, which requires careful attention.

Low brass to trumpet
: Treble clef must be learned; fingerings present no problem, but change from an instrument requiring less embouchure tension to one requiring more is difficult.

Violin to viola
: Time is needed to learn alto clef. Some authorities believe that all violinists should have at least a semester of experience on viola.[16]

Piano to string bass
: Pianists know bass clef and have an understanding of how bass part is organized in music.

Piano to percussion instruments with definite pitch
: Pianists read music and know keyboard; tympani roll can be learned without great difficulty.

Students who transfer will need special help at first, the amount depending on the difficulty of the change. It is helpful if the student can have access to a practice room during study hall, with the teacher stopping by occasionally. Perhaps the teacher can work with him after school. Progress will be most rapid, however, if the student can study privately with a specialist teacher. As soon as the student can play the parts on his new instrument, he should be moved back into the band or orchestra.

A special word needs to be said about French horn. Since the horn uses primarily the partials in the overtone series which are one octave higher than partials on other brass instruments, the pitches are much closer together in the series and are more difficult to play accurately. For this reason, there has been a persistent problem about how best to start young players. At one time the E flat mellophone was thought to be the answer, a solution from which a true lover of the French horn recoils in horror. The argument then centered upon the virtues of the F and B flat horns, with the former having the proper timbre and the latter being easier to play. Double horns are ideal, but few school systems can afford to provide them for beginners. More and more horn teachers now advocate starting the student on a single B flat horn. (He reads F horn music, but is taught

[16] Righter, *op. cit.*, p. 21.

B flat fingerings.) After about three years, he is transferred to double horn and taught to use the F horn for the lower pitches, gradually increasing its use for notes in other ranges.

Substitution of Instruments

There are occasions when an instrument called for in the score is not available. Rather than deny the rest of the players the opportunity to play the work, the teacher as an expedient can assign another instrument to substitute. Although there are no "good" substitutions, some may be a little more satisfying than others. Following is a list of common and passingly successful substitutions. An asterisk indicates that transposition is required to make the substitution. The E flat instruments indicated by the double asterisks may read bass clef by adding three sharps to the signature and reading the notes as if they were in the treble clef.

Oboe: muted trumpet*, viola
English horn: alto saxophone*, oboe*
E flat clarinet: flute*
Alto clarinet: alto saxophone
Bass clarinet: tenor saxophone
Bassoon: tenor saxophone*, bass clarinet*, cello
Tenor saxophone: bass clarinet
Baritone saxophone: bass clarinet*
French horn: alto saxophone*, clarinet*, cello*
Fluegel horn: cornet
Baritone: trombone
Tuba: string bass, baritone saxophone**
Viola: violin (Many publishers sell a Violin III part, which is the viola part put in treble clef with the lowest notes moved up an octave.)
Cello: tenor saxophone*, alto saxophone**
String bass: tuba, piano
Harp: piano

EQUIPMENT AND SUPPLIES

The physical needs of the instrumental music program are clearly in excess of other phases of the music curriculum. In addition to the administrative suggestions for the entire program mentioned in Chapter Six, the instrumental teacher must deal with matters of equipment and supply that are uniquely his own.

Supplies—items such as reeds, strings, rosin, valve and slide oil—can be sold at cost through a student supply store operated by the school or the music department. Some dealers will provide and stock a reed-vending machine which eliminates the need for handling. When the school makes supplies available, the students do not have to lose time waiting to get to the music store for a reed or string.

Repair on privately-owned instruments is facilitated if they are sent in with school-owned instruments to the repairman. The school pays the repairman for all work done, the teacher keeps a record of the cost of repair on the privately-owned instrument, and the student reimburses the school. If the student should prove forgetful or balky about payment of his bill, his report card can be held up in the school office.

In the purchasing of school-owned instruments, the teacher needs to inform the administration on the need for two grades of instruments. One is the rugged, adequate instrument for the beginner. The other is the good instrument (not artist model) for the high school player. Since most schools limit the amount of time during which one student has an instrument as a beginner, well-built plastic clarinets and instruments of similar or "student line" quality are appropriate. But for quality work in the high school band and orchestra, good instruments are needed. A cheap instrument at this level is poor economy. Many schools provide these instruments for competent junior and senior high school players: alto and bass clarinet, piccolo, oboe, bassoon, baritone saxophone, French horn, baritone, tuba and sousaphone, harp, cello, string bass, and percussion equipment. As was discussed on page 288, many schools provide all beginners with instruments.

As for the needs of particular instruments, the mouthpiece and reed have much to do with clarinet tone. A good medium to medium-wide lay mouthpiece and a reed not softer than 2½ in strength work best for most high school players. All hard rubber mouthpieces tend to warp over a period of two or three years. Refacing is not expensive and often improves the mouthpiece. Quality clarinets should be wood, as should the piccolo, which should be pitched in C, not D flat. Oboes and bassoons should be checked by a specialist on the instrument before a purchase is made. The good French horns should be double horns. If the school can afford both sousaphones and tubas, upright bell BB flat tubas are favored, with either a fourth valve or a compensating mechanism to improve the intonation. Cases and stands or chairs should be purchased for use with tubas or sousaphones. Percussion equipment of quality gives a noticeably better sound. There is something musically disappointing about hearing the group wind up to a beautiful climax and then comes a cymbal crash on a cheap, small pair of cymbals with handles. The advice of a percussion player from a symphony orchestra is well worth having on brands and the latest equipment. To preserve the percussion equipment and prevent the loss of small items such as maracas, triangle beater, and brushes, a movable cabinet should be made or purchased for housing the equipment. The cabinet should have a lock to prevent unauthorized use of equipment. String instruments should have Caspari pegs and tuners on the two highest strings (string basses excepted). The greater ease and efficiency of tuning is well worth the extra cost of the pegs.

When the time comes for the student to purchase a trumpet or clarinet, some parents hurry off to the nearest discount house. Often the "buy" they get is a cheap instrument which is hopelessly out of tune and carelessly made. To combat this, the teacher should in a letter or other communication with the parents try to establish the point that a cheap instrument may be the poorest buy of all. Next, he should urge parents to have a trained person inspect the instrument they plan to purchase, and he may announce his availability to consult with them about instruments. He should recommend all music merchants in the area who sell quality instruments and follow ethical business practices. He might also list good used instruments which families in the area have told him they would like to sell. Not only does this make it possible for prospective purchasers to buy a good instrument at less cost; it also lets them know that a share of their investment in an instrument is redeemable. In listing the used instruments, the teacher makes no contacts and suggests no price. The listing is only a service to interested parties.

PREPARATION ON THE SCORE

Just as an English teacher needs to study a poem or play in order to teach it, the music teacher must study and prepare the music he plans to teach. The instrumental music teacher must understand the transpositions and technical problems in a score containing as many as twenty lines occurring simultaneously. In addition, he must decide upon the correct tempos, phrasing, and methods for teaching the music.

More often than not, secondary school conductors face an additional obstacle: the condensed score. Since complete scores are expensive to publish, and since many school music teachers do not buy them even when they are available, music publishers are reluctant to prepare complete scores. So the instrumental teacher must learn to do the best he can with the condensed score. When the music is simple, as in the case of a chorale, a condensed score is usually sufficient. The more complex the music becomes, the more inadequate a condensation is. Its most limiting feature is that it does not indicate exactly what each part is playing; some parts, such as the E flat alto clarinet, are usually ignored. The condensed score is similar to a piano reduction of an orchestral score, even to the point of being in concert pitch. In fact, not too many years ago the part for the director was called "Piano-Conductor," probably as an outgrowth of the performance custom of the old theatre-pit orchestra.

Before directing a group from a condensed score, the teacher should compare it with the instrument parts. Pencil in hand, he should look through the condensed score and stop at the first place where the instrumentation is not clearly indicated. Then he can examine the parts at that point, writing in the conductor's score notes or abbreviations which indicate more accurately what is happening. In the case of marches written on the small march-size sheet, the teacher can take one first clarinet, first cornet, baritone, French horn, trombone, and percussion part, tape them together into one large sheet, and thus have a score of sorts.

A rehearsal can deteriorate fast when the teacher is not thoroughly familiar with the arrangement of parts.

> Mr. Morgan stopped the band and said to the second alto saxophone, "Say, Mary Ann, we missed your F sharp in the first chord at letter H." "I don't have F sharp there," Mary Ann answered; "I have a D."
>
> "Well, who has a concert A besides the second flutes? . . . (*no answer*) . . . Good grief! Tenor sax, what do you have?" "D natural," came the reply.
>
> "Bass clarinet, according to my score somebody has a concert A. Do you?" "No sir, I have a D."
>
> "Are you sure? Well, let's begin at letter G again and see if we can figure it out this time."

STAGE OR DANCE BAND

In schools where players of sufficient ability are available, a dance band or stage band can be a useful appendage to the music program. The case for the school stage band is this. Students interested in playing dance music are going to play it someplace. Therefore it is best that they have this experience in a situation properly supervised as to selection of music, hours and location of playing, and type of personnel. The stage band also helps bridge the gulf between popular and serious music. A strong case can be made for some popular musical forms, mainly jazz, as valid musical experiences, ones which the schools should not ignore.

There are disadvantages to the stage band. It can encroach on the main effort at music education. To prevent this, rehearsals of the group must be held outside of school hours, and should not make unreasonable time demands on the students or teacher. The music should be performed well, however. Sometimes the student attracted by the stage band is not the careful, hard-working type, and too often such a player is content to stagger through the music in a sloppy manner. Therefore it should be the *best* members of the concert band who are selected for the stage band, not the weaker ones. Hard work is necessary if the music is to sound acceptable and bad playing habits are to be avoided.

The affairs of the stage band must be managed so as not to violate the Code of Ethics with the American Federation of Musicians. Appearances of the group are limited to school events.

The past few years have brought forth many stage-band arrangements made specifically for a high school group. In general, the tunes are well arranged, without the technical demands and the *ad lib* solos of the commercial "stock" arrangements. The simpler arrangements can also be played with a more varied instrumentation. The group may not be able to learn enough pieces to consume three hours of playing time without some repetition of music. Repetition is preferable, however, to playing music on which the band is inadequately prepared.

Although stage-band music is written with the conventional nomenclature, it should not be performed in a strictly conventional way. The subtleties of the style are too numerous to go into here, and to some degree they change with the times. A few writings have been published on the style of stage-band music. Some music publishers also provide recordings of their arrangements, which help in teaching the proper style of the music.

MARCHING-BAND TECHNIQUES

The training and administration of the marching band is a specialized area of music education. Several books are available on the subject, and the person who feels in need of information on marching bands should consult one of these books:

Dvorak, Raymond F., *The Band on Parade*. New York: Carl Fischer, Inc., 1937.

Hindsley, Mark H., *School Band and Orchestra Administration*. New York: Boosey and Hawkes, Inc., 1940.

Hjelmervick, Kenneth, and Richard Berg, *Marching Bands—How To Organize and Develop Them*. New York: A. S. Barnes, 1953.

Johnston, Lawrence, *Parade Technique*. Rockville Centre, N.Y.: Belwin, Inc., 1944.

Lee, Jack, *Modern Marching Band Techniques*. Winona, Minn.: Hal Leonard Music Co., 1955.

Loken, Newt, and Otis Dypwick, *Cheerleading and Marching Bands*. New York: Ronald Press, 1956.

Long, A. H., *Marching to the Yard Lines*. Ponca City, Okla.: Luther Music Co., 1952.

Marcouiller, Don R., *Marching for Marching Bands*. Dubuque, Iowa: William C. Brown Company, 1958.

Wright, Al G., *The Show Band*. Evanston, Ill.: The Instrumentalist Co., 1957.

MUSICAL-INSTRUMENT REPAIR

A second specialized topic beyond the scope of this book is the repair of musical instruments. The reader who is interested in the subject should consult one of the following books:

Brand, Erick D., *Selmer Band Instrument Repairing Manual*, rev. ed. E. C. Schirmer, 1946.

How To Care for Your Instrument. Elkhart, Ind.: C. G. Conn Ltd.

Repair and Accessory Manual, Long Island City, N.Y.: Penzel-Mueller Company.

Sur, William R., and Charles F. Schuller, *Music Education for Teen-Agers*. New York: Harper & Brothers, 1958. Chapter V.

Tiede, Clayton H., *Practical Band Instrument Repair Manual*. Dubuque, Iowa: William C. Brown Company, 1962.

You Fix Them. Cleveland, Ohio: Scherl and Roth, Inc.

Questions

1. Suppose a boy has his heart set on playing the trumpet. The teacher already has more trumpets than he can use in a balanced group. Should the boy be allowed to start on trumpet, or should he be told to take something else or not be in instrumental music? Why, or why not?
2. Suppose a student is studying privately with a teacher who suggests that he withdraw from school instrumental music organizations "so that he won't get any bad habits." What arguments could you offer to persuade the parents of the student that he should also participate in the school group?
3. On page 291 the combination of singing-fingering is suggested. Why should the singing be done on the correct pitch level? From what was said in the chapter on principles of music teaching, why is it logical that this teaching technique is a good one?
4. Why is it a good practice from the standpoint of music education to utilize the procedure suggested on page 292, in which the student thinks of a note pattern, sings it, and then writes it down or plays it?

Projects

1. Using the criteria for the evaluation of beginning instrumental instruction books mentioned on page 289–90, make a study of all such books that you can secure for examination. Report your findings to the class. Compare evaluations with other class members.
2. Examine six of the group technique books listed in Appendix C. Note their level of difficulty, whether in unison or parts, and determine how each might best be put to use—for warm-up, rhythm, musical style, and so on.
3. Study the beginning instrumental program in a school system near your college. Find out at what grade level instruction is first offered, whether it is offered in subsequent years, how large the classes are, how homogeneous they are, whether the instruments are school-owned or rented, what instruction books are used, how much time is devoted to class sessions, and what instruments are offered beginners. Report to your class. Compare reports with other class members.
4. Study the complete instrumental music program in a secondary school in the area of your college. Find out how much variety it offers, whether there are "second" groups for the less talented students, whether there is an orchestra, what credit is given for private instruction, whether technical

instruction is included in group rehearsals, and whether there are small ensembles. Report your findings to the class. Compare evaluations with other class members.

5. Take a very simple melody, such as "Twinkle, Twinkle, Little Star," from an elementary instrumental instruction book. Look it over and decide, seriously, what you could teach the students about its *musical* qualities—important notes, phrasing, style of articulation, and repeated melodic patterns.
6. Practice the breathing exercises described on page 296 and see if they seem applicable to the wind instrument you may be studying privately or in class.
7. Think of analogies other than the one used on page 301 that might be useful in helping teen-age students understand the proper action of tongue and breath in starting a tone on a wind instrument.
8. Study the embouchures of fine wind players. On single reeds notice the appearance of the muscles of the chin, the appearance of the lower lip, and the angle of the instrument in the mouth. On brasses, notice the placement of the mouthpiece and ask the player to pull the mouthpiece away as he plays a tone so that the position of the lips can be observed. Watch the embouchure of a flutist as he slurs up an octave, and of a brass player as he slurs to a higher tone with the same fingering.
9. Take a simple community-type song, such as "America the Beautiful" and mark in all the bowings a violinist might use in playing it. Compare your bowings with those of others in your class.
10. From a condensed score, select eight consecutive measures that are fairly complex. Then refer to the individual parts, find the same eight measures and copy the parts in full score on manuscript paper. Compare and contrast the two scores, and evaluate the adequacy of the condensed score in giving an accurate picture of what the instruments are to play.
11. Visit several instrument dealers and look over the "student" quality instruments. If you are an instrumentalist, check your major instrument for intonation and tone quality, quality of construction, and case. Compare them with instruments of the next higher level in quality and cost. Report your findings to the class.
12. Write a letter to parents regarding the purchase of an instrument for their son or daughter. Explain the need for buying a quality instrument and offer your services in making a good selection.

Suggested Readings

Artley, Joe, *How To Make Double Reeds*, 2nd ed. Old Greenwich, Conn.: Jack Spratt, 1953.

Bate, Philip, *The Oboe*. London: Ernest Benn, Ltd., 1956.

Chapman, F. B., *Flute Technique*. London: Oxford University Press, 1958.

Farkas, Phillip, *The Art of French Horn Playing*. Evanston, Ill.: Summy-Birchard Publishing Company, 1956.

Goldman, Richard Franko, *The Wind Band: Its Literature and Technique*. Boston: Allyn and Bacon, Inc., 1961.

Hall, M. E., *Teacher's Guide to the High School Stage Band*. Elkhart, Ind.: H. & A. Selmer, Inc., 1961.

Keyboard Experience and Piano Class Instruction, William R. Sur, ed. Washington, D.C.: Music Educators National Conference, 1957.

Kuhn, Wolfgang E., *Instrumental Music: Principles and Methods of Instruction*. Boston: Allyn and Bacon, Inc., 1962.

Mayer, Robert and Traugott Rohner, *Oboe Reeds: How To Make and Adjust Them*. Glen Ellyn, Ill.: The Instrumentalist Co., 1953.

Mendez, Rafael, *Prelude to Brass Playing*. New York: Carl Fischer, Inc., 1961.

Normann, Theodore F., *Instrumental Music in the Public Schools*. Philadelphia: Oliver Ditson, 1941.

Righter, Charles B., *Success in Teaching School Orchestras and Bands*. Minneapolis: Schmitt, Hall & McCreary, 1945.

——————, *Teaching Instrumental Music*. New York: Carl Fischer, Inc., 1959.

Spencer, William, *The Art of Bassoon Playing*. Evanston, Ill.: Summy-Birchard Publishing Company, 1958.

Sprenkle, Robert and David Ledet, *The Art of Oboe Playing*. Evanston, Ill.: Summy-Birchard Publishing Company, 1961.

Stein, Keith, *The Art of Clarinet Playing*. Evanston, Ill.: Summy-Birchard Publishing Company, 1958.

The String Instruction Program in Music Education, Vol. I. Washington, D.C.: Music Educators National Conference, 1957. First of a ten-volume series on strings published by the Music Educators National Conference.

Weast, Robert D., *Brass Performance*. New York: McGinnis & Marx, Publishers, 1961.

Westphal, Frederick W., *Guide to Teaching Woodwinds*. Dubuque, Iowa: William C. Brown Co., 1962.

Willaman, Robert, *The Clarinet and Clarinet Playing*. New York: Carl Fischer, Inc., 1949.

XIV

the junior high school general music class

Steve Kowal's father lays cement for new highways. When a big project is finished, he and his family move on to a new place. Each time, Steve changes schools. He was enrolling in his fourth school in two years. The new principal gave him his schedule, and as he answered the phone he said, "All eighth-graders take general music every other day. I think it works best in your schedule second hour."

"General music . . ." Steve's mind began to run back over the other general music classes he had had. "I'll never forget old Miss Farot at Middleville," he thought. "She was nice, a lot like my grandmother. But I sure did get tired of filling out those workbook sheets for her. Don't care if I ever figure out another time signature or harmonic minor scale. Hope we don't do that here; I'd have to learn it all over again because I don't remember that stuff any more. Now at Edgerton, there was a class! That minstrel show sure was fun. We thought up all our own jokes 'cause ours were better than the ones the teacher gave us. Of course, those minstrel songs got kind of boring after a couple of months. Mr. McIntosh in Ohio Heights must have been born in a library. If the piece was real old, he thought it was great. Some of the songs were awful—singing cuckoo and all that stuff. That trumpet piece by Purcell and some of the other pieces weren't half bad, though. Wonder what general music will be like here?"

A good question, Steve! For years music educators have been trying to decide just what a general music class should be, and at present there is still little consensus on the matter. This is not surprising, in view of the fact that educators in general have differing opinions as to what the junior high school itself should be. Some teachers have conceived of the general music class as a "feeder" group for high school organizations, others as a recreational period, while still others have seen it as an extension of the elementary program. Music educators have not given general music classes as much attention as they have their bands, orchestras, and choirs, and so the course has fallen into somewhat of a second-class status. Only recently has there been an awakening to the importance of general music. Finally, the term "general music" is used in a variety of ways, sometimes referring to any required music course, sometimes to any non-performing course in the secondary schools. The term "general music class" in this chapter refers specifically to a junior high school course which all or most students take, and which offers varied experiences and learnings in music.

The organizational pattern of the school plainly affects the nature of what is done in the general music class. Some general music classes meet daily throughout the year or for a portion of the year, some meet twice a week, and others only once. Some schools require the course in seventh, eighth, and ninth grades, some in seventh and eighth, some only in seventh, and some not at all. Occasionally the classes are composed entirely of girls or of boys. Some schools group students homogeneously according to academic ability, and the grouping carries over into music. Sometimes students who take instrumental music are included, sometimes not. As if these were not enough variables, the elementary music program of a district largely determines the musical development of the students, and this is a prominent factor in shaping the ability of the students in the general music class; hence variations in the elementary schools help to explain the differences at the junior high level.

These many variables mean that there can be no single "right" content and method for general music classes. There is a difference between a heterogeneous seventh-grade class meeting twice a week, and an eighth-grade elective, composed largely of girls of advanced ability, meeting daily. What is good for one is not necessarily good for the other.

As in the total music program, the first purpose of the class is to teach music. But what is special about general music? One outstanding feature is the child/adult status of the students involved. All that was said in Chapter Three about new patterns of social development, varied physical development, the lack of ability to express, the easily set off emotions—all these become very real in the junior high school. A second feature is the fact that for students whose only music experience has been under the direction of an elementary classroom teacher, the general music class is their first experience in studying music under the tutelage of a specialist. Third, in many instances the class is compulsory and heterogeneous. Students of every type are there, whether they like it or not. The teacher must take into account the goal (teaching music), the conditions of the class (age of students, departmentalized organization, compulsory enrollment, homogeneous or heterogeneous grouping), and then organize and adapt the teaching of the subject so that it can be successfully assimilated by the students. It is not an easy assignment, but it is a vital one in music education.

THE GENERAL MUSIC TEACHER

There is no area of music teaching to which the idea of the "complete" music teacher, as presented in Chapter Four, is more applicable than the general music class. All the characteristics of the course demand ability, knowledge, and resourcefulness. Especially important is the rapport that the teacher must establish with the class. Indeed, unless this is present, the most perfectly planned lesson is largely worthless. The teacher has to understand and accept what one successful junior high school music teacher called, partly in jest and partly with respect, "the junior high mind." Teaching junior high school general music is as much a matter of feeling and attitude and understanding as it is of knowledge and intellect.

The teacher characteristics that will impress the junior high mind are enthusiasm and a sense of fairness. The problem for the successful teacher at this level often is not how to get enthusiasm from the students, but how to keep it within bounds. The response of junior high students to good teaching is one unequalled at any level. And the converse is true: at no level will the response to poor teaching be more vexing. It should be added that at no level is the response likely to be more unpredictable.

The statement that general music teaching requires much subject-matter knowledge may seem surprising. True, it is possible to get by in front of a general music class with little knowledge, but what is being discussed here is teaching in the best sense of the word. For this, knowledge is required. Suppose that the teacher wished to have a unit on music of the three major religious faiths in the United States—Judaism, Catholicism, and Protestantism. Are there hymns with different words but essentially the same melody to be found in all three faiths? in two? What source books could be used to look up an answer to such a question? Did Martin Luther write the words and music, or just the words to "Away in a Manger"? In Palestrina's day, it was a common practice to use boys on the treble parts; when and where was this custom changed? Are there choirs that still use boys on the highest part? The *Shema* in Judaism and the *Credo* in Catholicism are each a basic statement of faith. Why are the two settings so different? These questions have barely scratched the surface of what can be a part of one unit on "Music in Religion." And the teacher had better be prepared for such questions. The thirteen-year-old boy with big, clumsy feet and the twelve-year-old girl who giggles at everything can at times ask the most probing, serious, and difficult questions!

The teacher needs to be inventive and willing to try new ways of doing things. This requires effort and a certain spirit of adventure. There are real rewards for the imaginative teacher. He will find new zest in his work, to say nothing of the feeling of pride when an idea works out well. Suppose he wants the students to understand the significance of the half steps between 3–4 and 7–8 in the major scale. How can this be done so that the students *hear* the tonal relationships and remember them? Suppose the teacher wants to present operatic music so that it draws a favorable reaction. The class is made up of students who are well-versed in the latest hit tunes, but about opera they know only that they don't like it. What can the teacher do to circumvent the obstacle of attitude, without standing before the class and in effect saying, "This is good music. Now sit still and listen to it"? Suppose he wants the students to see a certain music program on television. How can he motivate them to watch without coming right out and requiring that they do so? How can the program be followed up in a meaningful way? Multiply these questions many times over and you have some idea of the need for inventiveness on the part of the general music teacher.

A comprehensive discussion of the general music teacher should mention the importance of skill at the piano. While the teacher does not need to be a virtuoso at the keyboard, he must play accompaniments easily and well.

CHARACTERISTICS OF SUCCESSFUL TEACHING

In addition to the personal characteristics mentioned, the teacher must seek to meet in his teaching six conditions that are called for because of the age of the students and the nature of the course.

Concreteness

Young teen-agers want and need learnings that are simple, unvarnished, and direct. They appreciate (although they may not show it at the time) the kind of straight-forward approach that was discussed in some detail in Chapter Five.

Students of junior high age tend to be literal in their interpretation of learned material. In one school a fine musician presented to his class a song called "Nymphs and Shepherds." The response of the class was disappointing; to an experienced teacher it would have been predictable. Teen-agers know there's no such thing as a nymph, they have never seen a shepherd, and they haven't the slightest intention of dancing and singing on the lea. To them, the whole idea is silly. They are too old to accept without question whatever the teacher gives them, and they are not yet old enough to look beyond the literal aspects of the work and enjoy the beauty and charm of the music. They are no longer naïve, but neither have they a mature perspective.

The correlation of learnings must be direct and concrete. A study of neumes, the *Bay Psalm Book*, or the harmonic form of the minor scale is worthy, to be sure. However, a class of thirteen-year-olds will not grasp the significance of any of it unless it is carefully related to what they know and can use. Copland's *Lincoln Portrait* is a work about a real person. Some of its music is derived from music sung and played by Americans of the mid-nineteenth century. The work has power and a definite mood, plus the concreteness of narrated words. This is a work that junior high school students can understand and appreciate.

The music teacher can use several practical ideas that make the learnings more concrete. One is the "Song Bag" described by Andrews and Leeder:

> A "Song Bag" is made by covering a cardboard form with burlap, bound at the neck with brightly colored twine, and labeled "Song Bag." The class then discusses the project and its objective, which is to place the name of each song, printed on a cardboard note (which may be half, whole or otherwise) on the song bag when the song is sung acceptably by the class. In this way the cumulative repertoire of the class becomes visible. The next step is to decide just how the class will interpret "sung acceptably." The class may set up certain standards, such as these:
>
> 1) The song must be sung correctly, and with good tone quality.
> 2) Everyone in the class must join in singing the song.
> 3) One verse should be sung from memory.
> 4) The song should be sung in the right mood, according to the composer's markings and the spirit of the words and music.
>
> These requirements or standards may vary according to the class that is setting them up. The teacher participates in the discussion which may be led by him or by the class chairman.
>
> Once the standards are agreed upon and accepted by the entire class, a committee is elected to judge when the song is ready to go "into the bag." This committee is changed frequently, so that all members of the class will have a chance to serve on it. When the class indicates its singing is ready to be judged, the committee listens to the singing of the song and renders a verdict, giving reasons why it does or does not believe the song is "sung acceptably."[1]

The significant feature of this procedure is not so much the concreteness of the song bag itself (the use of which is perhaps best confined to seventh grade), but the concreteness of the specific standards by which the students can judge their singing.

Another practical step is a music notebook or log. A notebook is kept by each student as a record of what the class has done—the songs sung, the records heard, the facts learned. In addition to keeping a record of class activities, the student is encouraged to supplement the notebook with pictures and articles from newspapers and magazines, reports on reading or records listened to outside the class period, a listing of questions that

[1] Frances M. Andrews and Joseph A. Leeder, *Guiding Junior High School Pupils in Music Experiences* (Englewood Cliffs, N.J.: Prentice-Hall, Inc., 1953), p. 72. Reprinted by permission.

come to mind as something is studied. Periodically the teacher can call for the notebooks and look them over, possibly using them in the determination of a grade. The notebook idea does have one drawback. The verbally able students can handle such a project easily, but the student who is weak in communication skills finds music another course in which success depends upon reading and writing. The teacher must stress to the class that the notebook represents a personal view of events in music class and indicates the degree of the student's interest in music activities; it cannot say much about the depth of the student's understanding, or the permanence of his learning.

"*Satisfaction Fast*"

Early adolescents are normally impatient; they lose interest in an activity that does not lead to satisfactory progress within a reasonable time. Read again the directions of Cooper on page 272 for finding the cambiata voices. He allows for no delay or dawdling. In less than fifteen minutes, the major undertaking of checking voices is finished. As an experienced junior high school music teacher, Cooper knows the importance of working quickly.

A second reason to strive for "satisfaction fast" is the limitation of time.[2] In most schools the class does not meet daily. It is hard for junior high school students to leave an interesting point on Wednesday and take it up again on Monday. Much of the impact of Wednesday's lesson will have dissipated in the intervening days. For this reason, every class period should be planned to give the students some sense of accomplishment, a feeling of "We can do that" or "We know what that means in terms of music and how it relates to us."

In practical terms this means a limitation on the complexity of class activities. In one class period, the students might learn to sing acceptably a song with a descant part, but they would have to leave unfinished a work in four parts. It is better to work on the third movement of Tschaikowsky's *Symphony No. 4*, which takes about five minutes, than it is to take the arm off the record in the middle of the twenty-minute first movement and say, "We'll hear the rest of it on Monday."

It means that the teacher must be amenable to the use of short cuts. Rather than teaching the tonic and dominant chords in the common keys, naming the notes in each chord, describing the tonal relationship between them, and explaining how to derive the proper chord from the symbols I and V^7 or F and C^7, the teacher can say, "Here's the Autoharp. When we sing 'The Cowboy's Lament,' John, play the F chord when I hold up one finger. Play it once on each heavy beat. When I hold up five fingers,

[2] The author is indebted to Mary E. English for the phrase "satisfaction fast." Miss English and Allen L. Richardson are the authors of *Living with Music* (New York: M. Witmark & Sons, 1956).

push the C^7 button, one chord to the measure. Just follow my directions."

The mention of short cuts, which get quick results without understanding, may raise the question "When do the youngsters finally get around to learning what they're doing?" Several avenues are open to the teacher for bringing about understanding after the act. He may ask, "How far is it from F to C? . . . All right, suppose we wanted to start singing with the G chord instead of F. What chord would we substitute for the C chord?" Or the teacher might say, "Donna, tonight I'll let you take the Autoharp home. Sing 'Down in the Valley' starting with a G chord. Don't look at any music. Just experiment with the chords until your ear tells you they sound right with the melody. Then write down the names of the chords, one for each heavy beat you hear. When you come to class Thursday, we'll compare what you found with what the book tells us, and we'll see if the ears of the class agree with yours."

Another approach might be to say, "Class, when Greg presses the F button, he's playing more than the note F. Susie, go to the piano and experiment, playing tones other than F until you find those that match what the Autoharp is sounding. The class can be the judge as to whether or not a note fits properly."

For songs with simple harmonies, the practice of vocal chording is useful, especially if there are a few changed voices in the class. The teacher can write the I, IV, V, I chords with symbols and names on the board. The structuring of the chords will vary depending on the division of voices in the class.

The class can sing them on a neutral syllable. Then they can sing the appropriate chord as the teacher calls it out by name or number during his playing of the melody on the piano. Better yet, the teacher can hold up the right number of fingers for the chord number, so that there is no extraneous sound intruding upon the music. Finally the class can divide, with one section singing the melody while the other sings the chords.

There are many more techniques a teacher could use to instill in the students a feeling for harmony and an understanding of it. But the underlying procedure and timing of the instruction are the important considerations. In the class that used the Autoharp, the students were given "satisfaction fast" in a musical experience–they sang a song with an attractive accompaniment. *Then* they proceeded to find out why certain chords made the music sound better.

There is a limit to how thoroughly a general music class needs to understand the tonic-dominant relationship and the intricacies of harmony. At some time in their schooling the students should be led to comprehend this, true; but not in a heterogeneous class of young teen-agers meeting on alternate days. Further understanding must await a theory class or at least an advanced class more homogeneous in its interest.

Relate to Students

Relating the subject to the students is crucial at the junior high school level. Sometimes students feel that much of what they do in music class is not very immediate or vital. Often the material seems distant in both time and geography. A song about flowers or a girl in Italy may be pretty, but it doesn't seem too significant. That Bach inverts the theme and that Bartók uses scordatura tuning for the violin does not seem very vital to most young people.

One way to relate general music more closely to junior high school students is for the class to keep up on current events in the musical world. Some teachers assign each student one week during which he is responsible for reporting music news to the class, or preparing a bulletin board or large wall calendar. If students keep a music notebook, one section of it can be reserved for current items. In covering the current scene, the class reporter should mention more than local concerts or musical events at the White House. Motion pictures and radio and television programs which have good music should also be mentioned, as should announcements, articles, and commentaries about music in newspapers and magazines. One class followed the writings of the music critic in a large metropolitan newspaper, found them written in a language difficult to understand, and wrote a letter to the critic asking her why such big and difficult words were necessary. Not only did the critic send the class a thoughtful and sensitive reply, she published the students' letter and her reply in the paper. Alive and relating to the students? Very much so!

The need to relate also affects the selection of music and activities. Gian-Carlo Menotti has written operas that have wide appeal as well as musical value. *The Telephone* is short and clever, while *Amahl and the Night Visitors* is longer and essentially serious. *The Telephone* involves the plight of a young man who is desperately trying to propose marriage to a giddy girl, who is laughing into the phone uproariously (usually as she sings) and inquiring about the well-being of her friend's pussy cat. This kind of story does not set a twelve-year-old boy's heart to pounding with excitement. Amahl, on the other hand, is a crippled boy of about twelve. He's quite human, telling tall tales and even thinking considerately of his mother upon occasion. With which opera do the students identify themselves? *Amahl.*

Not everything the class studies or sings needs to have a twelve-year-old boy or girl as protagonist. But the learning must start within the ken of the students, and move on from there. The teacher at times needs to point out to the students the relatedness between something in music and something in themselves. If the local school has no students who play string instruments, teen-agers can identify with community orchestras, or those in nearby metropolitan areas, or those whose playing is heard on recordings presented in class. Interest in tuning glasses or bottles of water will be heightened if the students realize that tuning is necessary on an instrument if it is to sound pleasing; they are in a simple way doing what the piano tuner does with the piano in the classroom or at home.

Another practical way of relating students and music is to set up a "Student Talent Day." At the seventh- and eighth-grade level quite a few students are still studying piano privately, and others may be in band or orchestra. Also included in the activity should be students who have studied guitar or accordion or have simply taught themselves to play the harmonica or ukulele. The purpose of the student performance is to demonstrate that music can be made in many ways. Simple efforts as well as the pretentious can be enjoyable and worth hearing.

Build on Student Maturity

As Chapter Three pointed out, teen-agers want to be like adults; they feel that they have left childhood behind. It is good sense on the part of the teacher to recognize this desire, and to predicate his planning on it. The type of music chosen, and even its appearance, should begin to differ somewhat from that used in the elementary school. More than one junior high school music class has wanted to sing from individual octavo music rather than books, because it felt that books are used only by children! The interests of junior high school students begin to broaden, and at times their perception can be surprisingly profound. The choice of music should reflect this. Gone from their repertoire, unfortunately, are many of the fine songs from elementary school days. They are not gone forever, though, for in a few years when the students are more secure in their adult image, they will again enjoy the music they learned years earlier.

The teacher can use their desire for maturity to attain other desirable objectives. At this age, teen-agers tend to dislike and reject that which they do not know or that which differs from their expectations. The teacher can say to the class, "One of the things that marks an adult from a child is his attitude toward people and ideas that are unfamiliar. Call it 'fairness' or 'tolerance,' but a person who is growing up always gives a fair chance to that which he doesn't know. Now, this Spanish folk song may strike you as being pretty strange. It's free in its use of rhythm. It sounds sort of made up on the spot—and it is. But different as it may seem, see if you can find three things about it that you like, three reasons why the song makes good sense musically." Students at this age are looking for new horizons. They are capable of viewing the world, of understanding those people who believe and act differently, of respecting music and customs of other nations. Several of the units to be suggested later will build upon the developing maturation of the students.

Stress Musical Qualities

If the essence of music is lost, the music class will be hollow and meaningless. This can happen when the instruction becomes "literary" or "academic" in the least desirable sense of these words. A student may learn that Mussorgsky was born in 1839, that he held a clerical position with the government, that he was a great Russian composer—one of "the Five" —and yet never comprehend his music. A student may be able to figure out time and key signatures, call out note names correctly, write scales, and still be musically ignorant. Such knowledge is fine *if* the students have grasped the musical idea first. Steve's teacher at Middleville, Miss Farot, failed music when she sought to make "facts" synonymous with music.

A second way in which music can be lost is by making the period solely a recreation time. Steve's class at Edgerton came dangerously close to doing this when it devoted its efforts to a minstrel show. No one is against enjoying music, but the indispensable combination consists of fun *and* learning. A good teacher can have both in his class. There is a place for the lighthearted song and the relaxing diversion. But then the students should move on to other things. General music classes exist to teach music.

Account for Variety

Variations are present to some degree in every class at every level, but in junior high school general music, the variety which is the spice of life nearly overpowers the recipe. Attempting to provide for these variations is no small undertaking. Essentially, it is best done by avoiding concentration on any one phase of class endeavor; a variety of activities is required. The principle is similar to the theory behind multi-packages of cereal: among the assortment at least one will be liked. The boy who is self-conscious about his singing can succeed by giving a report on high-fidelity sound systems. The academically slow student who has trouble understanding the factual material may possess a pleasant singing voice, and in this way get something from the class. As a bonus, the assortment of activities guarantees that the class will be stimulating for the teacher as well as the students.

ACTIVITIES AND MATERIALS

While hard and fast formulas are to be avoided, the teacher should usually plan for two or three different activities in each class period. Almost every session should include singing. Further work can revolve around listening, studying about music, playing instruments, or developing creative projects.

Singing in General Music

Singing in a choral music class and singing in a general music class have different purposes and must be approached differently. The singing of a song in general music class is not as involved technically as is choral singing, either from the standpoint of the music used or the degree of perfection of the singing. It is an activity that gives the students a personal experience with the music, develops their most important means of making music, and gives insight into a particular work. For many students, it is their only active encounter with music.

How is singing best taught in the general music class? First, the teacher must select songs carefully as to range, number of parts, text, musical quality, application to other class activities, and variety. Then he must make himself familiar with the music—accompaniment as well as voice lines—and think through the several possible ways of teaching the song.

In presenting the song, there are three approaches that may be used. One is having the class hear the song with books closed. This rote method is especially good if the song has a mood that the class should grasp. The second is having the students hear the song as they follow the music in their books. This procedure is the one most frequently used, and one which possesses elements of both rote and reading. When a song is presented to the class by either of the above methods, the teacher may sing it or play a recording of it. The teacher's singing is preferable, however, because a live presentation seems more immediate and holds more appeal for those students who in elementary school were taught music by recordings played by the classroom teacher. If the junior high music teacher is a skillful pianist, he can play the accompaniment while he sings the new song, but the piano should never *substitute* for the voice; the piano with its fading tones does not present a good model of singing style. A third method of presentation is having the students attempt to read the song through at sight. At times, this method should be employed because of its benefit to music-reading skill.

Whatever method is used for the first experience with the song, the teacher would next begin to draw attention to its musical content. For purposes of illustration, the following song "The Peddler" will serve as reference. The teacher can ask the class a question or two. "What's the mood—happy? sad? powerful? . . . Do any lines of music repeat themselves? Which ones?" If the students are experienced in sightreading, they

THE PEDDLER[3]

The melody of the verse moves from one vocal part to another.
Baritones may sing the alto-tenor part one octave lower.

Allegro
mp
Ah,
Ah,
mp
S.
A.-T.
1. Look down the street, see the ped - dler come, With his
2. "Tell me, now tell me, my fair - est maid, Will you
A7
d min.
mp
Ah,
Ah,
heav - y pack up - on his back;
buy some lace to help my trade?"
A7
d min.

[3] Russian folk melody, words by Margaret Lowrey, *Time for Music* by Walter Ehret, Lawrence Barr, and Elizabeth Blair (Englewood Cliffs, N.J.: Prentice-Hall, Inc., 1959), pp. 4–6. Reprinted by permission.

mf
Ah,
He is tired and his shoul - ders ache, But he must move
"Please, good man, you need not in - sist, For such love - ly
g min.
d min.
A7
mf
Ah.
rit.
on for mon - ey's sake, He is tired and his
lace I can't re - sist. Please, good man, you need
d min.
g min.
rit.
a tempo
Ah,
Ah.
shoul - ders ache, But he must move on for mon - ey's sake.
not in - sist, For such love - ly lace I can't re - sist.
d min.
A7
d min.
a tempo

Refrain
Hai - da, hai - da, hai - da,— hai - da,— hai - da,
d min.
A7
hai - da, hai - da, da!— Hai - da, hai - da,
d min.
hai - da,— hai - da,— hai - da, hai - da,— hai - da, da!
A7
d min.

can sing the melody only at this point, shifting their attention to the top part on each phrase beginning with the words 'He is tired.' In most cases, however, they should hear the song once more and then sing it themselves. Other features of the melody may then be pointed out. "Notice that the second time you sing the words 'He is tired and his shoulders ache,' the melody goes higher to make a high point of intensity. Let's try it—this is the second time the phrase appears—and make it dramatic." (Class sings.) "Now, what happens to the tempo at the refrain? . . . How about the dynamic levels? . . . All right, let's hear you make a difference; it's loud, then soft."

At this point the teacher must make a judgment as to what the class needs to do next on the song. Wrong notes may be the main flaw, or it may be a lack of concept of the aesthetic qualities, as evidenced by mechanical singing or other styles inappropriate to the music. Perhaps the first interval in the song is being sung inaccurately, or the high E natural is flat. Possibly the dotted rhythm is sung carelessly or sung where two quarter notes are written. It may be that the students are taking breaths at the wrong places, or are revealing a lack of attention to dynamic markings. The class should work on trouble spots or phrases as needed, and then sing the entire song again.

Depending on how quickly and well the class has learned the song thus far, the teacher will have to decide whether to go on or set it aside for the day. In any case, further study should insure that the music remains technically correct and properly expressive. The class might be divided in half, with each singing for the other and offering suggestions for improvement. A stanza may be read aloud and discussed as to its mood, important words, and how it fits in with the melody. Additional details can be discussed. "In what way are some of the phrases almost alike but not quite? Here's a hint—look at the words 'But he must move on for money's sake.' "

So far, the students have sung only the melody of the song. As in other music of this type, the melody is the essential vehicle for artistic expression, so it is desirable for the students to explore it completely before moving on to the learning of a harmony part. Most general music classes are able to sing simple part songs, so the teaching of the two parts of this number presents no serious problem. If the class is composed largely of soprano voices, as it sometimes is in seventh grade, the students should all learn the lower part as well as the upper melody. This keeps them interested and encourages flexibility in adapting to another part. The class can be divided arbitrarily, each half singing its part alone and then together. Later they may trade parts. If the class should have trouble with a second part, the teacher may sing or play the melody while the entire class sings the harmony part. In the initial stages of learning, the teacher should assist one part, then another, for a few notes as his help is needed.

If a class includes several boys with changed voices, it may be necessary to confine the choice of music to songs having a bass-clef part. However, when treble-clef music is of sufficiently good quality, it would be too bad to withhold it from the class simply because of imbalance in voice distribution. These boys can sing the melody an octave lower, as is suggested by the editors on "The Peddler," or a simple part can be worked out by the teacher, as was described on page 274.

When the song is sung well, the teacher may consider what in the profession of music education is known as "enriching" the song. In the case of "The Peddler" an Autoharp is effective, and a tambourine might be added on the "haida" section, playing this pattern:

Other techniques include clapping or stomping feet or other bodily movement, chants, rhythm or orchestral instruments, dramatizations. Many times the textbooks themselves suggest good possibilities. Generally, songs which contain a picturesque test ("The Caravan") or definite rhythmic patterns ("Ezekiel Saw de Wheel") are most suitable for additional musical elements. With other songs, the addition of clapping or rhythm instruments would be an artistic travesty ("Let Us Break Bread Together on Our Knees"). If piano accompaniment is used, a student can profitably be assigned to learn the part and play it. The accompaniment should not be continually present, however, because it tends to cover up errors in singing.

Craft Projects

Many teachers of general music classes have guided the students through such activities as the making of puppets, cigar-box ukuleles, miniature stage sets, shepherd's pipes, and soap carvings of instruments. These projects can be helpful, especially in providing variety and concreteness in the class. However, making puppets and carving soap are not musical activities, and such projects take about twice as much time as the teacher expects. Time is so limited, especially when classes do not meet daily, that the use of music class time for crafts work cannot be justified. For teachers who want to "keep the kids busy," a crafts project seems heaven-sent, but the concern should be for the musical education of teen-agers. If a crafts project can be undertaken jointly by the music and art or practical arts departments, so that the time need not be taken from music class, then the project may be desirable. Also, crafts work can be done on an individual basis outside of class. A musically less gifted student may be given the opportunity to contribute to the class by means of manual endeavor.

Teacher–Pupil Planning

The topic of democratic management of the classroom was discussed in Chapter Five. Since the students know vastly less about music than the teacher does, it is clear that the choice of what is studied in general music class cannot be abandoned to the students. As McDonald points out, it is the teacher's job to make decisions, based on his knowledge and his observations of how the class has done on its last learning project, as to what the class should do next. He further states: "We are not here discussing an issue that has been formulated as 'teacher-control' versus 'pupil-control.' The teacher's decisions are influenced by the goals, interests, and immediate behavior of the pupil."[4]

Teacher-pupil planning is a dynamic relationship—an exchange of views between students and teacher. The teacher attempts to motivate the class along paths leading to valid educational goals. At the same time, the students react, offer opinions, and make requests. Taking all these factors into account, the teacher then renders a judgment as to what should be done next. When the class first sings "The Ox-Driving Song," and John Mueller says, "Hey, I like that one," he is influencing in a small way what the class will do in the future. When Margie Lapcheck says, "Let's study another Broadway musical," the teacher may have to say, "I know, that would be fun. But there's so much to learn in music, and our time is so short, that I'm afraid for now we'll have to move on to other things. You'll find the new topics interesting, too." He knows that students learn best when they regard the subject as appealing, but he also knows from his mature perspective that he must occasionally lead them into areas that are new and strange.

Minimum Course Content

Since large numbers of students are often enrolled in general music classes, it is not unusual for more than one person to be teaching the various sections of the class. Without a minimum course content, students who change teachers at semester time or move from one grade to another run the chance of encountering duplication of what they already know, or being deprived of learnings they should have. Even if there is only one person teaching the general music classes in a school system, he should have in mind a minimum of learnings he wants to cover. This is only good planning. It serves as a floor upon which he can build according to his own interests and those of the students; it is not a straitjacket which is confining and unalterable.

The planning of a minimum course should involve the songs to be learned each semester, the units to be studied, including recommended recordings, and the skills to be taught and/or reviewed.

Audio-Visual Aids

The teacher of general music has more occasion to use films, filmstrips, flat pictures, tape recorder, record playing equipment, and other audio-

[4] Frederick J. McDonald, *Educational Psychology* (Belmont, Calif.: Wadsworth Publishing Company, Inc., 1959), p. 27.

visual aids than do the music teachers in other phases of the secondary school music curriculum. The nature of the course decrees that the students should explore every avenue of musical experience in order to uncover its infinite variety and scope. Such a comprehensive goal requires the use of imaginative and varied tools.

Audio-visual materials cannot in and of themselves teach a class. They are helpful only when used at the right time and place. When properly used, however, they bring about increased learning. Several studies, one involving seventh-grade music, indicate that a presentation by sound motion picture is between 18 and 34 per cent more effective than traditional methods of teaching.[5]

Films and recordings must be of high quality. A generation ago students accepted almost anything because there was a certain amount of novelty involved, but today teen-agers are accustomed to dazzling motion pictures on wide screens and stereo recordings played through equipment of the finest quality. No teacher can hope to win over a class by playing a scratchy record on an inferior record player. When films are shown, the room must be darkened enough to get the utmost contrast from the picture. Every film or filmstrip must be previewed before being shown to a class, to insure its appropriateness and quality.

Finally, never should the teacher say, "Class, today let's look at this film." The students must have some idea of what to look for, and the teacher must know what it is he wants the class to get from the film. At times, teachers have overprepared a class, spending an entire period on specific build-up for a twenty-minute film. To some degree the film must speak for itself, else why show it at all?

Bulletin boards and wall displays can aid the teacher's efforts to keep the class informed about current affairs in music, and can add concreteness to many of the learnings. The material should be displayed attractively, with a message or title that is unmistakably clear. The teacher can profitably keep a permanent file of good pictures suitable for mounting and display. These can be collected from magazines and newspapers, or purchased. Many music manufacturing firms put out attractive and educational wall charts, which are worth procuring. The bulletin board can provide a record of class activities by showing charts of individual voice ranges, a list of the current song repertoire, and pictures or written reports by the students. With most bulletin-board displays, the message is grasped rather quickly, so if the teacher can take time in his busy schedule, he should alter or replace the display about once a week. The preparation of bulletin boards is an excellent way to involve students, especially the more able ones, in the operation of the class. Student help should be used whenever possible.

[5] Walter A. Wittich and Charles F. Schuller, *Audio-Visual Materials*, rev. ed. (New York: Harper & Brothers, 1957), p. 392.

Books and Equipment

Students in general music classes should have access to material that supplements the books from which they sing. Several fine supplementary books are listed in Appendix F.

The teacher, too, benefits by the presence of more than one set of books. Some contain more factual material, others more music. In either case, an increased amount of resource material means more flexibility in choosing songs and planning units of study. Fortunately, in a departmentalized arrangement where the classes come to a music room, the number of books that need to be purchased is equal to only the number of students in the largest class, so the purchase of supplementary books is not a prohibitive expenditure.

The teacher should see that the records played in class are available to students through a school or city library. It is not uncommon for a student to become sufficiently interested in a work heard in class to want to hear it again by himself. The recordings that are manufactured for use with each book series are often exceptionally well done, and might well be purchased by the school.

The following equipment should be available for the teaching of general music classes:

A good piano that is kept in tune
A tape recorder of good quality with a good microphone
A good record player
Recordings
An Autoharp or Harmolin
Enough ukuleles for half the class
Simple rhythm instruments such as claves, large and small drum, maracas, tambourines, castanets, triangle
Xylophone, glockenspiel, or Resonator Bells
Motion picture projector, slide projector, screen
Room-darkening shades
Bulletin board
Plastic or cardboard simulations of piano keyboard

THE UNIT PLAN–WHY?

The traditional planning for general music classes has been based on units. The unit plan in the music curriculum involves songs, recordings, and other class activities centered around a unifying theme, such as "Songs of the South" or "The Sight and Sound of Music." The unit idea adapts well to a course that tends to be more extensive than intensive in its approach to the subject, because it allows for presentation of a wide variety of material while still retaining a thread of unity throughout. While it is not the only means of organizing lessons in the general music class, it is particularly well suited to the demands of the situation.

The unit plan can be overdone. Conceivably an entire year could be spent on the music of Russia, with all theoretical learnings, songs, recordings, and class activities reverting back to the one central theme. Instead of aiding learning, such an excess would be an intolerable bore.

The unit will have little value if it is essentially nonmusical. It is a matter of viewpoint. A unit could be developed around Shakespeare in music. Berlioz' "Romeo and Juliet" could be compared with Tschaikowsky's, and with "West Side Story"; "The Taming of the Shrew" could be compared with "Kiss Me, Kate"; the various songs alluded to in his plays, or derived from them, could be studied, and so on. The trouble with the idea is that the unit starts with Shakespeare and then examines music associated with his plays. Shakespeare is first, music is second. The difference is a subtle one, but nevertheless crucial to the teaching of music. Music may be brought in incidentally in social science when the class studies coal miners or rivers, and this is fine. In music, rivers and coal miners are relevant only as they increase the students' understanding of music.

Since class situations vary greatly, and since each unit has its own particular requirements, it is impossible to provide a model plan that is applicable to all units. Basically, the unit should center about some phase of music, integrating as much as possible singing, listening, discussing, and reading. It is neither possible nor desirable for every unit to encompass the variety of activities that should be found in each class period; some topics suggest singing, others invite more discussion and research. The teacher should not strain to achieve integration where it does not logically exist. If a prospective unit does not in itself suggest appropriate songs, then the class can work on songs which are not directly related to the unit, and neither the unit nor the singing will be of any less value for it. When possible, films, books, displays, field trips, and appearances by outside authorities should be integrated into the unit of study. Again, these features should not be forcibly incorporated into a unit.

The following eighteen units are a sampling of types of units that can be used with junior high school general music classes. These suggestions, along with moderate singing activity, probably provide more than enough material to occupy all the time for a class meeting every other day for one year. The units are presented in a simple, three-part format. "Value" states why the unit appears to be particularly appropriate for the general music class. The second part, "General procedure," contains suggestions for presentation of the unit. The suggestions are general because the wide differences among classes make detailed outlines impractical. Each teacher must work out the details to fit the needs of his teaching situation and the resources he has available. The third part, "Possible extension," is a listing of topics that might be studied as a result of the work on the unit. In a few cases, some of the ideas in this section could be used in place of the unit. The titles can be made more personal or eye-catching for the students if the teacher so desires. The units are presented in random order. There is some overlapping between units, which to some extent is desirable, since the learnings can reinforce each other.

"*The Nature of Sound*"

VALUE FOR GENERAL MUSIC CLASS. Correlates well with science courses and has special appeal to students who have an interest in scientific type of learning. Helps in understanding pitch, volume, and other musical factors.

GENERAL PROCEDURE. Play a recording containing experiments with sound, or possibly some electronic music. When the curiosity of the class is aroused, move on to describe and demonstrate how sound starts, how it travels, how the ear and brain function in perceiving sound, and how pitch and amplitude are determined. For demonstrations, prepare a trough holding marbles and manipulate it to show the chain reaction from one molecule to another. Suspend balls of cork close together on strings to illustrate the same reaction. On a string instrument, pluck or bow one of the larger strings to show the blur of vibration, and let the students feel the vibration by touching their fingertips lightly on the back of the instrument. Discuss the difference between sound and noise.

POSSIBLE EXTENSION. Learn about stereo recording and high-fidelity sound systems. Many students have fine record playing equipment at home, so this topic is useful and appealing. Make tape recordings of various sounds. Explore the realm of tuning and pitch; take eight to twelve glasses or pharmaceutical bottles of varying size, and fill each with water until the desired pitch is reached. A further extension of this activity is a "jug and bottle band," for which music has been published.[6]

"*Music in Religion*"

VALUE. Relates to an era of adolescent interest—religion.[7] Impresses students with the importance of music in all religions, and encourages tolerance toward people of all faiths. Opens to the students a vast store of the world's great music.

GENERAL PROCEDURE. Present musical high points of Protestant worship service, Catholic mass, and Judaic service. Show how the text affects the type of music used. Sing and hear recordings of Protestant hymns, chorales, or anthems; chants from the Catholic mass and chant-like melodies in modern notation; and musical portions of the Jewish service. Ex-

[6] Adam P. Lesinsky, *Fife, Jug and Bottle Band*, 2 vols. (Rockville Centre, N.Y.: Belwin, Inc.), Book I, 1952; Book II, 1956.

[7] Arthur T. Jersild, *The Psychology of Adolescence* (New York: The Macmillan Company, 1957), p. 331.

amine songs that have a background in more than one faith: "O Come, O Come, Emmanuel," or "God of Abraham" (Yigdal).

POSSIBLE EXTENSION. Listen to instrumental works such as Respighi's *Concerto Gregoriano* for violin, Mendelssohn's "Reformation" Symphony, or Bruch's "Kol Nidrei."

"*Man Expresses His Feelings Through Music*"

VALUE. Makes the students conscious of the universal nature of music and impresses upon them the oneness of humanity in its need for expression of feelings.

GENERAL PROCEDURE. From differing cultures and countries, select several folk songs that have essentially the same aesthetic feeling and thought in the text. Many textual themes are possible: human suffering ("Go Down Moses," "The Peddler," "The Pratties They Grow Small"), or ability to laugh at imperfect conditions of livelihood ("The Little Old Sod Shanty," "Eating Goober Peas"), or men at work ("Drill, Ye Tarriers, Drill," "The Ox-Driving Song," "Song of the Volga Boatman"). If the class consists only of girls, make a collection of beautiful lullabies from over the world. Become familiar with as much literature as possible, using folk-song collections and other sources to supplement the regular series material published for use at the junior high school level. Listen to recordings of good folk songs; use a world map to pinpoint the locations from which the songs have come.

POSSIBLE EXTENSION. Study a folk opera such as Weill's *Down in the Valley*. Listen to orchestral works that utilize folk music as thematic material (d'Indy's *Symphony on a French Mountain Air*, Op. 25; Tschaikowsky's *Symphony No. 4*, fourth movement; Dvořák's *Slavonic Dances*).

"*Popular Music—What It Is, and Why*"

VALUE. Provides a bridge on which the students can cross from the familiar (popular music) to the unfamiliar. Encourages rapport between students and teacher.

GENERAL PROCEDURE. Take a popular song and dissect it, analyzing its melody, form, rhythm, and harmony. Do not attempt to steer the examination of harmony into a study of chord function or anything that advanced; the class can merely hear the usually simple harmony part. Point out the difference between the beat and rhythm. Read the text aloud to evaluate it. Make a listing of themes from "classical" music that have become melodies for popular songs.

POSSIBLE EXTENSION. Examine reasons for the fact that a popular song must be short and simple. If the students are above average intellectually or more mature, share with them a resumé of "The Dialogue of Courtship in Popular Songs."[8] Find out how popular music is "plugged" and sold. The study of song promotion should include a presentation of the unethical practices that are found in some of the industry, as revealed by hearings before congressional committees.[9] Survey popular music since 1900 to see how its style has changed. Study the discussion recording "What Is Jazz?" by Leonard Bernstein (Columbia CL–919).

"Zeitgeist"—Music and the Spirit of the Times

VALUE. Serves as a different approach to giving students music of high quality and a sense of style in music. Increases awareness of the interrelatedness of culture and music.

GENERAL PROCEDURE. Introduce the term *Zeitgeist:* "Let's learn a new word, a German word." Write it on the board and give a translation. "Let's see how this word applies to music." Play two contrasting recordings such as "Bydlo" (Peasant Cart) from Mussorgsky's *Pictures at an Exhibition*, and Boccherini's famous "Minuet." Ask, "What kind of people are represented by this piece? Are they people who rush to go through revolving doors? Are they calm, simple? How do they think and feel?"

Use many types of music in addition to the usual Baroque and Classical works. Try Civil War songs, original American compositions for band, and music of one time period from a single country. When pointing out similarities or contrasts between pieces, use the same medium when possible—orchestra, piano, chorus. At this age the students find it hard to hear the similarity of style between a piano piece and a choral work by the same composer.

POSSIBLE EXTENSION. Present not only the music of a certain place and time, but also a sampling of the art and architecture, dress, and culture. Prepare bulletin boards and other displays to give the students information quickly without making demands on class time. Look for films that are appropriate in content and difficulty.

"You and Your Voice"

VALUE. Leads to a better understanding of the processes involved in correct voice production and explains the change in boys' voices. Some presentation of voice change is essential at this age.

GENERAL PROCEDURE. Through drawings, pictures, and films (*Your Voice* is an excellent film for this[10]), present the functions of the major bodily

[8] Donald Horton, *The American Journal of Sociology*, LXII, No. 6 (May 1957), 569.

[9] "Payola Blues," *Newsweek*, LIV (November 30, 1959), 94. Also "Royola," *Time*, LXXV (May 9, 1960), 68.

[10] Black and white, 11 min., Encyclopaedia Britannica Films.

parts involved in singing and speaking. Pay special attention to the change in boys' voices, answering such questions as when it will happen, how fast, and what happens to the vocal cords. Explain how this will affect the music sung. Have the students experiment with the physical setup recommended for correct singing: feel the abdominal wall move out during inhalation and in during exhalation; sing a high pitch and then a low pitch with the hand lightly on the larynx, noting the change in vibration and position. Check the singing range of each individual.

POSSIBLE EXTENSION. Make a range chart for each student and have him keep it in his notebook, or post the class results in the form of a wall chart. Keep the chart up to date throughout the year. Play recordings which represent the various voice timbres and classifications, then quiz the students on their ability to identify the easily recognized voice types.

"*The Virtuoso and His Music*"

VALUE. Provides a different approach to expanding the students' interest and knowledge of music. Presents music with "showy" qualities, which students at this age find attractive.

GENERAL PROCEDURE. Put the word "virtuoso" on the board and explore its meaning with the class. Mention the names of Liszt and Paganini, the great virtuosos on their instruments. Listen to a representative composition of each, giving special attention to the virtuoso techniques employed. Discuss the word "virtuoso" again, this time enlarging upon its meaning to include its use as an adjective to describe a certain quality in music. Study and listen to a movement of a virtuoso-type concerto, noticing especially the features that distinguish the cadenza.

POSSIBLE EXTENSION. Present the concerto grosso and notice how it differs from the solo concerto. Play a movement of Vivaldi's *The Four Seasons* to illustrate the combination of both. Listen to the "showy" virtuoso pieces associated with bands in the early part of this country—Herbert Clark, Arthur Pryor, and others. Invite an outstanding instrumentalist to visit class and demonstrate the techniques employed on his instrument.

"*Rhythm in Music*"

VALUE. Explores rhythm, one of the most basic and appealing aspects of music.

GENERAL PROCEDURE. Group rhythms into loose classifications according to their complexity and similarity. Point out the simple, strong beats that underline the rhythm in marches and popular songs; the syncopation of most types of Latin American music; the triple pattern of the waltz and minuet. Have the class clap and tap out patterns and beats, as well as hear and see them written on the board. Clarify the difference between the rhythmic pattern and the beat. With the help of suggestions from the class, take a simple melody, perhaps "Frère Jacques" or "Twinkle, Twinkle, Little Star," and rewrite it, using several different rhythmic patterns.

POSSIBLE EXTENSION. Continue study into the more intellectual, complex rhythms as found in Tschaikowsky's *Symphony No. 4*, first movement, and twentieth-century pieces with irregular measures and polyrhythms (although the term "polyrhythms" need not be used). Try Copland's *El Salón México* to demonstrate modern rhythms.

"*Music in the Community*"

VALUE. Impresses upon the students that music is a living, immediate presence in their surroundings. Informs them of musical activities going on in the area, encourages them to read newspaper notices and reviews, and stimulates their interest in live performance. When used early in the year, serves as a basis for reports on current musical events.

GENERAL PROCEDURE. Keep an up-to-date class calendar of musical events in the area: programs on radio and television, concerts by professional musicians, and performances by schools and amateur music organizations. Put up a map with concert locations marked on it, and post pictures of the conductors of local orchestras, as well as publicity material about the groups. Mention any local fund-raising drives for arts activities, so that students will be aware of the problems involved in keeping music locally available. Take the class to places where concerts are being broadcast or presented live.

"*Review of Fundamentals*"

VALUE. Provides periodic review of skills, such as music reading, which may be forgotten unless used frequently. May comprise virtually the first organized presentation of fundamentals the students have ever received, if the elementary program was weak on such training.

GENERAL PROCEDURE. Move the teaching along quickly and limit the amount of time given it. A student at this age level who requires extended explanation and practice on fundamentals lacks either interest or ability, and cannot profit sufficiently to make a major effort worth while. Handle fundamentals in a concise and interesting fashion, as indicated by this phrase used by English and Richardson: "Let's get our signals straight."[11] Limit teaching efforts to these three areas: note names, time values, and common signs found in music. Do not attempt the writing of scales and detailed examination of time signatures, since these efforts are of limited value in a general music class.

[11] English and Richardson, *op. cit.*, Vol. I, p. 4.

POSSIBLE EXTENSION. Encourage any desire on the part of the class to learn how to read music. (Yes, it has sometimes happened.[12]) Try *Two Part Reading Fun* and *Three Part Reading Fun* by Carl Vandre[13] for a class that indicates an interest in music reading. Combine work on music reading and rhythms by clapping out rhythmic patterns at sight. Make brief use of flash cards containing a measure of melody or rhythm. Have the students experiment at the piano keyboard, learning to play simple melodies and chords.

"So You Want To Conduct!"

VALUE. Contributes to an understanding of beat and rhythm, and leads to insight as to how musical groups play or sing together. Provides a degree of physical activity that is well received at the junior high school level.

GENERAL PROCEDURE. Start with the two-beat pattern. Draw it simply on the board

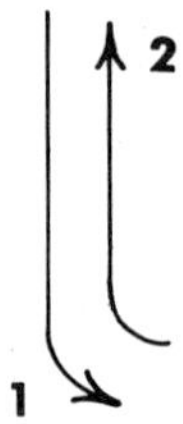

and have the students practice conducting the pattern while you conduct with your back to them (looking over your shoulder occasionally!). When the pattern is done properly, have the class sing through a song in the proper meter with no anacrusis, conducting as they sing. "Joy to the World" can be used for 2/4. Proceed in the same manner to the three-beat, and then to the four-beat patterns, writing them thus:

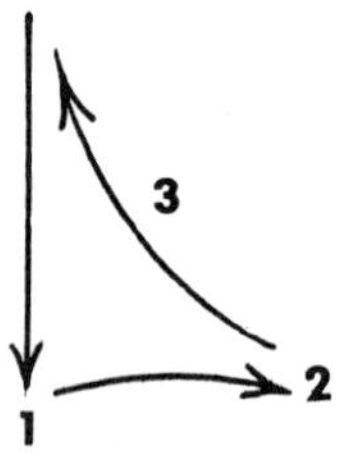

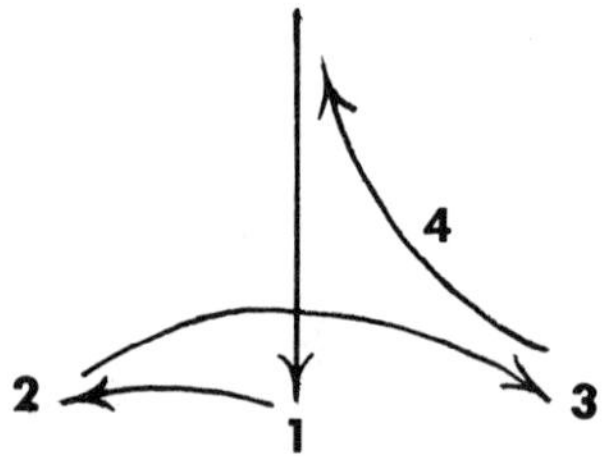

Try "America" for 3/4 and "Alouette" or "All Through the Night" for 4/4. Next teach the procedure for conducting an anacrusis, at which time

[12] Andrews and Leeder, *op. cit.*, p. 70.
[13] Carl Vandre, *Sight Reading Fun* and four similar books (New York: Mills Music Co.).

almost all common songs can be added to the conducting repertoire. Let the students take turns conducting the class as it sings. Instruct the class to follow the conductor even when he is wrong.

POSSIBLE EXTENSION. Teach the conducting of a hold and of a cutoff, and proceed to the use of the left hand. Encourage the students to maintain the conducting pattern in the right hand while at the same time indicating dynamic level and other points with the left. It is possible to conduct to records, but this technique is of limited value in teaching conducting.

"*Instruments of the Orchestra*"

VALUE. Increases the students' appreciation of instrumental music. Value of the unit may be limited if the students have covered the material in elementary school.

GENERAL PROCEDURE. Obtain some of the excellent teaching aids that are available—filmstrips accompanied by recordings; good pictures and wall charts in color and black and white; and recordings of individual instruments, to say nothing of works of music such as Britten's *The Young Person's Guide to the Orchestra* (available also in motion picture form as *Instruments of the Orchestra*[14]), and the ever-popular *Peter and the Wolf* by Prokofiev. If there are instrumentalists in the class, have them demonstrate their instruments, or invite outside students to give brief demonstrations. The students who demonstrate should be competent players but they need not be virtuosos; class interest will be high anyway. Divide the presentation into families of instruments to help the class recognize instruments by sight and, more important, by sound. Make a special effort to obtain and show instruments such as bassoon and oboe, which are not so well known.

POSSIBLE EXTENSION. Study the orchestra as a complete entity, its seating arrangement, instrumentation, and the conductor's score. Listen to a more advanced work featuring sections of instruments, such as Bartók's *Concerto for Orchestra*, or a record such as Howard Hanson's discussion of the orchestration of *Merry Mount*.[15] Compare the range and timbre of particular instruments with classifications of human singing voices; or study the use of instruments to represent characters in programmatic music.

"*Contemporary Concert Artists, Conductors, and Composers*"

VALUE. Brings life and currency to the art of music. Serves as a means of introduction to contemporary music.

[14] Black and white, 20 min., British Information Service.
[15] "The Composer and His Orchestra," Mercury 50175.

GENERAL PROCEDURE. Select about twenty of the most outstanding names among present-day concert artists, being careful to choose equally from the ranks of pianists, singers, instrumentalists, conductors, and composers. Present each briefly, his accomplishments and his background, making sure that they come across as human beings, not supermen. Show the class a picture of each musician, and from time to time give a sort of "flash-card" test on recognition of the pictures. A practical problem is the matter of spelling many of the names, which are especially difficult for junior high students of only average ability. The most feasible means of meeting the problem is to allow the use of phonetic spellings; otherwise, the emphasis may be diverted from music to spelling.

POSSIBLE EXTENSION. Tie in the study of contemporary musicians with an effort to keep up on current musical events; give special attention to well-known musicians when they appear in the local area. Make an inventory of the recordings owned by the families of class members, to determine the number that were made by the contemporary musicians studied in class.

"*Simple Instruments*"

VALUE. Teaches the fundamentals of harmony and provides experience in music-making. Increases interest in recreational music, which is a worthy outcome of such classes.

GENERAL PROCEDURE. Select and teach one simple instrument until the class has gained reasonable mastery of it, enough to be able to use it with only a little help. The most logical first choice is the Autoharp, because it is simple to play, and publishers of junior high school materials often include markings for Autoharp accompaniments. The ukulele has been used successfully in some schools. It is more difficult than the Autoharp, but it is inexpensive and has the advantage of being a favorite recreational instrument that enjoys periodic revivals of public interest. The Harmolin is similar to the Autoharp. Explore the possibilities of all three harmony instruments; each is appropriate for use in the general music class, and each can be learned in a group situation. Remember that the main function of these instruments is to accompany songs.

POSSIBLE EXTENSION. Teach the class a few recreational songs that can be accompanied by the instruments taught in class. Try improvisation. In *Living with Music*, simple parts are written for string bass, drums, piano, and other instruments.[16] The "other instruments" part uses a technique (called "vocalstration" in the book) which is common to the jazz musician: instrumentalists in the class are asked to create their own part using only the notes of a certain chord in one measure, another chord in the

[16] English and Richardson, *op. cit.*, Vol. I, pp. 21, 66; Vol. II, p. 17.

next measure, and so on, until a line based on the fundamental harmonies of the piece has been written. The new lines are then played with the original melody as an accompaniment or countermelody.

"*The Music of England*" (*Russia, Spain, Latin America, etc.*)

VALUE. Allows for comprehensive study of one culture.

GENERAL PROCEDURE. If England is the country chosen, have the class sing several fine English folk songs such as "Turtle Dove" and "Early One Morning," and some of the hymns of the Anglican Church such as "For All the Saints" (*Sine Nomine*). Choose several works that represent various periods of history—compositions by Purcell, Elgar, Vaughan Williams, and Britten. Compare the works of Vaughan Williams; some are arrangements of folk music, others are more complex and dissonant. Share with the class the Britten opera *The Little Sweep*. It is about an eleven- or twelve-year-old boy and includes a song for the audience to sing. Among the vast amount of fine music of Purcell is the *Trumpet Voluntary in D*, which is especially appealing to a general music class, as is Elgar's *Enigma Variations*.

POSSIBLE EXTENSION. Find out about England's relationship with Handel and *The Messiah*, the organ at Westminster Abbey, the tradition of boy choirs, the music for the coronation of the King or Queen, English folk songs that have become American folk songs, English sea chanteys, musical settings of great English poems, plus the music of several other fine composers not mentioned in this outline.

"*Musical Comedy, Operetta, and Opera*"

VALUE. Builds upon an interest that is already established: the teen-agers' interest in current musical comedies and dramatic shows. Expands the students' comprehension and acceptance of dramatic vocal forms, by proceeding from the known to the unknown. Aids teacher-pupil rapport.

SELECTION OF MUSIC. Much of the success of the unit depends upon the works selected for study. Avoid works which to a twelve-year-old appear to be pompous and long-winded, overly romantic, or odd and silly without being funny. Plots dealing with illicit love or romance on too mature a level are hardly appropriate. At best, the matter of love leaves a red-blooded twelve-year-old boy "cold," but idealized romance, as found in the poems *Evangeline* and *The Courtship of Miles Standish*, is quite appealing to girls. Of the standard operas a few are usable: possibly *Cosi Fan Tutte* and *The Marriage of Figaro* by Mozart, short operas such as *Gianni Schicchi* by Puccini, and perhaps one act from a few others. Explore the works of Britten, Menotti, and others which are more "down to earth" and hence are meaningful to students at this age. Gilbert and

Sullivan produced many fine operettas, but much of the subtle English humor and satire is lost on young Americans unless it is carefully explained. Romberg's operettas and contemporary American musical comedies usually find quicker favor.

GENERAL PROCEDURE. Start with a musical comedy, giving the general idea of the plot and pointing out the function of the overture, the relationship between orchestra and singers, and the variety in the songs. To present opera most effectively to the class, invite fine soloists to come and sing excerpts from the opera. The impact of live performance does much to win favor for operatic music. If the opera is very long, chóose one scene for concentrated attention, and merely tell the class about the plot involved in other scenes. Do not emphasize the interest which the plot alone creates, because on the basis of dramatic action, musical presentations come off a poor second to novels, motion pictures and television plays. Rather, focus attention on the relationship between the drama and music. In *Amahl and the Night Visitors,* the roles of two distinguished kings are written for deep voices. Why? How is the music affected when Amahl's mother slowly creeps toward the gold that she wishes to take for her son? Why does the oboe theme appear at both the beginning and end of the opera? Why is an oboe used for this melody?

POSSIBLE EXTENSION. Take the class to see a live performance of an opera, or if this is not feasible, obtain one of the several films on opera. Study in advance an opera that will be shown on television in the course of the year. Prepare a bulletin-board display on operas and opera singers, or on current musical comedies, and compare these forms with the oratorio.

"*Songs and Dances from around the World*"

VALUE. Builds upon the student's feeling for rhythm, and expands their knowledge of the music of foreign countries. Adds variety to the class through a limited amount of work on simple folk-dance steps.

GENERAL PROCEDURE. Group together those dances, preferably from different countries, which have similar steps, tempo, and style. This makes it easier for the students to learn and remember each dance, and it impresses them with the similarity among all peoples. Choose dances that call for a singing accompaniment, so that singing is involved in the unit. Point out that many folk dances are performed to music sung by the people participating in or watching the dance. Do not limit the class to the more usual type of dance and music, but let them listen also to music used in African tribal dances and American Indian dances. Check to see that there is sufficient space in the classroom for dancing. If space is limited, have only a portion of the class dance while the rest of the class follows the pattern on the board, sings, or accompanies on rhythm instruments. The unit may be done in cooperation with the physical-education teacher.

POSSIBLE EXTENSION. Lead into a study of music written for ballet, and ballet sections of musical comedy.

"*Music as a Career*"

VALUE. Gives the students a comprehensive idea of the vocational possibilities in music. Helps them understand why music is offered in the school.

GENERAL PROCEDURE. Present the various careers in music with descriptions as to training, working conditions, and opportunities. Include the following types of music occupation: music education (public school, college, private studio), professional performer (concert artist, symphony musician, dance-band musician), music therapist, music merchant, church musician. Several publications, such as *A Career in Music Education*,[17] describe the different careers, and these publications are brought up to date from time to time. As a part of the discussion on music education, ask the students to think through what they feel to be the purpose of the present class and of school music courses in general. Let them discuss curriculum content from the standpoint of need; they will undoubtedly agree that the three R's are necessary, but the need for music and the arts may not be as evident to them.

INDIVIDUAL LESSON PLANNING

Planning for a class in general music is in several ways similar to planning for a performing group. Over-all goals are considered, materials and techniques are evaluated, and a list of things to be covered is written down with an accompanying estimate of the time required to teach them. There are some differences, however. Performance may not consume as much time in the general music course, and there is a greater variety of class activity. Also, there is not as much on-the-spot decision-making as in the performing class, so more detailed planning is useful.

One practice that is especially valuable in the plan for general music is the use of "cues." These are reminders or questions for the teacher, briefly letting him know the manner in which something is to be taught or what question is to be used to bring out a point. Not everything the teacher plans to say can or should be cued in, of course; the cues are for the purpose of setting off blocks of activity.

Following is a plan for one class period of eighth-grade general music. To indicate better how the varied activities are incorporated, a unit has been selected that does not logically include singing, a film, field trip, or

[17] Washington, D.C.: Music Educators National Conference, 1962.

any other single time-consuming activity. The assumption is made in the selection of songs that over half the boys in the class are singing in the range of the bass clef. The class numbers about thirty students, of average ability and interest. For sake of clarity, the plan has been written out in more detail than would normally be used in a teacher's plan book. Many times the teacher uses his own unique abbreviations and one-word reminders.

Lesson Plan—8-3 General Music

9:30 Write "virtuoso" on board.
—What does it mean?
Piano virtuosos, Liszt.
Have students think of word to describe the following music as they listen

9:33 Listen to last half of *Mephisto Waltz* with no other prior comment.

9:37 —Was the piece sad? serious? wild? happy? breath-taking?
—What kind of man was Liszt? thoughtful? shy? a "show-off"?
—Piece was *Mephisto Waltz;* what does "Mephisto" mean?
—What kind of piece best depicts the devil?
—Why would a virtuoso like music about the devil?
Have students decide how music differs from other music they know, while they listen a second time.

9:41 Play last minute or two of piece again.
—What did you decide? How is this music different?
—Is it meant to be played by a talented amateur?
—Does it require you to think in order to understand it?
Have students decide what from this piece could be called "virtuoso."

9:45 Tell class the next instrument they will hear is a bassoon.
Play *Concerto in B flat for Bassoon,* Mozart, K. 191, third movement.

9:50 —Is this for a virtuoso? Why? What in the music makes us call it virtuoso?

9:53 Teach new song "Let Us Break Bread," *Time for Music,* p. 31.
Unison up to second line of p. 32. Point out melodic importance and dramatic quality of dissonant high E natural on p. 31.
Divide into high and low voices (baritones octave below A–T) for rest of p. 32.
Unison on p. 33.
—Is song for a virtuoso?
—Is it serious? simple? reverent?
Remind about good singing technique.
Try for *right expression;* observe dynamic markings.

10:00 Hear Betsy's report on current musical events.

10:03 Review "My Wild Irish Rose," *Time for Music,* p. 144.
Work with baritones on melody for good tone.
Introduce treble parts, let baritones hum melody during this.

–What is the effect of movement by half step in the treble lines?
Have class listen to effect of chromatics in the harmony.
–What are the words about?
–How important are they to the music?

10:10 Sing "The Ash Grove," *Music in Our Life*, p. 58.
Hear Julie, Wendy, and Tricia on the bell obbligato part they thought they could sing.

10:15 If time is left, sing "Dear Lahyotte," *Music in Our Life*, p. 22.

According to the plan, neither the unit on the virtuoso nor the singing of "Let Us Break Bread" will be finished in the period. "My Wild Irish Rose," may be, if the class does it properly. Betsy's report allows for a brief break in the singing. "The Ash Grove" is a song the students know, but to which three interested class members wish to add another line. The "if time is left" category allows some leeway for adjusting the timing of the class activities. Naturally the plan may be deviated from, if the situation warrants it, but even then, the plan has much value in that it outlines a workable direction for the class to take.

Projects

1. Share with other class members some of your experiences as a student in junior high school general music class. Describe the organization of the class, the type of activity carried on, and the strong and weak points of the course.
2. Make a list of songs common to the music books used in general music classes—songs which can be harmonized using only chords I and V, or I, IV, and V.
3. Examine books in the following categories and make a list of those that might serve as resource books for the teacher of general music: a) American folk songs, b) folk songs of other countries, c) religious music, d) musical instruments, e) music history, f) folk dances.
4. Examine these books published for use in seventh-grade general music:
   Birchard Music Series—Book Seven (Summy-Birchard Publishing Company)
   Time for Music (Prentice-Hall, Inc.)
   Living with Music (M. Witmark & Sons)
   Music in Our Life (Silver Burdett Company)
   Music Sounds Afar (Follett Publishing Company)
   The American Singer—Book Seven (American Book Company)

Sing Out (Summy-Birchard Publishing Company)

Singing Juniors (Ginn and Company)

This Is Music (Allyn and Bacon, Inc.)

Evaluate each with regard to: a) quality of music selected, b) variety in music selected, c) quality of musical arrangement in terms of voice part, range, accompaniment, d) extent to which music and text relate to seventh-grade students, e) logical organization of songs, f) availability of supplementary information and activities.

5. Look through music books for use in junior high school and through folk-song collections, and find six lullabies, each from a different country, that are suitable for use in a general music class.

6. Plan in detail a unit of your own choosing. If songs are to be included in the unit, indicate a source for each, listing the book title and page number. Identify precisely any films or filmstrips that might be used, and collect several pictures that are suitable for display. Describe any field trip or other activities that may be involved.

7. Using the unit developed for Number 6, make a lesson plan for a single forty-five minute period. Estimate the amount of time consumed by the various activities.

8. The unit "Rhythm in Music," suggested on page 342, contained general procedures for its presentation. Select specific songs, dances, and recordings that you would use in teaching the unit. A minimum of six to eight pieces seems necessary for this. Include in your plan any clapping or similar rhythmic activities that would be helpful.

9. On page 322 a question was raised about how a teacher could best impart the significance of half steps in the major scale. Describe what you would do to lead the students to this understanding in general music class.

10. Secure a sheet-music copy of any popular song. Plan how you would break it down to present it to a general music class in a manner that would be musically educational.

11. Decide upon two compositions or sections of compositions by each of the following modern composers; choose music that is characteristic of the composer's style and suitable for use in a general music class: Bela Bartók, Igor Stravinsky, Aaron Copland, Dimitri Shostakovich, Paul Hindemith, Samuel Barber.

12. Examine these three portions of operas and evaluate them in regard to their suitability for a junior high school general music class:

    Richard Wagner–*Tristan und Isolde*, Act II

    Giacomo Puccini–*La Bohème*, Act II

    C. W. von Gluck–*Orfeo ed Euridice*, Act III, Scene 2

13. Study *The Old Maid and the Thief* by Gian-Carlo Menotti. Plan how you would prepare a class for hearing this work, what learnings should precede its presentation, how much the class will hear in one period, and what you will say to the class about it.

14. In teaching "The Peddler" (p. 333), it was suggested that the melody be learned first, even though this would require the students to change temporarily from one part to another. Divide your class into two groups, one to argue the advantages of this pedagogical practice and the other to present its disadvantages. In preparation for the discussion, read what other music educators have written about the practice. Determine if any principles of music teaching are involved.

Suggested Readings

Andrews, Frances M., and Joseph A. Leeder, *Guiding Junior High School Pupils in Music Experiences.* Englewood Cliffs, N.J.: Prentice-Hall, Inc., 1953. Chapters III, IV, VI, IX.

Singleton, Ira C., *Music in Secondary Schools.* Boston: Allyn and Bacon, Inc., 1963. Pp. 73–84 and Chapter VI.

Sur, William R., and Charles F. Schuller, *Music Education for Teen-Agers.* New York: Harper & Brothers, 1958. Chapter II.

Weigand, J. J., "Experiences in General Music," in *Music Education in Action,* ed. Archie N. Jones. Boston: Allyn and Bacon, Inc., 1960. Pp. 92–107.

XV

music appreciation and theory

To some degree all music courses in the secondary school are classes in music appreciation and music theory. It is nearly inconceivable that there could be a band or a general music class that did not involve itself in the musical nomenclature or in understanding the qualities of the music it performed or heard. And this is as it should be. Indeed, one of the tenets of this book is that too much time is spent by performing groups in polishing numbers for public presentation. Not only should teachers involve themselves in teaching music understanding and theory; they should do more of it in the future than they have done in the past.

The special class in music theory or music appreciation will still be needed in the senior high school music curriculum, however, even if teachers of performing groups give more time to such matters in their classes. There are two reasons for this. One: many students do not have the time, interest, or ability for the performance-type course, and provision needs to be made for them. Two: even the best performing groups cannot cover the amount or variety necessary to acquaint the students with the vast world of music. For example, very few high school orchestras can play Brahms' *Symphony No. 4*, but they can study it in a music-appreciation class. Choral groups do not study instrumental music, and vice versa, but in a music-appreciation course, both media are explored. There is seldom time to write original works in a performing group; a music-theory class is needed for this. Because of the advantages of the performing group and the advantages of the nonperforming class, both types of learning situations are necessary if the music curriculum is to be effectively balanced at the senior high school level.

There is another important reason for including music-appreciation and music-theory courses in the senior high school curriculum. If well taught, these classes involve the intense, serious learning that can easily justify a place in the school day and the granting of credit. Unless the general music course is altered considerably from the broad and varied activities discussed in the preceding chapter, it hardly deserves full status in the senior high school. If the course is changed significantly, then a new name would seem appropriate.

It is unfortunate that courses in music appreciation and music theory are offered in only a minority of high schools. This is partly due to the confining six-period day in many schools—a pattern that seems likely to change in future years.[1] Some music teachers have felt that crowded teaching schedules eliminated the possibility of additional courses. Others have feared that such classes might draw students out of their performing groups for a year, a fear that the author has found to be largely groundless. Still others, recognizing the lack of precedent, have felt inadequate to plan the course content in new areas. These conditions do not negate the fact that such courses are needed in the music curriculum; they merely indicate that music educators must make a special effort to offer them.

Can music appreciation and theory be combined into one course to reinforce the learnings of each? Probably not in the high school, although taken at face value it appears to be a good idea. The general student in the music-appreciation course usually is not interested in nor can he profit from the work in theory. Moreover, at the high school level the study in each area becomes too sophisticated and specialized to allow for an easy combination of learnings. Using the Autoharp and vocal chording, a class can examine the harmonization of a folk melody, but the Autoharp and voices would be inadequate to study the harmonic intricacies of César Franck or Roy Harris. Finally, although the integration of music theory and music literature has been explored by many colleges, it has been attempted only rarely, with even rarer cases of success.

MUSIC APPRECIATION

Courses of this type have appeared under at least four names: music appreciation, literature, history, and understanding. Course titles using the words "history" or "literature" imply specialized courses that are more appropriate for the music major at the collegiate level. The term "music appreciation" has been abused and misunderstood in recent years, and somehow now carries the connotation of superficial and unmusical little lessons. The title "music understanding" is preferred because it

[1] J. Lloyd Trump, *Guide to Better Schools* (Chicago: Rand McNally and Company, 1961), pp. 40–45.

connotes knowing in the fullest sense of the word, as well as enjoying and appreciating. This chapter will utilize the more commonly used term, "appreciation."

The music-appreciation class, as generally conceived, must meet the needs of those students who have no special interest in making music but wish to be intelligent listeners. In large high schools it may be possible to section the course according to ability and interest. One section might contain students who are members of musical groups, and another non-musicians. Students may also be grouped according to academic ability. It is hoped that the students will be juniors or seniors, so that they can get the utmost benefit from a course that requires an intellectual effort equal to that of other courses in the high school, earns credit equal to that of other courses, and involves a textbook and homework.

By the time students reach their junior or senior year, a distressingly small percentage of them are still involved in music. For one reason or another, perhaps as a result of the drive for excellence on the part of the directors of performing organizations, perhaps because of the strenuous pace of required course work in academic subjects, most students with only a modest interest in music are no longer involved in the subject. Because the number of these students is so large, and because they usually have had no music study at all on a mature, high school level, the music-appreciation class is especially significant to the education of all teen-agers in music.

Course Content

In developing the content for this course, the teacher will have to consider the time available, the age and ability of the students, and what courses they have had in high school. Not only should musical training be considered, but other courses in the area of fine arts, English, and history. It makes a difference whether or not the students have had experience in English class representing rhyme schemes ABBA and the like. Also, much of the historical background can be passed over quickly if the students have had a good course in world history.

The music selected for study should be representative of the various styles and periods, and the various forms and media. In selecting the pieces which the limited time will allow him to present, the teacher should approximate the music chosen for performance in concert and recital halls today. This may appear to support the *status quo*, and to some extent this is true. But it is risky to pretend to be a prophet of what music will be in the future. It is also risky to extol the qualities of music that is not often performed publicly at the present time. For instance, should one teach electronic music? Should the music educator be teaching children music that uses quarter tones? Is the tonal technique of Schoenberg the wave of the future? Or is it Roger Sessions? Or Ussachevsky? Or Hába? Or Copland? Or Stravinsky? (Which phase of Stravinsky will remain?) The great Richard Wagner predicted the end of absolute music, but he was wrong.[2] Wagner's experience should cause the teacher of music appreciation to be restrained in forecasting music's future. The best solution is to present a variety of literature, slanted slightly toward modern music, *and do a good job of teaching it.* In the long run, it will be attitudes and skills of listening that the teen-agers of today will carry with them into the year 2000, far more than it will be specific pieces of music.

In most instances it is better for the teacher to do a thorough job on a limited number of musical works than it is to scatter the emphasis. He should use a "post hole" approach by which he permanently implants a particular work and composer. Between the post holes he will need to "string lines," in order that one area of concentrated attention can be logically connected to the next. This means leaving out some good composers and music—and how painful that is to the teacher! But better to do this than inundate the student in a vast sea of information and music.

Unfortunately, in many schools students cannot spare a full year in their schedules for this one course. If there should be sufficient enrollment for a full-year course, it is an easy matter to expand the content. Following is an outline of a post-holed course meeting daily for one semester.

Introduction	
Tschaikowsky	*Symphony No. 4*
Renaissance	
Palestrina	polyphonic vocal works
Baroque	
J. S. Bach	fugue, concerto grosso, suite, organ works
Handel	*The Messiah*, oratorio
Classical	
Mozart	symphony, sonata-allegro form, solo concerto
Haydn	symphony, minuet and trio, string quartets and other chamber music
Classical-Romantic	
Beethoven	symphony, piano sonata, changes in sonata-allegro form
Romantic	
Schubert	art song
Chopin	piano works
Liszt	virtuoso music, program music
Brahms	symphony, chamber music, use of forms
R. Strauss	tone poem
Puccini	opera

[2] Ernest Newman, *Wagner As Man and Artist* (New York: Alfred A. Knopf, 1924), p. 164.

Modern

Stravinsky	ballet, *Symphony of Psalms*
Bartók	*Piano Concerto No. 3*
Shostakovich	*Symphony No. 5*
Copland	*El Salón México*
Villa-Lobos	*Bachianas Brasileiras No. 5*
Ussachevsky and others	electronic music
Schoenberg	atonal technique
Menotti	*The Telephone* and *The Medium*
Harris	*Symphony No. 3*

Greater efforts at explanation by the teacher are needed for the Renaissance, Baroque, and Classical periods, simply because they are seldom familiar to teen-agers. The Romantic period contains more names in the outline because the students are somewhat more familiar with the names and music of that era. Since modern works present in varying degrees a departure from the style of music familiar to the students, the effort here centers on making the students accustomed to a few works by hearing them more than once. The presentation of electronic music and atonal techniques can be only a brief introduction, unless much time is available.

There are at least two difficulties in deciding on course content and order of presentation. One is the need to introduce musical forms and techniques, while at the same time progressing somewhat chronologically by composer and period. Clearly not every form can be introduced at the beginning of the course. Therefore it may be necessary to hold off on opera until the Romantic era, and at that time reach back and discuss a Mozart opera. In most cases, the high point of a particular form or medium is best presented within a particular period. Thus the song is presented with Schubert and the organ with Bach, even though songs and organ music have been written before and after these periods.

The second difficult matter is that of deciding just where and how to begin. Some teachers start with folk music and work into composed music. Others prefer to start with Gregorian chant and proceed chronologically. Some start with a unit on acoustics, others with a Broadway musical, and others with a standard symphonic work that almost all students are sure to like once they become familiar with it. The latter approach works well, since it also serves to introduce some discussion of form and terms used in the course, and starts the students to thinking about the purpose of serious composed music.

The classification system encounters trouble when it attempts to confine Beethoven or Impressionism within one period. In these cases the students must remember that some music is transitional, and almost all music, regardless of when it was written, carries within it the seeds of many styles.

A few specific compositions are mentioned in the outline to indicate the type of music selected. Some question may be raised about works such as *The Messiah*, which almost all students have heard at one time or another. But building on what the students know is a good thing. Students are encouraged when they hear music that is familiar to them. True, they may recognize only one or two portions of the work, and they may have little understanding of what they are hearing, but it is a basis on which to build. When students move from superficial recognition of the "Hallelujah Chorus" to a mature understanding of it, they are learning, in the best sense of the word.

Textbooks

It is difficult to find suitable textbooks for a music-appreciation course in the high school. (The junior high school teacher is more fortunate in this respect.) The problem is that almost all books are written for use at the collegiate level. They contain too many names and terms, and too much technical information for the high school student. Many times the orientation is heavily historical.

Textbook writers also face the dilemma of presenting material according to forms or chronology, so the teacher may have to use two books. One book may concentrate on musical aspects: harmony, form, media. The other may present the story of music chronologically with an emphasis on composers and styles. Both will need to be written in a down-to-earth manner, with a concentration on the highlights in music—"post holing," in other words.

Teaching Students to Listen—Not Just Hear

The key to a music-appreciation course is getting the students to hear in the music the points presented by the teacher or written in the textbook. All is lost unless the students develop this skill. The principle of music teaching that says "ear before eye" applies to the music-appreciation course. It is easy to forget the extent to which today's youngsters grow up learning to ignore sound. This resistance to sound is something formidable to overcome; it cannot be reversed in a few short hours so that the teen-ager suddenly begins to listen with keen sensitivity.

There is a need to develop selective listening in the students. The word "selective" here does not refer to choice of material, but rather to listening that is directed toward specific points in the music. For example, it is quite an achievement for many students to locate and follow the theme of a piece in the array of sound. Many students cannot even remember the original theme. In order to understand music, students need to hear counterpoint, contrasting lines, and the interplay between parts. They need the ability to listen selectively in order to keep their attention on the important features of the music. When music becomes a maze of sound, without any form or sense, it becomes a boring and pointless activity.

There is no foolproof way to teach teen-agers to listen carefully. The student has to be sufficiently motivated to put forth a minimum of effort, and he must possess the intellectual capacity to retain and make sense out of the musical ideas his ear transmits to his brain. The most the teacher can hope to do is persistently encourage, cajole, and prod students to listen selectively. Besides asking, "Did you hear this? Did you hear that?" or directing, "Listen for the melody in the horns," he can ask the students to verbalize about a specific portion of the music. For example, the arm of the record player can be set down near the canonic treatment of the melody in the introductory part of Berlioz' *Roman Carnival Overture.* Exactly when the imitation starts, the teacher can say to the class "NOW —what's happening?" After the section is done and the arm has been picked up, the class can attempt to answer the question. The teacher should generally ask several students in the class before he indicates if an answer is right or wrong. If only a few students get the right answer, the section should be played again, with the same procedure. Even a third time may be necessary. Of course, before students are asked to identify canonic treatment aurally, they must understand what the word "canon" means.

A second way to draw out the students is to take a work such as the last movement of Brahms' *Symphony No. 4*, the movement containing the chaconne. After being made familiar with the chaconne theme, the students listen to the first nine or ten variations, with the teacher indicating each new portion as it appears. The students are told to write down in their own words what happens to the original melody in each section. They should put down specifically what is heard in each particular variation. Answers are not acceptable which merely say that in the fourth section the violins are playing; the description must be specific. They must say exactly what the violins are doing. Are they playing in a rough, masculine style? Are they playing the very high notes in legato style? Are they playing the variation on the melody, or are they playing a contrasting line? If two students disagree on what is going on in a particular portion, the matter should be settled by hearing the music again, not by the teacher telling the class. The whole effort here is to get the students to listen as they have never listened before.

A third technique to encourage listening is one used successfully by elementary school music teachers. It is simply to count the number of times a melody appears in a work such as a fugue. The class can be asked not only to keep track of the number of appearances, but also to write down how the subject or melody is treated. Does it come back in a low voice, or in a high part? Is it complete? Is it played in the same style as the first time? Is the countersubject played with the subject?

A fourth technique is to ask the students what happens in the development section of a symphony. Assuming that they have heard the themes often enough to remember them, they are asked to indicate which theme is stressed in the development, and what is done with it.

A fifth practice used to assist in the achievement of selective listening is to have the students follow the theme in one movement. This works well with Mozart, since he presents themes in a straightforward manner with well-marked cadences and transitions, and most movements are not long. Students need not write anything in this case; the teacher merely picks the arm off the record and asks the students what is being done with the theme, and what this indicates about the form of the movement.

With so much emphasis being placed on careful listening, the question may come to mind, "What about ear training?" The usefulness of ear training in the music-appreciation course depends on the time available, because some time is needed before ear training efforts can bear fruit. Every music major and teacher can recall how much time was spent on ear training in theory classes at the college level, and then realize the time needed for this to be useful in the secondary school. Although simple ear training with scale numbers can be given, as mentioned on page 160, in order to reach full fruition it needs to be related to notation. This obviously creates problems with students who do not perform music, and for whom the musical nomenclature is somewhat of a mystery. If the teacher sets out to remedy this by teaching music reading, he has undertaken another extensive project. Ear training does help the students as far as tonal memory is concerned, and it helps in their selective listening. But unless a class meets daily for a year, formal ear training is seldom as wise a use of time as listening carefully for the particular phrases and techniques in the music studied.

How helpful is it for the students to see the music that is heard in class? To the experienced musician, seeing the score or a copy of the music is helpful, but to the nonmusician with limited ability to read music, an orchestral score is only confusing. Most students can comprehend something from seeing a theme written on the board; they can certainly read music to the extent of determining whether the notes go up or down. The teacher, therefore, should have a few scores available for the better-trained musicians, but he should also provide the class with a simply-written version of important themes and melodies.[3]

After a few weeks, rather than ask for the conventional term paper, the teacher of the music-appreciation course can assign the students a "listening project." He can give them a list of specific works to hear, or specific composers, or simply a certain number of major compositions from each period. The students are to listen to the music outside of class

[3] Edgar H. Smith, "The Value of Notated Examples in Learning To Recognize Musical Themes Aurally," *Journal of Research in Music Education,* I, No. 2 (Fall 1953), 97–104.

and prepare a complete report on it. In one way or another the students must commit themselves on each piece heard, by commenting on the form, style, unusual musical factors, or the expressive quality of the music. Not only does this eliminate the possibility of circumventing the assignment; it encourages the students to listen carefully, rather than just put in time hearing some records.

The emphasis placed on listening should carry over into the tests given in the course. After the students have studied some of the stylistic periods, they can be tested on their ability to listen to music and identify it by period only. The music played can be either familiar or unfamiliar. At first, there may be only two periods, Renaissance and Baroque, so the students find identification easy. With each additional period, identification becomes more difficult, although the students have the benefit of working into it gradually. Toward the end of the course, in addition to proper identification of the stylistic period, the teacher may ask about a particular recording, "Does it contain a cadenza?" "Is it a minuet and trio?" "Is it nationalistic?" In preparing the listening section of a test, the teacher must select works that are typical of the period they are intended to represent. Also, if he gives the organ attention only during the presentation of Baroque music, he will have to prepare the class somewhat on Romantic organ music if he expects them to correctly identify as to period a César Franck organ work. It should be added that listening examinations worry some students because there is nothing concrete to study in preparation. The testing on ability to hear is doubly valuable for them because it impresses on them the different nature of a course in a fine art such as music.

Getting Students to Think in Qualitative, Aesthetic Terms

When students first enter a music-appreciation course, they carry with them all their old patterns of thinking about subjects they study. They naturally expect music to be like the familiar academic disciplines, and do not realize that if they are going to get the point, the *raison d'être* of listening to Bach or Brahms, they will have to reorient their manner of thinking for the course. The teacher's success in getting students to use a new frame of mind will depend first of all on his understanding of the discussion in Chapter Two about the nature of and need for aesthetic experiences. Then, he needs to seize upon every opportunity to imbue the students with these basic propositions:

1) In a fine art one does not look for an answer, but rather for a representation or symbolization of experience. Many students are sorely disappointed when the teacher cannot supply an "answer" for Beethoven or any other composer. They are looking for gimmicks, and approach a work of art in the same way that they would approach a problem in mathematics.

2) In works of art one looks for quality, not quantity. Quantities can be stated with objective accuracy, but qualities must necessarily be based on subjective judgments. Since subjective opinion is a personal matter, growing out of each person's unique experiences, there can be no universal or unanimous agreement as to the meaning or value of a work of art. Furthermore, the qualities in life are far more important than the quantities. A crate can serve admirably as a table. It could be so used, except for the fact that human beings want their surroundings to be beautiful as well as functional. One crate and one fine table are similar in terms of quantity, but not quality.

3) There can be no single standard for evaluating a work of art. Certainly "prettiness" cannot be the only criterion. The effectiveness of a work of art lies in its ability to get across its point, to strike a response in the viewer or listener; and so a rough, harsh, masculine work may be aesthetically more effective than a lyric, sweet, docile piece. Nor does one always listen to music in the same way. As Copland points out in his discussion of "levels of listening," sometimes music is listened to more for its expressive qualities, while at other times one listens more analytically for musical factors.[4]

4) Works of art are not just one of the "good things of life," like a Caribbean vacation or wall-to-wall carpeting. A work of art is inexorably bound up with human experience. It stands on its own, and need not say anything or do anything in the utilitarian sense.

5) Technical knowledge of the arts is of little value for its own sake. A canon, rondo, or cancrizans movement in itself is of little consequence; its musical effect is the important consideration. Technical terms are introduced only to permit better understanding of the music.

Probably no teacher in one course can fully realign the thinking of the students on such concepts. But enlargement of the point of view should be begun. In the end, teen-agers should be able to see the pointedness as well as the humor in the "Peanuts" cartoon.

Because the frame of mind is the same for the study of all the fine arts, usually students who have had a course such as art appreciation are a step ahead when it comes to understanding music. Also, because of the similarity among the fine arts, the course which integrates them has some justification for its existence. The problem with the fine-arts course has often been the fact that each subject usually receives less time than it would get if studied by itself.

Developing an Understanding of Style

As has been implied in the sample course outline and in the discussion of examinations in music appreciation, the stylistic approach is suggested.

[4] Aaron Copland, *What To Listen for in Music*, rev. ed. (New York: McGraw-Hill Book Company, Inc., 1957), pp. 9–17.

Copyright 1958 by United Feature Syndicate, Inc.

One reason for this is that it places the emphasis on musical qualities. Furthermore, it adapts well to the post-hole approach. The periods represent a solid element of musical experience and knowledge for the student to hang on to—an element to which other aspects of music, and other fine arts, can be related. Although the classification of periods is by no means perfect, there is a Romantic movement in painting, sculpture, and literature, as well as in music, and the student's understanding of one will contribute to his understanding of the others.

The study of musical style should assist the student in approaching works that are unfamiliar to him. When he says he does not like this or that music, often the problem is that he missed something that was there, or he was looking for something that was not there. A course in understanding music should lead the student to look at a musical work through the proper pair of glasses, so to speak. He must not expect to be overwhelmed in a bath of sound when hearing Mozart, for example, because Mozart represents an age that proclaims reason, good taste, and the universal nature of truth and beauty. In Mozart's age, introspective emotionalism was wrong, not a valid experience. Knowing this, the listener avoids the disappointment of expecting to hear one thing and then hearing another. He can now listen devoid of illusions, and one serious obstacle to understanding Mozart's music has been removed.

The student must be able to hear selectively and consider aesthetically *before* he allows himself the luxury of deciding whether or not he likes a piece of music. The order here is important. To start from the "I-like-or-don't-like-it" position is bad for several reasons. It limits the student to only two poles of choice—"I like it" or "I don't like it." Generally, the new and different is not liked. Basically, however, this practice starts with the individual's opinion of the music, and consequently emphasizes a personal reaction, rather than the qualities to be found in the music. A student of music needs to be just that—a student of music—and not a referee. It is not a stretch of rhetoric to say that every music listener is, in a sense, a student of music. As he listens, he is analyzing, thinking, and considering, even though he may have heard the piece many times before.

Introducing a New Work

The teacher must first review his reasons for deciding to present a particular work to the class. In all probability these reasons will give him his cue as to how the work can best be presented and what the students are to learn from it. In almost every good major composition there are enough musical phenomena—themes, form, counterpoint, rhythm, orchestration, harmony—to occupy a class for weeks. So the teacher must select not only the composition but also the points he feels should be highlighted in the work. Mursell has stated the need for highlighting in this way:

> First, do not swamp the listeners. Do not ask them to notice too much at one time. It is far better to emphasize only a little, and to emphasize it clearly, than to try to cover a great deal and so make everything vague and baffling. . . . To highlight the principal themes only may be far better than trying to explain the entire structure of a symphonic movement.[5]

New music need not always be presented in the same way. There are times when a record should be played with no preparation by the teacher; he can then ask the class to describe the expressive quality of the music. He may wish simply to set a mood. In one case, during the playing of a Grieg number the class was shown color slides of fjords and other Norwegian scenery. Certain portions of the music can be played as "teasers" for the entire work. On other occasions the class can learn the theme and sing it before hearing it in context. This is especially helpful in enabling the students to follow sonata-allegro form more easily. Sometimes the themes can be placed on the board or on large pieces of paper around the walls of the room, and the teacher can point to them when they are heard in the music. Before an opera is presented, the libretto can be read as a play with acting. This works well with Menotti's *The Telephone*, for example. Perhaps the class can sing the first sixteen or so measures of three or four of the solos. In any case, the methods of presentation should be as

[5] James L. Mursell, *Music Education: Principles and Programs* (Morristown, N.J.: Silver Burdett Company, 1956), pp. 295–96. Reprinted by permission.

imaginative and varied as the works of music. The teacher must be much more than the record-player operator who announces the next selection to be played.

In many works of good music the points to be heard are not obvious or easily grasped upon first hearing, so a recording should be played twice, or even three times. These several hearings should not be one after the other, but on separate days with some new points to be listened for and some old ones to be reviewed.

The role of memory in understanding is a vital one. When a person hears music, he actually experiences only an instant of sound at any given moment. This exact instant of sound can have meaning only if the hearer remembers what he has heard prior to that instant and anticipates what he will hear in subsequent instants. Listening to music is like trying to view a picture that is entirely covered except for a small slit extending from the top to the bottom of the picture. The picture is seen only as the slit is moved across it. All that is in the picture on either side of the slit must exist in the viewer's mind in the form of memory or anticipation; in other words, the customary spatial comprehension of the picture is now changed to comprehension in time.

Memory and anticipation also exist in terms of style. If a trained musician listens to a new work composed in a style familiar to him, he finds it easier to remember what he has actually heard, and to anticipate more fully what is about to occur. It is as though a slit is being moved across pictures of similar subjects painted in a similar style. Thus another value of the stylistic approach.

Sometimes students enter a music-appreciation class with the notion that they must visualize something concrete as they listen—ships sailing, sunsets, horses galloping. This is an unfortunate carry over from some of the "music-appreciation" lessons of the past. While some pieces are written to express feelings aroused by specific incidents, the attention should be focused on what is happening musically. If students need to be persuaded on the inability of music to express specific stories or pictures, the teacher can try one of two devices. One: make up a new and different story to fit a programmatic piece of music. Tell it to the class and ask them to judge as they listen to the record whether the story is the one the composer intended to describe. Play the record, and after hearing the students' opinions, tell the right story. Two: without mentioning its title, play a short programmatic work such as "The Great Gate of Kiev" from *Pictures at an Exhibition*, or "Pines of the Appian Way" from *The Pines of Rome*, and ask the class to imagine a movie scene that would fit the music. Invite each student individually to describe the scene which the music suggests to him. Although the ideas may bear some resemblance to one another, the details will vary sufficiently to impress the students with the fact that music is not equipped to give an accurate description of pictorial or nonmusical observations.

MUSIC THEORY

Music theory, like music appreciation, enjoys a variety of names. Some colleges use an integrated approach rather than separate courses for ear training, sightsinging (solfeggio), partwriting, and keyboard harmony. And even the integrated course appears under such names as "Basic Music" or "Fundamental Musicianship." As with music appreciation, it is difficult for high school students to work a full-year theory course into their schedules. Many schools must settle for a one-semester course, while others can offer the class only in alternate years.

At this point, the similarity between theory and appreciation ends. The theory course is not for the general student; it is for the student with at least a minimal musical background. Its purpose is to teach the "facts and principles about the construction and notation of music."[6]

Except in a few specialized high schools, there is not enough enrollment to permit courses in several areas of theory. As a practical measure, the theory course in the high school must be an integrated one, or else significant topics will be left out. In any case, the unified approach to theory is more musically and educationally valid. Melody and harmony are interrelated, and upon them depends the usefulness of keyboard harmony; in a similar manner, the partwriting of music is related to the aural experience of that writing. Therefore, for practical and pedagogical reasons the work on theory in the high school should be integrated.

The teaching of theory in the secondary schools differs in three respects from that done at the collegiate level. One: the high school class may be more limited as to time, often being only one semester long. Two: the students are not as facile in the use of music notation, therefore they require more time to write out music. Three: the high school class is not as highly selected and able as the collegiate class. For these reasons, efficiency is of paramount importance in teaching the secondary school theory class.

Whatever is selected for work in the theory class should meet the twin criteria of being functional and versatile. The approach to harmony, for example, should be of sufficient scope to embrace the nineteenth-century as well as the eighteenth-century style; this will lead quickly into seventh chords, augmented sixth chords, and more drastic and frequent modulations. Harmonic analysis should encompass many forms: the chorale and hymn, the song accompaniment. A class should not become so involved with a certain style or approach to music that it never learns about other styles and approaches. Nor should it confine its study to highly specialized techniques and problems that pertain to only a very small portion of the world of music. Sometimes attention has become

[6] Peter W. Dykema and Karl W. Gehrkens, *The Teaching and Administration of High School Music* (Evanston, Ill.: Summy-Birchard Publishing Company, 1941), p. 261.

centered on intricate rules, especially in regard to partwriting. Not only does this teaching procedure violate the students' need to experiment with actual music, but the rules themselves are more complex than they need be, and are often applicable in only the rarest of circumstances. At times the rules have even been at variance with the practices of great composers.[7]

The learnings in theory should be so practical that the students on completion of the course will be able to write songs for a student musical, if the occasion presents itself. This requires a knowledge of fundamentals, an understanding of vocal and instrumental music, an ability to write and to arrange short, simple creative works.

Fundamentals

Even though a minimum musical knowledge is a prerequisite for the course, the first efforts should concentrate on fundamentals of the musical nomenclature. Although some members of the class are in many respects good musicians, their knowledge of theory may be spotty and not very cohesive. Few students are completely at ease with the double-dotted note, the 12/8 time signature, or the three forms of the minor scale. The work on fundamentals in the high school class should proceed rapidly, probably consuming not more than six to eight weeks of daily class meetings to cover this content:

- Note names, including bass clef
- Rhythm—note and rest values, meter signatures, borrowed units
- Major scales, constructed by interval and key signature
- Minor scales, constructed by key signature—pure, harmonic, and melodic forms
- Intervals, including inversion
- Chord types, including inversion—major, minor, augmented, diminished, seventh
- Chord functions, identified by name and Roman numeral

Several textbooks, some of which have workbook pages to be filled out, are available for the teaching of music fundamentals. Since the material to be learned is very specific, the teaching procedure is largely one of proceeding through the book and clarifying points for the students as the occasion calls for it. One point that bothers some students is the presentation of the circle of fifths as a means of understanding key signatures. Actually, it takes some musical training to fully understand the circle of fifths. When key signatures are introduced, the students do not yet know what fifths are, nor can they conceive of a "circle" of tonality. What seems more feasible with teen-agers is to teach them to write signatures properly, and after they have had intervals, then go back and show them the relationship between keys. Major keys are easily taught, at

[7] Vincent L. Jones, "The Relation of the Harmonic Theory to Practice from Rameau to 1900," unpublished doctoral dissertation, Harvard University, 1934.

least to the extent of writing them correctly. The students will find it easy to learn the order of flats, because the first four flats spell "bead"; next they can be informed that the order of sharps is the reverse of the order of flats. Then they need only learn that the name of the key is identical in name with the next-to-last flat, or the note a half step above the last sharp. This leaves only the keys of C and F to learn by rote.

Because of the specific nature of learning the fundamentals of music, it is likely that in the near future much of this will be programmed for use on teaching machines. When this is done, it may be possible for the teacher to progress to more advanced activities as the students learn the fundamentals individually and hence more quickly.

Keyboard Experience

Limited work at the keyboard should accompany the study of fundamentals. The word "keyboard" as used here does not encompass the complex activities required of many collegiate music majors. In the early stages, keyboard experience in the high school class involves playing the right notes on the piano. This is a necessary preliminary step because some students upon entering the course have only a sketchy acquaintance with the piano.

As major and minor scales are studied, they should be played at the keyboard, and the same is true for intervals and chords. Then as students progress into creative work, they will be more free and musical in their approach to the piano, especially in their writing and playing of simple accompaniments.

Ear Training

One of the most important and continuing phases of the theory class should be the work on ear training. Although the ability to listen carefully and selectively is not easily taught, a "good ear" is a necessity for any worthwhile musical effort, be it composing, teaching, or performing. Music is an aurally based art, and never should this fact be forgotten, least of all in the theory class.

In melodic dictation the use of numbers can save much class time. The "telephone-number" system, which utilizes scale step numbers without a staff, allows the students to get the essential experience of taking down what they hear without spending time putting it into musical notation. The use of numbers is, however, limited to phrases that do not modulate. The technique is this: the teacher tells the class the number of the starting note. Later, when the class is able to isolate a particular note in a chord, he can play the tonic chord and let them find the first number from that. It is not necessary for them to write down short phrases. For example, the teacher can play this figure twice,

and the students can memorize and/or sing back "1-3-4-2-7-1." As the phrases become longer, the numbers will need to be written down. To help the students see the relationship between numbers and musical notation, a melody that has been taken down correctly with numbers should occasionally be transcribed into musical notation.

Another practical way to relate musical sound with notation is for the students to recall a familiar melody, perhaps a popular song, and write it on the staff. This saves time normally spent in dictating the melody.

Whether numbers or notes are used, all melodic dictation should follow essentially the same procedure. First, the students should be told the starting pitch, or should be given a clue as to how to find it. Then the teacher should play the phrase *twice*. Long melodies should be dictated phrase by phrase. During the first two hearings, the class should *not* attempt to write anything; they should just listen. The no-writing policy trains the students to listen more closely and develops their musical memory. After the second hearing, the class can sing back the melody, in order to gain a concrete experience with it. Then and only then should they attempt to write down the melody. The teacher should play the melody two more times, with pauses between playings to allow for checking of work.

Some work in rhythmic dictation is helpful to the students, especially early in the course if melodic dictation is confined to numbers instead of the complete notation with its rhythmic symbols. The procedure for rhythmic dictation is similar to melodic, in that the students should listen carefully to the pattern the first two times it is tapped or played on the piano. As use of notation is increased in melodic dictation, rhythmic dictation becomes less necessary because rhythm is present in melody.

In addition to melodic and rhythmic dictation, the students should learn how to identify the soprano and bass members of a chord. Before actual identification is attempted, the class needs to have experience in singing major triads with numbers. The first singing should be from the root; later the starting tone can be the third or fifth. Once the triad pattern is established in the students' ears, these steps are recommended for dictation of chord members:

1) Play a triad using at least four notes. Arrange the tones so that the bass note is a distance of a fifth or more from the others, and play it more loudly. Hold the triad until the sound fades away. After a short pause, ask the class to sing back the bass note.

2) Play the chord once more, and again sustain it. Have the class experiment by assuming that the note sung is 1 and singing 1-3-5-3-1. If the starting pitch was not 1, this will be obvious to the class. Proceed then to 3, and to 5, if necessary.

3) When the class becomes proficient at singing patterns starting from the bass member of the chord, drop the singing and have the students merely identify the tone as 1, 3, or 5.

4) When the bass can be heard fairly well, use the same procedure to find the soprano member of the triad.

A fourth phase of ear training in the secondary school theory class is the identification of chord types. The initial attempt should be confined to a choice between major or minor chords in root position. Then the work can progress to inverted positions as well. This is followed by introduction of the diminished triad, and finally the augmented triad. For the first several weeks, practice in chord identification should involve hearing only two or three of the four types during one session. This avoids overwhelming the uninitiated ears of the students with too many types at once.

If the course meets daily for a year, it may be possible to begin work on harmonic dictation. The teaching procedure for this is quite specific and somewhat more extensive than those just presented. The teacher who wishes information on this phase of ear training should consult a book which specializes in pedagogy of theory, such as the *Teacher's Dictation Manual* by McHose.[8]

A certain amount of ear training can be handled with tapes and recordings in a language laboratory room. Some recordings of work in ear training have been available for several years, and the teacher should examine them to evaluate their usefulness for his class.

Creative Work by Students

When the students show a reasonable mastery of fundamentals and aural comprehension, they can turn their attention to simple creative efforts, which will involve the study of harmony and arranging and, most important, the application of ear training and fundamentals. The general approach to this portion of the theory class is similar in concept to that presented in *Creative Harmony and Musicianship*, by Murphy and Stringham.[9]

Generally, the term "creative work" brings to mind an original musical composition of some magnitude. In the high school theory class, however, the time available and the abilities of the students do not permit efforts at major compositions. At this level, creativity is best nurtured through limited works, sometimes not more than sixteen or thirty-two measures in length. Of equal importance with the brevity of the work is the degree to which the teacher structures the work. Never should the neophyte composer be told, "Go home and write a song." Such a direc-

[8] Allen Irvine McHose (New York: F. S. Crofts & Co., 1948).

[9] Howard Murphy and Edward Stringham (Englewood Cliffs, N.J.: Prentice-Hall, Inc., 1951).

tion is about as likely to succeed as pushing a child off a pier to make him learn how to swim. Although it may appear to be an inconsistency, creative work for most high school students is better fostered at the start when they are given a precise set of specifications for their work. What they need at first is a sense of how to go about writing music, and a successful experience at doing so.

Since song style is so fundamental in music, and since the writing of a song makes the students think in terms of expression through music, a good case can be made for starting with this medium. The teacher can pick a stanza from a poem that is definite in its emotional tone. He may reproduce on paper or have the students copy from the board the words written below the staff, with a time signature and measure bars already in place. For the first or second original effort by the students, the instructor may wish to suggest the note values to be used on each word. These can appear just above the text; they will look something like a percussion part. The reason for this degree of structuring is that many students have trouble grasping the simple and underlying quality of rhythm. It is not uncommon for the first unassisted effort to reveal a rhythmic pattern such as

There are several reasons why such rhythm might be forthcoming, one of them being the student's desire to make the rhythm "interesting."

The students should be instructed to write the melody only. At the next class session, the teacher plays the melodies and discusses them with the class, determining how well they meet the criteria of unity, variety, and appropriateness with text. The words "unity" and "variety" refer to the poles in the construction of melody, variety indicating novelty, and unity indicating a quality of cohesiveness. If the melody is a good one, the student can add a simple block-chord accompaniment. If the melody is not of good quality, another try is called for. At this point in the course, the writing of a good melody and proper chords is a sufficiently ambitious undertaking.

One or two more melodies can be attempted, using much the same procedure. However, each time the teacher should withdraw some of the specifications, such as the visual rhythmic aids. How long the structuring is continued depends on the success the students enjoy with their compositions.

After several block-chord accompaniments have been written, the teacher will have to devote some time to showing the class how to embellish the chords and make them more interesting. Pianists find this rather easy; nonpianists find it just the opposite. The class should hear many song accompaniments, especially those of Mozart and Haydn. Later the accompaniments to art songs can be examined. Through the study of accompaniments, students can be made aware of the countless ways of sounding the essential harmonic structure without resort to thumping out block chords.

Before the conclusion of the course the students should have an opportunity to write a melody for an instrument, with the accompaniment in two or three other instruments. As much as possible, instruments played by members of the class should be specified so that there can be live performances of the music. Composing for instruments will undoubtedly entail the teaching of transposition. The problem of range and orchestration is best handled under the condition of limited time by having the teacher specify the easy and practical ranges of the instruments for which the student plans to write.

As much as possible, the class should become a musical learning laboratory in which works are presented to the class for examination and evaluation. A most desirable outcome of the class, and one that does much to stimulate interest in music theory and composition, is performance of a student work by one of the school's performing organizations. Possibly the best student composition in each theory class can be arranged with the help of the teacher for performance by a large group. Again, the composition need not be pretentious. A march, a simply-arranged melody, or a song is adequate to make the point to the student body, and to provide plenty of educational benefits for the student composer.

Given time and student ability, there is no limit to the possibilities for work in theory. Clearly some counterpoint is a next logical step for such a class. Whatever the extent of its content, the theory course should be functional, versatile, creative, and above all, musical.

Questions

1. Why is a music-appreciation course more appropriate at the high school level than a course in advanced general music?
2. Suppose the high school principal asks the music teacher: "Why is a music-appreciation course so important for the high school students who aren't in band or chorus? After all, they had music all through school up to the eighth grade. Why do they need more? If they were really interested in music, they'd be in band or chorus right now." How would you answer?
3. On page 358, in the content outline of the music-appreciation course, the names of Robert Schumann, Felix Mendelssohn, and Richard Wagner were omitted. How is it justifiable to leave out these three important composers? Should they replace others listed? Why, or why not?
4. What are the advantages and disadvantages to beginning the music-appreciation course with folk music? with Gregorian chant? with acoustics?

with a Broadway musical? with a standard, easily accepted symphonic work? What could be the procedures for beginning with each?

5. Why is the music-theory course not for the general student? Could some of its value be given to the general student in some other way? If so, how?

Projects

1. Look over textbooks in music appreciation and evaluate them for use in a high school class. Consider the language used, amount of material covered, degree of emphasis on musical qualities, and ability to stress the points that are significant *for the listener.*
2. Look over textbooks in music theory and evaluate them for use in a high school class. Consider to what degree each book presents the learnings functionally, encourages creativity, and is versatile. Consider also whether the book is designed for use in an integrated theory course.
3. Listen to these recordings and decide what feature of the music could be suggested as a focus for the students' listening. Mention any particular teaching procedure that would contribute to the value of the listening experience.

Aaron Copland	*A Lincoln Portrait*
César Franck	*Violin Sonata,* fourth movement
J. S. Bach	*Brandenburg Concerto No. 5,* first movement

4. Practice giving a melodic, rhythmic, chord member, and chord type dictation exercise to one of the persons in your class.
5. Select a short stanza of a poem that would be suitable for the first attempt at song composition by a high school theory class. Structure the writing assignment as to rhythm and meter.

Suggested Readings

Copland, Aaron, *Our New Music.* New York: Whittlesey House, 1941.

————————, *What To Listen for in Music,* rev. ed. New York: McGraw-Hill Book Company, Inc., 1957.

Hartshorn, William C., "The Role of Listening," in *Basic Concepts in Music Education,* 57th Yearbook. National Society for the Study of Education, Chicago: University of Chicago Press, 1958.

Walton, Charles W., "Three Trends in the Teaching of Theory," *Music Educators Journal,* XLVIII, No. 2, November–December 1961, 73–76.

XVI

selecting music for school groups

Selecting music for school music organizations requires careful thought and planning. The teacher is not free to choose whatever his personal taste indicates; he is limited by the requirements of the situation in which he finds himself. Music studied and performed by secondary school music groups must meet certain specifications. First of all, it must be music of high quality. Time in the school day, as well as in the music class itself, is too valuable to be spent in learning music that has little worth. Second, the music needs to be simple enough for the group to perform creditably. Many fine pieces of music are too difficult for all except a few outstanding high school groups. Each teacher has to judge the performing ability of his students, and select his music accordingly. Third, most of the music must be interesting to the students and to the audience. Bach chorales are of unquestionable musical value, and most of them are not technically difficult. However, they can be used only in moderation with most school groups and with the audiences that listen to them. Most adolescents are not mature enough musically or psychologically to profit from a large amount of Bach chorales.

JUDGING THE VALUE OF THE MUSIC

Everyone seems to agree that students should attain an understanding of and a desire for music that is culturally significant. It is easy to say that a group should perform "good" music, but to define what is "good" is another matter! Fortunately, *among trained musicians* there is a rather high degree of agreement in terms of works of music. But when it comes to putting into words what it is that makes works of music good, there is little common expression. Music eludes the straitjacket of words, and the reader should keep this fact in mind as he studies this chapter.

In considering quality in music, it is necessary first to cast out any sets of absolute principles. At times, principles have been helpful to composers in understanding or developing certain styles. But many a fine work of music did not conform to the "rules" existing at the time it was composed. For example, from the time of the Baroque, parallel fifths were looked upon with disdain until in the nineteenth century Debussy came along and demonstrated their effectiveness. Music has so many variables of pitch, rhythm, and dynamics, that the composers of music and persons evaluating it must rely upon their judgment of its musical sense rather than its adherence to rules.

Music quality, then, is a comparative and relative thing; not an absolute. There is better or poorer music, not good and bad. Its worth can be judged, but not measured. Judgment involves subjective opinion, knowledge, experience, and an attempt to be analytical.

Purpose

In comparing and selecting works of music, one must keep in mind the purpose or function of the music. Some composers pour into their music their most profound thoughts and feelings, while other composers seek only to entertain the listener. So it is difficult to answer, "Which is better, Beethoven's *Symphony No. 9* or Offenbach's *Gaité Parisienne?* They are written to fulfill different functions.

Many times music is intended merely to enhance another activity. Some music is written to accompany dancing, some to highlight a play or a motion picture, some to serve as a prop upon which funny lines are hung. The music of the popular song functions as a rather unimportant vehicle for the lyrics, which are paramount to the purpose of the popular song: establishing vicarious communication between dating teen-agers.[1] In these instances music is only a minor partner to the achievement of an extramusical purpose. Music written to accompany some extramusical activity is usually poorer in quality than is music that has been composed for its own sake, with the exception of music for religious worship and for dancing which is primarily aesthetic in nature.

The dance form is an example of music that has fulfilled widely divergent purposes. The original minuet was a simple rustic dance, and the music was of secondary importance to the physical activity of dancing. Haydn took this dance music and refined it for use in his symphonies.

[1] Donald K. Horton, "The Dialogue of Courtship in Popular Songs," *The American Journal of Sociology*, LXII, No. 6 (May 1957), 569.

Thus his minuet had as its sole reason for existence the sense it made to the listener.

Often composers differ from one work to another in what they strive to express. In "Sing Ye to the Lord," J. S. Bach was praising and glorifying God; in the "Coffee Cantata" he was just attempting in a cultivated way to entertain and amuse the listener. Considered only in light of its effectiveness in accomplishing what it sets out to do, the "Coffee Cantata" might possibly be a better piece of music than "Sing Ye to the Lord."

Good music, then, can be partially defined as music that does what it sets out to do. If it is a fugue, then it demonstrates skillful use of contrapuntal technique. If the piece is ballet music, then it achieves a blend between the feeling of the story and proper rhythmic content. If the music appears in conjunction with a humorous song, then it is clever and fits the text.

Music written to stand on its aesthetic, musical merits is usually much more effective in achieving the goal of giving the students as much music as they are capable of assimilating. As Chapter Two pointed out, the use of music with aesthetic qualities is crucial if music education is to take place. It would be foolish for a teacher to emphasize the delicate relationship between text and music, the rise and fall of the melody, the stresses and relaxations in the harmony, and then have the class study a work of the quality and profundity of "How You Gonna Keep 'Em Down on the Farm After They've Seen Paree?"

The impression should not be gained here that a piece of music must be serious, yellow with age, difficult to understand, or surrounded with an aura of prestige. The trappings of the intellectual or the aesthetic are just that—trappings. As the old prospector said, "Gold is where you find it, not where it's supposed to be." Good aesthetic quality can be found in both entertaining music and serious music, in both simple and complex. Hence there is a place in the scheme of things for music that is not serious, including good current show tunes. Relief and variety are necessary for everyone, especially adolescents. Furthermore, many students in the junior and senior high school are not yet mature enough or are not innately able to comprehend the abstractions of complex, profound music. The appeal in secondary school music does with some students center in the entertaining type of music. Teachers of English have encountered a similar problem. They can get most of the students to like some Shakespeare, and even sense the greatness of the writing. But they feel that for some young people the appeal of *Macbeth*, for example, is based more on its fascination as a murder story, than on the insights into human personality that make Shakespeare's plays great. Is this not true in music? Some people are completely won over by the rhythm and color of Latin American music, but are unmoved by a slow movement from a Beethoven symphony.

Since the subject of popular music is a sensitive one in music education circles, what has been said about it should be clarified. There is a theory concerning appreciation of the arts which states that a person appreciates that with which he can make some self-identification. For instance, if an individual watching a graceful ballerina can make some identification with her dancing and can recognize it as the fulfillment of an ideal of perfection and beauty, then there can be real appreciation. If not, then to the viewer the dancing is a hodgepodge of senseless movements. This theory is significant for the music teacher. The teen-age student will better understand and appreciate music that is within his realm of identification and experience. Love songs can serve as an example here. With which type of love song can the twentieth-century, American teen-ager more easily identify himself: a sixteenth-century madrigal ("Since first I saw your face, I resolv'd to honor and renown you; if now I be disdain'd I wish my heart had never known you"), or a song from a twentieth-century Broadway musical ("I'm in love with a wonderful guy!")? Text is not the only difference; the music also varies greatly.

For this reason, it is justifiable and sensible to use a *little* of the *best* of the currently popular music which is in the realm of experience and identification of the students, even though it may not be "great" music. There is no place in the schools for the cheap, commercial fads in music ("Baby, All I Want Is You-Hoo"), but there is a place for the imaginative, tasteful, and musically logical piece which is widely known and liked. Such a number can do much to further student interest in music, and it can be a worthy vehicle for learning. Furthermore, it is preferable to uninspired attempts at serious music.

It is interesting to notice the changes in musical taste that take place as a group advances. In the beginning the students may be wholeheartedly in favor of entertaining music—and nothing else. As the year progresses, however, a gradual transformation takes place. The serious music becomes appreciated by more and more of the students. They have not turned against the entertaining music; rather they have added more kinds of music to the types they already like. A good way to demonstrate this musical growth in the students is to place the repertoire list on the board near the beginning of the semester and have the students vote on their preferences. When the voting is repeated at the end of the semester, the progress becomes evident. One of the great satisfactions for a teacher is having a work of musical worth, which was greeted with grunts and groans from the students, begin to be accepted and truly appreciated by them.

What Is the Norm?

The standards or norms for evaluating music are developed through hearing many different works. Heard in isolation without comparison to other works of the time, the symphonies of Karl von Dittersdorf (1739–

1799) are quite pleasing. But when the music of von Dittersdorf is compared with that of his contemporary, Wolfgang Amadeus Mozart, it is obvious that Mozart's music is much better. Mozart has set a standard for the music of that period which has nearly eliminated von Dittersdorf from present-day consideration. The same comparative factor operates in the music of Mozart himself. Not all of his 626 works are heard with equal frequency. Many of them have been largely forgotten because others of his works are, by comparison, more worthy of performance.

Experience or familiarity with a style is necessary before comparisons can be made. If a typical American music teacher heard a performance by a group of Hindu musicians, he would have little idea as to the quality of the performance. If he were to travel in India and become familiar with Hindu music, he could then make an evaluation of an individual performance or work. Familiarity is as necessary for judging "entertaining" music as it is for judging serious or folk music.

"*Inevitability*"

Assuming that there are no all-inclusive rules for judging a composition, how can anyone say that one work of music is better than another of similar purpose? The answer to this most basic question lies in the fact that a "good" composition has within itself a logical and consistent integration—a kind of "inevitability" or "rightness" of movement, as Bernstein calls it.[2] The rules of musical logic of one composer or style of music need not be the rules of another composer or style. Bach, Beethoven, Brahms, and Bartók each use a different approach to achieve a logical musical result, and yet each of these men is generally recognized as a great composer. In a fine piece of music the listener needs to feel that whatever happens in the work is so logical and right—so inevitable—that not a note could be altered without detracting from the music. Listen several times to a recording of Bach's *Cantata No. 140*, particularly the tenor chorale "Zion Hears the Watchman Calling," or to Brahms' *Requiem*, Part V, "And Ye Now Therefore Have Sorrow." In both works, the impression is that not a note could be changed to improve the work, and no part could be effectively expanded or condensed. Such music conveys the feeling that each succeeding note is the only possible "right" note. This is what is meant by "inevitability," and it is this sense of an inherently logical fulfillment that makes music effective and good.

The musical effect of the achievement of this logic is a continually evolving and developing organization of cohesive sounds. Copland refers to this as *la grande ligne*, and considers it the key to judging music.[3] A

[2] Leonard Bernstein, *The Joy of Music* (New York: Simon and Schuster, 1959), pp. 75, 93.

[3] Aaron Copland, *What To Listen for in Music*, rev. ed. (New York: McGraw-Hill Book Company, Inc., 1957), p. 32.

composer may have ample technical knowledge and good thematic material, but his works will fall short of greatness if he cannot put his ideas together into a coherent, logical whole. As someone has said of Anton Bruckner's music: "He lets the grass grow between the half notes." When the music has a logical development and reaches logical conclusions, the listener feels that "the music has something to say."

One reason for the high quality of most folk music is that in the process of formation, it has had the benefit of the work of many people. The less logical qualities have largely been eliminated. Then, too, folk music has withstood the "test of time." Music that did not seem to say anything was forgotten long ago. True, folk music does not have the individual touch of a Bach or Brahms, but it does have an aura of beautiful, unsophisticated directness and simplicity.

"Buy Brand Names"

Since it is obviously impossible for a teacher to examine all the music that is available, the judgments of musicians throughout the years can be a guide to the value of the music. Even though the evaluation of music is a comparative and subjective thing, some consensus as to the relative value of certain works does seem to evolve among musicians and music lovers. Concert audiences, conductors, performing musicians, all contribute to the slow and curious filtration process in musical history. J. S. Bach was largely forgotten until 1829, nearly eighty years after his death, but Mendelssohn and others found in his music the qualities which have stamped it as great. In the 1870's the popularly recognized composer in Paris was Charles Gounod, and few paid much attention to a humble church organist at Sainte-Clotilde named César Franck. His *Symphony in D Minor* was coolly received at its first performance, with Gounod himself calling it, "The affirmation of impotency carried to the point of dogma."[4] But through the intervening years, perceptive listeners have found a logic, a quality in Franck, and have weeded out much of Gounod's music. The passing of time does produce a perspective that is essential for the accurate appraisal of a work. For this reason, the teacher would do well to use music that has withstood the filtering process of history.

EVALUATING UNFAMILIAR MUSIC

Clearly the "test of time" cannot operate in the case of new music. Judgment in such cases is the most difficult of all. Time-proven works can serve as norms for assessing unfamiliar music. The following practical suggestions can serve as criteria to further assist in evaluation.

[4] Nicolas Slonimsky, ed., *The International Cyclopedia of Music and Musicians*, 6th ed. (New York: Dodd, Mead and Company, 1952), p. 621.

Melodic Quality

The most efficient way to judge a work being considered for study is for the teacher to play it through on the piano. (The condensed instrumental score has the advantage of being suitable for study at the piano.) The teacher needs to keep in mind that both voices and instruments will sound different from the piano because of their ability to sustain sound. Because the tonal characteristics are so different, it is necessary to develop the ability to hear in the mind's ear how a line of music will sound when sung or played.

To get a general impression of the music, the teacher can listen for its logic or inevitability. One way to check this is to attempt to sing back the melody after a phrase or two has been played. It is surprising how many of the works that miss being first-class music have thematic ideas and melodies that do not quite "jell." It is impossible to explain why they do not; they just seem to miss the mark as melodies. This test is not recommended for a work that is written primarily to achieve an effect or mood, because its melodic quality is of secondary importance. The test for such music will need to be on its effectiveness at expression. In other works, especially of the symphonic type, it is the development of the theme that makes for success. A beautiful melody is not necessarily a good theme for use in a symphony. The importance of the factor of melodic quality depends upon the nature of the piece.

Beginning and End of the Music

A test that is in many ways similar to the one just described is to play over the beginning page of a work, and then the last page. It is usually safe to assume that if a composition has an unattractive beginning and an ineffective ending, then the middle will not amount to much either. A good beginning in works of much length should somehow give the listener a "promise of things to come," as Bernstein puts it in praising Beethoven's music.[5] It should make the listener eager for what will follow. The conclusion of a musical work need not always be a glorious, full culmination; an appropriate ending is all that is necessary.

Trite Devices

The music should be checked for the use of trite musical expressions. One need only listen to some of the musical arrangements made for radio and television to become aware of many of these. Like slang, these devices come and go, and the out-of-date ones sound a bit humorous to a person accustomed to the newer clichés. Barbershop singing made much use of the Neapolitan sixth chord and sliding chromatic lines, and the 1920's

[5] Bernstein, *op. cit.*, p. 83.

developed a style now disdainfully called "ricky-tick." The writer of popular songs is not always alone in his predilection for hackneyed tricks; the serious composer sometimes demonstrates a similar weakness. In the latter case, however, this failing is more likely to show up in the lack of inspiration, rather than in an overuse of decorative stereotypes. What the teacher must do in considering music is to look for originality and freshness in the composition. Good music does not need to fall back on stock contrivances in order to attract the listener.

SELECTING MUSIC FOR A PARTICULAR GROUP

The most important point a music teacher should consider in the selection of music is its usefulness in furthering the music education of the students. Two requirements must be met before a piece of music can contribute to education. One: the music must be of quality, which has been the topic of the first part of this chapter. Two: the music must be suitable to the musical understanding and technical ability of the group. Music should be selected with a particular group in mind.

No music teacher should choose a number that sounds best with a hundred musicians and attempt to perform it with thirty. Neither should he pick music that is far beyond the ability of the student musicians. Some of the points a teacher must consider apply to the selecting of both vocal and instrumental music. They are as follows:

REPETITION. If sections of a work are repeated, this clearly will cut down on the amount of time required to learn the music. If a rhythmic or melodic pattern is repeated often in the piece, this also cuts down on the amount of music to learn. Repetition is especially helpful if the music is to be memorized, as is often the case in vocal music. One of the annoying problems in memorization occurs when the melody returns with different harmony parts; it is easy for the students to become confused.

LENGTH. All other things being equal, the longer the work, the longer it will take to learn it. In addition, there exists a certain amount of fatigue and loss of interest in learning music that requires a lot of time and effort. Teen-agers, especially in junior high, are not noted for their ability to stick to one activity for a long time.

RHYTHM. Adolescents are attracted to music that has rhythmic interest. They are able to perform difficult patterns, if these occur in almost all parts simultaneously, and if they contain much repetition. Rhythmic problems begin to appear when greater independence is required of the performer. One mistake, and the musician is lost in music in which it is hard to find the right place again.

METER. Meters that are less familiar to the students require more learning effort. Students find the music somewhat more difficult when the meter or the tempo require that the beat note be an eighth, half, or dotted note. A few vocal works are written with no meter sign, and this tends to bother inexperienced musicians.

MUSICIANSHIP OF STUDENTS. There is in music an essential quality that is more than pitches and their durations. The piece "How Lovely Is Thy Dwelling Place" from Brahms' *Requiem* requires a concept of tone color and, more than that, maturity of feeling. The notes of this work can be sung by a good high school choir, but the essential quality is not readily attainable. If such a number is to be undertaken, it will need to be worked on intermittently over a period of time, so that the music has time to "settle" in the students.

A work that is soft, slow, sustained, and subtle demands much musicianship and control. Debussy and Palestrina were great composers, but much of their music requires subtle interpretation, slow tempos, and sustained phrases. This is not to say that teen-agers should not perform anything that is too mature for them, but it is to say that there is a limit to which adolescents can be pushed in subtleties, symbolism, or profound emotion. The teacher wants to broaden horizons for the students, but he does not want to lose the students in the process.

QUALITY OF MUSIC. There are some works of music that are so logically written, and so clear in their musical intent, that many of the technical barriers are easily overcome. This explains why some secondary school choral groups can sing choruses from Handel's *Messiah* and why some bands can play difficult contemporary compositions. In good music with concrete challenges the students can overcome difficulties. The phenomenon may be due in part to the added zest of working on such music. Because most school groups must expend quite a bit of effort before a piece of music is ready for performance, the work needs to have lasting quality. Much entertaining music that has only a glittering surface cannot maintain its original appeal.

VOCAL CONSIDERATIONS

TEXT. It is necessary to determine the purpose of the work, then to evaluate it. Here are two texts that are comparable in purpose, but hardly similar in quality.

How Do I Love Thee?

How do I love thee? Let me count the ways.
I love thee to the depth and breadth and height
My soul can reach, when feeling out of sight
For the ends of Being and Ideal Grace.
I love thee to the level of every day's
Most quiet need, by sun and candlelight.
I love thee freely, as men strive for Right;

I love thee purely, as they turn from Praise.
I love thee with the passion put to use
In my old griefs, and with my childhood's faith,
I love thee with a love I seemed to lose
With my lost saints. I love thee with the breath,
Smiles, tears, of all my life! and, if God choose,
I shall but love thee better after death.
—Elizabeth Barrett Browning

When Roses Bloom

When roses are in bloom, my love, I think again of you,
And hear the lark that once did sing of love so pure and true.
'Twas in a garden far away beside a trellised wall
Where first we pledged eternally our hearts, our lives, our all.

And now the spring is here again; my heart should be in bloom,
But deep within my soul there is no rose amid the gloom,
Nor is there any lark to sing, since we did drift apart.
How silent now the garden spot that dwells within my heart!

The difference between the two examples is clear. The first is profound and sincere, while the other is trite and unimaginative. Teen-agers are more discerning about good and bad poetry than adults sometimes realize. They may not be able to say why one poem is better than another, but they sense the difference.

Teen-agers, especially boys, are often critical of the words to which music is set. They resent singing a text that has no thought worthy of communication. Unfortunately, students tend to be critical of any text which is abstract or symbolic. "Lo, How a Rose E'er Blooming" is a fine text, but its symbolism must be carefully explained to the singers to avoid a lackadaisical effort on the song. In schools with little choral music tradition, it is wise to select good music with concrete texts, ones that the students can comprehend easily. A distinction should be made between texts that are abstract and those that are serious. Teen-agers usually will undertake willingly a serious text that they can understand.

Some works of music have texts written in dialect. Too often these attempts at writing in the vernacular are grossly inaccurate; most dialects contain tonal characteristics that are impossible to indicate fully on the printed page. Furthermore, adolescents can seldom phonate them accurately, even though they may spend some time in practicing the strange pronunciations. "Mah soul done gwine to see de ribber of Jo'd'n" is a poor stab at the Negro dialect, and as such it is in bad taste. Unfortunately, many arrangers feel that a dialect is indispensable to music such as the Negro spiritual, and the result is a grotesque parody of sincere musical expression. The teacher should seriously consider whether the use of dialect in a particular number will produce the intended feeling of realism or unintentionally convey an impression of comedy and ridicule.

RANGE. The ranges of the various adolescent voices are discussed in Chapter Twelve. Generally the problem is not so much with those few notes that lie at the extremes of the range, but rather with a tessitura that is consistently too high or too low. Singers may be able to hit a few high notes, but they cannot sing many of them in succession without distorting their tone or singing with bad intonation. So in rating music as to its difficulty, the tessitura of the parts must be carefully checked, especially when changing voices are involved.

TENOR PART. The tenor part is of much importance in SATB music, but few teen-age boys have the experience and vocal development to sing the part well. This requires that the teacher be especially careful in looking over the tenor parts of prospective pieces of music. Tenor sections in school choral groups vary in their strengths and weaknesses, so each teacher has to know his tenor section. If the section is made up largely of boys whose voices are still changing, then high notes may present no problem. In other tenor sections, high notes are out of the question. One of the problems is that composers and arrangers have never quite agreed upon what a tenor voice is. Some tenor music demands a light quality, and some a dark, dramatic quality; some parts go to a sixth above middle C, others go to an octave below middle C. Adolescent tenors usually sing best about B flat or A below middle C, and they cannot be relied upon for much volume. The easier their part is, the better they will sing it.

ACCOMPANIMENT. Choral groups that are not musically advanced will usually sound better in a work that is accompanied. The piano gives them a feeling of confidence and supports their sometimes shaky pitch. There are two conditions under which an accompaniment might hinder rather than help a choral group. One is when the accompaniment is quite different from the singers' parts. In some modern works the rhythm is not the same, and the singers have to sing intervals such as E natural against an E flat in the accompaniment. The other occurs when the piano part is too difficult for the accompanist to play well, a not uncommon condition.

CHROMATICISM AND MODULATIONS. Teen-age singers can usually handle a small amount of chromatic movement and modulation to closely related keys. They find it more difficult, however, to sing accurately a piece containing many chromatics, frequent modulations, or modulations to remotely related keys. This is especially true if the work is sung *a cappella.*

INTERVALS. The singing of augmented seconds and fourths and unusual leaps in a melodic line present obvious difficulty. A less conspicuous problem is created when certain intervals are sounded harmonically. The trouble lies not so much in the actual intervals themselves, as in the way they are approached. The minor second in the following example can usually be sung with accuracy:

But when the approach differs, the same harmonic interval may become extremely difficult to perform well:

The character of the lines also affects the difficulty of the interval. For instance, if the singers are divided into two groups, and one group sings "Three Blind Mice" in G while the other sings "America" in F, they could probably sing the dissonances without too much difficulty. However, if the same dissonances occur between two lines that are unfamiliar or have little melodic character, the students find them almost impossible to sing accurately.

Unfortunately, the interval problem makes it difficult for secondary school groups to sing some fine works of modern music. This situation probably will not change until the modern idiom becomes more firmly planted in the consciousness of the population. This does not mean that all difficult intervals should or can be avoided. On the contrary, every group should sing some modern works each year. They may be difficult, but they are worth the effort if the teacher plans properly for them.

ARRANGEMENT BY VOICE CLASSIFICATION. Octavo music is classified by and arranged for different types of choral groups. In general, the more voice parts a piece contains, the more difficult it will prove to be. A TTBB work for boys' glee club is decidedly more difficult than a TB work. This is true for several reasons. The number of singers on each part is cut in half, requiring more independence from each singer; the length of time required to learn the notes may be much longer since there are twice as many parts; the highest and lowest parts are likely to be harder since the notes must necessarily be closer to the extremes of the voice range; and with each additional part there is a greater chance of error in notes or pitch. For inexperienced glee clubs, then, two-part music is much more suitable. The change from SA to SSA or from TB to TBB can be made without extensive reorganization of the group. In the girls' glee club some sopranos and altos will be able to sing second soprano on three-part numbers. The same is true of the boys in changing from TB to TBB music.

In boys' voices the tenor voice is usually the slowest to develop. Some mixed choruses, especially in the smaller schools, have a hard time finding enough tenors to make up a section. Arrangers have attempted to overcome this problem by providing SAB arrangements, in which boys with changed voices take the baritone part and boys with unchanged voices take the alto or sometimes the soprano. Although these arrangements are not completely satisfactory in harmonic structure, they do provide acceptable music for such groups.

The change from SAB to SATB is not made as easily as the change of voice groupings within a boys' or a girls' glee club. There is usually a greater difference between SATB tenor parts and SAB baritone parts than there is between the first and second tenor parts in glee-club music. The change can be facilitated if the teacher emphasizes to the prospective tenors that the "B" in SAB stands for baritone and not bass. However, it is no easy matter to create a tenor section out of a group of boys who are used to singing baritone. For this reason, SAB arrangements should not be used to the exclusion of all SATB arrangements, unless the prospects for a tenor section are nil.

Occasionally arrangements for one voice grouping may be used successfully for another grouping. For example, an SATB arrangement can sometimes be used by a boys' glee club that contains unchanged, changing, and changed voices. The music may have to be transposed, depending upon the demands of the soprano and bass parts. The unchanged boys' voices can sing the soprano line, the changing voices sing the alto line, and the changed voices the tenor and bass parts.

If the first tenors in the boys' glee club are weak, the most suitable arrangements are those that place the melody in the baritone or second tenor part.

MUSICAL ARRANGEMENT. Arrangements that teen-agers sing best are solid, "clean," and uncluttered with close harmony or excess parts. Members of school choral groups are not always talented, well-trained singers, so the use of complicated effects and extra parts can make the music sound worse, not better. There is nothing wrong with some of the arrangements cited here, except that they are not suitable for most secondary school groups.

In "Country Fiddler" (p. 390) the rhythm of the soprano, alto, and tenor parts is not conducive to accurate singing because it does not start on the beat and because it requires a precise release. Intervals of fourths and fifths are to be hummed and slurred, a difficult technique at best. If three-syllable words had been used, the figure probably could be executed more accurately. Moreover, the piano is of limited help to the singers in this passage.

"Prairie Home" (p. 391) is essentially a simple American folk song; the arrangement illustrated gives it a grandiose treatment. This song is effective as a solo with a simple accompaniment played on the guitar. The choral arrangement would sound better if it had emulated the solo version of the song. The melody here is almost lost in the complex fabric of parts. The parts are not merely doublings in different sections or at the octave, as they often are in eight-part music, but rather they present as many as

COUNTRY FIDDLER

PRAIRIE HOME

six distinct lines. The first and second soprano parts represent the type of passage that must be sung well, or it will sound terrible. Effects such as this do not usually add much to the music, and a few of them go a long way with most listeners. Then there is always the question: is the effect achieved worth the time and effort required to learn it properly? In many cases the answer is "no."

Too many teachers and arrangers have forgotten the beauty of hearing the simple done well. A well-sung unison is thrilling and beautiful. Notice how clean, solid, and in the character of the music, is this excerpt from a mixed-chorus setting of "There Is a Balm in Gilead," arranged by William L. Dawson. The top line is a solo for soprano or tenor.

The plea here is not to do away with eight-part music; there are some fine works that have to be sung in eight parts. Rather the plea is for clean, simple arrangements, and the elimination of musical bric-a-brac. There is no virtue in singing a work in eight parts when four parts will do just as well. Collegiate and professional choral groups can very well sing the more complex arrangements, but not most secondary school glee clubs and choirs.

INSTRUMENTAL CONSIDERATIONS

KEY. The easiest key for a band is B flat, while G and D are easiest for strings. The next easiest keys move toward more flats for the band and more sharps for the strings. In both cases the construction of the instruments and tradition in the keys used for instruction encourage this difference. In the case of the orchestra, it is considerably easier for the winds to learn to play several sharps than it is for the strings to learn to play several flats.

SCALEWISE RUNS. Sometimes the assumption is made that if the page looks rather black (that is, if it contains many sixteenth notes), it is automatically difficult. While this is sometimes true, it makes a difference whether the notes jump around without much pattern or move scalewise. Almost all students have minimal experience in playing scales, so they tend to know scales better than any other musical pattern. If the passage is in an easy range and key, the demand for alacrity in playing does not present too serious a problem.

RANGE. On woodwinds and strings, range affects the timbre and quality of intonation, and involves certain technical problems of fingering. On brasses, however, range is of first importance. Tones that are too high for the brass player may be missed entirely, or will be played with strain, accompanied usually by poor intonation. A high tessitura in a brass part is exhausting for the less mature player.

THERE IS A BALM IN GILEAD[6]

[6] Music Press, Tuskegee Institute, Alabama. Copyright 1939 by William L. Dawson. Reprinted by permission.

There is a Balm in Gil-e-ad, to make the wound-ed
There is a Balm in Gil-e-ad, to make the wound-ed
There is a Balm in Gil-e-ad, make the wound-ed
to make the wound-ed
whole, There is a Balm in Gil-e-ad, to heal the sin sick
whole, There is a Balm Hum
whole, There is a Balm in Gil-e-ad, heal the sin sick
whole, Hum to heal the sin sick

AMOUNT OF TECHNIQUE. The length of difficult passages must be considered. For example, the clarinets might rather easily play

but have trouble playing sixteenths of similar difficulty if they appear on four or eight consecutive beats. The longer runs require just that much more skill and training.

MUSICAL ARRANGEMENT. As with choral music, the easier, and often the better, arrangements for teen-age instrumentalists contain clear, basic outlines without needless decoration. There is, of course, considerable variation between music that is suitable for players with only a year or two of experience, and music that is possible for select players at the senior high school level. The simpler music requires fewer different parts and less independence of each part. The reduced number of independent parts may not be readily apparent in the score; even though the same number of instruments may be mentioned, many of the parts are doubled. With less experienced players, doubling is desirable because of the additional support it provides. But when the players are more advanced, it steals color and interest from the group's performance. An overuse of doubling tends to make the group sound the same no matter what it is doing.

On the following pages is a portion of the full score of *Concert Overture for Band*, by Robert G. Johnson. The parts are clean and solid. The tempo indicated for this portion of the work is "Fast (♩ = 152–160)."

Another difficulty in judging an instrumental arrangement is the disparity in the number of instruments on a part and in their amount of tone. On the score, the first trumpet, oboe, and flute each occupy a line and appear to be equals. The flute, however, is not as strong as the oboe, which in turn is not nearly as strong as the trumpet. Neither can the E flat alto clarinet play a concert B flat below middle C as fully as can the six third clarinets. The teacher needs to understand instruments well enough to evaluate an arrangement as to its ability to permit the important parts to be heard. He is advised to be on the lookout for bassoon solos that are accompanied by the brasses!

The band has suffered throughout its existence from an unstable instrumentation. The fluegel horn, saxhorn, valve trombone (often written in treble clef), C melody saxophone, E flat alto (peck) horn, B flat soprano saxophone, E flat soprano clarinet, E flat cornet, bass saxophone, all have come and gone. But the significant change has not been in the instruments that have undergone trial in the organization; the orchestra has tried out a few instruments itself, such as the tenor saxophone, cornet, and euphonium. The important change has been in the concept of what the band is, which in turn has affected greatly the nature of musical arrangements for bands.

CONCERT OVERTURE FOR BAND[7]

[7] Theodore Presser Company, Bryn Mawr, Pennsylvania. Reprinted by permission.

C Fl.
D♭ Picc.
Obs.
E♭ Cls.
I
B♭ Cls. II
III
Alto Cl.
Bass Cl.
Bsns.
Alto Sax. I II
Ten. Sax.
Bar. Sax.
I
B♭ Cors.
a2
II III
I II
F Hrns.
III IV
Euph.
I II
Trbs.
III
Basses
Timp.
S.D.
Cymb.
B.D.

For many years the band was thought of in "town band" terms; that is, a small but noisy group that existed primarily to give concerts on hot summer nights in the town park, and that played a diet of music consisting of novelties, light overtures, marches, and an occasional dazzling solo. Nobody took it very seriously.

Following World War I and on into the 1940's the band took on a new dimension. However, it could not shake some of its old habits, one being that it must still produce a big enough sound to be heard well outdoors. Because good original compositions for band were lacking, the repertoire became heavy with transcriptions—"Elsa's Procession to the Cathedral" from Wagner's *Lohengrin*, and many more. This style of band, which is probably still the dominant one in secondary schools, calls for many players, preferably nearly one hundred. When the band is good, the effect is that of a mighty organ. Because of its strong and sensuous tone, it is at its best with transcriptions of nineteenth-century masterpieces and Bach organ music.

Since World War II another concept has appeared in bands and band music. It strongly favors original compositions, which of course are largely by contemporary composers. Since these composers live in the twentieth century, they do not write for the romantic sound of yesteryear. Their music calls for fewer players and a less lavish use of instruments. This concept of a band sometimes prefers to call itself a wind ensemble. No longer is it interested in the lush, rolling effects of the generation before; rather, it is more intellectual and detached in its approach.

The instrumental music teacher, especially at the high school level, will find music that fits both concepts of band. What he chooses will depend on his own taste, and the size and ability of his group. Unlike the orchestra director, who can look at the first violin part and know that the composer intended it for fourteen or so players, the band director has to consider the music and its style and arrangement in order to determine what the intention of the music is. "Elsa's Procession to the Cathedral" is intended for a big band, and is not as effective when done with forty-five players. And the reverse is true: Persichetti's *Divertimento for Band* is not as effective when played by one hundred players. It is not a question of which style is "right," because both have musical value when properly used, but rather getting the right music with the right concept.

The orchestra teacher's most serious problem is having not enough strings to balance the wind and percussion, which are usually at full strength. Therefore, when looking over music, the teacher should check to see that the strings are permitted a chance to be heard. Some of the earlier arrangements for school orchestras seemed most concerned with keeping the music sounding, no matter how many strings might be lacking. The result was a "band with strings" effect that did not do justice to the orchestra. One collection written some years ago had violins on the melody part, and no viola part, yet the music could be played by a band using the wind parts of the set, and thereby do without strings entirely.[8]

A final word on orchestra arrangements. The piano is used infrequently in the symphony orchestra, and should be so used with the school orchestra, except for groups that have studied only a year or two. The arrangement should be complete without the piano. The only justification for the use of a piano in a school orchestra, beyond those valid for the professional orchestra, is for limited assistance to the strings in learning the music, and for strengthening a particular part that lacks adequate instrumentation.

VARIETY OF MUSIC LITERATURE

Each music organization should receive a balanced diet of the best music literature. In order to give the students the finest cultural experiences in music, the teacher should not allow his choice of repertoire to become narrow. When a teacher selects only works of a certain type, his students are receiving an incomplete music education. It is only human for a teacher to have personal preferences. But the use of some works that he likes less is often justified by the students' need for a broad education in music.

What are some of the areas that should be covered? The general categories have already been intimated. One is the geographical classification of music—Latin American, Russian, English, American, and so on. Second are the historical classifications such as Renaissance, Baroque, Classical, Romantic, Modern. If a teacher were to combine these two classifications and choose one work from each possible grouping, a large and varied selection of music would result.

Program Requirements

Sometimes there is a mistaken idea that certain music needs to be picked to fill a void in a concert, or to round out the program. Much of the problem is solved automatically if the teacher selects music of different types from different historical periods. Then each year he can vary his program format. One year the choral groups might do a cantata, another year a program of folk music and dancing. The instrumental groups might present a concerto program featuring three or four outstanding students, and another year the more usual program of concert music.

The teacher should try to determine the musical development of the community. He should hold to the ideal of using the best music without

[8] Cited in Charles B. Righter, *Success in Teaching School Orchestras and Bands* (Minneapolis: Schmitt, Hall & McCreary, 1945), p. 69.

losing his students and audience. There should be a little give and take between the teacher with his musical standards, and the students and the community with their lack of experience in music. It is a rare community that appreciates an all-serious program. On the other hand, there is no community in which some serious works cannot be presented.

It is difficult for listeners to sit through an entire concert of unfamiliar music. At Christmas time they want the program to include "The First Noel" or "Silent Night." A good arrangement of "The Battle Hymn of the Republic" is a stirring experience to them because they know the song. The average adult listener would much rather hear the familiar, established songs than current "hit" tunes.

Some teachers attempt to entertain their audiences by performing complex arrangements of "Polly Wolly Doodle" and similar music. They achieve their goal of pleasing the audience, but at what a price! There is nothing wrong with doing "Polly Wolly Doodle," but why a tricky, big arrangement that demands many hours of valuable class time? Is this a good educational investment? Probably not. In choosing the few songs that are chiefly for audience appeal, whether folk or popular, the teacher should select the easiest, best-sounding arrangement that he can find, and save the hours of rehearsal time for music that is worthy of meticulous care and attention.

Finding Appropriate Music

Where does a teacher find music for his performing groups? First, many pieces of music are presented in methods classes. The college student can start immediately to build up a "music log" or professional library of numbers that appear to be good and within the capabilities of the teen-age student.

Second, there are several excellent graded listings of music for use with school groups—lists such as those included in state festival guides. Other lists are contained in the following publications:

Andrews, Frances M., and Joseph A. Leeder, *Guiding Junior High School Pupils in Music Experiences*. Englewood Cliffs, N.J.: Prentice-Hall, Inc., 1953.

Band Music Guide, ed. Kenneth Berger and staff of *The Instrumentalist*. 2nd ed. Evanston, Ill., 1960.

Garretson, Robert L., *Conducting Choral Music*. Boston: Allyn and Bacon, Inc., 1961.

Handbook for Applied Music, Grades 7–12. Albany: New York State Education Department, 1957.

Leeder, Joseph A., and William S. Haynie, *Music Education in the High School*. Englewood Cliffs, N.J.: Prentice-Hall, Inc., 1958.

Materials for Miscellaneous Instrumental Ensembles, prepared by the Committee on Literature and Interpretation of Music for Instrumental Ensembles of the MENC, 1960. 90 pages.

Selective Lists for Instrumental and Vocal Solos, Instrumental and Vocal Ensembles, National Interscholastic Music Activities Commission of the MENC, 1963. 160 pages.

Selective Music Lists: Chorus, Orchestra, Band. National Interscholastic Music Activities Commission of the MENC, 1962. 71 pages.

Sur, William R., and Charles F. Schuller, *Music Education for Teen-Agers*. New York: Harper & Brothers, 1958.

A third practical step is the "program exchange" idea. Some teachers have standing agreements to exchange printed concert programs. A few music houses and instrument manufacturers publish programs that are submitted to them. Some professional organizations, the National School Orchestra Association among them, make an attempt to circulate programs among the membership.

Fourth, music can be ordered on approval from music stores and publishers. If a teacher does not know what pieces to ask for, the lists of music printed by various publishers can be examined and works by recognized composers selected from them. These numbers should be surveyed leisurely at the piano, then the pieces that seem musically inferior or unsuitable for teen-age groups can be returned. Choral teachers can keep those works that have good possibilities, and begin to build a personal library of single copies of choral music. This is somewhat expensive at first, but within a few years a valuable reference file will develop. This file can be catalogued by voice arrangement and difficulty, and comments can be written in the margins. The instrumental teacher can keep a written record on each piece, and maintain a file of free sample scores.

COPYRIGHT LAW

Before discussing the ways in which music may be changed to better fit the requirements of a group, it is necessary to examine what can and cannot properly be done under the copyright law as it now exists. The law states that copyrighted music cannot be copied. It does not matter whether the music is to be used at a performance for profit or in a classroom; it makes no difference whether it is mimeographed or copied by hand on manuscript paper or on the chalkboard. It is even illegal to copy the words on a slide and project it, or to print the text of an anthem in the church bulletin on Sunday morning. This is the letter of the law. Fortunately, laws are carried out by human beings and the spirit of the law as presently administered is more flexible.

Music publishing houses do not prosecute school teachers and church choral directors for *slight* infractions of the letter of the law. They are human, and do not want to be Shylocks about the copyright. Nor do they want unpleasant publicity. What the publishers are concerned about are the obvious violations of the law—the teacher who saves some of his budget money by making photostat, ditto, or mimeograph copies of the music.

If it is absolutely necessary for a teacher to make written changes in the music, he must write the publishers requesting permission. *If* the music is not published in the form in which he needs it, and *if* he has purchased several copies of an existing arrangement, the publisher will almost always give permission. This means that a teacher can, for example, arrange SATB material for SAB, if he has purchased copies of the SATB music, and if no SAB version is available. If an SAB version is available, he should buy the necessary copies or do without.

Music publishers want children to have music. But they do not want them to have it if it means robbing the composer or arranger of the income to which his ability properly entitles him, or depriving the publisher of his return on the investment in each piece.

The copyright law protects a piece of music for a period of twenty-eight years. This period can be, and usually is, extended for another twenty-eight years. After the fifty-six years have passed, that work or arrangement becomes public domain, and such material can be copied and reproduced at will. As one can surmise, all music copyrighted before 1900 is not now covered by copyrights, and this includes a vast field of fine music. A distinction should be made between music that is copyrighted, and an arrangement that is copyrighted. The original versions of such songs as "Home on the Range" are not copyrighted, but published arrangements of them are. A person can make his own arrangement of such pieces from the original but he cannot copy someone else's arrangement that is covered by the copyright law. The year in which the copyright was issued is always printed on the music.

ADAPTING MUSIC

There are several ways in which the teacher can simplify the music without infringing by rewriting it. Since the range of the voices in vocal music is frequently a problem, it is sometimes helpful for the accompanist to transpose the entire work. Intonation can frequently be improved by moving the key up or down a half step.

A second way to simplify and often to improve a work is to cut the number of parts or reduce the number of performers in one section of the music. In both instrumental and vocal music the amount of doubling can be reduced.[9] In choral music the singers can be told to sing other parts, while in instrumental music the player will have to rest unless a new part is written out for him.

Two other simplifications can be used in choral music. If a group is

[9] Alfred Reed, "The Instrumentation of the Band," *Music Educators Journal*, XLIX, No. 1 (September–October 1962), 61.

not very advanced, the B or bridge section of popular and semipopular songs can be sung in unison by one or a combination of parts. This portion of the music consumes about one-fourth of the performance time of the piece, and is frequently more difficult than the remainder of the work. The amount of time required to learn the full arrangement in the B section may not be justifiable in terms of its worth.

In some numbers the harmony parts are changed when the melody is repeated. The music can be simplified by merely instructing the singers to repeat the harmony parts as they were first learned—sometimes with different words. A good example of this is the Christmas carol "The Twelve Days of Christmas." The song can be complicated or quite easy, depending on the use of repeated harmony parts.

The music teacher should not be hesitant about trying changes in the music. Perhaps a soloist can perform one portion, or the teacher can compose a descant, a countermelody, or simple harmony parts. The use for teacher-arranged music is greatest at the junior high school level. The changing voices with their range limitations and the unique nature of each group make it desirable for the teacher to try his hand at occasional arranging. The instrumental teacher may also find it advantageous to do some arranging, especially if the group is of unusual size and instrumentation.

Projects

1. Listen to Beethoven's *Piano Concerto No. 5 in E Flat, Op. 73, "Emperor"* and then the *Fantasia in C for Piano, Chorus, and Orchestra,* Op. 80. Compare the musical qualities of the two works by the same person, written in similar style, using somewhat similar media.
2. Take a choral work and an instrumental work that are also available to two other members of your class. Independently make an evaluation of the quality of each work, its difficulty, and its suitability for use in the secondary schools. Then compare and discuss your opinions about the music with your two classmates.
3. Study the following SATB arrangements of the same piece. Compare range, tenor part, accompaniment, musical effectiveness, and appropriateness for secondary school choral groups.
   a. "Black, Black, Black"—Parker-Shaw (G. Schirmer)
   b. "Black Is the Color of My True Love's Hair"—Churchill (Shawnee)
   c. "Black Is the Color of My True Love's Hair"—Kirk (Schmitt, Hall & McCreary)
   d. "Black Is the Color of My True Love's Hair"—Smale (Summy-Birchard)

4. Compare the musical effect of each of these choral works:
   a. "Waters Ripple and Flow"–arr. Taylor, SSA (J. Fischer)
   "Waters Ripple and Flow"–arr. Taylor, SATB (J. Fischer)
   b. "God So Loved the World"–Stainer, SAB (Schmitt, Hall & McCreary)
   "God So Loved the World"–Stainer, SATB (Schmitt, Hall & McCreary)
5. Take a choral work that has been arranged in eight parts (SSAATTBB). With red pencil in hand, reduce it to a four-part arrangement (SATB), retaining as best you can the musical qualities of the work.
6. Try your hand at choral arranging. Take the melody "Prairie Home" on page 391 and write a clean, solid-sounding arrangement of the measures presented.
7. Study the original arrangements of two of Sousa's marches (Carl Fischer, Inc., or Theodore Presser), and the simplified arrangements of these two by Buchtel (Neil A. Kjos Music Co.), Harold L. Walters (Rubank, Inc.), Samuel Laudenslager (John Church Company), and James A. Scott (Rubank, Inc.). Note the changes that are made, and determine what effect, if any, the simplification has on the musical quality of the work. Also consider which are more suitable for performance by secondary school bands.
8. Compare the following works for school band as to difficulty, musical effect, key, and clarity of arrangement.

   Symphony No. 6, "*Pathétique*," by Tschaikowsky
   arranged by Ed Chenette (Rubank, Inc.)
   arranged by M. L. Lake (Carl Fischer, Inc.)
   arranged by V. F. Safranek (Carl Fischer, Inc.)

   Water Music Suite, by G. F. Handel
   arranged by H. Harty-Duthoit (Chappell)
   arranged by Hershy Kay (Presser)
9. Listen to and study the scores of William Schuman's *Chester* (*Overture for Band*), and "Chester" from the *New England Triptych*, which is for orchestra. Note the different use of instruments in each work, and how the musical effect is altered.
10. Study the orchestral score to Rimsky-Korsakov's *Scheherazade* and compare it with "Themes from Scheherazade," arranged by Frederic Fay Swift (Pro Art), and "Scheherazade Themes," arranged by Richard L. Weaver (Mills Music), in *Second Series Orchestra Transcriptions*. Observe which portions of the original work have been used, and note how the parts have been simplified. Make a list of the advantages and disadvantages of the "excerpt" approach in contrast to the performance of one movement from the original.
11. Compare the following works for school orchestra as to difficulty, musical effect, key, and ability of the strings to be heard.

    "Gavotte" from *Classical Symphony*, by Prokofiev
    arranged by Philip Gordon (Bourne, Inc.)
    arranged by Cyril Warren (Boosey & Hawkes)

Symphony No. 5 "New World" by Dvořák
arranged by Lotler (Boosey & Hawkes)
arranged by Roberts (Carl Fischer, Inc.)

12. Secure addresses of music stores in your area or in other cities that can supply "on approval" copies of a wide selection of choral and instrumental music.

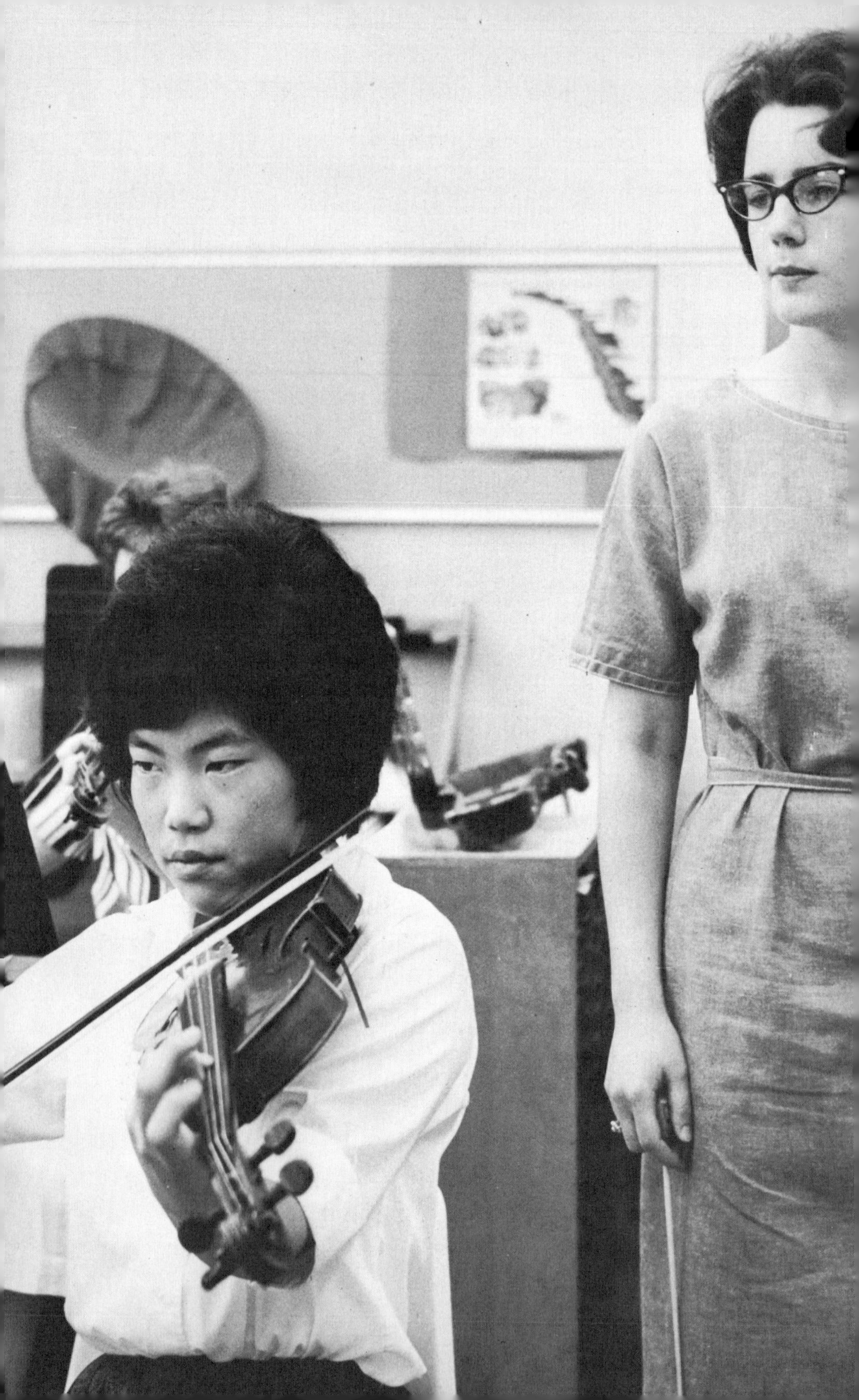

XVII

the profession and progress

A music teacher is never alone in his work, even though he may be the only music teacher in a school or district. He is a part of a profession and is so identified—whether he likes it or not. The results of his work are often affected by what others in the profession have done in the past and are doing now. This happens in several ways. For one, the teacher usually succeeds other music teachers. The music teacher inherits a legacy from his predecessors, as in the case of the vocal music teacher who followed a director whose main efforts were devoted to one big operetta each year. It was hard to wean the students, parents, and fellow teachers away from the annual spring entertainment.

For another, administrators and teachers are aware of what goes on in neighboring school districts, and comparisons are frequently made between schools as to the number of class meetings, size and quality of the choir or band, credit, and curriculum. There is an unfortunate tendency on the part of some school boards and administrators to be guided more by what like schools are doing than by what is best for their particular school. More than once the question has been asked of a music teacher: "Why should we start a string program when Duxbury and Westfield don't have one?"

A third way in which a teacher is affected by his profession is through the pronouncements of professional organizations and the statements of leaders in the profession. For example, the fact that the MENC has zealously promoted string instruction in the schools has undoubtedly contributed to the number and quality of string players.

These points represent what might be called a "minimum professional involvement." As was pointed out on page 62, the interested teacher can gain much more by participating in professional organizations and by being alert to happenings within the profession.

What are the notable features of the music-education profession about which every music teacher should be aware? First and most important, he needs to realize that the profession is alive and vital; it is evaluating its present practices and trying new ones to better itself in the future. To the first sentence in this book—"One who chooses to teach music in the schools has selected a profession that is interesting, worthy, and difficult"—should be added the word "dynamic" or "vigorous." This vitality is a good sign; it bodes well for the future of music education. Not only is it attracting the type of person who seeks excitement and a continuing challenge in his vocation, but it ensures that music education will progress and keep pace with education and society as a whole. Music education cannot afford to stop moving forward, and if the current scene is indicative of the future, the profession is in no danger of standing still.

An active and dynamic profession that is seeking to do an even better job tends to produce controversy and differences of opinion. And so it is in music education. A kaleidoscope of opinions can be found on almost every major aspect of music teaching. To the beginning teacher the lack of agreement can be confusing. He may wonder why a committee of recognized music educators cannot get together, say under the auspices of the MENC, and write a comprehensive and detailed book on the best way to teach music in the secondary schools. The answer is that music education, because it is trying many new practices and because it contains within it divergent views as to its role in the schools, can put forth only rather generalized statements on how music is best taught. But divergent views are not necessarily bad, since they generally indicate professional vitality, a most valuable asset.

CURRENT DEVELOPMENTS

Several of the more recent concerns of the profession merit mention here. Probably the most significant of these is self-examination. Music education is now looking at itself as it never has before. This was probably inevitable. The great effort to win some kind of place for music in the schools is largely over.[1] Not even the recent emphasis on the sciences and foreign language was able to weaken music's place in the schools, or inhibit its further growth.[2] Now music educators can afford the luxury of pausing

[1] "Report on Amateur Music in the United States—1962" (Chicago: American Music Conference unpublished study, 1962), p. 8. In 1962 in the elementary, junior high, and senior high schools of the United States there were 48,000 bands, 15,000 orchestras, and 6,000 stage bands.

[2] "Music in the Public Schools," *NEA Research Bulletin,* XLI, No. 2 (May 1963), 57–58. In the five-year period from 1956–57 to 1961–62 there were five times as many schools increasing their music curriculum as decreasing it, with 50 per cent of the secondary schools reporting an increased *percentage* in enrollment in music and only

to ask themselves: "What is music? Is this the best that can be taught in the name of music? Are the students really learning music?" Two other factors have also encouraged this self-examination. One is the emphasis placed on all education following the beginning of the Space Age in 1957. The other is the ending of the large increases in the percentage of students enrolled in the secondary schools.[3] This has encouraged a new emphasis on the quality of education in contrast to the previous attention on quantity of students.

One result of this reappraisal has been an increased realization of the values to be found in music itself. Music has become not only a means but also an end in education. The point of view presented in Chapter Two and in many other publications in recent years is that music should be studied because of its own aesthetic qualities and the need for these qualities in human life. This is a change from the predominant view of a generation ago that advocated "education through music," and stated its function in this way: "The teacher teaches children through the medium of music."[4] The word "through" is crucial here; it indicates the use of music to achieve a goal which by implication is more worthy than the benefits of music itself. Today music education might state its function in this way: "The teacher teaches music because the aesthetic quality in music is necessary for humanness." There is, of course, no uniform agreement among music educators on this newer view (ultimate needs in making mankind human are not easily explained or understood!), but the recent interest in the aesthetic, musical values in music instruction as contrasted with nonmusical values is undeniable.

The realization of the intrinsic value of music largely erases a dilemma that bothered many music teachers in the past: the question of which was more important, music or the students. The two are in reality inseparable when the students are helped most by knowing and understanding the subject. Also largely resolved is the old conflict between teaching for favorable attitudes (getting the students to like the subject) and teaching for knowledge and skill. Other things being equal, when the teacher organizes activities so that the students learn, the attitude of the students toward music will most likely be favorable. This is not to say that teacher-pupil rapport is no longer significant, because the quality of this relationship is crucial, but rather in the long run a student's interest is best promoted when he is truly learning.

The profession has looked to the related fields of psychology, sociology,

---

6 per cent reporting a decrease. There were also increases in the number of music teachers, number of courses, and both curricular and extracurricular enrollment.

[3] *Status and Trends: Vital Statistics, Education and Public Finance,* Research Report –R 13 (Washington, D.C.: NEA Research Division, 1959), p. 12.

[4] Peter W. Dykema, and Karl W. Gehrkens, *The Teaching and Administration of High School Music* (Evanston, Ill.: Summy-Birchard Publishing Company, 1941), pp. 380–81.

aesthetics, philosophy, and education to see what light they can throw on music education. Furthermore, it has communicated and worked with musicologists, composers, and professional performing musicians. Although this runs, as McMurray says, the "danger . . . that deeper thinking about the background of music education will become entangled in the dialectic disputes of systematic schools of thought in disciplines other than the discipline of music education itself,"[5] music educators have generally felt the risk well worth taking so that their field could be further strengthened. Scholars from related fields have been invited to contribute to music-education publications and to participate in professional meetings of music teachers. One such noteworthy attempt to draw upon related disciplines was *Basic Concepts in Music Education*, which was published in 1958 as the 57th Yearbook of the National Society for the Study of Education.

Closely related to the examination of subject matter is the increased interest in the music curriculum. An important phase of this activity (one which has been discussed at length earlier in this book) is the examination of the educational value of performing groups in the secondary schools. The brunt of the criticism about the lack of learning in performing groups has fallen on the marching band. Discontinuing this activity, however, would not solve the problem. Too many choral groups, concert bands, and orchestras have also concentrated on providing entertaining performances rather than in seeing that music learning takes place in the rehearsal room. Included at the end of this chapter are two articles that deal with the need for greater learning in performing groups. Anderson's article, "Survey of Musical Style for Band," outlines specific steps and works of music used in a high school band rehearsal. Nye's "Some Thoughts and Theories about Secondary School Music," which has been somewhat abridged for publication here, applies equally to instrumental or vocal music and suggests some practical steps for improvement.

Increasing interest in the educational process in music has led to more intensive experimentation. Thus, new practices in scheduling (some of which were mentioned on page102), ability groupings of students, teaching machines and programmed learning, and new teaching methods are being considered. Because many of the practices are in the process of being tested, it is impossible to say what will be the effect of any of them on music education. The significant point is that ideas are being tested, and the profession is continually seeking ways to do a still better job of teaching music. Indicative of the recent concern about handling differing levels of ability among students is the report published by the MENC and the NEA, entitled *Music for the Academically Talented Student.*

[5] Foster McMurray, "Pragmatism in Music Education," *Basic Concepts in Music Education,* National Society for the Study of Education, 1958, p. 36.

Excerpts from this report are published at the conclusion of this chapter.

Each year brings an ever increasing amount of new material for the assistance and education of the teacher and the teen-age student—books, filmstrips, educational recordings, music, and equipment. Recently, as a part of the interest in the quality of music studied, new emphasis has been placed on the quality of instructional books and teaching aids. The music teachers of today are indeed more fortunate than were their forerunners a generation ago with respect to the materials available. For example, Appendix C lists the many books available for a specific, limited use: the development of intermediate or advanced techniques in the full band or string orchestra. It is significant that the vast majority of these books have been published since 1955.

Summer music study enrollment at camps and colleges has increased more than 400 per cent since 1950, with more than two-thirds of all the 160 summer music camps organized since that time, and 20 per cent organized after 1959.[6] These figures speak for the dramatically rising interest in summer music study, and add importance to the discussion of summer music study in Chapter Six. Summer music programs are rapidly becoming a factor of real importance in music education.

The profession is also showing more concern for the general student, especially at the high school level. Music educators have become increasingly disturbed by the fact that in most high schools a great many students no longer study music. The more talented and interested continue in an instrumental or choral group, while the remainder of students lose contact with the music curriculum. Both Nye's article and the report on *Music for the Academically Talented Student* mention the need for a substantial course for the general student. Suggestions for meeting this need are included in Chapter Fifteen on the music-appreciation course in the high school.

No survey of the current scene in music education can omit the interest in creativity. This interest has taken several forms. One is the program of the Ford Foundation which places young composers in outstanding school systems for a year. The purpose of the program is twofold: to acquaint the composer with the limitations and rewards of writing for school groups and to interest him in doing so, and to stimulate the interest of school music teachers in new music. Recently the program has taken on the additional responsibility of seeking and encouraging creativity at all school levels.[7] Greater interest in the creative process has also been shown by psychologists and educators, notably Guilford, Getzels, and Jackson, who stress a newly recognized value of thinking which is divergent (expanding, elaborating) as well as convergent (reducing, abstracting, ex-

[6] "Report on Amateur Music," *op. cit.*, p. 10.

[7] Paul Hume, "Ford Grant to Start Six-Year Project to Develop Music Talent in Schools," *Music Educators Journal*, XLIX, No. 5 (April–May 1963), 40.

tracting).[8] The final article in Appendix A is by Donn Mills, who relates his experiences in teaching composition to students of junior high school age in a twice-a-week, voluntary class. The course had as its sole purpose the learning of music, and its teacher was not afraid to try new and different methods.

THE FUTURE?

While no one can say with certainty how the future will alter music education, it can be said with conviction that it will change. Probably, as in the past, there will be no sudden, startling, revolutionary developments. Rather the changes will be evolutionary, representing the sum of many small trials, experiments, and evaluations, and many attempts at thinking through basic issues. Although progress will probably be neither uniform nor consistent, the significant point is that *music education twenty years from now will not be what it is today*. Hopefully, by building upon current efforts of the profession, it will evolve into a more meaningful and effective portion of the school curriculum.

Speaking to the International Society of Music Education in 1958, Vanett Lawler, Executive Secretary of the MENC, listed for the music educators from other countries what she saw as some trends of the profession in the United States. Because of her wide contacts, her observations as to future trends are worthy of mention.

1) Increased professional autonomy enjoyed by music educators in the fields of music and education.
2) Increased realization of the fact that the music education profession demands teachers trained in two professions—music and education.
3) Increased recognition by music educators, administrators of school systems, boards of education and directors of curriculum of the importance of a well-balanced program of appropriate music courses which will contribute to the objectives of general education. This means planning for the entire student body in schools—elementary, secondary and colleges and with more than perfunctory courses in music appreciation.
4) Increased utilization of school music performing groups as functional parts of total school programs.
5) Increased recognition by administrators of schools of music and schools of education within State universities and colleges of education, of the professional organization, the Music Educators National Conference, the Music Teachers National Association, the National Association of Schools of Music, and the National Coun-

[8] J. P. Guilford, "A Revised Structure of Intellect," *Reports from the Psychological Laboratory*, No. 19 (Los Angeles: University of Southern California, April 1957), pp. 6–9. Also: Jacob W. Getzels and Philip W. Jackson, *Creativity and Intelligence: Explorations with Gifted Students* (New York: John Wiley & Sons, Inc., 1962), p. 14.

cil for the Accreditation of Teacher Education, as the source for guidance in developing curricula for education of music teachers.

6) Increased insistence upon balance in education of the music teachers, as musicians and as educators. . . .
7) Increased recognition of the importance of quality of materials used in the schools.
8) Increased opportunities for cooperation between music educators and musicologists, composers, private teachers and professional musicians. . . .
9) Increased awareness of the public relations aspects of music education—of the importance of a non-isolationist policy of the music educators as regards their community.
10) Increased attention by music educators and administrators of school systems and colleges to the pre-service education (before entering the profession) and in-service education (after entering the profession) of the general elementary school teacher.
11) Increased attention to the importance of music education for exceptional children, including the physically handicapped, the mentally retarded as well as the gifted child.
12) Increased interest throughout the music education profession in the United States of America of the importance and effectiveness of music education in international relations and intercultural education.[9]

When sails propelled ships across the seas, sailors used to speak of "favorable" winds. At the time of this writing, the "winds" are clearly favorable for music education. Two circumstances in American society account for this. One is the increased emphasis on education in general; the other is an increasing interest in the fine arts, especially music. Partly because of the vast sums of money it involves, but more because of society's need for it, education is receiving more public attention than ever before, and most of it is favorable. Not only are more people going to school, but they are staying in school longer, and many others are returning to school in adult education programs.[10] The mass-communication media publicize education as they never did before, and betterment of the schools has become a major political issue in many states—something that was unheard of thirty years ago. The Federal government is taking a new interest in education, and big foundations, such as Ford, Rockefeller, and Carnegie, have invested large sums of money in educational studies and research, the results of which may affect music education. Although there have been temporary, local setbacks, for each of these there have been several successes.[11] In fact, the *percentage* of income spent on edu-

[9] Vanett Lawler, "New Trends in Music Education," *Music in American Education* (Washington, D.C.: MENC, 1955), pp. 47–50.

[10] *Digest of Educational Statistics*, Department of Health, Education, and Welfare (Washington, D.C.: U.S. Government Printing Office, 1962), p. 13.

[11] "What Taxpayer's Revolt?" *Michigan Education Journal*, XLI, No. 1 (September 1963), 64.

cation has increased from 3.06 per cent in 1941, to 4.05 per cent in 1951, to 6.17 per cent in 1959.[12]

As for the fine arts, greater leisure time and affluence (both of which seem destined to increase) have enabled artistic interests to develop among the mass of the population, as have radio, television, and the electronic reproduction of music. For the first time in man's long history, there are the means, the time, and the financial resources to make great music and the other fine arts available to virtually everyone. Certainly the great American experiment in mass education can also claim some credit for the burgeoning interest in culture. Evidence of this trend is abundant: the figures on community orchestras cited on page 97, the sales of serious "classical" recordings, the number of musical instruments purchased, the amount of money spent for concerts and musical events, and the establishment of fine-arts centers and arts councils in many cities.[13] Probably equally as indicative of the trend is the *percentage* of personal income spent on new musical instruments, sheet music, and musical accessories. (The figures exclude recordings and recording equipment.) Since 1941 the percentage of money, not only the gross amount, has increased slowly from 0.110 per cent to 0.177 in 1962.[14]

Never has the future of music education been more promising, and never has music education been more vital and more eager to move ahead. To be more complete and accurate, the sentence that opened this book, to which the word "dynamic" was added, should now be further amended to read: "One who chooses to teach music in the schools has selected a profession that is interesting, worthy, difficult, and dynamic, and one with an unlimited future."

[12] *Digest of Educational Statistics, op. cit.*, p. 21.
[13] "Report on Amateur Music," *op. cit.*, pp. 3, 9.
[14] "Report on Amateur Music," *op. cit.*, p. 11.

appendix a

*SURVEY OF MUSICAL STYLE FOR BAND**

Donald Anderson

MUSIC USED IN THE SURVEY OF MUSICAL STYLE FOR BAND AND ARRANGED BY THE AUTHOR

I. Polyphonic
  Kyrie I, by Guillaume Dufay
II. Baroque
  Sonata Piano Forte, by Giovanni Gabrieli
  Prelude and Fugue in G Minor, by J. S. Bach
III. Classic Period
  Octette in F Major for Winds, by Joseph Haydn
IV. Romantic Period
  Prelude No. I, op. 28, No. 7, by Frederic Chopin
  Prelude No. II, op. 28, No. 20, by Frederic Chopin
V. Modern
  Prelude in E Flat Minor, No. 14, by Dimitri Shostakovich

MUSICAL STYLE

To the Band Student: The purpose of the survey is to acquaint you with the different styles in music. We have taken musical examples from the following main periods in music.

Polyphonic	1000–1600
Baroque	1600–1750
Classic	1750–1820
Romantic	1820–1900
Modern	1900–

We will approach musical styles by using the tools that a composer uses in creating a composition.

COMPOSERS' TOOLS

Rhythm: Everything related to the duration of musical sounds, including emphasis and frequency of occurrence.

Melody: A succession of musical tones which comprise a musical idea.

Harmony: Musical tones sounded simultaneously.

Form: The plan of construction; the way the music is put together.

Color: The different types or combination of voices or instruments used.

Texture: The thickness or thinness

* Originally published in *Missouri Journal of Research in Music Education,* Vol. I, No. 1, 1962.

of voices occurring either homophonically or polyphonically, i.e., horizontally or vertically.

Dynamics: Loudness or softness of the music.

This should provide you with a foundation that will make all the music you play more interesting and meaningful.

POLYPHONIC PERIOD
1000–1600

Rhythm:

a. In the early part of the polyphonic period no regular meter was used or bar lines that we use today.

b. You will notice the independence of each part as it is played. Also note the interweaving of independent rhythms.

c. Rhythmical accentuation of each part is free, but the composition as a whole conforms to a fixed metrical scheme in which strong and weak accents succeed one another in predetermined order.

Melody:

a. Melodic lines were well proportioned, with upward movement, balanced by descent.

b. Melodic skips, major and minor thirds, perfect 4ths and 5ths, octaves (minor 6th ascending only) were used.

c. Church modes were used but by alteration and breakdown the primary ones left, in the latter part of the period, were major and minor.

d. Melodies were written for voices, but instruments played the same parts.

Harmony: In the early polyphonic period, harmony was the momentary result of interval relationship between voices, progressing horizontally.

Form: Standard polyphonic forms were used, such as the motet, the mass, and the madrigal.

Color: There was little interest in differentiation between vocal and instrumental color.

Texture: Methods used were polyphonic and chordal (strands moving simultaneously in homophony).

Dynamics: Few dynamic changes were indicated in the scores.

Suggestions for Rehearsals:

a. Play each part separately (I, II, III, IV).
b. Show the interval skips.
c. Show where momentary harmony occurs.

Some Important Composers of the Period:

a. Guillaume Dufay
b. Josquin Des Pres
c. Orlando Di Lasso
d. Giovanni Da Palestrina

BAROQUE MUSIC
1600–1750

Some Important Composers of the Period:

a. J. S. Bach
b. G. F. Handel
c. G. Gabrieli
d. A. Corelli
e. H. Purcell

Rhythm: Regularity of beat.

Melody:

a. Range of melodies increased.
b. Establishment of tonality.
c. Major and minor mode.

Harmony:

a. More organized development of tonal harmony using 7th and 9th chords (major and minor).

b. Development of counterpoint.

c. New emphasis on homophony, but does not replace polyphony.

Form:

a. Examples: Baroque sonata, concerto grosso, cantata, opera.

b. Basso continuo (bass part with numerals below the notes to indicate harmony).

c. Polyphonic music at its peak at the end of this period.

d. Increase in importance of homophony.

Color: Instrumental color; interest in specific instrumental harmony.

Texture:

a. Perfection of the fugue.

b. Homophony (see above).

c. Thorough-bass technique.

Dynamics: Terraced dynamics, either forte or piano.

Suggestions for Rehearsals:

Point out:

a. A period of dramatic expression, more spectacular and with more grandeur than polyphonic period.

b. An era of ecstasy and exuberance of dynamics, tensions, and sweeping gestures.

c. Music of the period developed in two directions, one homophony and the other polyphony. (Bach wrote in both styles.)

d. Instrumental music of the early Baroque period as typified by Gabrieli through his use of dynamic contrast between two groups, and combining for dynamic climaxes.

e. Culmination of Baroque, Bach and Handel.

CLASSIC PERIOD
1750–1820

Rhythm: Regularity of rhythm; simple rhythms.

Melody:

a. Mainly diatonic with chromaticism, becoming more important in later part of period.

b. Simple light melody.

Harmony:

a. A period of harmonic revolution, change from polyphonic to homophonic.

b. Diatonic harmony, with chromaticism.

Form:

a. Sonata allegro form, e.g., concerto, symphony, etc.

b. Form conscious–larger sectional structures that are simple and clear.

Color:

a. Standardization of orchestra.

b. Piano used as important solo and ensemble instrument.

Texture: Homophony; melodies with chordal support.

Dynamics:

a. Greater use of dynamic marks.

b. Terraced dynamics and crescendo and diminuendo both used.

Suggestions for Rehearsals:

a. Play melody alone, pointing out lightness and brevity of melody.

b. Music is generally restrained, impersonal and objective.

c. This period gives a feeling of stability, clarity, balance, self-reliance, grace, refinement, and elegance.

d. Notice the composers' use of relatively simple diatonic harmony.

e. Notice the use of terraced dynamics at measures 9–11, crescendo at measure 3.

f. Notice the diatonic use of notes at measure 5.

g. Rhythm of the piece is triple.

Some Important Composers of the Period:

a. Franz Joseph Haydn

b. Wolfgang Amadeus Mozart

ROMANTIC PERIOD
1820–1900

Rhythm: More complex rhythms being used.

Melody:

a. Flowing melodies, strong emotions in music, more personal.

b. Chromatic intervals.

Harmony: Still tonal (key centered) but also becoming more chromatic.

Form:

a. Longer forms in symphony and sonata but also many short piano pieces.

b. Development of the symphonic tone poem.

c. Less rigid form than preceding period.

d. Program music.

Color:

a. Composers preoccupied with color effects.

b. Change of color by use of new instruments.

Texture:

a. Prevalence of homophony.

b. Sonorities–rich and full.

Dynamics:

a. Varied dynamics.

b. Sweeping effects.

Suggestions for Rehearsals:

Point out:

a. Enrichment of music by poetry, fiction, philosophy, and painting of the Romantic period.

b. Use of flowing melody with much emotion in Prelude No. II.

c. Full color of the chords in Prelude No. II.

d. Melody with rich chordal accompaniment.

e. All dynamics used.

Some Important Composers of the Period:

a. Richard Wagner

b. Franz Liszt

c. Frederick Chopin

d. Johannes Brahms

e. Franz Schubert

MODERN PERIOD
1900–

Rhythm:

a. More complex rhythm patterns and syncopation used.

b. Mixed meters, exotic rhythms, experiments in metric schemes.

Melody:

a. Wide range.

b. Serial techniques.

c. Microtones.

d. Modes.

Harmony:

a. Dissonance is greater in melodic intervals.

b. Atonality and modality, polytonality, seven-tone scale, microtone, multi-tonality, chords built on 4ths and 2nds.

Form:

a. Many of the classic forms being used.

b. Renewed interest in polyphonic texture.

c. Experimentation with new forms.

Color:

a. Expanded technique being used in all instruments.

b. New electronic instruments.

Texture:

a. Much experimentation.

b. Horizontal and vertical direction.

c. Monophonic, polyphonic, homophonic, non-melodic.

d. Thin and clear sonorities.

Dynamics: All dynamic markings used, extreme effects.

Suggestions for Rehearsals:

Point out:

a. Change in time at measure 24, 3/4 to 5/4.

b. Wide range of melody, low in beginning to high flute at measure 24.

c. Syncopation at measure 26.

Some Important Composers of the Period:

a. Vincent Persichetti

b. Leonard Bernstein

c. Dimitri Kabalevsky

d. Igor F. Stravinsky

e. Anton Webern

f. Dimitri Shostakovich

g. Darius Milhaud

h. Paul Hindemith

*SOME THOUGHTS AND THEORIES ABOUT SECONDARY SCHOOL MUSIC**

Robert E. Nye

Once there was a high school music teacher who was very busy meeting the demands of his school and community. His music groups, small ensembles, and soloists served the P.T.A., the Kiwanis Club, the Athletic Department, the Ladies Literary Society, the Assembly Committee, and myriad other school and community agencies. The teacher felt that he had little time to do more than get the boys and girls ready for their next public appearance. The major musical objective of his music program was performance for school and community.

The teacher was disturbed when his first-chair trombone player came to him and said, "I have discovered that while I can play my trombone well enough to place in first division in the Competition-Festival, I still don't know much of anything about music." The teacher knew that this was true. When he shared his knowledge of music literature, structure, and theory with the students, it was unplanned and amounted to chance comments. He regretted this, but felt that nothing could be done about it since there was not time in which to teach such things.

Some weeks later his friend, the principal, spoke with him. The principal had attended a national education conference at which a speaker presented an analysis of the secondary school curriculum. He asked the music teacher a number of questions:

> Is the present music program reaching the number of students you think it should?
>
> Is there grade-level planning? Is the junior year in chorus or band different from the sophomore year? Why should your first-chair trombone player continue in band rather than take some other course or activity next term, since he has already advanced as far as he can in band?
>
> Should there be some subject matter taught in band, orchestra, or chorus, or should the content of these courses be limited to the learning of skills necessary for performance?
>
> What does the public think is the purpose of music in the high school?
>
> Should our music program serve only those who possess superior musical talents, or should it (like United States History and English) serve every boy and girl in some measure?

* From Robert E. Nye, "Some Thoughts and Theories about Secondary School Music," *Music Educators Journal,* Vol. 45, No. 2 (November–December 1958), 26. Reprinted by permission.

> Can you give me some reasons to present to the Board of Education why the music program should not be reduced to make way for more sections of science and driver-training?

The teacher was caught off-guard and could not give logical answers to these questions. His first reaction was defensive and stemmed from a feeling that the principal knew little about music. Upon second thought however, since he could not answer the questions, he was forced to conclude that he too knew little about these aspects of music education. He told the principal that he would seriously consider these questions and give him more complete answers at an early date.

SEEKING ANSWERS

At first the music teacher could not find a starting point at which to begin to analyze his music program. . . . He knew that his program was geared almost entirely to one major goal—public performance—which was largely extracurricular. Now his professional work was being seriously questioned. Did that mean that performance was somehow bad? He did not think so. "What good is music if it is not experienced through performance?" he asked himself, and answered, "No good at all." Without performing music or listening to others perform music, there could be no real music program. He knew how much boys and girls want to sing and play in chorus, band, and orchestra. He also knew that these activities are physiologically and socially sound for this age group. . . .

The teacher asked a number of his friends in the community what they thought was the purpose of the high school music program. Most of them said that it was to let the boys and girls sing and play. Several said it was to give the children something to do "keep them off the streets." Too few mentioned aesthetic and spiritual values. However, one wise woman replied with another question, "When you were in music school, of what did music consist?" The teacher remembered that in music school there were courses in music history, music theory, form and analysis, and performance. The woman asked, "How much *music* are you teaching at the high school? Are you spending all of your time rehearsing for performances, or are you teaching music classes?" The teacher explained that he was rehearsing for performances, not teaching classes in music as such. The woman said, "The other teachers teach academic courses, with the possible exception of the coach. Maybe some of your problems would be solved if you taught music classes instead of holding rehearsals." The teacher answered that if he did, he would lose his job because the school and community required him to serve them with dozens of performances of many types. Besides, high schools were not music schools. The woman responded, "Performance is certainly essential, but it would seem that you should teach music at the same time you rehearse, and do this in a manner compatible with the American high school."

ANALYZING THE SITUATION

Many conversations with townspeople helped to clarify the situation for the teacher. He began to realize that his present music program had some disadvantages. One was that it had led to a widespread belief on the part of the public that music in the high school was limited largely to preparation for public-relations-type performances, and that it included little concerning the larger world of music. Moreover, the program was geared to those students who possessed above-average musical ability, because those of little ability were of no help in producing programs for the public; this limited the music enrollment. There was no presentation of the subject matter of music in any organized way; therefore, the graduating seniors knew little about music except those skills and knowledges believed essential to passable performance.

The teacher then tried to compare his teaching procedures with those of the good classroom teacher. There was little comparison, because his own techniques of instruction were limited largely to drill and rote procedures designed to hurry boys and girls into acceptable skills for public performance. Missing from his teaching were such things as guides to outside reading, mimeographed material to aid research and comprehension, and such activities as extensive teacher-pupil planning, pupil participation in evaluation, student research and reports on significant subject matter. He prepared no lesson plans, and his music courses had no organization of subject-matter content.

Suddenly he realized that he had not taught many musically essential things in his rehearsals. . . . He made a humbling confession that he would have to alter his objectives, his procedures, and his materials of instruction, to some degree. . . .

Second Objective

As the teacher continued to ponder the state of music in the high school, he decided that while purposeful performance must always remain as the major objective, a second objective should be gradually raised to approximately equal status with it. This second objective could tentatively be called "teaching the subject matter of music" until he could think of a better term. He further decided that the presentation of this subject matter should be in *integral relation* to the music being performed; it should make performance better, not detract from it. After further thinking along these lines he could see that performance and subject matter, which he first perceived as twin objectives, were really only one—to help boys and girls develop genuine musical competence and understanding. He decided that one vitally important key leading to improved teaching was the establishing of new criteria for the selection of music to be used in this way of teaching. The older criteria would still be there:

Is the music's degree of technical difficulty appropriate in terms of performing ability?

Is the music suitable and desirable for either teaching essential techniques of playing and singing (as for beginning classes) or for use on public programs?

The new criterion would be:

Is this music of superior value in teaching the subject matter of music?

A Frontier

The teacher had never seen a materials list which met the third criterion in any detail. He realized that his thinking had reached a frontier of secondary-school music education, and he needed help. He decided to reveal his problems and anxieties to his co-workers in nearby schools; perhaps their problems would be similar to his.

A time was arranged and the music teachers of high schools in the area met in an effort to solve their several problems. Their first task was to try to agree on the general approach to improved teaching stated by the teacher who had called the meeting. They soon agreed that the subject matter of music should be taught, if possible, by a well-organized approach through the use of carefully selected music. They also agreed that another way of saying this was, "The performance of selected music, the preparation of which has been a matter of organized planning by the teacher, should result in both the learning of some of the subject matter of music and in improved quality and sensitivity of performance." . . .

PLANNING FOR EFFICIENCY

An immediate concern of some of the teachers was how all of this could be done without interfering with musical performance. All agreed that this was one of the things which would require continued study. Some time-saving techniques mentioned were (1) writing information on the chalkboard before class time, (2) mimeographing material such as study guides for students to use outside of class time, (3) using one wall of the room for a large music history and world history chart to which the boys and girls could refer at a glance, and (4) instructing the student librarian to mark the students' copies of music with red pencil to underscore or label aspects of the music through which the learning of specific subject matter was to take place. A fifth idea was the writing and use of program notes in a manner which relates to the subject matter under consideration and also in a manner which would give parents a knowledge of the "twin objectives" of the music program. The teachers were certain that other devices useful in preserving sufficient class time for drill on the technical skills of performance would be found as their experimenting proceeded.

They became increasingly enthusiastic about the future of secondary school music.

The teacher went to his principal and told him what he and the other music teachers were attempting to do to improve the music program. The principal said, "I can now tell the Board of Education that a good music teacher not only prepares for performances of his music groups and soloists, but also like all other good teachers, teaches the subject matter of his area." . . . He looked into the future and believed that the prestige of music and of the profession of music educators would improve progressively when the public and the teaching profession became aware of what constitutes good music teaching. The transition to the new program would take place according to certain steps, he thought.

Step one would be gaining acceptance of the larger concept of good music teaching. Step two would be the selection and study of the music to be chosen according to the criteria. Step three would be the developing of techniques (many of them time-saving) which would be needed in teaching the subject matter of music by means of the selected music. . . .

Music for Everybody

Another suggestion was that in reorganizing the music program, opportunities for non-performers and mediocre performers should be considered. He believed that in this age of science, automation, and the shorter work-week, music will be more necessary than ever to the people of the United States. He asked the help of the music teacher in establishing music's place in a balanced school program.

The music teacher was anxious to continue working on more of the new activities he was planning for the boys and girls. Soon he was on his way to the librarian's office to confer about ordering books on music and musicians, and recordings to be placed in the library for the students to study as the music they played and sang in their music classes related to them. A record player with sets of headphones was being installed in the library. The teacher was confident that he could eventually give a good answer to the principal's question regarding grade-level planning in the music program by developing an understanding-of-music approach. . . .

The Rewards

The music teachers planned and worked and organized more diligently than they ever had before; they also enjoyed their teaching as never before. They knew as they built a library of music suited for better teaching, and as they organized study outlines and developed other teaching aids, each successive year would be easier because of the information they had assembled previously. They were becoming teachers who could not only direct a musical group, but who could use musical performance as a logical and powerful means to guide students to learn about the various aspects of music. Some learned to plan capably for music classes which did not have performance as a major goal. These teachers made General Music a valuable course which grew in popularity, necessitating the addition of more sections. Some ceased thinking of certain music classes as "feeder groups" and planned these as terminal classes for boys and girls whose abilities and interests were not such as to admit them to the performing band, orchestra, and chorus. . . .

The values of music were revealed more clearly because of the improvement of music instruction.

*MUSIC FOR THE ACADEMICALLY TALENTED STUDENT IN THE SECONDARY SCHOOL**

William C. Hartshorn

CURRICULUM

Since the over-all purpose of music education for academically talented students is their musical growth, and since the essential characteristic of growth is continuity, the curriculum should provide for a continuity of musical experience which will promote the progressive development of understandings, insights, judgments, and skills. A program which does not provide academically talented students with such a continuity of experience deprives the best minds of the quality of music education they deserve.

The purposes and activities suggested in this publication cannot be considered to be separate from the total instructional program of the school. Indeed, they should take their place as a significant part of the school's curriculum, and, as these opportunities are made available both to academically talented and musically talented students, the result should be a strengthening of the over-all existing program.

In some situations, the purposes, activities, and content suggested for academically talented students may constitute the basis for scheduling a particular course for them. The intent, however, is not so much to recommend the organization of a specialized course in music for academically talented students as to indicate the types of learning most appropriate to

* Report of the Music Educators National Conference and the National Education Association Project on the Academically Talented Student, 1960. Reprinted by permission.

them. These kinds of learning may involve one course or several; a course organized primarily for performance and which also provides for other musical activities; a course organized primarily around listening activities and which also includes some performance, as well as related reading, analysis, and discussion; or individual or small group activities outside of any organized class structure. The situation in which the learning takes place is, from the point of view of this publication, less important than the scope, depth, and quality of the learning itself.

It is to be expected that the special characteristics of academically talented students (curiosity, imagination, initiative, and self-propelled desire to learn) will lead them to explore areas of learning related to, but outside of, the scope of the course in which they are enrolled. Obviously, such activity should receive strong encouragement, including provision of necessary source materials and student presentations to the class of the results of particular studies undertaken. It is also desirable that the total resources of the music department be made available to academically talented students, e.g., a student in a performing group may desire the assistance of a teacher of theory or of music history. The academically talented student should be given every opportunity to move at will across the boundaries that separate the various subjects in the music curriculum.

The activities through which the academically talented student grows musically will differ from those of most students, chiefly in the extent to which they are characterized by a greater degree of intellectual involvement and self-initiated, self-directed performance, listening, research, and creative activity.

For the academically talented student whose previous experiences have included a high level of vocal or instrumental performance, or both, it is important that this performance be continued with uncompromising adherence to the highest standards of repertoire and technical proficiency. It is essential, however, that ample provision also be made for listening, analysis, reading, writing, and discussion, so that he can grow in understanding the meaning of the music he performs, as well as of other music. Skills alone are not enough for the academically talented student.

There may be some academically talented students for whom performance has become an activity of minor importance and, perhaps, one in which they have had only moderate success. These students need not abandon performance altogether, but their activities should involve a greater emphasis upon listening and related studies that are intellectually oriented.

For one reason or another, large numbers of academically talented students may have no desire to perform music with any serious intent. For this group, the curriculum should provide musical experiences that consist chiefly of listening, analyzing, reading, and reacting to these experiences through writing or discussion. These opportunities should result in a high level of enjoyment, involving responses that are both emotional and intellectual. They should also lead to deep understandings and insights, and to discriminating judgments of value.

For these three groups of academically talented students, the program will vary chiefly in the relative emphasis placed upon performance, for the other activities are essential in all cases if these exceptional young people are to be musically educated.

Academically talented students may wish to relate learnings from other subject fields to their musical activities. This is desirable and to be encouraged, provided a direct and authentic relationship exists, and provided that it strengthens learning in the field of music.

PERFORMING GROUPS

The academically talented student whose musical experience qualifies him to participate in selective performing groups should participate in them, provided they include opportunity for learnings other than performance skills. These other learnings should include an understanding of form, harmonic idiom, the expressive significance of the music he is rehearsing, and other factors that may have helped to determine the nature of the music. If the rehearsals of the performing group do not provide for learnings other than performing skills, the academically talented student should enroll in courses, independent study groups, honors classes, or seminars which meet during or after the school day. These activities are essential for his growth in understanding the nature and meaning of music.

Academically talented students, allowed to serve as assistant conductors or assistant teachers, strengthen their own learning as they attempt to teach others, develop social competence in leadership and a taste for teaching which may encourage them toward a career in this field.

These students cannot be expected to remain in performing organizations semester after semester if their experiences continue to be simply "more of the same." In addition to a different repertoire, they have a right to expect that something new will be added in terms of more advanced ear-training, increasing understanding of theory, and associative concepts which will both broaden and deepen their musical understandings. The fact that this may be difficult to achieve, with new students enrolling each semester, simply serves to emphasize the necessity for flexibility in scheduling. Such a schedule will make it more possible, in a performing ensemble, to meet the varying needs of students with divergent abilities.

It is important for the academically talented student (as well as other students) to develop and maintain a sense of responsibility to the performing groups of which he is a part. However, it is also important to remember that the performing group is a part of the music curriculum of the school and exists to serve the needs of students, rather than to provide a vehicle through which the student will serve his school and his community. The values of public performances are fully recognized, and to the extent that they provide a goal which motivates rehearsing that is more careful than it otherwise would be, they are of value. However, to the extent that public performances consist of repertoire chosen in terms of what the prospective audience will enjoy, regardless of its intrinsic merits or its appropriateness to the musical and technical needs of the participating students, they are miseducative ventures that deprive students of high quality musical experiences.

LISTENING

Listening is an indispensable part of every musical activity. Members of performing groups must listen to each other in order to achieve blend of tone, accuracy of intonation, and unity of ensemble. Even the personal, emotional, and social values of participation in group performance depend upon the participant's aural recognition of the musical results he has achieved. His realization of success can come only when he has heard what he has done.

Listening is also essential in the theoretical phases of music education. Without relevance to music that has been heard, a study of theory is mechanical routine, without meaning.

Listening to music should be a major part of the study of music history. The reading of factual information about music, particularly about design, and form and characteristics of style, has little, if any, significance unless it is related to direct experience with the music to which it refers.

Listening provides the individual with the opportunity to come into contact with music beyond that which he is able to perform. No matter how skilled a student or even a professional performer may be in some type of performance, his musical experiences would be tragically restricted if they were limited to those of his own performance. Virtually the entire world of music is available to the academically talented student through listening, for there is little music of importance and worth that has not been recorded. Selection of recordings for listening should be made in terms of the intrinsic worth of the music, its educative potentialities as related to the immediate needs of the student, and the quality of the performance and the recording itself. . . .

FLEXIBILITY OF SCHEDULING

An examination of the considerable quantity of material that has been written during the last two years concerning the education of academically talented students reveals a definite trend in the direction of greater flexibility in scheduling. Evidently, school administrators have taken a sharp look at the practice of scheduling all subjects for an identical number of periods per week. They are now moving from a policy of determining the master schedule on the basis of administrative convenience to a policy of providing the flexibility necessary for a broader and more effective educational program. Increasing attention to the needs of academically talented students is leading also to planning for flexibility in the number of subjects which these students may take.

Freedom from rigid class attendance has been reported:

> Schools where academic programming is not unduly rigid have sometimes permitted students to work "on their own" during class time. The student is completely responsible. Because of his special abilities, however, he is permitted to be absent from the classroom during a specified number of periods each week in order to carry on an approved individual program for independent research. This may involve working with a more advanced group, or simply availing himself of the facilities offered by the school or by the community. The independent work is undertaken, of course, under the supervision of a faculty member.[1]

Thus, there is a growing recognition of the fact that it is unrealistic to presume that all subjects should have the same time allotment per week. Some subjects can be adapted to a schedule which calls for meetings of only two or three days a week. If there are a sufficient number of these subjects, students can program two of them during one period. Such subjects might include foreign language, mathematics, physical education, typing, music, art, home economics, and industrial arts. An arrangement of this kind can give greater flexibility to the schedule and permit the academically talented student to choose electives in accordance with his talents and interests. Under the hour-long, six-period day schedule, gifted students seldom have time for free electives in the art fields, unless they use summer-school study and out-of-school seminars to free their schedules.

Another possibility for saving time for more electives is to offer some subjects, such as art, music, home economics, industrial arts, science, and other laboratory-type classes in double periods. Because of the time spent during each class period in setting up and putting away materials and equipment, two full double periods per week are equal to approximately the same amount of instructional time as five standard single periods.

Apart from the master schedule of the school, academically talented students can be given varying degrees of latitude with respect to their own schedules. For example, on the basis of individual ability and interest, it should be possible to permit a given student to share one period between two subjects. In the traditional schedule, the academically talented student is often bored because of repetitive activities which are carried on for

[1] *Administration—Procedures and Practices for the Academically Talented Student* (Washington, D.C.: The National Association of Secondary-School Principals, National Education Association, 1960), p. 93.

the benefit of the student of lesser ability. These activities seldom are of value to the academically talented student. Learning is not directly related to the amount of time which a student spends in a class. A superior performer should not be required to remain daily in an orchestra, band, or choir where considerable time is spent in rehearsing passages which he already knows. Such a student should be permitted to put this time to better use. It is quite possible, too, that the music class is not the only one in which he is bored and wastes time while waiting for other students to "catch up."

Frequently a student, in making out his program of courses, must choose between two subjects, thus depriving himself completely of one of the subjects for which he perhaps exhibits a keen interest or a real talent. Electives usually suffer when such choices must be made. A better practice is to permit the academically talented student to participate in both classes on an alternate day basis or to follow some other partial attendance plan agreed upon in advance. Such cases should be evaluated carefully, on an individual basis, by counselors and teachers. Experiences of this kind help the academically talented student to learn to use his time wisely and profitably. It is conceivable that some highly gifted students could be involved in 8 or 10 different subject fields during a given year.

Within the framework of the music class itself, there are additional possibilities for flexible arrangements. In the large ensemble class, interminable repetition of material which the academically talented student already knows well is a waste of time for him. This student, with guidance from the teacher, should be able to spend part of the time rehearsing with a few other selected students in a small ensemble, or be allowed to spend part of the period assisting less able students.

Some of the most talented performers, who are also academically talented, may plan to enter college as music majors, perhaps in preparation for music teaching. These students often have musical deficiencies because of their preoccupation with a single medium of musical performance. Instead of devoting each full period to the large group rehearsal, the time of selected students may be spent to better advantage in developing skill on a second instrument, learning to read from a different clef, engaging in functional piano practice, carrying out activities in music theory assigned by the teacher, or hearing and analyzing representative works in music literature that are beyond their ability to perform. . . .

If band and orchestra meet during the same period, the best wind players can participate in both groups. This provides students with the opportunity to become better acquainted with twice as much musical literature as could be learned in only one group. There are also possibilities for the academically talented student to have both vocal and instrumental experiences during the same period. Instrumental students are often deprived of any opportunities to sing because of schedule problems. Flexibility in programming within the music department can frequently solve this problem for individual students, e.g., by permitting them to participate in both a choral and an instrumental class during the same period.

THE ROLE OF THE TEACHER

The trend is in the direction of a longer day, more periods per day, greater flexibility in the scheduling of those periods, and in the use of time outside of school for seminars and independent study. We should be eager to contribute to this movement in every possible way. The time is at hand for teachers of music, who are traditionally among the most devoted of professional educators, to be resourceful, imaginative, and energetic in promoting every possible scheme that will broaden and deepen the musical experiences of all students, and those of the academically talented, in particular.

This may call for some unselfishness in certain quarters. It may not be quite so pleasant to conduct a rehearsal of a large vocal or instrumental performing group without the best performers for one or two days per week, but it is quite possible that those who remain in the group will develop greater independence and confidence because they are thrown on their own resources. The best performers, in turn, may be having other types of musical experiences, which should make them more knowledgeable participants upon returning to the group.

*TEACH COMPOSITION IN YOUR GENERAL MUSIC CLASS**

Donn Mills

. . . Recently I conducted an experimental class in composition for a group of average children, ages 11 through 14, who had only a classroom music background. They had volunteered to join the class, and agreed to meet twice each week after regular school hours. Each session lasted one hour.

In the six weeks of the class we covered the basic musical materials available to the composer, and did a great deal of actual composing. The interest was phenomenal, and the results amazing.

We began by talking about the basic elements of music: rhythm, melody, harmony, counterpoint, and form, and discussed each of these

* From Donn Mills, "Teach Composition in Your General Music Class," *Music Educators Journal*, Vol. 49, No. 5 (April–May 1963), 43. Reprinted by permission.

elements in turn. As you can imagine, rhythm structures had great appeal. We clapped, stomped, and "da-da-da'd" through countless patterns. We analyzed the rhythms of familiar melodies, and the class wrote some "percussion music," the percussion being limited mostly to small hands and feet. These "pieces" were performed in class, much to the delight of all, except perhaps the teacher next door. Some surprisingly complex rhythms were attempted, too, I might add.

When we discussed melody we began by looking back into history—way back. They liked the mysterious sounds of the Greek modes, and tried improvising a few plainchants. They compared their efforts with their models, and were quick to criticize any unstylistic patterns. We tore melodies apart from Palestrina to Berg in an effort to determine what constituted a "good melody" (within a given style) and talked about such things as conjunct and disjunct motion and tonality. When the time came for them to become "composers," a steady flow of melody was uncorked which surpassed anything you might imagine. I doubt if even the old masters were more prolific than this crew of melodists. Few of their melodies were conventional; most sounded quite contemporary, intentionally so.

Moving on to harmony was a big step, but we tackled it by experimentation. Each student "composed" a chord of three notes. He could choose any three notes which pleased him when sounded simultaneously. Of course, except for a few "modernists," the natural selection of root, 3rd, and 5th was most often chosen. We discussed the major and minor triad and its traditional evolution, and eventually were able to harmonize and even analyze some simple chorales in a slightly crude fashion. Since it was not my intention to give a complete class on the subject of harmony we left most rules and conventional practices undiscussed. The important thing was to see how harmony "worked," and how composers suited "the action to the word."

The fascination the students had for counterpoint was unexpected. After demonstrating the basic principles of free counterpoint (melody against melody) the class was eager to try it. We used some of the previously written melodies and added a second voice. These two-part inventions were sung by the class with great enthusiasm. A discussion followed which proved to be revealing. The natural, instinctive taste and musical sense of these children turned out to be surprisingly mature. Their judgments on good and not-so-good counterpoint were generally correct, both technically and aesthetically. I gave them many differing examples of contrapuntal writing, and they tried them all. Introducing the canon was fun. Youngsters love a game, and writing canons became just that, a game.

The final element—form—was more challenging to present because it doesn't deal with actual sound. I wanted to avoid the usual diagram explanation of the forms until the students could discover them for themselves, and sure enough they did, quite suddenly. As they listened to some short pieces, played on piano and phonograph, they were asked to determine what held the pieces together. "Why does a piece sound complete." For the purpose of comparison, I also wrote out some badly constructed pieces which had no form. Immediately they realized that there was contrast and repetition involved in the better pieces, and no sense of order in the bad examples. The way was then clear to explain the various ways a composer can extend and build his musical ideas, from the motive to the long symphony.

I enjoyed this group, and feel the class was highly successful. Whether those students ever write another note of music or not, I know that they will at least understand the processes involved in creating a work of art. The craftsmanship side of creativity was revealed to them, and I'm sure they'll appreciate the music they perform or hear more, too, knowing a little about the way it's put together.

Why don't you try six weeks of "composition" with your general music class? Since children learn by discovering and doing, let them discover music by writing it. It's an exciting experience for both teacher and student.

appendix b

TEACHER-RATING FORM

You have all waited for such a chance! Now, here it is! This is your chance to criticize me. All year I have been quick to point out your errors, so now I am giving you the opportunity to correct me. Please notice that nowhere on this paper are you asked to write your name. I shall have no way of knowing who said what. So feel free to criticize me fairly and frankly.

All you have to do is circle the words that seem to be the best answer. The following is an example:

How tall would you say I am?

Very tall	(Medium)	Very short

All the other questions are to be answered in the same way. There are a few which ask for extra suggestions. If you have none, skip those questions.

1. In general, I use words that are

Too complicated to understand	About right	Too simple

2. How much do I talk in rehearsal?

Too much	About the right amount	Too little

3. My speaking voice is usually

Too loud; practically a shout	Just loud enough to be understood clearly	Too soft

4. How effective am I in what I try to say?

Very convincing	Moderately convincing	Not at all convincing

5. How clear am I in presenting my ideas?

Very clear	Sometimes hazy	Very difficult to understand

6. In rehearsal do I clearly state where we are starting in the music?

Usually	Only occasionally	Seldom

7. How often do I go over spots in the music that are hard for you?

Too many times	About the right number of times	Not enough times

8. When rehearsing various numbers, I tend to

Stay on one piece too long	Rehearse a piece about the right length of time	Skip around too much

9. Do I make it clear how I want the music to be performed?

Instructions are seldom clear	Part of the time such things as speed, loudness, are made known	Instructions are almost always clear

10. As a rule, my conducting is

Very hard to follow	Fairly easy to follow	Very easy to follow

11. How sensible is my conducting?

Looks like a madman	A little funny sometimes, but usually O.K.	Looks quite sane and sensible

12. How much do I seem to expect of you when it comes to learning and performing music?

Too much	About the right amount	Not enough

13. Do I have any annoying habits such as mouthing words, scratching my head, and so on?

Several such habits	One or two such habits	No bad habits

14. If I do have annoying mannerisms, what are they?

15. How much do I look at the music when conducting?

Too much	About half the time	Very seldom

16. "Clothes make the man," they say, so how about me?

Too flashy	About right for a teacher	Too conserv-ative

17. How often do I smile?

Not nearly often enough	Enough to be con-sidered a pleasant person	Face just beams most of the time

18. Do I tend to pick on certain students? This includes both favorable and unfavorable contacts.

Very much so	A little bit	Everyone treated equally

19. How much interest do I take in you personally?

A great deal	Some interest	Very little

20. How do you feel about making requests and asking questions of me?

Afraid to request anything	Willing to request something if necessary	Very much at ease in making a request

21. How am I about letting you students "in" on what is going on?

Plans are kept secret	Group gets in on some planning	Plans are reviewed and discussed

22. How about my sense of humor?

Difficult to find	About average	A tremendous wit

23. Do I inspire you to do your best in music?

Very much so	Sometimes	Not at all

24. How strict am I in disciplining you?

Too easy	About right	Too strict

25. Do you think that next year I should "crack down" more, or less?

Crack down more	Be about the same	Relax rules a bit

26. Are my demands reasonable on small details such as chewing gum, sitting up, and so forth?

Too rigid	About right	Too easy

27. How patient am I?

Very hot-tempered	Average	Very even-tempered

28. How much time do I spend in bawling out the group for talking, etc?

Too much | About average | Not enough

29. Have I ever humiliated anyone in front of the class?

Never | Once or twice | Several times

30. How am I about giving out grades?

Tough | About average | Easy

31. How about the number of tests?

Not enough | About the right number | Too many

32. How fair is my system of grading (attendance, citizenship, musicianship, and tests)?

Very fair | O.K. | Very unfair

33. In general, do you like the music we have studied this year?

Very much | O.K. | Not much

34. Please check the following items that you feel are TRUE.
This year we have done too many numbers that are:
serious (classical) ____
popular ____
difficult ____
easy ____

35. Do you have any suggestions as to the type of music we might do next year?

36. Do you have any other comments to make about the teacher or the class?

Class ________________ M or F ____
(fr., soph., jun., sen.)

appendix c

The following band and string orchestra books are for the purpose of aiding playing technique at a level beyond beginning instruction. All are intended for use with either full band or string orchestra.

BAND TECHNIQUE STUDIES

Buchtel, Forrest L.	*Intermediate Scales and Etudes*	Kjos 1948
Chenette, Ed	*Advanced Technique*	Rubank 1945
Ford, John, and Elliot Hadley	*Classic Chorales, Carols and Hymns*, with vocal part	Pro Art 1963
Freeman, Elvin L., and Maurice C. Whitney	*Band Reader*	Edwin H. Morris 1954
Fussell, Raymond C.	*Exercises for Ensemble Drill*	Schmitt, Hall & McCreary 1939
Gordon, Philip	*42 Chorales for Band*	Bourne 1962
Hindsley, Mark H.	*Fundamentals of Band Performance*	Belwin 1950
Hovey, Nilo W.	*TIPPS for Bands*	Belwin 1959
Hudadoff, Igor	*Adventures in Rhythm*	Belwin 1960
	A Rhythm a Day	Pro Art 1963
Laas, Bill	*Fun with Fundamentals*	Belwin 1963
Lake, Matthew	*Sixteen Chorales by J. S. Bach*	G. Schirmer 1938
Magnell, Elmer P.	*68 Pares Studies*	Belwin 1957
	Schantl Studies	Belwin 1959
Ostling, Acton	*Basic Band Balance*	Belwin 1960
	Reading Around the Notes	Belwin 1958
Paulson, Joseph	*Get in Rhythm*	Pro Art 1948
Peters, Charles S.	*Master Drills: Scales and Skills*	Kjos 1962
Prescott, Gerald R.	*The Magic of Tempos*	Belwin 1959
Rusch, Harold W.	*24 Arban-Klose-Concone Studies*	Belwin 1955
	25 Lazarus-Concone Studies	Belwin 1956
	55 Ensemble Studies	Belwin 1958

	Barrett and Jancourt Studies, style emphasis—unison or ensemble, solo & accompaniment	Belwin 1960
Smith, Leonard B.	*The Treasury of Scales*	Bandland 1952
Weber, Fred	*Belwin Progressive Band Studies*	Belwin 1949
	Rehearsal Fundamentals	Belwin 1956
Yaus, Grover C.	*"All in One" Studies*	Belwin 1960
	20 Rhythmical Studies, unison	Belwin 1952
	40 Rhythmical Studies	Belwin 1958
	47 Foundation Studies	Belwin 1961
	54 Harmonized Rest Patterns	Belwin 1954
	59 Studies in Unison	Belwin 1959
	101 Rhythmic Rest Patterns	Belwin 1953
	127 Original Exercises	Belwin 1956
Yaus, Grover C., and Roy M. Miller	*150 Original Exercises*	Belwin 1944
Yoder, Paul	*Smith-Yoder-Bachman Technique*	Kjos 1943

ORCHESTRAL TECHNIQUE STUDIES

Applebaum, Samuel	*Scales for Strings*	Belwin 1962
Bergh, Harris V.	*String Positions*	Summy-Birchard 1958
Green, Elizabeth A. H.	*Musicianship and Repertoire*, Vol. I	Theodore Presser 1962
Underwood, Rex	*Bow-Art for Strings*	Remick 1959
Waller, Gilbert R.	*Waller Vibrato Method*	Kjos 1951
Whistler, Harvey S.	*Introducing the Positions*, 2 vols.	Rubank 1955–56
Whistler, Harvey S., and Herman A. Hummel	*Elementary Scales and Bowings*	Rubank 1955
	Intermediate Scales and Bowings	Rubank 1957
Wikstrom, Thomas	*Techniques for Strings*	Carl Fischer 1963

appendix d

Band

RATING

Use no plus or minus signs in final rating

Order or time of appearance________ **Event No.**________ **Class**________ **Date**________**19**__

Name of Organization________________

School________________ Number of Players________

City________ State________ District________ School Enrollment________

Selections________________

Adjudicator will grade principal items, A, B, C, D, or E, or numerals, in the respective squares. Comments must deal with fundamental principles and be constructive. Minor details may be marked on music furnished to adjudicator.

TONE (beauty, blend, control)________ ☐

INTONATION (chords, melodic line, tutti)________ ☐

TECHNIQUE (articulation, facility, precision, rhythm)________ ☐

BALANCE (ensemble, sectional)________ ☐

INTERPRETATION (expression, phrasing, style, tempo)________ ☐

MUSICAL EFFECT (artistry, fluency)________ ☐

OTHER FACTORS (choice of music, instrumentation, discipline, appearance)________ ☐

***May be continued on other side.**

Signature of Adjudicator________________

Adjudicator's private comments for________________**, to be detached by *adjudicator***
(Name of Director)
and sealed in attached envelope furnished by Festival Chairman.

Use reverse side for additional comments

B-1, Official Adjudication Form. Copyright 1958 by National Interscholastic Music Activities Commission, 1201 Sixteenth Street, Washington 6, D.C. Reprinted by permission.

Choral—Large Group

RATING

Use no plus or minus signs in final rating

Order or time of appearance________ **Event No.**________ **Class**________ **Date**________**19**___

Name of Organization________

School________Number of Singers________

City________State________District________School Enrollment________

Selections________

Adjudicator will grade principal items, A, B, C, D, or E, or numerals, in the respective squares. Comments must deal with fundamental principles and be constructive. Minor details may be marked on music furnished to adjudicator.

TONE (beauty, blend, control)________ ☐

INTONATION________ ☐

DICTION (clarity of consonants, naturalness, purity of vowels)________ ☐

TECHNIQUE (breathing and posture, precision, rhythm)________ ☐

BALANCE________ ☐

INTERPRETATION (expression, phrasing, style, tempo)________ ☐

MUSICAL EFFECT (artistry, feeling of ensemble, fluency, vitality)________ ☐

OTHER FACTORS (choice of music, discipline, stage presence and appearance)________ ☐

***May be continued on other side.**

Signature of Adjudicator________

Adjudicator's private comments for________ (Name of Director) **, to be detached by *adjudicator* and sealed in attached envelope furnished by Festival Chairman.**

Use reverse side for additional comments

V-7, Official Adjudication Form. Copyright 1958 by National Interscholastic Music Activities Commission, 1201 Sixteenth Street, Washington 6, D.C. Reprinted by permission.

Orchestra or String Orchestra

RATING

Use no plus or minus signs in final rating

Order or time of appearance________ Event No.________ Class________ Date______ ______19___

Name of Organization_______________________________________

School____________________________Number of Players________

City_____________State____________District____________School Enrollment________

Selections____

Adjudicator will grade principal items, A, B, C, D, or E, or numerals, in the respective squares. Comments must deal with fundamental principles and be constructive. Minor details may be marked on music furnished to adjudicator.

TONE (beauty, blend, control)________________________________ ☐

INTONATION (chords, melodic line, tutti)__________________________ ☐

TECHNIQUE (articulation-bowing, facility, precision, rhythm)________________ ☐

BALANCE (ensemble, sectional)________________________________ ☐

INTERPRETATION (expression, phrasing, style, tempo)___________________ ☐

MUSICAL EFFECT (artistry, fluency)_____________________________ ☐

OTHER FACTORS (choice of music, instrumentation, discipline, appearance)___________ ☐

*May be continued on other side.

Signature of Adjudicator____________________________

Adjudicator's private comments for________________________**, to be detached by *adjudicator***
(Name of Director)
and sealed in attached envelope furnished by Festival Chairman.

Use reverse side for additional comments

OSO-3, Official Adjudication Form. Copyright 1958 by National Interscholastic Music Activities Commission, 1201 Sixteenth Street, Washington 6, D.C. Reprinted by permission.

appendix e

SIMPLE STAGE CONSTRUCTIONS

Figures and letters have an embroidered effect when made of pieces of crepe paper in chicken wire. Figures formed by this technique must be simple and block-like. The chicken wire is first tacked onto a wooden frame using a staple-type nail. Then the outlines of the figure, which has previously been plotted on graph paper, are put in according to scale. This outline is made by placing pieces of crepe paper at fifteen or twenty key points, such as the top, bottom, and extremities of the figure. Then the remaining pieces of paper, which have been cut into squares about 4 or 5 inches in size, are inserted into the mesh. Each piece must be taped down on the back side with a bit of masking tape. This is necessary to prevent the pieces of crepe paper from coming out when the figure is erected. The taping process is difficult and tedious. A large frame may require different groups of three or four students to work every hour of the school day for two or more days. When this type of construction is finished, it looks very attractive, almost as if it were made of flowers.

Another way to make simple figures is to have them cut from fiberboard. The figure is first traced or drawn on pieces of fiberboard. The art teacher may be willing to do this, or the music teacher can work out a sketch with a talented art student. Then the shop teacher or a student can cut out the figures on a power jig or band saw. Enamel paints add a bright finishing touch to the figure. Fiberboard does not usually come in sizes larger than four feet, but half the figure can be done on one piece and half on another, and the two halves put together on a stand.

A third type of scenery or prop utilizes poster paint on heavy paper. Since the scenery is made of paper, it should be hung. If a large piece is put on a frame, the weight of the paper alone will cause some tearing, and the chance for accidental punctures is great. The piece can be hung by being tacked to a board or pole extending horizontally across the top.

Several lengths of cord are attached to the pole, and the entire device is then suspended from the pulling apparatus. This type of prop makes an effective backdrop.

Some stages do not have facilities with which to pull up scenery or props. In such cases a standard must be made for each prop. The best standard is made by using pieces of 2 × 4's and metal shelf braces which can be purchased at any hardware store. Screws should be used rather than nails, because nails work loose very quickly. It is not necessary to use an expensive grade of lumber for these projects; cheaper grades are entirely satisfactory for holding props. The standards should be saved, because they can be used on other pieces in future years. Two views of the standard are shown here.

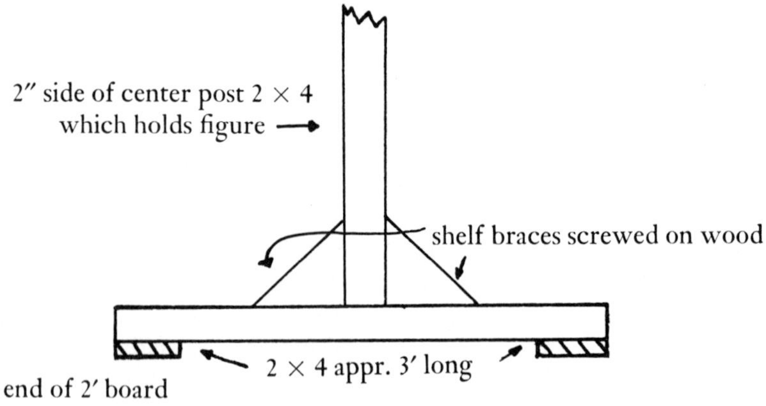

SIDE VIEW

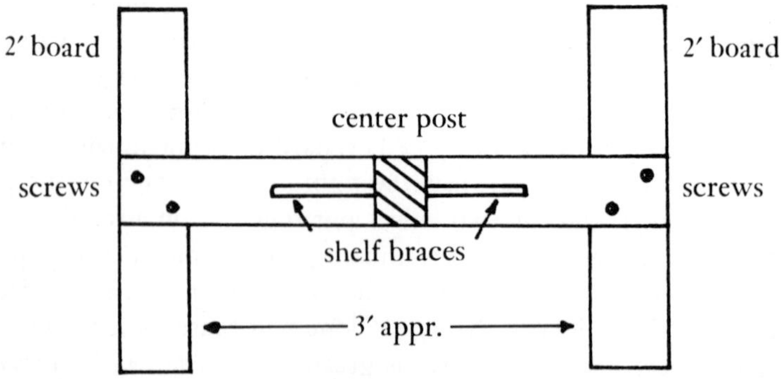

TOP VIEW

appendix f

SUPPLEMENTARY INFORMATION BOOKS FOR STUDENTS IN GENERAL MUSIC

Baldwin, Lillian, *Music for Young Listeners, The Blue Book.* Morristown, N.J.: Silver Burdett Company, 1951.

______________, *Music to Remember.* Morristown, N.J.: Silver Burdett Company, 1951.

Barbour, Harriot, and Warren Freeman, *A Story of Music.* Evanston, Ill.: Summy-Birchard Publishing Company, 1950.

Buchanan, Fannie R., *How Man Made Music.* Chicago: Follett Publishing Co., 1951.

Cotton, Marian, and Adelaide Bradburn, *Music Throughout the World.* Evanston, Ill.: Summy-Birchard Publishing Company, 1953.

Dike, Helen, *Stories from the Great Metropolitan Operas.* New York: Random House, 1943.

Hartshorn, William, and Helen S. Leavitt, *Prelude, Progress, At Home and Abroad, and New Horizons,* in *Making Friends with Music* series. Boston: Ginn & Co., 1940.

Kinscella, Hazel, *History Sings.* Lincoln, Nebr.: University Publishing Co., 1948.

McKinney, Howard, and W. R. Anderson, *Discovering Music.* New York: American Book Co., 1943.

McKinney, Howard, *Music and Man.* New York: American Book Co., 1948.

McKinney, Laurence, *People of Note.* New York: E. P. Dutton & Company, Inc., 1940.

Miller, Ralph G., and Martha Pearman, *Music from Across the Seas*. Cincinnati: The Willis Music Co., 1956.

Swift, Frederick, and Willard I. Musser, *General Music in the Junior High School*. Vols. I, II, III, and IV. Rockville Centre, N.Y.: Belwin, Inc., 1954.

Wheeler, Opal, *Frederick Chopin, Son of Poland*. New York: E. P. Dutton & Company, Inc., 1948. (Books concerning other composers are available from this company.)

index

A

N

V

W

Y

Z